CW00971699

A CONCISE
ECONOMIC HISTORY OF
BRITAIN

A CONCISE
ECONOMIC HISTORY OF
BRITAIN

FROM 1750 TO RECENT TIMES

BY

W. H. B. COURT

CAMBRIDGE UNIVERSITY PRESS

CAMBRIDGE

LONDON · NEW YORK · MELBOURNE

Published by the Syndics of the Cambridge University Press
The Pitt Building, Trumpington Street, Cambridge CB2 1RP
Bentley House, 200 Euston Road, London NW1 2DB
32 East 57th Street, New York, NY 10022, USA
296 Beaconsfield Parade, Middle Park, Melbourne 3206, Australia

ISBN: 0 521 09217 5

First published 1954
Reprinted 1958 1962 1964 1965
1967 1974 1976

Printed in Great Britain
at the
University Printing House, Cambridge
(Harry Myers, University Printer)

PREFACE TO
THE 1964 IMPRESSION

Economic history is the record of economic acts and decisions.
It is concerned with the decisions and acts which arise out of
men's need to make the least wasteful and most effective or,
as we say, the most economic use of their resources. Necessity
compels them to apply what resources they have, whether these
are vast or scanty, part of the material world or part of their
own person, to the purposes of life as they see them. It
demands that they shall allot those resources as best they can,
according to the customs, the techniques and the values which
they know, among competing and often conflicting ends. This
is the unchanging basis of economic history at all times and in
every kind of society.

How men in Great Britain have handled their economic
resources and the social income derived from them, forms the
subject of modern British economic history. Between 1750 and
1850, the peoples of the British Isles became, not suddenly
but none the less decisively, the first great industrial community that the world had ever seen. They stumbled through
the door, one might say, which led mankind into a new age and
a new organization of society, at that time equally unknown
both in its potentialities and its dangers. They bore in their
own persons the hardships, the shocks and the triumphs of
that astounding transition. During many years of the nineteenth century, in the long Victorian age, they led the countries
of the West industrially and those of them who were in a
position to do so, at all levels of society, saw to it that they were
suitably rewarded. For in a world full of uncharted possibilities, with resources waiting to be mobilized, they displayed
all the virtues and many of the failings of pioneers—the will
to work, to face the unknown and achieve the impossible, the
speculative fever, the readiness to leave to late-comers the
bill marked social cost. But the pioneering age was relatively
soon over. Between 1870 and 1914, the notable advantages
which British industry had possessed in early Victorian days
over those of all other countries were abolished by the swift
industrial growth of great nations in Central Europe and North
America. Foreign competition was not the only problem in

sight. Within the industrial cities of Great Britain, at the turn of the century, social questions of immense range and complexity, conditioned by the industrial development of many years, were coming to political maturity and could no longer be postponed.

The thirty years of crisis in Europe that followed the outbreak of war in 1914 brought with it for Great Britain an acquisition of economic experience far different from the lessons of Victorian times. An industrial people had to learn that the age-old institution of war was becoming industrialized and scientific. They twice faced the economic demands of total war. In the twenty years between the fighting, novel and intractable difficulties arose in the redevelopment of national resources, of a kind that could only emerge in a mature industrial economy, and they brought new riddles of social obligation with them, to add to those inherited from the nineteenth century. During those inter-war years, an economy and its resources, a society and its values, a world and its politics, were all in violent motion together. Then, as before 1914, general changes were taking place inside and outside Europe that might lead to catastrophe—fundamental shifts of power between nations and classes long held in a kind of traditional equilibrium, based upon the new development of resources, and the transformation of political ends which went with the acquisition of so much new material means to effect them. The British economy and the society it served were highly sensitive to these extraordinary changes. But they ran a course and took a shape which were characteristically British, because influenced by national circumstance and tradition.

These are among the major topics of modern British economic history before 1939, considered in its broad setting in the life and development of British society. It follows that no historian could possibly do justice to them. The present book, first written as a companion piece to Sir John Clapham's volume[1] was intended simply as an introduction to a vast subject. It is as such, written to help the general reader rather than the professional economist, that it is now reprinted as a paperback. The essential statistics of modern British economic development are nowadays to be found in the admirable collection by B. R. Mitchell and Phyllis Deane, *Abstract of British Historical*

[1] *A Concise Economic History of Modern Britain from the Earliest Times to A.D. 1750* (Cambridge University Press).

Statistics (1962). Much that is here said can be, and should be, checked against the relevant figures.

So many people helped me in one way or another to write this history that it would be hard to mention all the names. To the few who were mentioned in the preface to the first edition and to many others, I am deeply grateful, even if less than I ought to be, considering the magnitude of the debt.

W. H. B. COURT

July 1963

CONTENTS

BOOK II

The Victorian Economy and After, 1837–1939

Book I

THE GROWTH OF AN INDUSTRIAL STATE

1750 TO 1837

Chapter I

Population

THE OLD STATE OF POPULATION

The economic problems of men begin in the scarcities and inequalities of nature, although they may be sharpened beyond measure by the unwisdom and injustice of human arrangements. In approaching the economic history of modern Britain, it is natural to start by inquiring into the relations between her population and her resources about the middle of the eighteenth century, when her modern history begins.

Behind the economic problems of Great Britain in the eighteenth century lay the growth of Europe's population and of British population as a part of this. The causes which have controlled Europe's population and the fluctuations which have come over it in historic times are far from clear. It seems certain, however, that population in Western Europe, which since the late Middle Ages had been increasing only slowly, began to grow at a faster rate in the seventeenth and eighteenth centuries. Behind this increase lay many things; economic development, peaceful administration and medicine all played a part.

The new influences which were at work may perhaps best be understood from observing the older conditions which had kept numbers down in other countries as well as Great Britain. In Sweden, where official vital statistics, beginning in 1749, are the oldest in Europe, we may see how a society largely agricultural in its interests, living under conditions perhaps rather harder than in some other parts of Western Europe, was restricted in its numbers by what the eighteenth-century writer, Malthus, described concisely as 'periodical returns of severe want, and the diseases arising from it'. The rates of marriages, births and deaths among such a people varied with the crops. No great import of foodstuffs into Sweden existed or could exist under the conditions of the time. When the harvest failed, people went short; if times were exceptionally bad, they starved. When they were weakened by hunger or a poor diet, disease attacked them. Smallpox and typhoid were endemic, although tuberculosis, which was to flourish in the ill-built towns of the nineteenth century, was comparatively rare. All members of the population suffered together; when the death-rate among adults was highest, the children died fastest too. Following each period of dearth, perhaps because death had removed the weakest members of society, the mortality would be unusually low for some years, giving rise to an abnormally rapid increase of population. Any progress made from time to time in the production of food owing to the extension or improvement of agriculture seems to have been absorbed by a rise in numbers, so that a substantial improvement in the material standard of living was out of the question. The rise in population in eighteenth-century Sweden under these severe conditions was less slow than might perhaps have been expected. But it struggled in natural bonds, set by want and pestilence, with war as a third taskmaster, chiefly important because it gave rise to disease, brought home by soldiers whose exposure to disease was high and for whom little was done in the way of medical attention.[1]

These conditions were in many respects characteristic of all Europe before the nineteenth century. The high death-rate was the main check to population increase. Its causes were the low standard of living and the absence of medicine. The rate of mortality was highest in the towns, so much so that many of the towns, could they have been isolated, would presumably have died out. The prejudice of contemporaries, who believed that the towns devoured the country, was to this extent justified only too well.

Reliable figures about British population do not go back as far as the Swedish. The device of the census, when it was first proposed in 1753, was rejected by Parliament as an invasion upon the liberties of Englishmen and a danger to the realm, since it might reveal the extent of its weakness. The first census of England and Wales, an imperfect one, was not taken until 1801, during the wars against Revolutionary France. The Registrar-General of England and Wales did not begin to register births, marriages and deaths until the passage of the Marriage Act, which established his office, in 1836. Without these modern sources, we are forced back upon the records kept by the churches and chapels and by the tax-collectors for

[1] E. F. Heckscher, 'Swedish Population Trends before the Industrial Revolution', *Econ. Hist. Rev.*, 2nd series, vol. II (1950), pp. 266-77.

their own purposes. They are often unsatisfactory for the reckoning of numbers, and they tend to become more unsatisfactory the further back we go. The bright light of central statistics only falls upon the scene when the older conditions had broken down. Great Britain was already passing through a revolution as regarded the increase of its population, as the first decennial censuses showed.

The population of Great Britain in 1801 appears to have been just over ten millions—10,501,000. It was to multiply itself by three and a half times between that year and the census of 1901, when it was 37,000,000. The rate of increase is as significant as the total. The early censuses disclosed that this rate was very high. The addition to the population of England and Wales in the first three decades of the nineteenth century was more than equal, so far as we can see, to the increase which had taken place in the period of 140 years between the Restoration of Charles II in 1660 and the first census. This high rate of increase persisted throughout the first half of the nineteenth century and longer. Between 1801 and 1821, the number of people in Great Britain rose by 34 per cent; between 1821 and 1841 by 32 per cent; between 1841 and 1861 by 25 per cent. After 1870, and especially in the present century, the rate of its growth slackened considerably,[1] and this was marked after 1910. Two generations after this slackening had begun, statisticians between the two World Wars were beginning to discuss the possibility of a stationary or falling population. The trends which they were discussing then have not proved constant. But whatever happens, it is most unlikely that anything resembling the nineteenth-century rate of population increase will ever be seen in this country again. Had it continued with its greatest force, the population which tripled itself between 1801 and 1901 must have tripled again between 1901 and 2001.

To understand how human life in Great Britain looked and felt two centuries and a half ago we have to begin therefore by removing six out of every seven persons in its present population. This is, it must be agreed, a drastic mental operation. It presents us with a type of society whose problems are in some respects hard for us to understand, saturated as we are with the experience and with the ways of thinking and feeling of the great age of population growth so recently past.

[1] See Table III in *Report of the Royal Commission on Population*, Cmd 7695 (1949), p. 8.

Perhaps it is curious that we should feel the difficulty as gravely as we do. The demographic character of Great Britain before the great upward swing of population in the eighteenth and nineteenth centuries was that common to great parts of Western Europe over a long period. In this country, at the beginning of the eighteenth century, we read 'both the birth-rate and the death-rate were high, and there cannot have been a great difference between them. It is probable that fewer than half of the children born survived to adult ages....In some years—for example, when there were outbreaks of epidemic disease—deaths may have exceeded births, but this was not normally the case. In most years births exceeded deaths, and the population therefore grew, but only slowly.'[1] Great Britain of the eighteenth century broke with the long-established standards of the past in the growth of its population, as other parts of Europe were preparing to break.

THE LARGE FAMILY AND THE CONDITIONS OF ITS SURVIVAL

What were the causes of the revolution in population, already far advanced when the first census was taken? The decennial census revealed a population growing at the rate of 10 per cent every ten years. This rate of increase could only have been attained as the result of a long series of cumulative changes in the habits and the conditions of the population concerned. Why had the barriers, whatever they may have been, which had proved so effective for centuries in preventing any rapid increase been broken down and swept away?

This is not a question which it would be easy to answer, even if the takers of the census had begun their work much earlier. An explanation depends on knowing a great deal about marriages, births and deaths at the time—not only statistics, but also information required for their interpretation—much of which cannot easily be got in any society at any time. But it happened that the great population increase at the end of the eighteenth and the beginning of the nineteenth century coincided with and also helped to stimulate the rise of scientific inquiry into problems of this kind. A considerable literature developed and theories were worked out and widely adopted.

[1] *Report of the Royal Commission on Population* (1949), p. 6.

Such a theorist was T. R. Malthus.[1] Speculation on the relations between human reproduction, food supply and the happiness or misery of nations began in the mind of Malthus, a young clergyman in the Church of England, in a mood of youthful scepticism provoked by the optimistic extravagances of his father. The elder Malthus was a Godwinian and a friend of Jean-Jacques Rousseau, a believer in the perfectibility of man according to the ideas of the late eighteenth century. Differences between father and son are not uncommon, but it must be rare in history for a great scientific theory to arise out of a difference of that kind. In his *Essay upon Population* (1798) and in the long series of inquiries which filled the later years of his life, Malthus considered the relations between the growth of human numbers and those forces, which he called preventive checks, which had prevented population from increasing rapidly over long periods of European history. Thinkers before Malthus had noticed the relation between population and subsistence, which formed the heart of his argument—the tendency of the one to outrun the other—and the part played by war, pestilence and famine in keeping human numbers in check. But no one had attempted to work out their relations with the acumen and learning which he brought to the task.

Malthus's speculations would hardly have had their public influence but for his political interests and his view of the immediate situation. What many contemporary Englishmen came to know of Malthus was not his theoretical and historical inquiries, on which his scientific fame rests, but his judgement that the practice of the Poor Law authorities had much to do with the increase of population in Great Britain. Malthus pointed to the public relief given to the labourer in receipt of wages, in proportion to his family and to the cost of living, measured by the price of bread. This system of relief had been adopted under the direction of the justices of the peace for Berkshire in 1795, in order to meet the distress created by the low wages of the farm labourer in face of the upward movement of prices after the outbreak of war with France in 1793.

[1] Thomas Robert Malthus (1766–1834) was for many years Professor of Modern History and Political Economy at the East India College at Haileybury, where he taught the cadets who went out to rule British India, then under the administration of the East India Company. He wrote widely upon economics as well as population and was, with his friend Ricardo, one of the founders of the classical political economy.

Population

The practice, not new among the Poor Law authorities, had been regularized in law soon after and widely adopted in the country. Introduced as a war measure, it persisted over many years of peace, until the legislative and administrative reform which the Whig Government aimed against it in 1834. Under the influence of Malthus, the so-called 'Speenhamland system'[1] of poor relief came to be regarded by educated people as a main, if not the principal, influence behind the contemporary rise of population. It was argued that it cheapened subsistence to the poor and encouraged large families. Propounded in this narrow way, the thesis never squared with the development of numbers in Scotland and Ireland, where the English system of poor relief did not prevail. It broke down completely upon the continuing increase revealed by the census long after the giving of out-relief in aid of wages had been curbed in 1834. But throughout the first half of the nineteenth century the idea was a political force and swayed powerfully the opinions of the governing classes.

Allied to what one might call the 'Poor Law theory' of the population increase was the more respectable proposition that every increase in food supply tends to be taken out in a more than proportionate growth of population. This happens because the returns to human labour provided by the land tend to diminish in the absence of any marked improvement in agricultural methods and a rising population does not adjust itself easily to this limit upon its resources. This observation had such powerful backing in old and new experience, as Malthus amply demonstrated, that it led the best English economist of the middle nineteenth century, John Stuart Mill, to take a sombre view of the economic prospects of Great Britain, for precisely this reason, as late as 1848. Events at the time when Mill was writing—the dearness of bread in England during the 1840's, the Irish famine of 1846, the struggle over the laws restricting corn imports—lent force to his argument. The habit of regarding the contemporary history of their country as a race between population and food supply did not die out among educated Englishmen until the second half of the nineteenth century, by which time their country had ceased to depend exclusively upon a home-grown food supply. Then the doctrines of Malthus and of the classical economists, of whom Mill was

[1] So called from the name of the district in Berkshire, now part of the town of Newbury, where the Berkshire justices held their meeting in 1795.

one of the latest representatives, came to seem irrelevant, if not incorrect.

Later generations accepted other explanations of the great rise of population. In the early years of the present century, writers who saw how far industrialism had been carried and were critical of its achievements, suggested that the demand for labour in the new mills of the Industrial Revolution led to the increase. This view never had much to commend it. For one thing, the millworkers, even as late as 1830, were a small minority of the population, older and more widespread occupations such as domestic service being more important. For another, it failed to explain adequately the increase in the country districts. No county in Great Britain, whether agricultural or industrial, recorded anything but a substantial growth of population, decade by decade, between 1801 and 1851. We must look elsewhere than the factories for the key to rising numbers.

Generally speaking, a rise in population may be due to fewer people dying or to more being born; to a fall, that is, in the rate of mortality or to a rise in the rate of births, expressed as a proportion of the whole population. Or the increase may, of course, be due to simultaneous changes in both rates; the two rates are not independent of one another.

Were more persons being born, to put it in that way, during these years? The crude birth-rate, the rate of births, that is, every year for every thousand of population, was certainly, according to what information exists, high in the middle of the eighteenth century compared with earlier years. It had been rising throughout the first half of the century since about 1710, and continued to rise gently in the later decades, to fall again gently but distinctly, after 1790.[1] Changes in social convention, standards and arrangements would no doubt account for part of this increase. Behind it lay changes connected with the organization of industry and the decay or obsolescence of the system of apprenticeship in many trades, which in the past had acted as a restraint upon early marriage; the growth of new industries outside the sphere of apprenticeship altogether, such as the cotton and the coal industries; the possibility of full earnings at an early age, whether as a result of the higher

[1] Birth- and death-rates for the eighteenth and early nineteenth century are discussed in G. T. Griffith, *Population Problems of the Age of Malthus* (1926); see also his Diagram I. There is much room for disagreement on this subject; see the criticisms of T. H. Marshall, 'The Population Problem during the Industrial Revolution', *Econ. J. Supplement*, January 1929.

productivity of machinery or the widening employment of
young people in industry, about which nineteenth-century
social reformers were to have much to say; and, after 1800, the
immigration of Irish people, whose penchant for large families
was in those days certainly not less than the British. In the
country districts, changes in the organization of the land, begun
at a far earlier date, may have had the effect of breaking down
gradually these rules of habit by which many peasant peoples in
past times, and perhaps the English among them, have deferred
marriage and limited the time within which they may have
children, so as to make sure of possessing the land required for
the maintenance of a family. The opening of alternative occupations in industry, in an age when much industry was rural, may
have worked in the same direction. All these things might and
probably did alter the age at which people married and affected
the fertility of their marriages, over a long period of years.

The rising fertility may also have been due in part to an
increased chance of survival and the cumulative effects which
this would have on the age composition of the nation. This is
easily seen. If fewer children died at birth or in their very
early years, or if at the other end of the scale of life more
married women lived out the whole natural period within
which they could have children, the size of surviving families
would increase. The greater number of prospective parents
and the survival of their families when they came to marry
would tend to create, over a series of generations, a type of
population distinguished by a large average size of family, not
only born but surviving and propagating itself over the full
period of human fertility. This population would be in a state
of rapid increase, comparable with that revealed by the early
censuses in Great Britain.

In eighteenth-century Britain we are watching the gradual
rise of the large average size of family which prevailed in this
country in Victorian times. Its triumph over the forces which
in earlier ages had tended to limit families and population
appears to have been due both to influences, such as those we
have been discussing, which raised the rate of marriages and
births, and to those which reduced the rate of deaths, but
mostly to the latter.[1] To put the matter more exactly, the large

---

[1] For a recent discussion, see K. H. Connell, 'Some Unsettled Problems
in English and Irish Population History, 1750–1845', *Irish Hist. Stud.*
vol. VII (1951), pp. 225–34.

surviving family was, so far as can be seen on imperfect evidence, mainly the result of forces which diminished mortality, but which had as their secondary effect the increase of fertility, meaning by fertility the number of children born to a family. The saving of children at birth or in the first years of life and the lengthening in the expectation of life among mothers may account for the greater part of the advance of population in the eighteenth century. These things formed part of a general reduction of the death-rate going on at that time, but their influence would be widely felt in an enlargement of the size of the average family. It is worth remembering that, as late as 1850, only two-thirds of the female population ever reached the age at which they would marry and only one-half of them reached the end of the child-bearing age.[1]

The general fall in the death-rate was due to many things. An improvement of medical services was one of them. Medical knowledge in the eighteenth century was beginning to show what it could do, although much of the knowledge was empirical rather than scientific in the strict sense. That century was a great age in the building and establishment of hospitals, dispensaries and medical schools. The Foundling Hospital in London was started by the kind-hearted Captain Coram in 1742 to save children left to die of exposure in the streets. The oldest of the London lying-in hospitals dates from the middle of the century. Medical training was being put upon its feet, under the influence of Continental models. The medical school at Edinburgh, which owed much to the Dutch school of Leyden, began teaching about 1725. Maternity was becoming a specialized branch of medicine, and John Hunter was laying a scientific foundation for surgery. Of course, not all knowledge of the rules of health flowed directly from the trained men from the medical schools, although they were the spearhead of the movement. A man like Dr Johnson's friend William Levett, unqualified, practising in the poor parts of London among patients as poor as himself and taking his fee in the shape of a meal, may have been useful in his own way. Knowledge of the rules of health, however, could not have helped very much, if the slow improvement in the water-supply, paving and sanitation of English towns had not made it possible to apply them.

The course of events is not clear, but it appears that the death-rate in London was clearly falling after 1750, in Man-

[1] Table X in *Report of the Royal Commission on Population* (1949), p. 20.

chester a little later. Taking the country as a whole, the rate of
deaths per thousand of population began to fall, as far as we
can tell, after the first quarter of the century and declined
markedly from 1780 onwards, despite the rapid growth of
town life. Between the end of the French wars in 1815 and the
cholera epidemic of 1831-2, the death-rate rose sharply, but it
never regained the old levels.

Other influences, less easily traceable than medical services
and the elements of sanitation, may have been equally if not
more important. Every increment in the productivity of
British agriculture and industry, from the end of the Civil
Wars onwards, had a bearing on the increase in numbers in the
subsequent century and a half. The population of Tudor and
Stuart England had lived a hard life. Every change for the
better, however small, in their food, clothes or housing, must
have affected the chances of survival. Many changes of this
kind took place in the late seventeenth and early eighteenth
century, not least owing to improvements in agriculture. The
introduction of root crops, the feeding of cattle throughout the
year and the addition to the supply of meat, a growing consumption of wheaten bread instead of poor mixed cereals—
maslin, rye and barley bread—and the increased use of
vegetables, all helped. In a remote Hampshire village at the
end of the eighteenth century, a country curate noted how the
diet of his parishioners had improved within living memory, with
a consequent improvement of health.[1] Gilbert White's Selborne
cannot have been the only village in which this happened.

Industrial production provided cheaper and cleaner under-
wear, cotton and soap and greater cleanliness increased the
resistance to disease. And the late eighteenth-century towns
with their street improvement commissioners and water
companies did improve on the very low standards in public
convenience and amenity of an earlier time, even if they left
the men of Victoria's day with the feeling that there was
almost everything still to do.

If we interpret subsistence to mean, not only the harvest,
but all that under the conditions of life in a northern country
is necessary to survival, then Malthus's view of the relations
between population and subsistence, which was broadly that
they tended to rise and fall together, appears to have been in
general correct for the Britain of his time and of some genera-

[1] Gilbert White, *The Natural History of Selborne* (1789), Letter LXXIX.

tions before. To a population living for the most part at a very low standard, even a slight improvement in the margin upon which it had to live was important, and the addition to its resources tended to be taken out in a more than proportionate increase of numbers. The rise of population in the time of Malthus was in a sense the alternative to a substantial improvement in the material standard of life. It was accompanied by severe privation for many persons and from time to time a widespread fall in living conditions, under the influence of bad harvests, trade fluctuations, and other causes. Hard times might go so far as to drive the general death-rate up, as they seem to have done in the generation after the Napoleonic Wars, during the 1820's.

There were, therefore, powerful forces playing in the eighteenth and early nineteenth century upon the old high mortality which British population had suffered along with that of other countries, and they brought it down. What was happening to the rate at which people died cannot be separated from the other influences which were altering the traditional attitudes towards marriage and child-bearing. The saving of lives among young children and child-bearing women promoted a high birth-rate; but as more children were born and survived, the greater proportion of young people in the population may be assumed to have brought the average death-rate down, for an old population dies faster. These interactions must have been important, but they cannot with the surviving material be easily traced and weighed.

THE ECONOMIC PROBLEMS OF AN INCREASING POPULATION

The picture presented by the British population after 1750 is therefore one of a land in which the old conditions of life had been sufficiently modified to permit a rapid increase of numbers. By the end of the century, between 1780 and 1820, the rate of increase was very high indeed. The time was within sight when, as in the 1840's, the population would be added to at the rate of three hundred thousand persons a year. This, if coming from abroad by immigration, would have been regarded as a formidable addition to the population of a country the size of Great Britain. It was no less impressive because it was the result of what men were coming to call natural growth.

The continuance of so high a rate of increase depended upon the persistence of the conditions which favoured it. It was maintained, in point of fact, far down into the nineteenth century, until the birth-rate began to fall and new population conditions to come into sight after 1870. Owing to this swift growth of numbers over so many years, the nineteenth century was to prove even more revolutionary in its effects on the settlement of the island than its predecessor. The population of the United Kingdom, despite the fall in the Irish population after the famine of 1846, overhauled by the end of that century's last decade the more slowly growing population of France. Yet the French people had been for more than two centuries by far the greatest unit of population under a single government in Europe. Despite her small size, Great Britain came to support a population which in 1947 was the largest in Europe, outside of Soviet Russia and Germany, and the eighth largest of any state in the world.

At this point we are concerned not with the distant results of rapid population growth but with its beginning in the late eighteenth and early nineteenth century. Many interesting questions might have been asked about that population, and were so asked, at one time or another, by thinking contemporaries. One man might have wanted to know how and on what principles it was to be governed. The short answer would be strange. After being directed for over twenty years, in Malthus's lifetime, between 1789 and 1815, in conscious opposition to the French Revolution and its heir Napoleon, British society in the nineteenth century was to become a leading proponent of the ideas of political and civil liberty which the Revolution had brought anew into the world. Another might have wondered, how was such a society to be civilized? In point of fact, it was submitting itself at this very time to powerful influences, born out of its Christian past and from the philosophies of the eighteenth century. The mighty part-contemporaries and opposites, John Wesley (1703–91) and Jeremy Bentham (1748–1832), might serve as examples and types. Out of the flowing together of such widely distinct currents was to emerge in due time the peculiar amalgam of piety with rationalism which distinguished the Victorian mind. Finally, a man might have inquired, how was such a society, so rapidly growing, to be kept alive and provided with the resources necessary for peace and war? At the end of the seventeenth century, just before the Union with England, Scotland had passed through 'the dear years' when dearth followed six bad harvests and some Scottish parishes lost one-half or one-third of their inhabitants. Ireland, during the years from 1780 onwards when the English population was rising so fast, was moving towards the tremendous calamity of the famine and its aftermath (1845–50), in which she lost one-quarter of her population.

The question of subsistence as the thinkers of that time put it, of income as we would say today cannot be dismissed as academic. Assuming, as we must, that the leap forward of British population in the eighteenth century is inexplicable without the modest economic progress of earlier centuries, we have still to ask where the materials, human and natural, were to be found for the creation of additional income, matched to the need for it. The materials of economic progress were thoroughly discussed by eighteenth-century thinkers, notably by Adam Smith.[1] They appeared to resolve themselves into the three factors; labour, land and capital. The classification was convenient and easy, perhaps deceptively so.

The immediate requirements for an increased national income were from this point of view comparatively few and simple. The wealth of the nation was the annual product of its labour. Of the prospect of a continued increase in the nation's numbers there could be no doubt, nor of an increase in the numbers of the population occupied in work, provided capital was there—that is, a correct proportion of the national income put aside every year for the purpose, not of immediate consumption, but of investment in the business of providing more work and income in the future. The modesty of Great Britain's natural resources, which were indicated by the term 'land', might be overcome by a judicious commercial policy. This would permit the exchange of what Britain could produce best against what other parts of the world, with other resources, had to offer. Considerations of this order, however, give little idea of the real difficulties in the way of securing a new growth of incomes, still less a powerful or a steady growth, in eighteenth-century Britain.

Later students of the process of economic growth, recognizing its extreme complexity, have assigned its causes to numerous

---

[1] Adam Smith's *Inquiry into the Nature and Causes of the Wealth of Nations* appeared in 1776. He died in 1790.

and subtle propensities at work in society, such as the propensity to seek material advance, to apply science to economic ends, to accept innovations, and so forth.[1] The view is certainly sound which keeps clearly in mind and directs our attention towards the elementary but easily forgotten fact that the first requisite of increased wealth is a society of the kind required to produce it. Here the limiting factors on economic progress begin to come into sight and they are seen to be by no means confined to a few arithmetical quantities, in the way of land or minerals available, numbers of people or sums of money put aside for investment. The full powers of society must be brought into play. Society must be tolerably agreed upon what it regards as wealth and upon the validity of its reasons for seeking it, within the circle of existing values and customs. If wealth is to increase, society must be bent on increasing it. Not only must it have numerous and multiplying ends in view, both private and public, for the disposal of the additional resources which it wishes to have. It must be skilled in the distribution of existing resources and prepared to submit to new skills and disciplines in using new ones, whether this skill is that of the craftsman choosing between materials or the operative learning the use of a new tool or machine or the banker deciding a choice of investments or the industrialist resolving to drop one line of production and begin another. Such a society must even be ready to go further; however reluctant, it must be prepared for changes in its laws and its politics, in its scale of values and its social conditions, consequent upon its own economic strivings—changes which may be as wide and catastrophic in the heart of an old civilization as those which have been forced upon other societies in recent times by the application of Western enterprise in the undeveloped parts of the world.

In the process of economic change, size of population is of less importance than its adaptability, the investment of capital is of less importance than a willingness to accept all its consequences, which may ramify far and wide. This is perhaps only another way of saying that in any society where large-scale economic change is to take place there must exist, somewhere or other, a strong sense of economic values and considerable powers of economic calculation. The members of such a society may be much or little given to examining the

[1] See the discussion in W. W. Rostow, *The Process of Economic Growth* (1953).

fundamental values by which they live, but they will certainly be much concerned with the search for ways and means to give their current values effect. They will also have developed considerable intelligence, ranging perhaps the whole way from rule-of-thumb skill to scientific exactitude, in disposing of resources between the many uses to which they mean to put them and in perceiving what the alternative results are likely to be.

Eighteenth-century Britain was becoming this kind of society. Habits of valuation and device are the creation of time and the existence of such a society on the edge of Western Europe in the middle of the eighteenth century was the upshot of a long and complicated history. This cannot be described here. It must be enough to say that the economic revolution which accompanied the growth of population and which to some extent made it possible, took its rise not only in the physical circumstances of Britain but far more in the existence and the strengthening of these special economic qualities in British society. They were already widely diffused by the middle of the century. The cake of custom had been broken up. We must conceive of eighteenth-century economic history as the result of the economic decisions of a vast multitude of people, now almost all forgotten, going to live here or to work there, to learn this trade or abandon that, to build this ship or to sink that mine, each contributing his or her mite to determine events the ultimate shape of which no one foresaw or could have foreseen.

The decisions of some men were, however, more important than those of others, for reasons which were well known to the eighteenth-century economists. The relative scarcity of capital gave an extraordinary importance, from an economic point of view, to all those who by whatever means, good or ill, old or recent, had acquired property and the income which came from property, whether small or large. The larger the property and the income the greater the importance of the command of capital which they conferred, given an interest in acquiring more property and income and an ability to judge prospects and to turn opportunities to account. Much of the drive and the initiative, the entrepreneurship of change, came from men who in the first instance were owners of small or medium amounts of capital or who rose out of the unpropertied mass. But because the disposition of resources waited most upon the decisions of capital-owners, their choices were of particular importance, and the economy which they did so much to build is properly called a capitalistic economy.

Economic reasoning, for by far the most part plain, prosaic, and lowly; frequently mistaken; often unscrupulous, narrow, and mean, created a new economy in eighteenth-century Britain. But since its centre was calculation exercised upon daily affairs it is not to be understood except among the circumstances of everyday life. We must leave generalization in the chapters which follow and trace in some detail its workings in the main economic activities of the age. Only in this way is it possible to grasp how, step by step, economic growth rose to the creation of the world's first industrial state, so that the evolution of Great Britain in the eighteenth century became an epoch in the history of the world. Only so may we retain a proper sense of the essentially limited, imperfect and even ambiguous nature of that great achievement.

Chapter II

Agriculture and the Land System

At a time, from 1789 to 1848, when the position of the peasant was one of the prime questions in Western and Central Europe and when his emancipation from surviving feudal dues and services was indispensable to further social and economic development, no such controversy disturbed British politics. A still deeper gulf separated British from Continental social conditions. Not only was feudalism no longer a living tradition, but the class of independent cultivators called peasants, in whose hands so much of European agricultural production lay, had ceased to be the main force, if indeed they ever had been, in the British land system. It remains true, however, in Britain as in the rest of Europe, that the special turn which economic development took in the nineteenth century, when industry provided new incomes for new population and caused a new growth of cities and towns, cannot be understood without considering what was happening to agriculture and the supply of food.

Agriculture was by far the most important industry in Great Britain in 1750. For centuries past the greater part of the population had lived by farming. The growth of industries had much diversified the pattern of Britain's occupations, but agriculture continued then and long afterwards to make the greatest call upon the labour of her people. A hundred years later, in 1851, the industry still employed one-quarter of the men in the country above the age of twenty, as well as a considerable number of women, greatly surpassing as an employer at that date the next largest occupations, which were domestic service, cotton textiles, building and general labouring.

With the fortunes of the farming industry were tied up the interests of many classes, professions and occupations, besides those of the farmer and his labourers. The aristocracy, which had never lost direct touch as it tended to do in France and Italy, with the country estates to which it owed most of its wealth; the Church, with its interest in tithe and glebe; the educational and charitable institutions which were also land-owners, such as the colleges of Oxford and Cambridge; the lawyers, through whose offices much business relating to real property passed; the merchants who sold the corn, the cheese, the cattle, and the other produce of the farms in hundreds of markets, ranging from Covent Garden, Smithfield and Mark Lane in London, to that of the smallest country town: all those whose income, in whole or in part, derived from the land, were affected by and influenced the agricultural industry.

No agricultural or land system ever stands still. The economist, Alfred Marshall, who was a keen student of Victorian British India, once remarked that the apparently timeless communities of Indian peasant cultivators were subject to important changes over long periods which he held to be explicable only in terms of economic calculation by land-owners and cultivators, independent of the effects of war, civil disorder or the monsoon. Similarly, the quietness, even the stagnancy, of country life in many agricultural districts of England and Scotland in the middle eighteenth century should not deceive us. Important changes had taken place in British agriculture and landholding during the ninety years since the Civil Wars had ended and were still proceeding in 1750.

One obvious sign of change was the continued extension of the cultivated area. Britain had been in 1700 a country in which considerable areas of land, in England and Wales perhaps as much as a quarter of the whole area, stood unused or relatively unused. Considerable portions of this waste land were within the capacity of contemporary farmers to cultivate, but the moment for exploitation had not yet arrived. Britain still wore a certain semi-colonial air, perhaps especially so in the north and west of England, although such land was to be found in many parts. As population and the towns grew, as communications by road and water improved, as banking and commercial services penetrated the country districts, the value of land rose and much of this waste land came into use.

The extension of the cultivated area continued a process which had been going on throughout the sixteenth and seventeenth centuries. Important land reclamation had been undertaken in Stuart times, as the demand for agricultural products grew and capital for exploitation became available. Some of this work continued into the eighteenth and nineteenth centuries, such as the drainage of the Lincolnshire and East

Anglian Fens, where more than a thousand square miles were added to the farming resources of the kingdom.[1] Work of this kind, smaller in extent, went on at all times, on marsh, moor, heath and hillside, as local conditions favoured.

The greatest incentive towards the cultivation of the waste came late in the eighteenth century from the wars against France between 1793 and 1815. The cutting of many trade connections with the Continent during the Napoleonic struggle separated Great Britain from the main sources in Poland and East Prussia of imports of wheat and agricultural products. The uncertainty of credit and the high war freights for shipping made more difficult the problem of food supplies. Great Britain had been a corn exporter in the first half of the eighteenth century; she had had a surplus to spare in years of good harvest for other European countries, although she imported from them too. Towards the last quarter of the century, as her population grew, she was becoming on balance a net importer of wheat, although the conditions for growing, transporting and handling it from abroad were slow in building up. The interruption of the trade formed a strong inducement towards the reclamation and enclosure of the waste, as it did towards all forms of agricultural activity. The attack on the waste lands by landowners and farmers was especially vigorous after 1802, when the brief Peace of Amiens ended in the resumption of the war and a long period of hostilities was in sight. The reclamation of Exmoor, in the district around Simonsbath, by members of the Knight family in the 1820's may be regarded as the last grand chapter in the story of enclosure of the waste which had been so largely written in the war years.[2] By 1830, the waste as it had once been known was a thing of the past. The cultivated area continued to expand, by small amounts, here and there, to the end of the nineteenth century; but its main outlines as they exist today were firmly drawn by the earlier date.

This filling in of the agricultural map was important both economically and socially. On the one side, it made a contribution to national food supply in Napoleonic times estimated by a contemporary, Joseph Lowe, at something a little less than fifteen per cent of the war-time increase in tillage crops.[3]

---

[1] On this see H. C. Darby, *The Draining of the Fens* (1940).
[2] C. S. Orwin, *The Reclamation of Exmoor Forest* (1929).
[3] Joseph Lowe, *The Present State of England in regard to Agriculture, Trade and Finance*, 2nd ed. (1823), Appendix, pp. 36–7. Lowe thought that Ricardo

Together with improved agricultural methods, it made Great Britain difficult to starve out in Napoleon's time and largely self-sufficient in food, although at high cost, until well on into the nineteenth century. On the other side, it marked the strengthening in British rural life of those interests which had successfully carried out this work and the decline of other interests opposed to it. Broadly speaking, those benefited who could bear the expenses of the work of drainage, reclamation and enclosure. There was a dwindling of those people who had flourished where there was much unsettled land—the squatter, the itinerant trader and tinker, the poacher—of all those whom Gregory King, a statistician and writer of Charles II's time, had described, too harshly, as hanging upon the skirts of society and contributing nothing to national wealth. Much more serious was the loss by labourers and small cultivators of prescriptive rights on land of this kind, such as to turn out an animal or two for pasture or to cut turf and wood for fuel. For poor men, these rights of common upon the waste were of some value and the loss was felt, the more because it came at a time when the cost of living was high owing to the war and various forms of bye-employment, such as spinning, were beginning to die out in country districts in face of competition from the industries of the towns. No legal right was involved and there was nothing which could be disputed in a court of law. In equity, however, some compensation was due and the allotment of land in lieu, which was sometimes done, undoubtedly ought to have been general. As it was, considerations of equity were allowed to be overridden by what were regarded as the superior claims of private interest and national urgency. The question of common right upon the waste was, however, but a small part of the reconstruction of rural life which was now going forward under the impulse of new demands, new uses for the land, and new methods of farming it.

NEW DEMANDS AND NEW USES FOR LAND

The extension of the cultivated area was associated with important changes in the utilization of land, affecting the system of cultivation as a whole. The pull of the metropolitan

and other economists overrated the importance of the extension of cultivation during the war compared with improved agricultural methods. The opinion may have influenced his estimate.

market of London for cheese, meat, cider, hops, poultry and many other agricultural products had been felt for centuries. In the eighteenth century it was stronger than ever. Daniel Defoe had described in his *Tour of the Whole Island of Great Britain* (1724–6) how distant parts of the country specialized in kinds of farming suited to London's needs, from the cheese-farming of Wiltshire to the turkey-rearing of East Anglia. The growth of other towns led in the first half of the century to considerable extensions of pasture-farming for milk and meat. The rising importance of stock upon many English and Scottish farms was a direct consequence of the growth of population and income. They were marked in such a county as Leicestershire, where the grazing grounds were dependent on the London market for their profitable use.

In the second half of the eighteenth century another influence began to make itself felt with increasing force. This was the rising price of wheat after 1760, which, for reasons already mentioned, became acute in the years that followed the outbreak of war with France in 1793. To Englishmen living in the years of war against Napoleon and the uneasy years of peace which followed, the extension of cultivation meant primarily corn-growing. This was because wheat had become in the course of the eighteenth century the national bread-corn. It was in England that the rapid growth of towns and town incomes created the greatest demand for wheat, but the same tendencies could be seen in Lowland Scotland. William Cobbett described the great farms which he saw in the Lothians in 1832 as 'factories for making meat and corn'.[1]

The old bread-meal of Britain had been diversified, both regionally and in the mixing bowl. Barley, oats, rye and maslin, a mixture of rye with wheat, had played a large part in English diet at the beginning of the eighteenth century; oats in Scotland, barley in Wales, oats and rye in England north of the Trent. By 1800, even the poorly paid country labourer had 'lost his rye teeth', as some Nottinghamshire men remarked, when they were urged to counter the rising cost of living in 1796 by returning to the older breads. Given the change of diet, it was not unnatural that the discussions of English economists upon the relations between the margin of

---

[1] In their size, these farms were exceptional in Scotland, but not presumably in the growing attention to town markets; see Miss I. F. Grant, *Economic History of Scotland* (1934), p. 115.

cultivation, rent, wages and the cost of living in the years after Waterloo should be about corn and mainly about wheat. They reflected, in the terms of their argument, the long-standing preoccupations of the landowner, the farmer and the consumer in the towns.

While the production of wheat, beef and mutton for the family table was gradually becoming the main business of British agriculture, it would be a mistake to think of the uses of land wholly in these terms. In the Highlands of Scotland, during the same years of high wheat prices, the most economical use of land was coming to be associated with sheep-farming and the price of wool. Hence the fall in the population of the glens at a time when the population of the Highland counties was rising. The landowners, who were turning out sheep upon the hill pastures, evicted their tenants and threw the farms together on the lower-lying ground to provide winter shelter for the flocks.

The Highland clearances form a celebrated and distressing chapter in modern Scottish history. They may also serve as a reminder of what we might be tempted to forget, in watching the development of experimental farming in the eighteenth century, that the agricultural movement of that day was primarily economic, not technical or legal. It was a question of the most economic use of the land, measured in terms of the financial returns which could be wrung from it.

Before a more profitable use of the land became possible, certain conditions had to be fulfilled, given a potential market for farm products in the towns. One of the first and most easily satisfied conditions was the maintenance of an adequate working population upon the land. There could be no difficulty about this, at a time when the growth of population in country districts was beginning to become marked and alternative employment was relatively scarce. The problem was rather the reverse. Men had to be weaned from a wasteful use of labour, whether it was their own or that of others, and from an abuse of the labourer's weak bargaining position.

Experience suggested, however, that little was to be gained merely by extra labour. Additional employment might be created by the reclaiming of land or the extension of arable farming as against, say, rough grazing. But the more effective and therefore more profitable use of labour on the land depended on an investment of new capital in stock, houses, roads, field drains and ditches, buildings, barns and implements. Capital investment at a high level, such as was needed to have substantial effect upon farm output, was not, however, entirely a matter of routine. To be successful in supplying existing markets and in creating new demands, it needed the addition of a certain amount of originating ability, which might be modest or exceptional. There had to be a certain willingness to use the resources of the land in new ways.

THE LAND SYSTEM

The possibility of agricultural progress depended upon the decision to invest more heavily than in the past in new and fruitful methods of cultivation. Such modifications of existing agricultural practice might require serious changes in the system of landholding and the adaptation of the agricultural population to a new kind of life. Who took decisions so momentous, and who saw that they were enforced? On the Continent of Europe, during the nineteenth century, the man who settled how much money should go into the land and whether it should be spent in new ways or not was often a peasant. He was both small landowner and agriculturist, and as the towns and cities grew, the supply of food depended upon his calculations and actions. He was the man who carried through, in many parts of Western and Central Europe, the transition from subsistence to commercial farming, from one standard of cultivation to another.

In eighteenth-century Britain, this was not so. The trend of landownership and holding, particularly since the Civil Wars had been unfavourable to peasant-farming, if we mean by this the cultivation of the land by the small owner-occupier. A contrasting land system had developed, and by the middle of the eighteenth century was already strong in many parts of the country. It was based upon large ownership by men accustomed to make an income by letting a large part if not the whole of their land, and upon tenant-farming by well-to-do tenants who brought capital of their own to farming. This system, which gave the authority and the influence in the countryside to the territorial aristocracy, and to a wealthy upper middle class, represented by the squire and the country gentleman, was by 1750 sufficiently old and well established to be regarded by many Englishmen as the natural order of society.

It was in point of fact largely the product of the history of
the sixteenth and seventeenth centuries.[1] The squires and the
landed gentry owed some part at least of their strong position
in England to the catastrophes which had overtaken landed
property during the Reformation and in the later struggle
between Crown and Parliament. The dissolution of the
monasteries with their great endowments of land had had the
effect, between Henry VIII's time and the Civil Wars, of
throwing much land into the hands of the untitled but
business-like men who stood just below the aristocracy in the
ranks of society, although they were often equal or superior to
it in wealth and ability. The break-up of the family estates of
bankrupt noblemen in Elizabethan and Jacobean times and
the sales of crown lands during the same two generations
before the Civil Wars further advanced changes in ownership,
as did the sequestration of Royalist estates during the Civil Wars.

Religious and political violence were not the only source of
change. England was becoming a country of rich merchants,
perhaps all the more so because much of the trade of the time
was of a monopoly character, while taxation bore lightly on
mercantile and industrial incomes. Until the Revolution of
1688 and the rise of the practice of investing in the public
funds, land was the favourite investment for capital which, for
one reason or another, was no longer wanted in trade. The
merchants of London, Bristol, Newcastle and other towns,
over generations, had been buying their way into society, and
seeking at the same time a safe return on their money. Together
with members of the professions, especially wealthy lawyers,
and those many individuals and families who made money as
holders of high office under the Crown, they were purchasers
of estates, both those which had snapped their family moorings
in the revolutions of the period and those which had not.

Mercantile investments played a smaller part in the building
up of great landed properties when the city of London through
its financial institutions began to offer an alternative employment for capital after 1700. The chief incentive towards the
concentration of landownership after that date seems to have

---

[1] These paragraphs can only skirt the complex and contentious subject
of the history of landed property. See R. H. Tawney, 'The Rise of the
Gentry', *Econ. Hist. Rev.* vol. xi (1941), and the comments of H. R. Trevor-
Roper 'The Gentry, 1540–1640', *Econ. Hist. Rev.* Supplement (1953); for
the eighteenth century, H. J. Habakkuk, 'English Landownership, 1680–
1740', *Econ. Hist. Rev.* vol. x (1940).

come from the family pride of the aristocracy and the workings of primogeniture, armed, since the Restoration, with new refinements in the land law, which assisted the unbroken descent of vast estates. The squires and the smaller country gentlemen, who were feeling the effects of the heavy taxation required by the wars of William III and Marlborough, appear to have lost ground in the first half of the eighteenth century to the great aristocratic houses from which they had gained so much in the past.

The net result of many alterations in social and economic conditions was to give to the English land system a high concentration of ownership together with an attitude towards land ownership which was commercial rather than feudal. The mere existence of the great houses in the countryside and the unchallenged position which their owners occupied in society did not suffice to make them homes of economic enlightenment. The expenditure of the aristocracy and the country gentlemen on building, politics, horse-racing, and their many other interests was always great. As a class, they were not ashamed of their debts. Their incomes had to pay for the glories and the follies of the aristocratic age between the Revolution and the Reform Bill of 1832, as well as for any economic development in which they might care to invest. But it is remarkable and important that many English landowners, such as the famous Coke of Holkham,[1] possessed an acute sense of the new value given to land and agricultural products by the growth of population, commerce and manufactures and showed much shrewdness in exploiting it. They turned to account new agricultural knowledge and the increasingly important profession of estate management, which placed much business-like ability at the service of the landowner.

During the same period of the eighteenth-century aristocratic revival, when the large country estate was becoming more than ever fashionable for the sake of the political and social power which it conferred upon its owner, the actual supervision of agricultural operations was coming more and more into the hands of the well-to-do tenant-farmer. This was due, in the first place, to the decline of the small independent

[1] Thomas Coke, first Earl of Leicester (1752–1842), was not an inventor of new techniques, but he raised the art of estate management on the light soils of West Norfolk to a high level. Mrs Stirling's *Coke of Norfolk and His Friends* (1910) needs to be corrected in the light of Miss Naomi Riches' *Agricultural Revolution in Norfolk* (1937), on the point of Coke's originality.

owner of land, the so-called yeoman. (The word was coming to be more loosely used to cover tenant-farmers too in the eighteenth century.) Men of this sort formed a kind of intermediate middle class in the countryside. Sitting on the jury, voting for the county member of Parliament, fighting as soldiers on both sides in the Civil Wars, they had played a notable part in national history during the hundred years before the Revolution of 1688.

The decline of the social group to which the yeoman, the English analogue to the well-to-do peasant on the Continent, had belonged is obscure. It seems to have begun in the century before 1750 and to have been particularly marked during the fifty or sixty years which followed the Revolution. For it was caused by political and social as well as economic conditions. Taxes, the new habit of preserving game for sport on the grand scale, the rising value of land, the wish of the large estate owner to hold everything he could see from his windows or to increase the rent-roll, whether for private or political purposes,[1] all played their part. The decline of a class did not always mean social descent for individuals. The yeoman often improved his economic position by selling his property. The decline of his class was neither steady nor complete in the eighteenth century. The yeoman during the Napoleonic wars (1793-1815) was so far from disappearing that he made money out of high food prices and was more often a buyer than a seller of land. The fall of prices after the war, in the 1820's, together with the more costly standard of living he had become used to during the wars, was a disaster for the men who lived as he did. Many owner-occupiers were sold up between 1813 and 1835. Even so, yeoman families survived, only to migrate in many instances to the Middle West of the United States of America during the British agricultural depression of the 1880's. The yeoman never became extinct, although the name disappeared from general use. But in 1750, although still strong in parts of the country, such as Lincolnshire or the Cumberland of Wordsworth's boyhood, he had already lost, so far as we can see, the national position from which he might possibly have played a distinguished role in the transformation of agriculture. He was tenacious, but he continued to lose ground.

[1] In the eighteenth century, the political influence of a man in his county was roughly measurable by his rental; see L. B. Namier, *Structure of Politics at the Accession of George III* (1929), vol. I, p. 88.

The 'husbandman' or small tenant was a common figure in almost all counties. But although common, he was neither economically nor legally strong. The tenant of from 10 to 30 acres—by leasehold or copyhold, or as a tenant at will, or from year to year—the slenderness of his resources made him rather a subsistence farmer than a seller to market. The nature of his tenancy was such that he could often be ousted without much trouble to his landlord. Owing to his poverty and his ignorance of the world, he was not well fitted to make the most of his opportunities; yet unless he did so, his holding was in peril. In an age when the commercial value of land was rising, the temptation to the landlord to evict him and bring in someone financially stronger, who could exploit the land more successfully and pay a higher rent, was strong.

The small cultivator was therefore not well placed to play in Britain the part which fell to him in the economics and the social politics of great Continental states such as France and Prussia in the same age, where it raised him to European significance in the years after 1789. Unless some strong attempt had been made by the State to alter the balance in favour of the weaker elements in English rural society, the initiative in commercial farming lay naturally with the larger owner of estates and the wealthier type of tenant-farmer. The structure of rural society in 1750 was already such that the question was how, rather than whether, these men would make use of their advantages. The composition and temper of Hanoverian Parliaments deprived the small cultivator of the possibility of protection, beyond the minimum required by the strict letter of the existing law; and unless he was first helped, he was unlikely to help himself.

The small cultivator was weak in capital and in knowledge of the market. Even in the nineteenth century, in parts of Europe more favourably disposed towards him, he needed all the help he could get from co-operative credit and marketing, sometimes State-assisted, to adapt his type of farming to the needs of the market. In eighteenth-century Britain, his weakness was technical also. He did not easily come by a full knowledge of the resources of the land and would probably have needed some form of instruction to do so. This instruction he did not possess and he was living in an age of comparatively rapid change in agricultural practice. Even the larger farm could not have produced upon the scale required, without some sort of effort to increase the return from the soil. It was because the large holding came to be associated, although not invariably so, with advances in the technique of farming, that many contemporaries, especially towards the end of the century, came to favour the concentration of agricultural holdings and to regard the small occupier or tenant as the enemy of good husbandry.

THE TECHNIQUE OF FARMING

Changes in agricultural practice were not new in 1750; neither were they new to the small farmer. Considerable local variations in farming methods, to meet different conditions of soil, rainfall, market and so forth, had been developed over long periods of time. Many must have originated with small farmers in the past, and their soundness was indicated by the success with which the fertility of the soil had been maintained, despite centuries of exploitation. What distinguished innovation in English (and, one might add, Scottish) farming increasingly from the Restoration onwards was the consciousness of the experimentation and the linking of it with scientific knowledge.

After the Civil Wars, men returning from exile on the Continent, in the Low Countries and France, brought new standards of comparison to the business of farming and estate management. The same age, which saw the first great English naturalists, Ray and Willughby, the foundation of the Royal Society, and the work of Newton and Boyle, brought into currency an interest in science and its applications. This was the hobby of the few, but it bore upon practical interests, because of the new critical attitude which it brought towards the age-old concern with the breeding and rearing of plants and animals.

In the century after 1660 important new steps were taken towards raising the yield of crops and the number and quality of livestock on English farms. Men were experimenting particularly with the introduction of new field crops, which could be grown in years when the soil was by old custom left fallow to recover its powers. The significance of these was double. They made it possible to eliminate the loss of a crop, without injury to the soil by over-cropping, because the new crops restored indispensable chemical elements to the soil. At the same time, they provided winter food for stock. The need to lay down land to a bare fallow, because there were no artificial fertilizers, and the extreme difficulty of keeping cattle through the winter without cake or silage had constituted serious wastes in the old-style farming. The two wastes aggravated one another. Scanty crop yields made it hard to keep as much stock as the land was capable of carrying. Few and ill-fed stock deprived the farmer of the manure which might have rendered the bare fallow unnecessary by supplying the soil with the chemicals it wanted. This statement represents the older farming at its worst or most difficult. Farmers had achieved various compromises towards reducing these wastes according to their resources. Not all were reduced, at the winter's end, to the sadness of a Highland or a Welsh mountain cattle lifting.[1] But to eliminate them altogether was an important object of good land management and farming practice.

What we see in British agriculture in the eighteenth century is the gradual building up of a new technical system, adapted to the massive production of the wheat and meat which were becoming the staple diet of the population, and associated with the financial and legal conditions which made large-scale agricultural organization possible. This development in farming was specially marked in such districts as the wheat country of Norfolk and Suffolk, which became the home of an advanced type of estate management and tenant-farming; Leicestershire, in the heart of the grazing country; Hertfordshire and Essex, both near the London market. But its influence came to be generally felt, granting that types and standards of farming continued to vary immensely, even on different sides of the same hedge. The new methods made themselves felt in rising yields per acre. These are difficult to measure and compare in an industry of wide local and seasonal variations, but by the opening of the nineteenth century in some parts of the country they were beginning to approximate to modern yields, in wheat, oats and barley.[2] They were also felt in the improved weight and quality, from the butcher's point of view, of beasts sold.[3] The doubling, and more than doubling, in the

[1] The need partly to lead, partly to carry, half starved beasts from their winter quarters to spring pasture was the natural consequence of the scarcity of hay and winter pasture in hill country.
[2] R. Trow-Smith, *English Husbandry* (1951), p. 143.
[3] Lord Ernle, *English Farming, Past and Present*, 4th ed. (1927), p. 188. There can be no doubt about the improvement, but the estimates are confused: see G. E. Fussell 'The Size of English Cattle in the Eighteenth Century, *Agricultural History*, vol. III (1929), pp. 160–82.

size and weight of beasts sold at Smithfield market between
1710 and 1795 has been often quoted, although it is an unreliable index for the state of British farming as a whole. The
general measure of the change they brought is the relative
success with which agricultural output kept pace with the needs
of a population which doubled itself between 1710 and 1810.

The rise of the new mixed farming owed much to personalities
and individual enterprise. The introduction after the Restoration of the new crops for rotation, the roots and the clovers,
remains anonymous. Many of the ideas successfully applied in
the eighteenth century had been hinted at or anticipated by
agricultural writers of the seventeenth century. But the contributions of Jethro Tull (1674–1740), a Berkshire farmer, in
arable cultivation, partly under French influence; of Viscount
Townshend (1674–1738) in Norfolk, the champion but not the
introducer of turnips as a field crop; of Robert Bakewell (1725–
95), the Leicestershire grazier, in stock-breeding, above all the
improvement of sheep for mutton, remain distinct, although
they have sometimes been overrated or misunderstood. So,
too, in their different ways, do those of Arthur Young (1741–
1820) and William Marshall (1745–1818), the agricultural
writers and propagandists. Very often we find men building on
foundations laid by others. Many were imitators. After 1780,
it might be said, the improvement of estates became fashionable
among wealthy landowners.

It was not only fashion, however, which spread the influence
of the new farming after that date. The expectations, both
realized and false, of high profits and rents during the war with
France, between 1793 and 1815, did much to stimulate investment in agriculture by farmers and landowners. High prices
rewarded, of course, the bad farmer as well as the good, and
they must have helped to keep alive much poor farming. Nor
did the new investments always pay. The collapse of prices
after the war brought heavy losses to many farmers in the
1820's and early 1830's, as a war-inflated agriculture struggled
with indifferent success to adapt itself to peacetime conditions.

OPEN-FIELD AND ENCLOSED FARMING

By 1830, the progress of capitalization, the growth of large
holdings, the adoption of new methods, and the commercializa-
tion of agriculture had had important effects upon the structure

of farming and the interests of the various classes and groups who lived by it. The investment of new capital in the land, although it cannot be measured and is known to us only in fragments, was certainly the heart of the economic revolution in agriculture in the eighteenth century. But investment could not take place upon that scale without remoulding rural life. The decline of the open-field village was the outward and visible sign of social change.

Open-field farming was an organization of agriculture and of rural society which still remained strong at the middle of the eighteenth century, particularly in the eastern, north-eastern and east midland counties of England. In other parts of the country, it appears never to have been known; for example, in large parts of the south-western counties of Devon and Cornwall, in the north-west (in the Lake District), and in the south-east counties near London. In Scotland, there existed a type of agriculture much resembling it, known as 'run-rig', although this differed in important respects from the English system. But Scots custom and law and Scots social conditions were different. The main enclosure movement of the eighteenth century was English, and it is English conditions that are in question.

Open-field farming was a system of agriculture in which land was held in severalty, that is, by individual tenure. Tenures were well defined, but cultivation was carried on in common. The system perhaps had its origin when settlement was still going on and the fair distribution of the valuable and highly variable commodity land, as it was brought under the plough for the first time, was an important consideration. Equitable shares apart, the method of cultivation in earlier times had been largely dictated by the narrow resources of the farmers. They made up among themselves, as few owned a complete team, the plough-teams on which the main work of cultivation depended and carried out, according to rules carefully laid down in the court baron of the local manor or at the parish vestry meeting, the principal operations of the farming year, ploughing, sowing and reaping. They were usually short, not only of capital in the form of ploughs and plough-teams, but also of good meadow land to feed their beasts, including plough animals. Hence the practice of pasturing stock upon the arable fields, after harvest, and of making an annual distribution of what meadow lands there were. The uncultivated waste played an important part in their sort of farming. It was additional pasture for cattle and poultry, a place to find wood for fuel and fencing, to be used only under elaborate customary rules. The open fields, in which lay the unfenced arable holdings, gave their name to the system as a whole. But the arable fields formed only a part of it. The cultivator's livelihood and that of his family depended upon his cluster of rights in arable, meadow and waste land all taken together and upon a proper balance in his holdings between land for bread-corn and pasturage for beasts, for he depended on both.[1]

Open-field cultivation had to its credit the relatively dense settlement of Britain over centuries, without serious exhaustion of the soil. Being a bundle of devices to meet practical conditions, it probably never was stationary as a land system and had been considerably modified in the course of time, especially by two developments of high importance. One was the growth from very early times of wage-labour, hired in money or in kind, often in both, among men who had no land or too little to keep them and their families. This made it possible to run enclosed, that is, hedged or fenced holdings of considerable size, as an adjunct to or in replacement of open-field holdings. Many factors besides the farmer's ability to meet the wages bill determined, however, the size of enclosed holding which actually emerged in any part of the country, such as the availability of land and the product dealt in. The other development was the accumulation of capital among some of the cultivators themselves and the willingness of the richer to risk part of it in cultivation and stock-breeding. They might do this inside or outside of the common field.

Open-field farming was more adaptable to the needs of commercial farming than has sometimes been supposed. There are traces in the sixteenth and seventeenth centuries of variation and growth in open-field communities. Given careful nursing the old system might perhaps have been made to serve as the basis for a rural reconstruction which would have preserved some of its essential features, especially the relatively wide distribution of landholding and the community of interest which existed, although this should not be exaggerated, among the cultivators. But this was not the direction in which

[1] The system, which cannot be done justice to in a few lines, has been many times described, but best in C. S. Orwin, *The Open Fields* (1938).

the English land system had developed for many years before 1750. As farming became commercialized, the tendency was to take land out of the open field and to cultivate it as an enclosed holding, which might be and often was a larger unit than the farmer's open-field holding. Landlords might and often did terminate small tenancies and consolidate holdings as enclosed farms. The efficiency of enclosed farming should not be overrated. The growing of a hedge or erection of a fence did not necessarily mean that the methods of the farmer were better than those of his open-field neighbours or than those used on that part of his holding, if he had any, which lay in the open field. But enclosure did permit a specialization of the land in the direction rendered most profitable by the existing state of demand. There had been much enclosure of open field for sheep pasture and wool in the sixteenth and early seventeenth century, and there was much for cattle and dairy purposes in the early eighteenth century. In that century, resources in capital grew. With many agriculturists, their savings must have grown almost automatically with their incomes. The contemporary increase of population in country districts turned on to the labour market a multitude of men and women without land of their own, often without alternative employment. The enclosed farm in the late eighteenth century was consequently becoming a formidable competitor for the use of the land, as better able to extract the maximum product for commercial purposes. The open-field farmer did not disregard the market, but he remained nearer than the capitalist tenant-farmer to the subsistence farming of his forebears.

The rising price of wheat after 1760 and the demand for meat in the towns both encouraged a type of business-like farming on enclosed land which was increasingly common and increasingly profitable. Moreover, the encloser could quote strong arguments of public advantage for what he was doing. That Great Britain depended on her fields to feed a rapidly multiplying people was something that few understood. But everyone could appreciate the pressure of that unseen demand reflected in high prices and the contention that open-field practice stood in the way of a higher yield of corn and more and better-fed cattle. The argument of demand was reinforced by war. Of the fifty years after 1760, more than a half were for Britain years of war. During the war with the American colonies and France (1776–82) command of the seas was temporarily lost to the French and self-sufficiency became indispensable. In the war against Revolutionary and Napoleonic France (1793–1815), British command of the sea became absolute after the battle of Trafalgar in 1805, but the pressure of population upon home food supplies was acute. In years of poor harvest, in 1800 and 1801, and again in 1810, 1812 and 1813, wheat prices at well over 100s. a quarter were little short of famine prices. It is not surprising that the two periods of war were also periods of rapid enclosure. The atmosphere which they created favoured quick action and was adverse to the cool consideration of agricultural and rural policy.

In centuries past, open-field holdings had been exchanged or enclosed from time to time by agreement among the parties concerned. The agreement might or might not be formally registered by the court baron or the local vestry. As many parties were sometimes concerned, agreements were slow to arrive at. A minority or one man might hold them up. Hence the practice which sprang up in the seventeenth century of ratifying such agreements in the Courts of Chancery or Exchequer, often after a collusive action, so as to obtain a decree which would bind the minority. What now happened, from about 1760 onwards, was that the older processes of private agreement and Chancery decree were abandoned in favour of the private act of Parliament, by men who were too deeply impressed by arguments of private profit or national need to be willing to wait. The private act was at first used to give legislative effect to an agreement already reached. Later, the practice was to appoint, as soon as the act was passed, officials known as enclosure commissioners to visit and survey the parish and re-allot the land in an award which became legally binding upon all the parties concerned.

There were some 5000 enclosure acts and enclosure awards under general acts after 1760, and they affected some 6 million acres of English land out of a cultivated area which Gregory King had reckoned in 1688 at 21 million acres.[1] The effects of eighteenth-century enclosure were therefore of national importance. These effects were mostly felt in some of the counties

[1] The estimate of the acts and their effects is that accepted by a recent student of the legislation, W. E. Tate, *The Parish Chest* (1946), p. 266. The figure for Gregory King combines his estimate of arable with that for pasture and meadow; see Gregory King, *Natural and Political Observations, 1696*, ed. W. E. Barnett (1936), p. 35.

containing much waste in the north, such as Yorkshire, and in the east midland and eastern counties. Some of it was enclosure from the wild, but there were a number of counties where a quarter, sometimes more, of the land already in open-field cultivation was enclosed in the course of the century.[1]

There can be little doubt that enclosure did much to improve the use of the soil. The landlord could achieve this not only by the consolidation of small subsistence tenancies into large farms but also by a careful choice of tenants, by the application of types of tenure, such as the long lease, which attracted the good farmer at the same time as it brought in an improved rent, and by the insertion of cultivation clauses in the agreement with his tenant. Finally, he could encourage the farmer by investment in the land, in buildings, roads and cottages. The farmer could and often did put much capital into the land in other ways, in stock, seed and implements, and might and often did make a more intelligent use of labour. These were not invariably the results of enclosure, but that there was a substantial rise in the technical efficiency of agriculture between 1760 and 1830 is indisputable. It cannot be dissociated from enclosure or from the reclamation of the waste land which had formed a part of the open-field farmer's resources.

The social consequences of enclosure were none the less serious. After 1830, large tenant-farms of from 100 to 500 acres were responsible for the greater part of the product of English farming. The tenant or occupier of less than 100 acres was still common, but he was no great contributor to national income. The continued growth of large tenancies meant, however, the extinction of many small ones. What happened to the small tenant depended on local economic conditions and on the degree of protection afforded by his tenancy. Where it paid the landlord to throw holdings together, enclosure provided an opportunity to do so, although it was not always taken. Tenants at will or for life could not resist eviction. The tenancies of other men were more secure, being heritable or protected by custom. They might, however, be bought out or exchanged. In the enclosure fever of the war years after 1793 there was a good deal of eviction. The men concerned went to the towns or declined into the agricultural labourer class. Unfortunately for them, they entered that class at a low point in its fortunes.

[1] E. C. K. Gonner, *Common Land and Enclosure* (1912), p. 448.

THE COUNTRY LABOURER

The agricultural labourer, sometimes owning a scrap of land, but dependent mainly and often wholly on earnings in money or kind, had existed in Britain for many centuries. His class had multiplied with the opportunities for wage-labour and with the rise of population in a country where the chances of forming new holdings out of the waste had become increasingly rare. The English country landscape is his memorial, as much as it is that of the country gentleman or the farmer, whether yeoman or tenant; his hand had made or remade much of it. How numerous labourers were is a difficult question to answer. But it has been suggested that in 1750 they stood in relation to landowners and landholders of all types in the ratio of rather less than two to one. Their numbers were to rise to between two and three to one in the next eighty years.[1]

The eighteenth century was an important period in the history of the country labourer. The limits of land settlement, in a country so small as Great Britain, with a greatly increased population, were becoming uncomfortably close. So much so that the advance of cultivation upon what appeared to be the last of the waste led Ricardo and other economists to propound in the first quarter of the next century a theory of rents, based upon the cost, in terms of labour, of cultivating such marginal land. The country labourer was beginning to be more cut off from access to land than ever in the past. Many men must have been born into that class who had no expectation of holding at any time the smallest scrap of land, whether by inheritance, purchase or prescriptive right. This had long been so in some districts; but to the extent that it became increasingly the condition of a larger and larger proportion of the labouring class, it presumably weakened their ability to bargain in the labour market.

What land the labourers possessed appears to have been respected during enclosure, not only as regards scraps of land but also gardens. They retained their gardens, while they received compensation for legally recognized rights in land or in money, which did not have the same meaning for them as land. Here, as in the treatment of the small tenant, the

---

[1] The figures for 1750 are from Sir John Clapham, *Concise Economic History of England to 1750* (1949), p. 210; for 1830, his *Economic History of Modern Britain*, vol. I, 2nd ed. (1930), p. 113.

behaviour of the larger landowners and of the enclosure commissioners appears in almost all cases to have been perfectly
correct, according to law. It was equity and the large sense of
fairness that were wanting, in matters where legal right was not
concerned.

Access to land was not confined, however, to landowners
under the older conditions of country life. Customary rights
to the use of land, especially waste ground, for such needful
purposes as cutting fuel or grazing poultry or an animal or
two, were more important to many labourers than rights
in land, which few had. Small allotments of land were sometimes made in lieu of the customary rights of common, but
they were the fruit of the generosity of a few landowners. It
was in this respect that the labourer was a loser by enclosure,
to an extent not easily measured by the apparent triviality
of his loss, which must be put against the slenderness of his
income.

The prospect of continued agricultural employment the
labourer often owed to enclosure. The spread and the intensity
of cultivation promoted the volume of employment. Where
employment declined, owing to enclosure or to new types of
cultivation, the decline was local. Until the mechanization
of farming began in the 1840's and 1850's, conditions in
agriculture were favourable to the extension of employment, often owing to enclosure of the waste, especially when
this took place for arable purposes. It did not follow that
there was employment to be had all the time or that the terms
of employment were good.

Since enclosure did not, so far as we can see, diminish farm
employment nationally, it follows that the new industrial
towns of this period were not created by evicted tenants and
dismissed labourers, as has sometimes been supposed.[1] Their
rapid growth was rather due to the migration of an over-
abundant rural population, in the search for employment and
income, however poor and wretched. On the other hand, the
fluctuations of new investment in farming during the war and
after were extremely serious for the country labourer and far
worse than the consequences of enclosure. They left him often
with no option but to leave the countryside. He was fortunate

---

[1] This question has been thoroughly examined by J. D. Chambers,
'Enclosure and Labour Supply in the Industrial Revolution', *Econ. Hist.
Rev.*, 2nd series, vol. v (1953).

if he did not find industrial investment and employment equally depressed in the towns.

Employment could not of itself solve the country labourer's daily problem, how to maintain himself and, if he were married, his family. The competition of industrial employments was forcing up farm wages in the north of England towards the end of the eighteenth century; the northern labourer was becoming better paid than the southern. Where industry was decadent or was hardly to be found, as in large parts of the western and southern counties, agricultural wages were low. Furthermore, the value of those wages in terms of what they would buy varied with prices. There were considerable regional differences in cost of living in that age of poor communications. Some labourers lived in 'dear counties', others in cheap ones.

Far more serious than these local variations was the steep general rise in the cost of living which followed the outbreak of war with France in 1793, and which proved to be the beginning of a long-continued and memorable inflation of prices. This inflation was symptomatic of an inflation of incomes, but the country labourer's income was not among the first to rise. He found himself faced with the highest living costs that any man could remember, just when his common rights, if he had any, had been or were about to be impaired or lost by enclosure and when various forms of bye-employment pursued by the families of small farmers and labourers, such as spinning and flax-dressing, were being swept away by the progress of factory textile production. Severe privation was only alleviated by an extension of poor relief in aid of wages, particularly agricultural wages, from 1795 onwards. This expedient, 'the Speenhamland system' mentioned earlier in this book,[1] was continued after 1815, as war-time expedients often are, into the peace.

With the arrival of peace, the inflation and high prices came to an end. If this was depressing to the farmer and landowner, who had pitched their expectations for a continuance of the wartime levels of rents and profits which they had enjoyed for the best part of a generation, it was a relief to the labourer. The cost of living fell in the 1820's, and at the same time, employment diminished and wages, which had risen in the later war years, were reduced. What the position of the labourer was, at the new levels of prices and wages, is imper-

---

[1] See above, p. 8.

fectly known; but there seems something to be said for the view that, assuming equal regularity of employment, some English or Welsh country labourers in the mid-1820's lived a trifle better than in the first years of the war, before prices rose. Many were worse off; many others could show no change in their condition.[1] Where deterioration had occurred, the Poor Law stepped in.

No profound scientific application had been necessary to work a revolution in eighteenth-century British farming. A certain willingness to experiment, to try new things, to lay out money and energy in new ways, were the qualities chiefly demanded. It says much for the healthy state of many elements in rural society that they were forthcoming. They enabled farming to play an important part in the process of industrialization by providing an adequate supply of food, which in those days could not be obtained overseas, and so set labour free for town employments. Agricultural rents and profits assisted the expansion of industry, as we shall see.

Other sides of rural society were in a far less satisfactory condition. Little of the immediate benefit to agricultural incomes from the supply of new markets in the towns had gone to the small tenant-farmer or the agricultural labourer. These men paid part of the price of the establishment of a new economy, as the peasant has helped to pay it in other countries since. The wartime boom, which did much for the expansion of industry, brought hardship to them. Bitterness was the consequence, all the more so as men seldom look for the source of their troubles, but consider only those through whom their troubles come. It is hardly surprising that relations between farmer, landowner and country labourer, especially the first and last, were bad. This was so especially when wages were reduced after 1815, as the disturbances in the south of England in 1830 were to show. Many men and women left the country then and later, carrying with them a dislike and hatred of the ruling men in rural life, the landowner, the parson and the farmer. The deep-rooted memories and emotions of an intelligent but inarticulate class became one of many ingredients in the radicalism of the towns, then about to enter into the long political battle over agricultural protection and the Corn Laws.

[1] Sir John Clapham, *Economic History of Modern Britain* (1930), vol. 1, 2nd ed., p. 131.

Chapter III

The Path of Innovation in Mining
and Manufacture

THE OLD AND NEW LOCALIZATION OF INDUSTRY

Agriculture provided the food for Great Britain's additional
population between 1750 and 1830, saving the small amount
of food that was imported. It could not put into the hands or
pockets of people, unless they worked on the land, the incomes
with which that food could be bought. Herein lies the significance of the towns, for it was in them that, through industry,
commerce and finance, new incomes were being created at an
unusually rapid rate. Industrial growth and town life did not
always go together, nor had either as yet got very far. For
centuries, manufactures had existed in country districts,
scattered through industrial villages and the cottages of a population which still retained many ties with the soil. From about
the middle of the eighteenth century, these ties were being
quickly broken. The forty years between 1780 and 1820 were,
so far as can be seen, years of particularly swift urban growth.
This left the balance of the national life still tilted in a rural
direction, as late as the Reform Bill of 1832, which gave parliamentary representation to many of the towns for the first time.
The representative Englishman and Scotsman was not yet a
town-dweller, nor was he to be until the second half of the
nineteenth century. None the less, the developments of those
eighty years before 1832 were extremely significant. Town life
was becoming a kind of index of industrial activity, as it was
later to be throughout Europe and North America. Industrial
incomes were coming to form a larger proportion of the
national income than anyone had supposed possible in the past.
This happened because a long and unexampled process of
industrial investment and activity offered some sort of alternative employment to men and women prepared to quit the
familiar scenes of rural life in order to escape from the depths
of poverty, under-employment, social depression and isolation
which existed there. If the measure of their escape appears
less obvious to us than it did to them, or even delusive, as it

sometimes undoubtedly was, we have to remember the sharp spurs which drove them on; the unromantic needs for food, shelter and warmth in a northern land; hunger, cold and unwantedness at the hearth.

Great Britain in 1750 was already distinguished by the variety and prosperity of its industries. Many went back in origin to the Middle Ages as did the greatest, most generally distributed of them all, woollen clothmaking, and important industries such as ironmaking and shipbuilding. Others, such as printing and papermaking and the glass and copper industries, had been introduced in the sixteenth and seventeenth centuries when a considerable industrial expansion had taken place, much assisted by the immigration of skill and capital from the Continent. By 1750, industrial employments were common and widespread.

The older county and market towns had their own crafts and industries, working usually for a local market. But much industrial organization, including that of some of the most important industries in the country, took a rural form, as it had done for centuries since the sharp distinction between town and country of the high Middle Ages had broken down. The typical industrial area, even in those parts of the country where industry was growing fastest, was a countryside of industrial villages peppered with small collieries, isolated ironworks or the cottages of workers, making cotton or woollen cloth, gloves, stockings, lace, nails, chairs, or whatever it might be. This rural organization was characteristic, to take some of the most important industries of the time, of the coal industry, in its great strongholds in the northern counties, in Cumberland and around Tyneside and Weardale; of the early cotton spinning and weaving of Lancashire; of the woollen cloth manufacture of Yorkshire and the West of England; the silk stocking making of Derbyshire and the cotton stocking making of Nottinghamshire; the primary branches of the iron industry, with their furnaces and forges, in the woodlands of Shropshire, Furness and elsewhere; the hardware manufactures of the Staffordshire and Worcestershire villages, and many others. The village or small town setting for industry was general. Yet many of these industries worked for a market which was national or foreign.

One great city was also one of the largest of industrial centres. London was both a great consumer and a great producer of industrial goods. She sheltered a great mass of unskilled men, drawn by her port, ships and markets, and also a multitude of skilled trades, such as the clockmakers of Clerkenwell, the silk-weavers of Spitalfields, the tanners and curriers, coopers and builders of the riverside parishes. But while London was an important element in the industrial life of the country and while many of the county towns were prosperous, it was not in the existing cities that the main industrial advance of the eighteenth century took place.

The economic problem which faced many men engaged in industry and which was becoming acute in certain branches was to increase production, and to do this without increasing costs and with costs, prices. The world of the time offered many markets, both at home and abroad. They were not, of course, to be found without effort. Some of the men most to the fore in adapting the methods of British industry in that century were also among the keenest commercial travellers of their time, perpetually sounding and tapping new demand. Such a man was Matthew Boulton, the Birmingham industrialist and partner of James Watt in the development of the steam engine. But the steady expansion of markets, home and foreign, in war and in peace, only made the problem more acute. How to increase production, so as to meet that part of demand which could be satisfied at existing prices, and how to reduce the cost of every unit of output, so as to secure the half-known markets which could be had at a lower price—this was the economic puzzle in which the problems of technology and industrial organization took their rise.

The problem did not face all industries in the same degree. The fashionable trades of London, like those of the great cities of the Continent, such as Paris, Vienna or Rome, were only moderately interested in expanding their sales. Not only was their market limited, but the value of much of what they had to sell depended upon the constant change of fashion, even upon the maintenance of an artificial scarcity and a high price. The goods sold in such markets were the products of an exquisite civilization. The craftsmanship which produced them was often superb. It was not in these industries or in these markets that men found it worth their while to ponder the economics of large-scale production or that British industrialists and industrial workers first made for themselves a world name. The luxury trades of the great Continental centres remained

almost without serious challenge from Britain in the next
century. The significance of British industrial growth lay in the
fact that it was largely directed towards the supply of goods
which were wanted at a medium or a low price and in quantity.
The type of industry so created served the needs not of small
and wealthy circles but of large markets and of large and
increasing populations, to an extent rare or altogether unknown among the industries of the past.

Much of the new industrial development which marked the
later years of the eighteenth century went on in districts of
Great Britain which had been undistinguished as industrial
producers in the past and were economically poor and backward. The new industries sometimes owed initial advantages
to that fact, in competition with older and more expensive
industrial centres. They owed even more to the growth of local
incomes and markets. In the new localization of industry,
East Anglia, the South of England and the West of England
lost much of the industrial weight they once had, although they
were to regain part of it at a much later date. The new
industrial growth tended to be concentrated in the Midlands,
the North of England, South Wales and Clydeside. This
shifting of the balance against the south and the west tended,
of course, to be countered in some degree by the constantly
expanding mass of London's industries and population. The
gradual redrawing of the industrial map, first clearly displayed
by the census of 1801, had begun much earlier than 1750. It
was one of the most obvious features of British industrial
development during the late eighteenth and early nineteenth
century. It was the outward sign of a new deployment of the
industrial resources of the island, not only in raw materials but
also in capital and labour, and was connected with profound
changes in the technique and organization of important
industries.

THE HEAVY INDUSTRIES

The altering economic geography of Great Britain was
especially due to the continued growth and revolutionary
development of the industries which have since come to be
known as the heavy industries. The coal and iron industries
had been important in British economic life since later Tudor
and early Stuart times. Late in the eighteenth century, their

renewed and rapid expansion became linked with steam engineering, with the heavy castings trade and with the beginnings of the new professions of the civil and mechanical engineer. This great associated group of industries and professions did much to transform, as it grew, the structure of British industry as a whole, as regarded both products and methods.

The development of heavy industry was an especially marked feature of British industrial activity after 1780. It was a true industrial revolution, distinguished by sudden and momentous innovations and rapid developments, linked with the names of individuals. But like many other economic developments it owed much to the work of earlier generations. These had laid broad and solid industrial foundations, which daring and energetic men might build on, often enough in contempt of the past.

The use of coal for industrial purposes had become common since the time of Elizabeth I. The burning of coal for domestic purposes had been known even earlier; hence its mining, in open workings or shallow pits, on private estates. London had come to depend over the centuries upon coal, imported by coaster from the North of England, for its domestic fires. But an increasing tendency to substitute coal for wood for industrial purposes was the result of the gradual exhaustion of forest resources. Denser settlement brought into old woodland districts farming and enclosure and also industries such as glass-making and iron manufacture which made use of charcoal. The point of exhaustion of the forests and woods came earlier in Great Britain than in neighbouring parts of the Continent. The concern of government with the working out of the woods began as early as Elizabethan times. Hence the rapid spread before 1700 of the use of coal among the makers of copperas and alum, the soap and starch manufacturers, the sugar refiners and brewers, the preparers of dyes, owners of brick-kilns and glass-ovens and metalworkers of all sorts. Great Britain was becoming the country in Europe using the most coal, taking both domestic and industrial consumption into account.

The consequent growth of the coal industry had been one of the most important developments in British economic life in the seventeenth and eighteenth centuries. Even before the Civil Wars, coal and corn had become the principal articles of internal trade. Coal was also an export to the Continent. Coal production was becoming fundamental to the output of British industry as a whole, even as early as 1750. It was fortunate for industrial development after that date that the limits of coal production were not easily reached. The British found themselves in possession of the largest coal reserves in Western Europe outside of the Ruhr, and upon this foundation they reared an industrial state. Had Ireland also possessed mineral fuel, the economic history of the two countries might not have diverged so much.

The coal industry, which did so much to make possible a mechanical revolution in other industries, never went through a mechanical phase at this time. Coal-getting in the main centres of eighteenth-century coal-mining, the Midlands and the North Country, in the valleys of the Tyne and the Wear, was carried out by hard and exhausting manual toil. Some animal and mechanical aids were coming in. It seems to have been in the first half of the eighteenth century that ponies began to become common below ground, bringing with them an extension of child-labour in the shape of the boy driver. In the century's last decades, the Watt steam engine was turned to winding and drawing in the shaft. But in Scotland, at that time, the 'fremd-bearer' continued to carry her load of coal, one hundred and seventy pounds weight, strapped to her forehead and her back, from the coal-face up the shallow shaft to the pit-bank.

In technical matters, the coal industry became the most advanced industry in the kingdom. This was chiefly owing to the need to solve its problems of drainage and traction. The Newcomen steam pump after 1711 and James Watt's improved steam engine after 1769 were successfully used to keep down water and handle men and coal in the shaft. Iron rails replaced wooden for the surface carriage of coal after 1767, when they were first used by the ironmaster Richard Reynolds in Shropshire. Hundreds of miles of these iron 'tramways', as the colliery men called them, had been built in the North of England by 1800 to handle the movement of coal by pony cartage or the pull of stationary engines. The coal-mining industry thus made important contributions towards the steam railway. The first experiments with the steam locomotive were made in the mining districts of South Wales and the Tyne by a mining engineer, Richard Trevithick, and the standard gauge of rolling stock on British railways today is that of the coal-waggons used in the North of England over a century and a half ago.[1]

In other respects than the technical, coal-mining was backward and primitive. This was partly because it was growing up in sections of the country, such as the mountain valleys of Glamorganshire and the fells of the north, remote from the older centres of habitation. To overcome the shortage of labour in these districts in that age of bad communications, relations sprang up between colliery-owners and their workpeople which were exceptional and which later became the proper target of attack, sometimes by the law, more often by the trade unions and the employers of the mid-Victorian era. Scottish mining-bondage (which permitted the sale of miners with the mine, although the miners' families could not, however, be broken up) was prohibited by law in 1774, two years after Lord Mansfield had declared in the Somersett case that slavery could not exist under the law in England. But it was thirty years before emancipation was complete. The Scottish collier-serf was a well-paid man, by contemporary standards; but his status was already becoming a social anachronism. Nothing so primitive as this existed elsewhere; but the yearly bond entered into by the colliers of the North of England, the annual hiring of the South Wales collieries, and the butty or charter system, by which men were hired on a sub-contract, through a butty or charter-master, common in the Midlands, were all of them devices which, while they had a practical purpose in obtaining labour for the mines, were open to the gravest exploitation and abuse. They were swept away later partly for that reason, partly by changed conditions. Abuses in the employment of women and young children were not abolished until the famous law introduced by Lord Shaftesbury in 1842 which prohibited their employment below ground—the symptom, late in the day, of an altering public mind on these matters.

While the coal industry was primitive and harsh in the general relations between employer and employed, it was also a dangerous industry, increasingly so as mines went deeper and the problems of flood and fire became more acute. The first safety lamp, Sir Humphry Davy's, did not appear until 1815, after public opinion had been roused by the great loss of life in

[1] T. S. Ashton and J. Sykes, *The Coal Industry of the Eighteenth Century* (1929), p. 69.

explosions in the pits in the North of England. The lamp came rapidly into use, but its first effect was not to protect the miner. The colliery-owners were tempted to work coal which they would previously have let alone. The public recognition of coal-mining as a dangerous industry and the development of a special code of safety legislation did not come until mid-Victorian times, with the Mines Act of 1850, which first imposed regulations for safety and inspection. Meanwhile, in the hundred years between 1750 and 1850, this big, remote and rough industry was becoming the foundation stone of British industrialization. In 1850 its output was estimated at 56 million tons of coal;[1] very little of this went abroad.

At the beginning of the eighteenth century, one great industry had not yet negotiated the change from wood or charcoal fuel to coal. This was the iron industry. Smiths working iron at the forge into small articles such as horseshoes or nails had long used a coal fire. But the primary branches of the iron industry, the furnaces which smelted the ore to make pig-iron for the foundry and the forges which hammered the reheated pig to make bar-iron for the smith, still needed charcoal, as did iron-producers throughout Europe. There were serious technical difficulties to be overcome in turning coal to account, although its potential usefulness was obvious. As wood and charcoal grew scarcer in the seventeenth century and their price rose, many attempts had been made to smelt iron with coal. But if any 'projector' of Stuart days ever made coke-smelted iron successfully, which is highly doubtful, he never produced it on a commercial scale.

The iron industry had to meet the problem of its fuel costs by migration to those parts of the island where wood was still plentiful or where other costs were unusually favourable. The smelters' furnaces came to be located near the woodlands which provided them with charcoal fuel and the streams and rivers which worked their bellows and heavy hammers. They were sometimes distant from the ore, which had to be carried to them. The forge-masters' works, where the smelters' crude pig-iron was turned by reheating and hammering into forge-iron for industrial use, tended to be near the markets where the iron was sold and the water-power which they required. They were often distant from the smelters. Not only its fuel costs, but also the transport costs of the industry, were high.

[1] G. R. Porter, *Progress of the Nation* ed. F. W. Hirst (1912), p. 222.

The growing scarcity of suitable fuel had the effect of scattering the organization of the iron-producers over the kingdom. The main centre of ironmaking in England in the sixteenth and early seventeenth century had been the Sussex Weald and the Forest of Dean. But the balance of costs had turned against these old forest lands. By 1750, the furnaces of the ironmasters were well established near the woods of the Lake District, around Workington and Furness, and in the wild woody country of Shropshire and Hereford. They had also penetrated here and there into South and North Wales. Iron-smelters even carried their operations as far north as Inverness-shire and Argyllshire, although the Highlands of Scotland in those days were both distant and unsafe. The occasional importation of iron from Ireland and from the American colonies did not much assist national production. The dependence of Great Britain throughout the first half of the eighteenth century for the greater part of her iron supplies upon imports of iron from the forest and mineral lands first of Sweden, later of European Russia, was one of the most striking features of her economy. It was a direct consequence of the inadequacy of native production in face of the rising consumption of iron. Iron-using industries were well developed, especially in Birmingham and South Staffordshire. But the availability of supplies was an important limiting factor upon their development, sometimes painfully felt in times of Continental war. The considerable iron-ore resources of North and South Wales and the Scottish Lowlands, which were to be the foundation of much later Welsh and Scottish industrial development, still awaited the use of coal, or rather coked coal, for smelting.

Curiously enough, by 1750 the process of coke smelting was already known, although its practice was local and obscure. Its inventor, Abraham Darby, a Quaker, manager and part-owner of an ironworks at Coalbrookdale in Shropshire, died at the age of forty, in 1717.[1] He seems to have become interested in the smelting process owing to his desire to cast iron domestic utensils to replace brass and copper ones. He perfected the commercial use of coke for smelting iron-ore, after so far as can be seen prolonged experiment, about 1709. In doing so, he created that link between the coalfields of the

[1] The little that is known about the personality of this man, together with an excellent account of the firm which he founded, is now to be found in Dr A. Raistrick's *A Dynasty of Ironfounders: the Darbys and Coalbrookdale* (1953).

world and its iron industries which has shaped modern
economic history. But for forty years after Darby's discovery,
the use of his process was confined to ironmasters in Shropshire
and Denbighshire, while other men still continued to experiment and to take out patents.

Abraham Darby was an ironfounder by trade. The chief
importance of the new process for many years was in providing
the casting-shops with iron at a reasonable price and a suitable
quality. This led to a great expansion of ironfounding. The
Coalbrookdale works became one of the most important
foundries in the country under Abraham Darby II, its manager
from 1732 to 1763, and Richard Reynolds, who controlled it
from that year until 1768. The business extended far beyond
the pots and pans which had interested the first Abraham
Darby. That inventor had also patented a method of casting
iron in sand, which proved important for industrial as well as
domestic casting. Long before James Watt's day, Coalbrookdale built steam engines, of the Newcomen variety, fitted with
a cast cylinder made of iron instead of brass. The third Abraham
Darby, with the ironmaster John Wilkinson and others, put an
iron bridge over the Severn, to avoid ferrying across the river,
which was the first bridge of the kind in the world.

The Coalbrookdale works became, in the quiet way which
befitted a Quaker enterprise, one of the first centres known to
history of mechanical and constructional engineering. Its
association with the most important technical advances in the
iron industry over a period of sixty years was very striking, in
contrast with thriving centres of ironmaking, such as Yorkshire,
where the steady growth of the industry was associated with no
such inventive fertility. At Coalbrookdale in 1766, two
brothers, Thomas and George Cranage, successfully manufactured with coal fuel wrought-iron, that is, iron refined from
the crude pig-iron and made suitable for the purposes of the
smith and the engineer. This they did with the aid of a
reverberatory furnace. The method continued in use until in
1783 and 1784, first Peter Onions, an ironfounder at Merthyr
Tydfil, then Henry Cort, a naval agent with works of his own
at Fontley, in Hampshire, who had set himself to produce
English wrought-iron as good for naval and ordnance purposes
as that imported from the Baltic, patented a combined puddling
and rolling process. This process made possible the large-
scale production with coal fuel of wrought-iron. The iron was

produced at such a quality and price that it soon drove out charcoal iron for most purposes, except for making steel.

The part played by steel in the metallurgical revolution of the eighteenth century was small. The conversion of charcoal iron of the finest quality into steel by the cementation process, for use in the manufacture of cutlery, tools and weapons, had long been known. A considerable advance upon this method was made between 1740 and 1742 by a Quaker clockmaker of Sheffield, Benjamin Huntsman by name, who was on the look-out for an improved material for clocks and pendulums. He devised the process of making steel, in small quantities but of high quality, in crucibles, making use of coke fuel and casting the steel in moulds afterwards. Cast steel, by its excellence and its lower price, did much for the Sheffield cutlers and some other industries. But steel remained an expensive raw material until the second half of the nineteenth century, when a new series of inventions brought about its production on a great scale and effected the almost universal substitution of steel for iron.

The work of Darby and Cort made possible the replacement by the inorganic raw material, iron, of some of the organic materials then in use for domestic and industrial purposes; for example, the wood and leather out of which some of the earliest textile machines were contrived. The wide adaptability, the uniformity and other good qualities of iron were to be of immense industrial importance. Iron became the raw material of the new industry of mechanical engineering.

British iron supplies became now adequate for all home purposes, including industrial expansion and the equipment of new industries. British iron production trebled between 1788 and 1806, by far the greater part of the output coming from coke furnaces. The decline of the older charcoal smelting process was rapid after 1760. By 1812, exports of bar-iron already exceeded the imports of foreign iron retained for home consumption, although Swedish iron continued to be brought in for the use of the steelmakers. The revolution in Britain's international trading position which was one consequence of the new methods of production was felt even in such far-distant centres of ironmaking as the Russian Urals.[1]

[1] The peak of iron production in the Urals was in 1781. This coincided with the peak of the export of iron to England, which fell rapidly in the years that followed; see E. Koutaissoff, 'The Ural Metal Industry in the Eighteenth Century', *Econ. Hist. Rev.*, 2nd series, vol. IV, no. 2 (1951), p. 255.

Great Britain thus possessed an iron industry the most modern and up-to-date in Europe by the end of the Napoleonic wars. This she owed partly to the exploitation of coal fuel, but partly to the use of steam instead of water-power at all stages of iron production. The Coalbrookdale Company had turned to its own purposes some of the Newcomen steam engines which it manufactured. But the transformation of the iron industry by steam was due far more to James Watt and the powerful and efficient engine which he introduced after 1769. The un-amiable but enterprising John Wilkinson (1728–1808) was a leader in this process of innovation. He seems to have been the first to use steam to blow blast at the furnace, to work the forge-hammer, and to slit and roll iron. Where he led, a host of other men followed, and would perhaps have gone even if he had not led. The iron industry of his time owed much to the new metallurgical and mechanical applications, and it owed hardly less to the growth of the canals, which supplied it with much of its transport.

The development of iron technique and of inland transport brought new centres of the iron industry into being, besides augmenting old ones. This accounts for the swift rise of output after 1780. John Wilkinson was one of the first to take coke-smelting from its home in Shropshire to South Staffordshire. He was consequently one of the creators of the Black Country. He also used the new method in Denbighshire, North Wales, although that part of the country failed to grow into the industrial region which it once looked like becoming.[1] Much more important was the entry of the new-type iron industry into Scotland and South Wales. The establishment of the Carron ironworks near Falkirk by Samuel Garbett and Dr John Roebuck in 1759, and of the Dowlais ironworks by John Guest in 1760, marked the beginnings of the large-scale exploitation of Scottish and Welsh mineral resources, the wealth of which was coming to be known. In the next half-century, Scottish and Welsh developments did much to alter the balance of the distribution of the heavy industries in Great Britain, and to transform social life in Lowland Scotland and South Wales. The break with the past came more suddenly than in England. This was in some respects unfortunate. Minerals lend them-selves to rapid, wasteful, even destructive development. It cannot be pretended that the swift growth of the Scottish and

[1] See A. H. Dodd, *The Industrial Revolution in North Wales* (1933).

South Wales iron and coal industries, which now began, was by any means all gain to those countries.

While coke-smelting and the new puddling and rolling processes were coming into commercial use in the iron industry, other developments of extreme importance were taking place, which had to do with the foundation of civil and mechanical engineering. The engineer of the seventeenth and early eighteenth century had been a military man, skilled in the building and taking of fortresses. Industry was now undertaking operations comparable in scale with those of the military engineer of the past, and some were related to war. John Wilkinson, for example, was an ordnance specialist, who supplied Wellington's armies in the Peninsula, and made important advances in the boring of cannon. His works and the works of other ironmasters, such as the Carron enterprise, owed much to government contracts for cannon and munitions of war. It is of some significance in the history of the iron industry that of forty years, from the opening of the war with the American colonies in 1776 to the end of the war with France in 1815, only eleven were years of peace. Wilkinson, however, is chiefly famous because his attention to the problems of boring iron brought him into association with James Watt and Matthew Boulton of Birmingham, who were then exploiting the patent granted to Watt's improved steam engine in 1769. Watt and Boulton had become consulting engineers,[1] who got Wilkinson to make parts for them, especially the cylinder of the engine. Wilkinson was to the Watt engine what the Coalbrookdale ironworks had been to the Newcomen engine; he was manufacturer-in-chief. It was not until Boulton and Watt discovered that Wilkinson had been cheating them that they broke with him and decided to turn steam-engine manufacturers themselves. The opening in 1795 of their new foundry at Soho, just outside Birmingham, brought into existence the largest and best-managed engineering works of the day. It became intimately connected with the development of the steam engine, not only in mining and manufacture, but also in steam navigation. The road towards steam engineering, as a business, a livelihood and a profession, and as a branch of

[1] James Watt's first partner, Dr John Roebuck, went bankrupt in 1773, and Matthew Boulton took over his share in the exploitation of the steam engine. Watt removed to Birmingham in May 1774, and the new partnership, protected in its monopoly by a special Act of Parliament, began business in 1775.

export trade of high economic significance to the rest of the world, lay direct through John Wilkinson's shops at Bradley and Bersham and the Soho works of Boulton and Watt and their two sons.

Heavy constructional engineering was growing up in the same age, with the coming in of iron, steam-power and the first machine-tools. The iron bridge built by John Wilkinson and the third Abraham Darby across the Severn and opened to traffic in 1779 has been mentioned. The civil engineer's profession, which may be said to have begun with the canals, blossomed in the next generation with the road and bridge builder Thomas Telford (1757–1834) and with John Rennie (1761–1821). The foundation in 1818 of the Institution of Civil Engineers, of which Telford was first President, marked its emergence.

While heavy iron castings were making possible the steam-engine business and heavy structures, the lighter castings opened the way to other branches of the engineering industry. One of the most important was the making of textile machinery. Richard Roberts (1789–1864), the inventor of the self-acting mule for spinning cotton, played an important part in building up this highly specialized industry in Manchester. Down to 1825 the export of machinery and the emigration of skilled men was forbidden by law. This limited but did not make impossible the growth of export business. With the repeal of the law and the spread of modern textile industries on the Continent, the export of textile machinery became one of the characteristic trades of mid-Victorian England, through which the new textile industries of Europe and North America were in part created.

THE TEXTILE INDUSTRIES

From the history of the coal and iron industries, it appears that the large unit of production, employing perhaps several hundred persons, as well as considerable quantities of equipment, and representing a substantial investment of capital, was not new in 1750. The large plant had an old history. In alummaking, brine-boiling, sugar-refining, brewing, shipbuilding, brassmaking and some other trades of real and growing importance, seventeenth- and early eighteenth-century England was already well acquainted with the centralized capitalistic undertaking. Factories or works, sometimes on a considerable scale, appeared in other industries during the eighteenth century as industrial output expanded. Sometimes, as in the Midlands tinplate japanning industry, it was the need for the constant supervision of industrial processes that led employers to bring their workpeople together. Sometimes, as in the heavy chemical industry, the growth of which in Scotland and England forms an important part of the industrial history of the age, or in the bleaching and dye works, it was the special nature of the plant required, which brought men and equipment together.

The course of industrial organization was therefore not always from small, scattered units of production towards large scale units. The technical and economic conditions prevailing at particular times decided whether the advantages of large-scale production at low cost, which were increasingly sought, were obtained through the small or the large unit. The unit which was large in capital and in output, compared with the total production of the industry, might come in at the start or it might be adopted at an early date. In the industries producing the primary materials of industry, such as coal or iron, units of fairly advanced capitalistic type tended to act as suppliers to the makers of finished articles, who were often organized in a different way. Thus, collieries and ironworks in the Midlands furnished coal to the rising metal trades of Birmingham and South Staffordshire. The majority of these trades, such as the making of nails, which gave much employment in that district, were domestic. They were run in a room of the craftsman's house, sometimes with the help of his family. The Midland trades were great employers of men, women and children at forges attached to the cottages in which they lived. At the most, the industry might rise to the dignity of a small shop with assistants run by a garret-master. The expanding production of coal and iron had the effect for many years of facilitating the growth of industry of this domestic type. The larger works fed with raw material, generation by generation, new swarms of small producers, as the local population gradually detached itself from the soil and went óver to industrial occupations. Long after James Watt's steam engine had been first adapted for factory use, by the patenting of rotary motion in 1781, and indeed far down into the Victorian age the small shop and the domestic producer remained overwhelmingly powerful in the Midland trades, outside of the primary industries.

Is it untrue then that the years between 1780 and 1830 saw, as it is often said, a great development of factory organization in British industry? By no means, but this adaptation was less universal and was more confined to particular sectors of industry than has sometimes been supposed. In the heavy industries, large undertakings became markedly stronger with the adoption of steam-power and with the continued increase in the demand for their products which followed. The coal and iron capitalists were among the most important figures of their time, by virtue of the scale of their operations and the influence their decisions had upon the course of trade. Some of the engineering concerns of the time, such as the Soho works, were not far if at all behind, whether in the scale of their employment of men and equipment, or in the care which their owners and managers, who in those days were usually one and the same, devoted to the problems of large-scale management. They brought to bear upon industry powers of administration which, at their best, were equal to those reserved by earlier ages for the conduct of war or other business of the State.[1]

By far the most striking change in the scale of organization took place in the large and well-established group of textile industries. The textile industries, especially the cotton industry, first conclusively showed that every process of industrial production, from the preparation of raw material down to the making of articles for sale to the consumer, might be mechanized and organized upon a basis of power production. This was to carry the use of machinery and large-scale capital equipment much further than had ever been done before. The process of innovation was crowded into a relatively short span of years, and had such profound effects upon British economy and social life that it is not surprising that it has sometimes been regarded as the main industrial event of the eighteenth century. This is to forget the developments in coal, iron and engineering which made the machine age possible. But the mechanization of textile manufacture was, none the less, a revolutionary and transforming event.

The textile group of industries included a number of

---

[1] E. Roll, in *An Early Experiment in Industrial Organization* (1930), tells the story of the firm of Boulton and Watt between 1775 and 1805, and gives a good idea of eighteenth-century industry at its largest and most intelligent.

different trades. A textile industry of which much was heard in eighteenth-century Parliaments was silk. Great Britain was not so well suited to maintain a natural silk industry, as were, say, France and Italy. The silk industry had to be heavily protected. It enjoyed exclusive possession of the home market down to 1830, except for valuable smuggled supplies. Much of its product went to another textile industry, the hosiery manufacture of Derbyshire and Nottinghamshire, for the making of silk stockings. Linen manufacture was less dependent on protection. Flax-growing was widely scattered in Great Britain and the flax was spun and woven by the spinning wheel and hand-loom. The industry had been firmly established in Ireland since the seventeenth century. Power-driven linen mills were first erected in Scotland and the North of England at the end of the eighteenth century, the stimulus coming from the example of the cotton industry. They were followed by a great growth of the industry in those districts. After 1835, Northern Ireland became the main centre of the trade.

Silk, hosiery and linen, to say nothing of lace, fishing-nets and ropes, had an interesting development of their own.[1] But the main textile industries in Great Britain were wool and cotton. It is to them that we must look to understand the changes which were coming over textile manufacture. These changes helped to determine the organization of textile industries, such as jute, which were unknown in Great Britain at this time, but which were introduced later.

The making of woollen cloth was by far the older industry of the two and went back in its origins to medieval times, if not before. An industry of many centres, its strongholds in the eighteenth century were Yorkshire, the West of England from Gloucestershire to Devonshire, and East Anglia. Much of the trade was for export, and down to the later years of the eighteenth century woollen cloth was the largest single British export. The capital invested and the number of persons employed, although neither can be accurately measured, must both have been great, and much experience and ingenuity had been brought to the manufacturing and trading organization of the trade. The cotton industry, although later in its introduction, was far from new in 1750. Cotton spinning and weaving had been known in Britain since the seventeenth century, and

[1] See J. D. Chambers, *Nottinghamshire in the Eighteenth Century* (1932) and E. R. R. Green, *The Lagan Valley, 1800–1850* (1949).

by the middle of the next century had already found its chief centre in Lancashire and Cheshire.

Cotton spinning and weaving, from being complementary to wool in the making of mixed cloths, soon became a considerable industry in its own right. It incurred in so doing the jealousy of capitalists in the older industries of silk and wool and the opposition of the East India Company. The Company were importers of cotton cloth from India, then the chief cotton-manufacturing country in the world. Until the end of the eighteenth century, fine cloths continued to be imported from the East. The British industry grew up, as other such industries have grown up since, by exploiting the market for the simpler and coarser cloths, which it could easily make. It built up a large market for these cloths in the course of the eighteenth century, at home and then abroad. This widening demand helps to account for the technical inventions which at last permitted the Lancashire man to challenge the Indian maker upon his own ground and in his own land. In doing this, he reversed trading relations between Europe and the East which had been established for centuries.

The broad course of technical change in the cotton industry is well known. The first half of the eighteenth century saw considerable experiment; for example, Lewis Paul and John Wyatt's early attempt at mechanical spinning and Kay's flying shuttle for use upon a broader loom. In the second half, the organization of cotton spinning upon a basis of power-driven machinery was successfully accomplished. This was the work of the mechanical genius of James Hargreaves (d. 1778) and the inventor of the mule Samuel Crompton (1753-1827), the organizing power of Richard Arkwright (1732-92) and James Watt's device of rotary motion. From the 1770's onwards, the spinning side of the cotton industry was going over to power— first water, then steam—and to the machinery driven by power which displaced hand spinning. Power-weaving, a more difficult operation, was not successfully attempted until Edmund Cartwright's invention of the power-loom in 1785, and it was not until after 1805 that it began to establish itself. The pace at which these innovations were adopted must not be exaggerated, although it was headlong from time to time, for example, after Arkwright's patents were annulled and thrown open in 1785. As late as 1830, when the cotton industry might truly be said to have lived in a turmoil of invention for

sixty years, there were still in England and Scotland at least
200,000 hand-looms working in cotton. It was the next decade
which was decisive for the unfortunate men and women whose
fate was bound up with the older form of production.

The cotton and wool industries shared important technical
characteristics. Both had made use of the spinning wheel and
the hand-loom. In both, the older hand methods of production
went out, although the process of decline in wool was slower.
Power-loom weaving in wool did not establish itself until the
years 1825–35, and the hand-loom weaver survived for many
years after. Both industries had also much in common in the
type of their early industrial organization. In 1750, both made
use of the smallest possible unit of production, the cottage and
the family of the spinner or the weaver. But long before that
date, the need to obtain production on a large scale had created
forms of capitalistic organization which brought the domestic
producer into subordination to a larger unit, for purposes of
finance, the supply of raw material, and marketing.

The time came, and came soon, when the cottage-worker
did not know enough of the variety of wants in the market or
the prospects of sale, sometimes in lands wholly unknown to
him, to be able to make the most of his opportunities. The
initiative in organizing production to satisfy an intricate pattern
of demands passed to the shrewd men who knew the markets
best. By virtue of their knowledge, they became employers of
other men, purchasing the raw materials on an estimate of
sales, handing it out, personally or by agent, to domestic
workers, paying them for the finished product, and disposing
of it on the markets.

Production for sale on large markets required an ability to
give credit and to await payment, while continuing to meet
payments for raw material and wages at the same time. This
might be done to a limited extent out of small savings. But as
the market became wider and more risky, such as the woollen
industry's large Central European market, liable to the interruption of trade and credit by war, revolution, or financial
panic, the man of capital enjoyed an immense advantage. He
could keep himself and his trade together until times improved.

The resources of the ordinary cottage-worker were, on the other hand, narrow in the extreme. Even if he possessed a scrap of badly cultivated land on which he and his family might fall back, he found it difficult to survive the least interruption of his earnings. The instability of trade was a most serious matter for him; it tended, outside and beyond any question of personal prudence or extravagance, to throw him into debt. But he was often already in debt to his employer for materials. In other textile industries, which worked upon the same system, he owed money for expensive tools, such as the stocking-frame required by hosiery workers, which they hired from the master-hosiers.

The old-time system of industry in the textile trades and in many others was shot through with debt. The story of its industrial relations makes sorry reading. The social gulf between the capitalist employer and his workpeople was often just as wide as that under the later factory system. There was a tendency to go behind the wage-contract, by both employer and employed. The one used his powers to alter the rate of payment, to make deductions for bad workmanship or waste of material, or to recover small debts. The other embezzled the materials or scamped the work. There was little which was idyllic about the old domestic system of industry in the countryside. It suffered from many of the evils of the sweated domestic industry of cities, such as London, at the end of the nineteenth century, which was organized in a similar way.

The amalgamation of capitalist finance and enterprise with the manual technique of the cottage-worker has been sometimes described as the domestic system, because of its cottage character, and sometimes as the putting-out system, because its centre point was the putting out of work to workers in their homes by the large employer. This was the system that was threatened in the cotton and woollen industries at the end of the eighteenth century by the drive towards expensive buildings, machinery and power, by the centralized plant and the new discipline of factory industry. The old system had never been the same everywhere. Thus, in wool, the power of the capitalist employer in the mid-eighteenth century was far more marked in East Anglia and the West of England than it was in Yorkshire. But under the domestic or putting-out system in its many variants, multitudes of persons had worked in Britain for centuries past and still did so. Outside of Great Britain, it was common in many parts of Western Europe, wherever the handicraftsman found it impossible to sell direct to his customer. Adam Smith, the best of the economic thinkers of the eighteenth century, was well aware of its existence, and he entertained few illusions about the degree of freedom which it left to domestic workers who sometimes chose to regard themselves as independent.

The old system offered, however, certain solid advantages to both employer and employed, which helped to keep it in existence for many years, despite the technical efficiency of the factory. From the capitalist's point of view, the putting-out system had proved itself well adapted to the conditions of an age when industrial capital was scarce and timid. It concealed the extent of the employer's operations, scattered as they might be among the cottages of an entire countryside, and protected him from Government control and taxation. There was another feature of the system which was more important now that industrial capital had become more abundant. Trade depression might bear hardly on the owner of fixed capital in the shape of mine or factory, for with fallen receipts he had to maintain outgoings which could not easily be reduced. The old-time domestic capitalist simply ceased to put out work or he reduced the amount put out. He threw the burden of trade depression upon his workpeople while his fixed capital and costs remained of the smallest. The superior earning power of the new system finally overcame these considerations. But it is not surprising to find that employers at first hovered between the two systems and even ran both side by side, especially as it was a long time before factory methods could satisfy the demand for fine quality cloth.[1]

The craftsman or workman had his own attachments to the old system. They were not always financial, but they were sufficient to make him pause either in accepting factory employment or in deciding to send his sons and daughters into it. For some men, the older form of employment was congenial, because it made room for part-time agricultural work, as among the linen workers of the Lagan valley, in Northern Ireland, although many industrial domestic workers had little or no

---

[1] For an account of a capitalist, Samuel Oldknow, who began as a putter-out and ended as a pioneer in factory organization, see George Unwin, *Samuel Oldknow and the Arkwrights* (1924). Oldknow spun fine cotton at Stockport in Cheshire, and at Mellor in Derbyshire.

connection with the land. There were also social considerations of great force in determining the attitude of industrial workers towards factory employment. One was the confusion which existed in many minds between the new factory system and the old and bad practice of letting the parish workhouse out on contract to speculative employers. This confusion seems to have helped to give the factory, in its early days, an ill name, as if it was an extension of the same practice. Far more important was the abiding sense of the craftsman that he belonged to his local community. He was unwilling to abandon it to seek permanent employment and a residence elsewhere. The new factories were localized by their source of power, whether water or coal. The worker was expected to go to them and the break with his past was a big one. He was expected to give up, not only one form of employment for another, but also the immediate society in which he had been born and brought up. This reluctance was particularly strong among people who were still half peasants. It broke down gradually, partly because work ceased to go out to the country districts, partly from such financial attractions as the mills had to offer. Money earnings were not, however, the only consideration in the worker's mind. The industrial discipline of the factory was new, real and hard. Many preferred to stand by a falling system even if working conditions were bad.

The social resistance to the rise of the factories was strong, apart from the recognition of abuses connected with their running and management. Hence the long and hopeless struggle of many hand-loom weavers in the North of England to maintain themselves by their old trade—one of the gravest causes of social distress in the 1830's and 1840's. Official inquiry, in 1841, brought no remedy for this. The nailer of the Midland counties followed the same dreary road to extinction when the machine-cut nail began to come in after 1830.[1] The lot of the hand-loom weaver was made no easier by the immigration of Irish workers in the early decades of the nineteenth century, who found his trade relatively easy to learn. They were prepared to compete for work even at his low wages, as an escape from their own dismal condition. How serious had been the extent and the effects of technological unemployment, as a consequence of the new methods of

[1] See *Birmingham and the Midland Hardware District*, ed. S. Timmins (1866), pp. 111–15.

production, especially among the older generation of workers, was easily forgotten amid the comparative prosperity of mid-Victorian England. But they persisted in particular industries for many years and they formed, between 1839 and 1848, one of the many roots of the great social and political movement known as Chartism.

By the 1840's the battle had been decided in favour of the new industrial system in the theatre of the textiles. This was a verdict of European significance. Men could see how rapidly the new industrial methods were being turned to account and improved upon the Continent, especially in France, Germany and Belgium. The strongest testimony to the dramatic quality and importance of British industrial evolution is to be found in the writings of foreign observers. French writers, as early as the 1820's, seem to have been the first to speak of an industrial revolution, comparing English industrial developments with the catastrophic political life of their own country after 1789, and striking out by analogy the phrase which has been usually applied to the industrialization of Britain ever since.[1] The German, Friedrich List, since 1819 had been urging his countrymen to develop their industrial resources on the same scale as the British, although in a more balanced way, if they would see Germany united, strong and free. In 1848, Karl Marx and Friedrich Engels utilized their knowledge of the gathering forces of industrial change to denounce the existing order of society in the Manifesto of the Communist Party. Thus early, we see the powers of industrialism seized upon for their own purposes by what were to prove the ruling forces of the next hundred years in Europe, the spirit of nationality and the spirit of social revolution.

[1] The history of the idea and the phrase has been traced by Sir George N. Clark in *The Idea of the Industrial Revolution*, David Murray Foundation Lecture, 1953.

Chapter IV

Transport and Overseas Trade

COMMUNICATIONS ON THE EVE OF 1750

National income rises, speaking roughly, with the increase of new capital invested. The large investments in agriculture and industry were the immediate cause of economic progress in eighteenth-century Britain, and they took place in the pursuit of profit by private persons in a society which was markedly commercial in its outlook, even before it became industrial. But they do not exhaust the many forms of new investment which took place. There were also important increases of capital in transport and trade, without which the expectation of profit in agriculture and industry would have been less. Investment in those branches of the national economy may be said to have been induced by the investment in communications and commerce. This in turn owed much of its profitability to the capital going into industry and agriculture.

The practical purpose of improved transport in England and Scotland during the eighteenth century was the service of markets. There was a great expansion of markets as production grew, and their importance in leading to improvements in inland communication can hardly be exaggerated. The London corn-market would be a good example. This market, which bought and sold corn for the kingdom as a whole, became steadily more important as the population and agricultural production grew. It dealt both in imported and home-produced corn, but although imports rose, nine-tenths of its business at the outset of the nineteenth century was in corn of home origin. The influence of a market of this kind was felt throughout the kingdom, although the buying and selling of industrial products in the provinces, particularly coal and iron, was to prove even more decisive in its effects upon transport.

About the middle of the eighteenth century, the communications of Great Britain lagged behind general economic development. The only age of systematic road building which the island had ever known had been under the Romans. The canal and railway eras were as yet in the future. Since the close of the Civil Wars, some improvements in communications both by road and water had been carried out. On the roads the first turnpike trusts, instituting a new system by which local companies raised loans for repair and maintenance, which they paid back out of a revenue derived from tolls charged upon the traffic, dated from the early eighteenth century. The turnpikes represented a method of financing and managing the roads which might succeed where the parish had failed. The maintenance of roads by the parish through its highway surveyors, instituted by Tudor law, had become a jest as early as the time of Shakespeare. The indictment of parishes for neglect of roads and bridges had done little to improve the matter. But the turnpikes, warmly commended by such travellers as Daniel Defoe early in the eighteenth century, included only a fraction of the roads at that time and never the greater part of the total length of highways at any time. In the first half of the eighteenth century, Parliament trusted to what has been called 'broad-wheel' legislation. This prescribed by enactment the breadth of wheels for vehicles, so as to preserve road surfaces. The adaptation of the traffic to the roads, rather than the roads to the traffic, was a confession of failure. Meanwhile, the growth of traffic in coal and iron threw a load upon the local roads, especially in the Midlands and the North of England, they had never had to bear before. In these districts, road conditions deteriorated, rather than improved. The countryside was far from the town, and the towns were far from one another, to an extent we can now hardly understand.

Coaching times are a good test of the travelling difficulties of the period. Stage-coach lines had come in after the Restoration. They represented a considerable advance in passenger and mail transport, but the difference was wide between the coaching speeds then and after the later improvement in the roads. About the middle of the eighteenth century, Edinburgh and Exeter were both the greater part of a fortnight distant from London; Manchester and Liverpool three to four and a half days; Birmingham two and a half days.

There were remote parts of the country where no private or public coach or any form of wheeled vehicle could easily go until a much later date than 1750. There the traveller, or perhaps one should say the youthful and active traveller, was still the man astride a horse. Goods and the mails were still carried by pack-horse in moorland parts of Yorkshire in Charlotte Brontë's childhood in the early years of the nineteenth century, and on Exmoor until the railway reached Devonshire. In the Lake District of Wordsworth's boyhood, the travelling pedlar and chapman continued to play a necessary part in the social life of the dalespeople. Cattle travelled on the hoof, to the detriment of their quality. Sir Walter Scott (1771–1832) wrote one of the best of his short stories[1] out of the still living traditions of the old cattle road over the waste of Cumberland. This continued to be followed by drovers taking their charges from Falkirk Fair into the southern kingdom, until with the coming of sheep into the Highlands the cattle trade declined, and the arrival of the railway at last made the drove road extinct. Similarly, drovers from the annual Welsh fairs took their herds of cattle, sheep and ponies over the Brecon hills into the Midlands and the home counties or to Bristol and the West of England, providing on their return, out of their English sales, much of the currency used in the Welsh country districts.

It would be wrong to judge transport and communications throughout the island by the standards of its most secluded regions or to neglect the fact that the first half of the eighteenth century was a time of slow, if limited, improvement. But there was little sign of any great readiness to improve the roads by devoting to them additional labour and capital, down to a period long past the building of military roads by Government in the Scottish Highlands after the Jacobite rising of 1715 and, broadly speaking, both in Lowland Scotland and England, until the industrial and agricultural improvements of the century's second half.

The roads being what they were, the rivers played an important part in economic development. Their role in inland transport stood higher in the century and a half from 1600 to 1750 than at any time before or since, as the trade of the country grew. Unreliable and inadequate as river carriage was, it did well enough for heavy and bulky goods such as coal, building materials or grain, where speed of delivery was not urgent, and it was cheaper than by road. The merchant dispatching goods by English rivers was fortunate in being free from the many tolls and inland duties which burdened the merchant using the great rivers of Continental Europe. Rivers such as the Thames and the Severn were routes of much com-

---

[1] *The Two Drovers* (1827).

mercial activity, and the smaller rivers were used to an extent which appears surprising, considering the difficult and restricted navigation which was all that many of them had to offer.

As trade grew, the widening and deepening of channels and other improvements of river navigation came to be urgent. Of the many efforts, the improvements on the Bedfordshire Great Ouse and the Warwickshire Avon in the seventeenth century, and on the Aire, the Calder, the Mersey, the Don and the Dee in the North of England during the eighteenth century, were good examples. The local country gentlemen and the merchants, especially the latter, assumed the lead in these enterprises and found the finance. The state took no hand. At first, improvements tended to be the ventures of isolated projectors or speculators, paid for out of their own pockets; but the methods employed with more success as time went on reached out towards the joint-stock finance by which the later canals were built. River improvement represented a substantial addition to the facilities of transport. The canal system of the second half of the eighteenth century did not so much supersede river navigation as round out and complete, by the creation of artificial channels, a system of inland water communications of which the rivers formed the original framework. Into the subsequent building of the canals went engineering knowledge first acquired in the process of river improvement by, for example, such men as the Hores of Newbury on the Kennet. But at the beginning of the eighteenth century, although the construction of locks and canals had already been imported as an art into this country from the Continent, the Englishman was inferior in the practice of it to the Frenchman and the Dutchman. There was at this date nothing to compare in Britain with the great works carried out in France, under the direction of the Government of Louis XIV and Colbert.

The employment of rivers was never independent of sea transport. Few parts of Britain were remote from the sea even by eighteenth-century standards of travel and carriage, and there were many decently navigable small rivers to act as connecting links. The century and a half before 1750 witnessed an 'uninterrupted expansion'[1] of the coasting trade. This trade was carried on from a vast variety of ports. Some, such as

[1] T. S. Willan, *The English Coasting Trade, 1600–1750* (1938), p. xii.

Bristol and London, were large and were overseas traders as well. Others were small places, such as Weymouth and Lyme Regis, which owed their existence to the coasting trade. Down to the building of the main-line railways in the 1830's and 1840's and the filling out of the railway system with branch lines in the middle of the nineteenth century, the coasting trade occupied a place of peculiar importance. It was handled by all sorts of craft, from open boats to the three- or four-hundred-ton colliers engaged in the east coast coal trade between London and the Tyne. The coasting business might almost have been described as the only form of bulk transport which was available, handling mainly bulky and heavy commodities, such as coal and grain. A great part of the trade centred on London, with its demand for all kinds of goods, but some branches of traffic, such as the movement of china clay from Cornwall to the Potteries or the Continent, or of coal from Newcastle and Sunderland into East Anglia through the port of King's Lynn, had little or nothing to do with the metropolitan market.

EXPANDING TRADE AND TRANSPORT

The quickening growth of British industrial and agricultural production in the second half of the eighteenth century and the many exchanges of goods and services which were developing between different parts of the country and between Britain and other states, created a demand for speedy communication and heavy transport which could not be satisfied by existing means. New developments took place, which are sometimes regarded as revolutionary. They are perhaps better understood as the continuation by more effective methods of the search for improvement which had marked the whole century since the Civil Wars.

The two chief improvements of the period between 1750 and 1830, by which time the steam locomotive had arrived, were an increased speed and importance of wheeled traffic on the roads and a wide extension of water transport by canal. As a result of these developments, Great Britain entered the nineteenth century in possession of internal transport and communications superior to anything which she had had before. They gave her temporarily an important economic advantage over other countries.

The age of wide improvement on the roads is usually said to have begun with the spread of the turnpikes after 1748. The turnpike system was certainly an important agency, especially in the period of rapid turnpiking during the quarter-century before the outbreak of the American war in 1776. The turnpike trusts were local bodies formed with Parliamentary sanction by local landowners, merchants, professional persons and other fairly well-to-do people directly interested in the roads of their district. Their chief function, as has been said, was to raise money, usually by borrowing, for repairs and maintenance. They recouped themselves by tolls collected from the users of the roads. The roads of the country came to be divided into two groups, the highways maintained out of the statutory parish rate, under the care of the surveyors of highways in the parishes, and the turnpiked roads, financed and controlled by the trusts. There was no national system of roads. Authorities controlling wide areas of road were not favoured by Parliament except under what were regarded as special circumstances, as in the Highlands of Scotland after 1803, and on the eighty-five miles of the Holyhead road to London, in North Wales, after 1815. In the latter instance, it was the pressure of Irish members of Parliament, after the Union, which wrought a change.

The management and finance of roads remained unsatisfactory, whether they were turnpiked or, as most roads were, maintained by the parish. Parliament failed to make the best of the turnpike system. Dealing with the trusts piecemeal by private legislation and conferring powers upon each as it was formed, it allowed most of them to be too small. As they managed, on the average, ten to twenty miles of road only, they could not pay their way. Many were incompetently run, others corrupt. By the time the railways came on the scene, most of the trusts were heavily in debt and the whole system of road management and finance was ripe for an overhaul which it never received.

Despite bad organization and corruption, progress in the construction and maintenance of roads was obtained, mainly by the fortunate employment of a few able men who represented in their own persons the rising profession of the civil engineer. Scientific road- and bridge-building was new in Britain. It was the creation, in its first days, of such men as the blind man, John Metcalfe (1717–1810), who did much work upon the roads of the North of England, in Yorkshire and

Lancashire, Cheshire and Derbyshire, of Thomas Telford (1754–1834), the builder of the Menai bridge, and of John Loudon MacAdam (1756–1836), who gave his name to one of the most celebrated processes of road surfacing. The road authorities and engineers of the first years of the nineteenth century created, not a national system of good roads, but many first-class roads on important routes. This made it possible to raise coaching speeds. Thus was produced that fast-travelling England, still bound to the horse, which was the admiration of visiting foreigners after 1815 and the natural home of Mr Pickwick. These were the roads used by the new-type commercial traveller, carrying his sample books, and by the mail-coaches which carried the fast-growing commercial correspondence of the country.

The economic effects of improved transport would have been limited if they had been confined to passengers and mails. The development of production required a transport system capable of handling a much larger quantity of goods, with reasonable speed and certainty of delivery, and at rates which people were prepared to pay. What a high-capacity transport system may be varies according to time and place. For eighteenth-century Britain it was represented by the canals. The building of the canals is properly associated with the name of James Brindley (1716–72). Brindley's work in Lancashire, where he linked Liverpool and the Mersey with the industries of Manchester and the country round about, and upon the Grand Trunk Canal, doing much to link the Cheshire salt-works and the Staffordshire Potteries with the outside world, showed what canals could do for the rising industries of the Midlands and the North of England. But Brindley died before the greatest age of canal-building had begun. Between 1780 and 1800 there was a kind of canal mania, resembling the railway manias of the 1830's and 1840's. In those twenty years, the greater part of the present canal system of Great Britain came into existence.

The canals represented an employment of savings, labour and material resources most remarkable for their time. Like improvements on the roads, those in inland navigation were carried out by companies of local people, anxious to develop their district and to reap a dividend and prepared to put up the capital. A surprising store of savings came forward for investment. But the canal system was never looked at as a whole, either by the canal companies or by the Parliaments

which granted them their legal rights. Hence the lack of
uniformity in the canals, even in such necessary matters as
width of channel and size of lock. Despite all the sound
engineering work that was put into them, the neglect of
facilities for through traffic made the canal system a good deal
less than perfect.

Failures in conception and execution notwithstanding, the
canals must be reckoned a major element in British industrial
development before the railways. The light and perishable
produce of agriculture did not provide ideal cargo, and in
farming districts canals often failed to pay. The assistance given
to the heavy industries, such as coal and iron, and to the
building and constructional industries was, on the other hand,
great. The canals did not sell their services cheap; in the rising
industrial centres of the Midlands and the North of England
they tended to become lucrative monopolies and so promoted
their own doom, once railway-building began. But it is hard
to see how much of the contemporary growth in towns and
industries could have taken place without them. Great investments in themselves, they were the cause of much investment
taking place, as may be seen by the multitude of works and
yards which sprang up along their banks.

PORTS AND SHIPPING

One effect of the canals was to cheapen transport between
inland points. Another was to bind together inland developments with the ports, with coastal and foreign trade. Improvements were made in the ports and in the navigation and
lighting of the coasts, just about the time when the new inland
waterways and the better roads were beginning to have their
effects. Much of this development had to do with distant trade.
This was particularly true of the extensions to the docks at
London during the French wars, which served, without much
addition, for ships using the port of London until the middle
of the nineteenth century. But London was a great centre not
only of the long-distance trades but also of the coasting and
short sea business. Almost all ports of any size and importance
improved their equipment between 1800 and 1830. There were
advances also in the putting of lights and buoys round the
coasts. Off Scotland, lighthouse building was controlled from
1786 onwards by a new body, the Commissioners of the

Northern Lights, with whom and their Surveyor-General Robert Stevenson, Sir Walter Scott visited the Hebrides, the Shetlands and the Orkneys in the year 1814. There was a certain competition in lighthouse building between them and the older authority, dating from Henry VIII's day, the Brethren of Trinity House, who managed lighthouses and floating lights around the English coasts. Such activity represented a gain to commercial shipping, as well as to the fleet which protected that shipping.

The main fact about these developments in British transport and communications was that they came to form part of a new and comprehensive transport system, the various parts of which acted together, which penetrated to all important centres of the national economy, and provided the kingdom with external communications superior by far at that time to those of most other European states. This was a fundamental condition of the new type of economy which was being created in industry and agriculture. It was partly by virtue of excellent communications that Great Britain rose to economic leadership in the eighteenth century, as Holland had risen before her.

If economic leadership in the world before the nineteenth century tended to fall to small countries on the edge of the sea, this was largely because of the immense advantage in long-distance communication enjoyed by countries possessing marine transport, before the world's railways were built. Sea transport is to this day the cheapest form of long-distance transport. Before the nineteenth century, it represented the only means by which goods and men could be carried at all over large spaces of the globe. Hence the special importance of the developments which took place about this time in British merchant shipping and the organization of foreign trade. Adam Smith, who saw something of them before his death in 1790, was fond of pointing out that the home trade was more important than the foreign, and that the role of the export merchant in the national economy had been exaggerated by politicians. This was certainly so. It is equally true that the home trade and the foreign formed part of a single system of communications and exchange. No survey of markets and communications would be true to life which separated them.

Britain had been linked to the Continent of Europe by commerce for untold centuries, and in modern times her trade had been expanding notably. The rise of European activity upon the Atlantic and Indian oceans in the sixteenth and seventeenth centuries put her at the centre of the mercantile world. Before the war with the American colonies and France (1775–82) commercial expansion was marked, although it may possibly have fallen short of the rate of growth of British industrial production during the same period. It fluctuated under the influence of wars, and between 1697 and 1815 there were for Britain more years of war than of peace. War did not, however, prevent economic development. Both Britain and her great antagonist in that century, France, strode forward commercially. There does not seem to have been much to choose between them in the rate of their commercial expansion. In both countries, large fortunes were made at ports and commercial centres such as Bordeaux and Bristol. By the end of the century, the merchant and the merchant banker, interested in the finance of foreign trade, were important figures in English and French society.

The progress of British overseas trade, which had been substantial down to the American War, quickened remarkably in the last twenty years of the century. The growth of new industrial production and the revival of trade with the infant United States of America seem to have been responsible for this. The sudden spurt was a foretaste of things to come, an anticipation of the prodigious rise in exports and imports half a century later. But the outbreak of war with France in 1793, while it did not bring about a decline of Britain's trade, did produce a temporary stagnation in the rate of its expansion. The commercial situation during the war was mixed. Great Britain's freedom from invasion, her command of the sea and the temporary advantages, both naval and economic, which the war gave her over old rivals, such as the Dutch and the French, were such that she continued to drive a great trade. At the same time, the new industrial equipment which she was acquiring was prevented from having its full effects on world markets. Neither did it find opportunity in the years immediately after Waterloo. Old competitors revived, as competitors do, while the slowness of Europe's economic recovery after long years of war and blockade limited commerce. Prices fell, and the British tariff system after the war, which levied many duties not *ad valorem*, that is, at a proportion of the value of the article, but specifically at so much per pound of coffee, and so forth, became a growing burden to trade as values fell.[1]

The work of the export merchant, often in those days both shipowner and merchant, in whose hands the overseas trade of the country lay, at Liverpool, London, Bristol and many other centres, was hindered both on the import and the export side of his business by the economic effects of the war and a commercial policy which stood in need of overhaul. It was not until the 1820's that signs of recovery showed. Then the expansion which had been so marked just before the war was resumed, although the rate of growth of overseas trade was relatively modest, compared with that of the mid-Victorian era.

In 1830, the business of exporting manufactures was still being built up. There was also a qualitative change going on in British foreign trade which was no less important, in some respects more significant, than the increase of its quantity. It affected the character both of British exports and imports.

The export of manufactures was not new to British merchants. It was one of the oldest branches of their trade. Woollen cloth remained the most important single article of export trade down to the eighteenth century. The first effect of the new changes going on in British industry was to displace woollen textiles from their old pre-eminence. It was during the later years of the Napoleonic wars, after 1802, that the export of cotton fabrics began to exceed that of woollen. As a consequence of the rise of the cotton industry, textile fabrics became a more important export than ever before, to the extent that cottons formed 40 per cent and woollens 22 per cent of the value of all exports in 1816.[2] Twenty years later, in 1835–40, the average annual export of cotton yarn, cloth, hosiery and lace reached nearly £24,000,000, compared with something under £6,000,000 for woollens and about £20,000,000 for everything else.[3] By that time the country was spending £20,000,000 a year upon the three most important of its imported raw materials, cotton, wool and timber; cotton was by much the most important of these three. The years when these great cotton imports and exports were being built up produced a new type of merchant

---

[1] A. Imlah, 'Real Values in British Foreign Trade', *J. Econ. Hist.* vol. VIII (1948), p. 151.

[2] A. Imlah, 'Terms of Trade of the United Kingdom', *J. Econ. Hist.* vol. X (1950), p. 184, footnote.

[3] Sir John Clapham, *Economic History of Modern Britain*, vol. I, 2nd ed. (1930), p. 479.

community in Manchester and Liverpool and introduced new conceptions of commercial policy.

There was another change in the composition of Britain's overseas trade between 1780 and 1830, no less important for the future than the huge growth of textile exports. This was the rise of the export trade in iron and coal, an effect of the progress in the heavy industries. Great Britain did not cease to import iron of special quality, but as her home production grew after 1800 foreign imports came to form a small proportion of the iron she used, although they had at one time been about a quarter of the whole.[1] She began to export iron to other countries. The trade grew rapidly, even more quickly than the trade in cotton, and the United States of America was by far the largest purchaser. The fall in iron prices owing to increased production, rising technical efficiency, and lessened Government demand after 1815 had much to do with this, combined with the rapid opening up of American resources and demand for capital equipment. The export trade in coal, on the other hand, was European and old. It entered on a new stage of growth with the beginnings of industrialization upon the Continent, but did not exceed one million tons until the year of Queen Victoria's accession, in 1837, and took place mainly through North Sea, Baltic and Channel ports. The export of coal and iron were the beginnings of the trades through which Great Britain helped to industrialize Western lands.

The most important single market for British exports was Europe, reached through the North Sea, the Baltic and the Mediterranean. Hence the question of foreign trade policy which was just beginning to take shape in the years after 1815 was largely a European question—whether any greater readiness on the part of Continental nations to take British manufactures could be expected, so long as Great Britain remained unwilling to take Continental corn owing to her policy of agricultural protection. The traditions of commercial policy in Europe, including Britain herself, were not liberal and they had become more exclusive than ever under the influence of the economic warfare of Napoleon's day. The heavy decline in the price of British textiles, both woollen and cotton, in the generation between 1816–18 and 1849–51 and the growing economic importance of Britain for the Continent and of the

[1] G. R. Porter, *Progress of the Nation* (1912), p. 241; also Clapham, op. cit. vol. I, p. 483.

Continent for Britain were beginning to make such policies look out of date.

Outside of Europe, the largest market in the past had been the American colonies, now the United States. The United States still held that position. In years of active trade, as in 1835–6, she might take nearly a quarter of all British exports, representing more than a quarter of her imports.[1] It would be difficult to exaggerate the importance of the American trade in those days, when 80 per cent of Lancashire's raw cotton came from the Southern States and American manufactures were only incipient. The United States market for British exports was to lose some of its relative importance later, as American factories and tariffs rose, and markets opened in other parts of the world.

Next to the United States as theatres of British trade in that generation after the Napoleonic wars, stood Asia, where the old direct trade to India, carried on by the East India Company, had been extended by the 'country traders' (that is, merchants basing their trade on Indian ports) round the Indian Ocean, and by the Company east of Singapore to the China coast. British North America; the old, still important market of the British West Indies; and Central and South America, the scene of much of the trading and speculating boom of the mid-1820's came next in order of importance. Africa, where Englishmen had done business for many years, including slave trading (which by 1830 was prohibited to them by law), was a market hardly more important than the non-British West Indies.

Here were the materials of world-wide trade. But as world-wide traders the British had long been known. The special significance of overseas trade to Great Britain and of British trade to the rest of the world, in the early years of the nineteenth century, lay in the deep changes which had begun in the structure of the British economy itself and in the changes which were beginning to take place in the structure of the economies of other peoples.

Great Britain had developed to a point where, with growing population and manufactures, foreign trade was more important to her than ever before. The Industrial Revolution was taking place, not in the heart of a self-sufficient continent, but upon a small island. Foreign trade was beginning to be necessary to supply not only the luxuries and conventional comforts

[1] L. H. Jenks, *Migration of British Capital to 1875* (1927), p. 67.

of life and special necessities such as naval stores, but food and raw materials required for the daily subsistence and employment of the mass of the nation. The growing significance of imports gave a fundamental character to the disputes over commercial policy which became a feature of British public life in the first quarter of the nineteenth century. Commercial policy was coming to be popular politics.

A large import trade was indispensable. This made it all the more necessary that means of payment for imports should be found, assuming that other countries were prepared to act as suppliers of food and raw materials. Fortunately for this latter assumption, Britain's chief sources of supply for foodstuffs and raw materials, including corn and cotton, in the early years of the nineteenth century were the same countries of Europe and North America where markets were opening up to her manufactured goods. She had been divided for a generation from the Continent by the wars of 1793–1815; the wars had increased her manufacturing advantage, while they retarded the development of her competitors. There was a foundation for direct commercial exchange which might be built upon for some time to come.

The comparative ease with which Britain built up the import trade which was so necessary to her development in the early decades of the century was remarkable, all the more so because until the 1840's her exports grew rather slowly, while her need for imports was pressing. From a surprisingly early date, about 1820, perhaps from time to time earlier, for the statistics are defective, her balance of trade tended to be passive;[1] that is to say, in any one year commodity imports tended to outweigh commodity exports.

The explanation of her ability to foot the bill abroad lay partly in the great and growing mass of payments which fell due in London at all times for commercial services rendered to other nations, so bringing foreign exchange into the hands of importers. The capital invested in the two to two and half million tons of shipping which made up the merchant marine after 1820 formed, apart from its services to export manufacture and merchanting, an independent source of income. While British shipping did not depend upon the carrying trade to the extent that the Dutch had done, it earned foreign

---

[1] A. Imlah, 'Real Values in British Foreign Trade', *J. Econ. Hist.* vol. VIII (1948), p. 149.

exchange by its services to foreigners. Similarly, a flourishing system of marine insurance had been built up in London during the eighteenth century for the use of British merchants and shipowners. The services of Lloyd's underwriters, which expanded during the naval war after 1793, had become international business. The services of ships, of the marine underwriters, of merchant bankers, of merchant houses of all kinds to the rest of the world brought into Britain a flow of payments which fluctuated with the course of trade. They enabled the country, together with the earnings of commodities exported, to meet the bill for imports with ease, except in seasons of rare difficulty. Such periods of strain usually came accompanied by grave complicating elements, such as war, large-scale speculation or short harvests, as in 1797, 1825, 1839 and 1847. At these times, claims from abroad might be met with what gold had been accumulated in the country in the ordinary course of trade.

Circumstances were therefore favourable to the state of Great Britain's balance of payments—a fact of much importance for her future industrial development, which in turn was to give new strength to her international economic position. The surest sign of the prosperous condition of her foreign balance was the growth of her ability to lend abroad, or, what amounted to the same thing, to leave debts due to her outstanding. In the generation after Waterloo, wealthy men in Britain began to interest themselves for the first time in the business of lending money to foreign governments and business men. Great Britain herself in an earlier age had been the scene of investment upon a small scale by wealthy foreigners, particularly Dutchmen. In the eighteenth century there were Dutch holders of British government funds, East India stock and Bank of England stock. The long wars on the Continent did not break the connection, and Dutchmen still held shares in the Bank when those wars came to an end. The finish of the wars and the fixing at the Congress of Vienna of an indemnity to be paid by the French to the victorious allies led to what is usually regarded as the first step in the development of British lending to Europe. This was the loan arranged by Baring Brothers, of London, in 1817, to the French Government, so that that government might pay off the indemnity. The Rothschild loans to the restored governments of Europe followed in the 1820's. So did a miscellaneous business in lending to the governments of South and Central America, and a foreign investment boom in 1822–5 included much unsuccessful speculation in the shares of mining companies in that part of the world. British money had been invested in the securities of the government of the United States of America before the end of the eighteenth century but it was not until the 1830's that Britons were prepared to finance development in the United States on a considerable scale, by the purchase of the bonds of the State Governments and the securities of American banks and railways.

British investment in other countries, whether in Government bonds or private shares, represented a potential means of financing through loans British industrial exports and of paying with the interest due upon them for imports of foodstuffs and raw materials. Foreign investment business, risky and unsound as much of it was, was a natural outgrowth of the London merchant-banking which had grown up during the eighteenth century. The firms handling the issue of foreign loans in the 1820's, including the Barings, were mercantile houses, not banks. They were engaged in a large way in foreign trade.[1] Their connections, special knowledge and resources enabled them to enter a branch of business which was remote from the acquaintance of most of their countrymen, but it was hardly more strange to them than the financing of foreign trade which was the normal field of their activities.

---

[1] R. Hidy, *The House of Baring in American Trade and Finance* (1949), gives a picture of the growth of foreign investment in its early days. The firm of which Alexander Baring (1774–1848) was for many years the head began as woollen merchants in the West of England, at Exeter, but later opened a merchanting house in London.

Chapter V

Investment, Banking and the Instability of the Economy

THE CONDITIONS OF INVESTMENT

The sum of money laid out in the great investments in agriculture, industry and trade, must have been very large by the standards of the eighteenth century, although we do not know how big it was or what proportion of the national income it represented. Where did the savings come from? How was the money provided? What were the financial habits and institutions which made it possible to furnish Great Britain with the fixed capital of an industrial State—the factories, mines, farm-buildings, roads, canals, ships, wharves, warehouses, counting-houses and so forth—and with the circulating capital, in the form of payment for farm stock, raw materials, salaries and wages, required to keep the fixed capital instruments in working order?

The economic development of many countries in modern times has been financed in part by borrowing on the world's money markets. In this way, the United States of America, Russia, Canada, the Argentine and other countries built during the nineteenth century many of the railways, docks and harbours and other equipment which they required for the exploitation of their resources. The economic and political conditions of the eighteenth century made impossible any such resort to foreign credit. There were rich men in Europe, in Amsterdam, in Hamburg, Geneva and elsewhere, who were prepared to lend beyond the borders of the state they lived in. But they were chiefly interested in loans to governments. They played a negligible part in the industrialization of Britain, which had therefore to be financed from domestic savings. Such an internal effort laid, and was bound to lay, a heavy burden upon her people.

Many schemes of economic development in recent times have been financed by governments. They have often been conspicuously successful, from the financing of the Japanese heavy industries after 1868 onwards to the building up of

Russian industry in our own time. Such a use of the public credit in eighteenth-century Britain might not have been impossible. After the Revolution of 1688 and the foundation of the Bank of England in 1694, the political stability of the country and the resources of the moneyed interest in London, organized in the Bank, permitted the rise of a system of public finance which, with all its faults, was one of the best in Europe. But the events which led to a change of dynasty in 1688 had been part of a long struggle to limit the authority of the Crown. The results of this were felt throughout the next century in an extreme suspicion by Englishmen of government initiative or action of any kind. A public debt was not beyond the understanding of the men of the time. The National Debt may be said to have begun with the foundation of the Bank and its loans to the State. It mounted steadily during the eighteenth century, largely owing to incessant wars. But public investment was an idea too foreign and dangerous to be entertained in the political and social atmosphere of that age. Public investment, if it had existed, might have contributed little towards the events which we know as the Industrial Revolution. Statesmen and civil servants preferred to deal with the known and successful; what was wanted was bold investment in the unfamiliar and the improbable. There were no precedents for industrialization. In these circumstances, only private investment could fill the gap.

THE RISE OF A NATIONAL MARKET FOR CAPITAL

For many generations before 1750, landed property had represented the favourite field for the permanent or quasi-permanent investment of funds by rich or well-to-do men. Some knowledge of the properties and possibilities of land was widespread in a predominantly agricultural community. Land offered a stable income, although not always a high one; and a secure investment, except in time of civil disorder. The social prestige which attached to landed estates was high. It was reinforced in the eighteenth century by the struggle for political power between the Whig and Tory parties and the need to lay one's hands upon tenants who would also be obedient voters and Parliamentary seats which would be in one's gift. The value of land at the end of the century during the years of war after 1793, when agricultural prices, profits and rents were rising, stood higher than ever. The slump in prices and rents which followed the wars and the severe agricultural depression of the 1820's brought some lessening of its value, but throughout the period down to 1830 there was much to enhance and little to detract from the value of landed property.

Much of the capital invested in land had been mercantile, while some of it had been accumulated in industrial under-takings. With the growth of regular government borrowing early in the eighteenth century, the public funds became an alternative form of investment for the wealthy, as well as a new way of making money for professional financiers, who placed and contracted for government loans. About the same time, the growth of commercial and industrial undertakings and of joint-stock undertakings, in which shares could be taken up, expanded the field of investment.

Many landowners were prepared to take an interest in com-mercial and industrial investments. Landlord investment had been conspicuous for centuries in the iron and coal industries. The iron industry in the Sussex Weald had always been associated with the local landowners. As the iron and coal industries spread in the Midlands, the North of England and South Wales during the seventeenth and eighteenth centuries, local landowners similarly ventured their capital, whether as sole undertakers or as partners. During the same age, landed families came to invest in commercial undertakings and to place their younger sons in them. The rise of companies with transferable shares, such as the East India Company, and the increasing ease of investment through friends and through the London jobbers facilitated this kind of connection between agricultural capital and mercantile activity.

Merchants, on their part, placed capital in industrial under-takings. There was an old tendency for the merchant to take an interest in his sources of supply. The first large development of the South Wales coal and iron industries, after the war with the American colonies, owed much to London and Bristol merchants. Capital was scarce in South Wales; all the more important was the willingness to lend shown by men who had close knowledge of the district and its products and who could judge the possibilities of profit.[1] There were similar develop-ments elsewhere. The Darby ironworks at Coalbrookdale on

[1] A. H. John, *The Industrial Development of South Wales, 1750–1830* (1950), chapter II.

the Severn owed much to the support of a Bristol Quaker merchant and banker, Thomas Goldney.[1] Merchant capital also found its way into the cotton industry of Lancashire.

There was some tendency therefore for capital in the eighteenth century to go where the most profit could be found, irrespective of its former history. One of the forces making for the growth of a national capital market was the rising importance, already mentioned, of the public funds. Rich men came to make comparison between the rate of interest they would obtain by lending to the government with what they would gain by investment elsewhere. How far this habit went at any given time it would be hard to say. From time to time forms of investment which required large quantities of capital, such as house-building and the turnpiking of roads, may have suffered from the raising of the rate on government borrowing due to war. But the importance of the funds and their effect on the investment of capital can be exaggerated. It is also possible to overrate the significance of the joint-stock company, with its public issues of capital.

After 1720, the foundation of joint-stock companies was controlled by the so-called 'Bubble Act' of that year, a panic measure passed by Parliament as a direct consequence of the public scandal caused by the collapse of the South Sea Company. This law prohibited the formation of new joint-stock companies unless sanctioned by private Act of Parliament or Crown charter. The law stood unrepealed until 1825. It never affected the continuance of those aristocrats among the older public companies, the East India Company (founded in 1600), or the Hudson's Bay Company (founded in 1670), or the Bank of England. Long before it was repealed, as the need for collective capital increased, the ingenuity of lawyers and business men got round the act by promoting the formation of unincorporate joint-stock associations. Good lawyers were divided on the legality of this device, but Parliament could not be persuaded to prohibit it or to tidy up the law until the early Victorian age. The unincorporate association, although without the powers and privileges in law of the full corporate company, allowed a considerable growth of company enterprise in certain fields, such as insurance. Meanwhile, pro-

---

[1] The Goldney family for many years held a majority of the shares; see A. Raistrick, *A Dynasty of Ironfounders: the Darbys and Coalbrookdale* (1953), chapter I.

fessional dealers in stocks and shares had acquired a position in English business and society. Working in London, they were at first to be found in the coffee houses which were the recognized resorts of professional men and their clients, in the days before chambers and offices away from home became common. After 1773, they foregathered at the Stock Exchange. The Exchange dealt regularly in East India and government stock and the shares of public utility and insurance companies. The struggle to acquire sought-after investments was keen; but it was the preoccupation of a small circle, for the most part of very rich men. The number of investors resorting to the Exchange remained few, until the railway investments of the 1840's. The early lists of the Exchange make it clear that the shares dealt in there must have formed a trifle of the whole invested capital of the country. The Stock Exchange had nothing to do with the large proportion of national wealth invested in agriculture; until the middle of the nineteenth century it did not deal in industrial stocks and shares.

THE CAPITALIST ENTREPRENEUR

The most striking feature of the investment of capital during the years between 1750 and 1830 was that it was over-whelmingly local. Men invested in land or business usually from family connection or in partnership with friends and relations. They did not always ask themselves whether they could make more money elsewhere, although some part of their money tended to be mobile between employments. Most investments were small compared with those of a later age, owing to the predominance of single owners or partnerships and the rarity of companies. Those who invested usually managed the business; they undertook the risks and reaped the profits. There was nothing like the wide gap which was later to spring up between the investor on the one hand and the manager and director of the enterprise on the other in the joint-stock concern.

The law relating to partnerships sometimes inflicted heavy penalties. A man was liable for the debts of any concern in which he was a partner to the full extent of his private fortune. It was not until the coming of general limited liability, after 1855, that it became possible to run businesses in which the liability was restricted to the extent of the shares held. The old

law of partnerships, acting in an age of much business instability, brought down men with better business heads than
Sir Walter Scott, who was ruined as a partner in Ballantynes,
the Scottish publishing firm, in the crash of 1825. It heightened
the risks facing the capitalist who took up some new undertaking. A man such as Matthew Boulton, who ran many
enterprises, was forced to resort to a number of partnerships.
Any one of these might have brought down all his enterprises,
sound or unsound.

The state of the law and the undeveloped state of company
finance, while they handicapped and even destroyed individuals, do not appear to have seriously restricted the supply
of capital. Whether this was forthcoming or not depended in
the main on other things. It owed much in the first place to
political conditions; to the undisturbed state of the country
after 1688; to the protection, sometimes grotesque and
excessive, afforded to property by English law; to the fact that
England's wars were on the whole successful and that her
failures did not badly frighten rich men; to a system of taxation
which never (until the introduction of the income tax in 1799
and then only for a short time) dipped deep into the rising
wealth of the country, but left capital, partly by design, partly
by accident, to accumulate in the hands of the receivers of rents
and profits.

The economic conditions favourable to investment were a
level of national income and savings which had notably risen
since the Civil Wars. This was combined with a readiness
among many men to invest in any undertaking which looked
profitable. By 1750, Britain had already left behind the
troublesome circle which has impeded the economic development of many countries where savings do not find their way
into productive undertakings, although they may go into
government loans, or landed properties. In such countries,
incomes and savings remain at a lower level than they might
otherwise be at and a rapid accumulation of capital and
incomes is out of the question.

The development of farming and of industry both took place
by a process of local investment and reinvestment. This
ploughing back of profits might occur upon an immense scale,
as in the South Wales iron industry in the last years of the
eighteenth and the first years of the nineteenth century. In
other concerns it was a matter of small annual additions.

The industrial revolution of the eighteenth century was thus self-financed. What we cannot tell is what proportion of the national income found its way into industry or how far the growth of that income may have accelerated the accumulation of savings and the rate of industrial investment. At the first stages in the industrialization of a country, when the standard of living of most of the nation remains about subsistence level, while the opportunities of industrial profit are as yet known and exploited only by the few, and while government has not so far begun to tax the new wealth for its own purposes, both the rate of growth of industrial incomes and the volume of savings finding their way back into industry may temporarily reach levels far above the old ones. The half-century between 1780 and 1830 may have been such a period in British economic history. It may be too that the increase in the demand for the products of many industries which followed government expenditure for war purposes after 1793 and was maintained for many years, although it raised industrial costs as well, further heightened the rate of growth of the industrial part of Britain's economy. Certainly it was during and just after the wars that the attention of contemporary statisticians and others seems to have been first strongly drawn to the rapid accumulation of capital and the expansion of the national economic system.

The century between 1750 and 1850, before the invasion of industry by joint-stock finance and limited liability, was the heroic age of the private owner of risk capital. Like most heroic ages, it had a deeply sordid side. But its achievements in furnishing the country with the fixed equipment of an industrial state, the first such state to be known, amply account for the role which the private capitalist played in the economic thought of the time, from Adam Smith and Ricardo to John Stuart Mill. There he appeared as the prime mover of the economic world, in so far as it did move and was not sunk in the lethargy of the past, nor had reached whatever stationary state might be feared or hoped for in the future.

This dynamic role belonged to the capitalist entrepreneurs and the ablest of these men were well aware of it. Found at almost all levels and ranks, from the aristocratic land improver to the garret-master in a Midland trade, from the small employer of a Lancashire weaving shed risen from among his own workpeople to the wealthy son of wealthy parents, they were less a class than an element in society. The entrepreneurial activity of the Industrial Revolution might almost be defined as a phase of British society, called into being by circumstances which had played upon the energies and the desires of many generations, since the discovery of America and the opening of the Cape route to the East.

Many historians, from Arnold Toynbee to Mr and Mrs J. L. Hammond,[1] have written the history of investment in the Industrial Revolution in the form of a sharp commentary upon the public morals of the capitalist entrepreneurs in industry. Their criticism is often just. Later historians have pointed out that the capitalist entrepreneurs were not a class or an homogeneous group in the society of their day; that many variations of education and family upbringing and religion and social position and individual personality were to be found among them; that they were representative of the nation, as much as of a class or a social group. It follows that there were among them different standards of management, different attitudes towards their investments, different kinds of employers.

But it also remains true that there was a hard and ruthless side to the process of extracting from a people which in the middle of the eighteenth century were hard pressed to make ends meet the savings required for acts of capital investment which were of unparalleled magnitude. No other people in modern times has carried out a comparable programme of national industrialization, which has not been driven hard, whether by private or State enterprise. Eighteenth- and early nineteenth-century Britain was the first country to experience such driving. The strongest incentives were probably less those of personal greed, though it is tempting to suppose that they were, than motives which commonly pass for good, such as the advancement of one's family. Economic man, as Marshall long ago pointed out, was nothing if not a family man.

The matter is no doubt more complicated than is sometimes supposed. New investment was the only source from which new income could come. For a nation whose numbers were rapidly increasing on limited agricultural resources, as were those of Britain after 1780, there was no escape from great

---

[1] Arnold Toynbee, *Lectures on the Industrial Revolution of the Eighteenth Century in England* (1884). The books of the Hammonds here referred to are *The Town Labourer* (*1760–1832*) (1917); *The Skilled Labourer, 1760–1832* (1919); and their *Rise of Modern Industry* (1925).

hardship except by a high rate of investment in capital equipment generating industrial incomes. This must, to the extent that it called for a great volume of savings, be at the expense of current living standards. It must remain a matter of opinion whether the rate of capital accumulation achieved and the sacrifice of current consumption was justified, taking all the circumstances into account. The question is not soluble as a matter of mere economics, even if all the necessary economic information was available. It was clear to the bystander that the methods resorted to by many employers to add to their gains and their capital stood condemned. If some thinkers were tempted to throw a cloak over them in the name of contemporary utilitarianism, looking to results and the general good, this was an argument that has been often heard before and since, whenever powerful interests are at stake, and it did not pass without challenge at the time.

The record of incomes and of conditions of employment during the Industrial Revolution deserves a brief examination elsewhere.[1] Considering the multiplication of incomes that new investment gave rise to and that low incomes and wretched conditions of employment were after all not new, it may be that too much importance has been attached to them, by comparison with other things. In considering the virtues and defects of the new economy, instability and the insecurity of incomes appear among its gravest evils. To understand how this came to be, it is necessary to consider the operations not only of the capitalist entrepreneur, investing and managing his capital, but also those of the banker, upon whom many contemporaries were inclined to blame the high instability of the new economic system.

THE ROLE OF THE BANKER

The private investor would never have got far with the task of remodelling the national economy on lines which no one could foresee if he had not enjoyed the support of financial institutions such as banks. The origins of the English banks are to be found among the goldsmith-bankers in the seventeenth century. They were the first Englishmen who accepted deposits of money on which they paid interest, with the intention of lending them again. They also issued cheques against the deposits. The goldsmith-bankers were, however, London men.

---

[1] See below, pp. 128–39 and 144–6.

The remarkable aspect of banking towards the end of the eighteenth century was that so much of it was a provincial movement and existed to serve the convenience of farmers, manufacturers and merchants distant from London. The country banks, as they came to be called by contrast with the London banks, had a diversity of origin. The early banks were small, doing business only in their town and district. The line between merchanting, with its use of credit, and banking was ill drawn. There was little to prevent any man or woman who had accumulated a little money in business from setting up as a banker to his neighbours. Few of the many country banks started in the eighteenth century—there were said to be nearly 400 in 1793, over 700 in 1810[1]—had a long life before them. Of those which did, the bank started at Birmingham in 1764–5 by the ironmaster Sampson Lloyd and his partner, Taylor, and the bank established by the Gurney family at Norwich in 1775 were the origins of the present Lloyds Bank and Barclays Bank.

Between banks south and north of the Scottish Border there was a difference of organization. The Bank of England, founded in 1694, was believed to have possessed ever since legislation of 1707 and 1708 a monopoly from Parliament of joint-stock banking in England. Any other banking institution of more than six partners was understood to be prohibited. The other English banks, as they grew up, took the shape of family businesses or small private partnerships. Only in Scotland did the joint-stock company become a common form of banking organization, although private banks existed there too. This difference between English and Scottish banks persisted down to the end of the first quarter of the nineteenth century.

Then the English law was altered, largely owing to the work of Thomas Joplin, a Newcastle stockbroker familiar with Scottish banking practice, and of those who thought with him. The question was discussed at the time largely in terms of the superior stability of joint-stock banks. The terrible financial panic of 1825, when many English banks failed while the Scots banks were almost untouched, lent urgency to the debate. In 1826 Parliament passed legislation which restricted the Bank of England's monopoly to an area within sixty-five miles of Charing Cross. The Bank in compensation got permission to open provincial branches, which it had never yet done, at Gloucester, Swansea, and Manchester. In 1833, the last

[1] Sir John Clapham, *The Bank of England*, vol. II, 1944, p. 1.

remains of the prohibition of English joint-stock banking were swept away and the joint-stock banks entered London, on condition that they issued no notes. From 1833, a new chapter in the organization of British banking begins.

By that time, the functions of the country banker had become specialized and important. His neighbours expected him to do what bankers had done since the goldsmiths' time and to hold in safe keeping that part of their savings which was not invested in government stock or other security or in their business. The banker became custodian for considerable sums, especially in those wealthy agricultural counties of the east and south which were making much money from farm profits and rents, without possessing many outlets for the investment of this money, once the needs of agriculture had been satisfied. But the well-to-do Englishman expected of his banker something more than safe-keeping. He was anxious that his money should go on earning while in the banker's hands. The banker was able to promise to pay him interest, because he had not the least intention of letting the money left with him stand idle. What was deposited with him by one person could be lent, as a short-term loan on adequate security and at a suitable rate of interest, to some other person, who would know how to make good use of it in the course of business. So long as the banker took the trouble to keep a safe proportion between the money deposited with him and his lendings—a matter of nice judgement in the early days of banking, when frequent crises of confidence led to runs upon the banks for repayment—this delicate business of lending money could be both safe and profitable. It differed entirely from the age-old profession of the moneylender as this had been known for centuries past. The main borrowers from the banks needed money, not for immediate personal consumption but as circulating capital to keep the farm or workshop going, by paying wages, purchasing raw materials and meeting their other running expenses.

The banker filled many gaps in the economic life of the eighteenth century. He alleviated the old and chronic shortage of cash in districts where industry was growing up. He also came to be the main supplier of short-term capital to agriculture and industry. Long-term investment in business enterprises he mostly left to the landowner or the industrial capitalist. The country bankers as a class neither played nor attempted to play the part which in Germany, in the late nineteenth century, was played by the German banks in fostering and developing industrial expansion and in associating themselves with the management of industrial enterprises. The English country banker did not usually feel this to be the line for him to take, although there was no absolute rule and bank advances played a part in building up the fixed capital of the South Wales and West of England iron industry. He found enough to occupy his attention in discriminating men who did from those who did not deserve short-term credit, in the new, fast-moving and unstable economy which had begun to develop.

The safe-keeping of deposits and the making of short-term loans did not exhaust the functions of the banker. They were associated with a third and most important function which many people held to be indispensable to the business of a banker. This was the issue of bank-notes or paper money. The country banker first accustomed Englishmen, and the joint-stock bank at an even earlier date Scotsmen, to the use of paper money. But the sort of paper money in use between the banker and his clients varied from time to time and from one part of the country to another.

The first banker's notes or bank-notes came into use in London among the goldsmith-bankers after the Restoration. They were written acknowledgements by the banker of his obligation to pay cash for sums left with him by his customers. No clear line of distinction seems to have been drawn in early days between this document and the cheque. Both were used by the depositor in drawing upon his account. In the course of the eighteenth century, however, the only London bank which maintained its issue of notes was the Bank of England. Its notes tended to be for large denominations only, in multiples of £5 or £10. Until 1793, it never issued a smaller unit than £10. Bank of England notes passed from hand to hand in settlement of accounts among the men of the City of London, circulating freely there and for thirty miles around, but no farther. The Bank's notes, which could be changed at any time into gold coin by presentment over the counter at the Bank, met the need of the merchant or the shipowner for a paper money which would enable him to settle accounts without the need to pay out or receive intolerable quantities of cash. The other London bankers also used the Bank of England note and the cheque in dealings with their customers; they no longer issued notes of their own.

The provinces had different arrangements, largely determined by the rarity or frequency of their dealings with London and the local character of their economic life. Down to the end of the eighteenth century, the merchants and industrialists of Lancashire and the West Riding and other counties who had large payments to make made extensive use of bills of exchange. Bills of exchange had been used for centuries in foreign trade. The inland bill like the foreign bill was a promise to pay, issued in advance against goods on their way to market, in this case the largest market in the country, London. A promise to pay, drawn by men in the provinces against men in London, both parties being known to be reliable traders, was as good as gold, since cash would certainly be forthcoming when the goods were sold. Meanwhile, the bill was willingly accepted by third parties in payment of debt. As it represented an advance of money before the sale of the goods, men paid interest for the privilege of using it. It passed from hand to hand until the time came when the bill fell due for payment and was extinguished.

The bank-note was rapidly becoming in the last quarter of the eighteenth century a commonly circulating form of paper money. These notes, like the notes of the Bank of England, were issued by local banks in the form of loans. The banks found it desirable to pay a modest interest to get their customers to accept them. They circulated freely only in the locality served by the bank, where they were more highly prized than the Bank of England notes. Branch banking was rare in England, although it was common enough in Scotland. It followed that a wide variety of notes passed current, each in its own district. Nothing resembling a national uniform paper currency existed.

Something more important than a uniform currency was coming into being as a result of the banks' activities, although it was veiled behind the variety of bank paper. This was a national structure of credit. Local as the country banks were, they could not live entirely to themselves, because the economic life of the provinces was not self-sufficient. The link between the provinces ran through London. Here much that was produced in the provinces, whether agricultural or industrial, was sold and here there had long existed a number of well-developed banks, including the Bank of England, already the largest and the most powerful of them all.

One circumstance that brought together the country banks and the London banks, including the Bank of England, has already been mentioned. This was the constant tendency of some persons and parts of the country to receive more income than they knew how to invest locally, while others could always lay out more money in profitable business than their incomes afforded. The agricultural districts, such as East Anglia and the West Country, tended to be the saving districts; at certain times of the year the farmers and landowners of those districts had much money on hand. The borrowing districts were to be found in the Midland counties, Lancashire and the West Riding, where there were men, particularly in times of good trade, anxious to borrow for the expansion of production and willing to pay interest upon a loan. The London banks did an extensive business in the City, receiving the idle balances of London merchants and others and making loans on an overdraft and cheque basis in the manner familiar today. They were also receivers, through the country banks whose correspondents they were, of the savings of the agricultural provinces. The money came up to London to be laid out at a profit. The London banks thus came to be the means by which the resources of one part of the country were put at the disposal of the needs of another, by their readiness to lend money against bills of exchange. These became their favourite investment for the large sums of money which they had in hand. The country manufacturer, raising money on a bill through his local banker and the local banker's corresponding bank in London, was able to draw upon larger than local resources and so at a lower rate of interest than he must otherwise have paid. This was an important advantage for him, while it placed in the London bankers' hands an extensive and profitable business. For many years, the lending of money on bills of exchange drawn in the provinces against London was most important to the London bankers and formed a principal tie between the country banks and the London banks. Just as the country banks 'discounted' their bills—as the process of borrowing upon bills of exchange was called, from the rate of discount or interest charged—with the London bankers, so the London bankers discounted bills at need with the Bank of England. The Bank competed with the London banks in the business of purchasing and lending money at interest upon commercial bills. But the Bank's terms and the volume of business were such that there was plenty of room in the bill market for the sixty-odd London banks which existed in 1832.

During financial panics, when their customers were demanding their money back, the country bankers obtained the cash they needed from the London bankers and the London bankers in turn the 'cash they needed from the Bank of England, by raising money on discount against good securities in their hands, which consisted largely of inland bills. At such times, the depositor demanded gold. He was not prepared, generally speaking, to receive his money back in bank-notes. Much of the art of banking consisted in maintaining a proper proportion between cash which was in hand or readily available and the issue of loans in the form of notes, so as to avoid being broken when a run came. The paper money of the country, which was a useful and economical currency, for it allowed a growing volume of commercial business to be done with the minimum use of cash, had to be backed by gold.

In the course of the eighteenth century, gold had come to be the standard coined money of Great Britain. The coin in use was the gold guinea, first issued in 1663 and so called because the first guineas were made of gold brought by the Royal African Company from the Guinea coast in West Africa. When Sir Isaac Newton was Master of the Mint, in 1717, he assigned a value of twenty-one shillings to the guinea. Gold, like other commodities, came and went freely in and out of the country, in the ordinary course of trade, although dealings in it tended to be restricted to specialists, working in London.[1] It could be sold freely to the Mint for coining, by anyone who was prepared to accept the Mint's price, and gold coin and bullion could be freely exported, as the value of gold altered from time to time and chances of profit offered. There was, in other words, a free market for gold in eighteenth-century London. Silver coins, like gold, were legal tender, that is to say, could not be refused if offered in payment of a debt, up to any amount, until 1774, when silver ceased to be payable by tale for amounts over £25. This was the first step on the part of Parliament toward making silver a token coinage. The definitive measure was not passed until 1816, when silver became legal tender only to the amount of forty shillings and

[1] Miss L. Sutherland's *A London Merchant, 1695–1774* (1933) describes such a man.

gold coin was declared to be the sole standard of value and legal tender without limitation on the amount.

The legal recognition of the gold standard was the upshot of a long process by which gold coins had driven out silver as the effective standard coinage in the first half of the eighteenth century. This happened partly because of the increasing demand for coins of a larger denomination than silver for commercial purposes and to pay salaries and wages, and partly because of the fixed price policy of the Mint and the variations which were taking place in the world supply of gold and silver and in their relative commercial values. By 1816, gold had long been in effect the standard, as was now tardily recognized.

The significance of gold to the banker lay in its universal acceptability which made it standard coin and also made it his reserve against the time when, for good reasons or bad, men refused his notes. The growing together of the credit business of the country had the important consequence that, as the provincial bankers got into a habit of keeping their reserves with correspondent London banks, where in good times their money could go earning interest, the reserves at the London banks, above all the Bank of England, came to form the prop of national credit.

This might have mattered little, if credit had been stable. This was, however, far from the case. Credit and the production which was based upon it passed through phases of prosperity and depression which were marked. From 1763, when a financial crisis followed the close of the Seven Years War onwards, they can be traced in great detail and formed an important part of the general history of the century. The collapse of the Ayr Bank and the panic of 1772; the crisis which succeeded immediately upon the close of the American War in 1783; the sharp, fierce storm of panic in 1793; the suspension of cash payments at the Bank of England in 1797—these form the landmarks.

The London bankers found themselves at the centre of these events. They reaped many of the profits of a speculative boom, and they had to stand the strain when panic and slump arrived. The alternations of prosperity and gloom seemed as natural as the weather, the product of, so to speak, the natural laws of the money market and of the economy as a whole. The position and policy of the Bank of England were particularly important. The national credit structure which was arising centred upon London, where this was the strongest bank. This made it the bank of last resort, as a London banker Francis Baring described it in 1797, for the whole country. It had therefore the potential leadership of the money-market. Its role could not be entirely passive, and it must from time to time forecast events and decide whether to encourage or avert them.

It was in this way that the Bank came to assume what nowadays would be called the functions of a central bank. The Bank approached the fluctuations of the money market, which were sometimes wild, with its own interests and the interests of its clients in mind. It was only gradually that it realized that its power and influence were such that more might properly be expected from it than from other banks. It might forestall trouble on its way, by contracting credit when speculation appeared to be reaching a dangerous height, and it might with its credit support the market from too precipitate a fall. These were not simple measures to take, for the results might be both complicated and unexpected. There were also statutory obstacles in the way of the Bank's assuming, even if its Directors wished to do so, the leadership of the credit market. One was the ancient law which prohibited the rate of interest for money being raised above 5 per cent. This legal maximum continued to be imposed until the repeal of the Usury Act in 1833. Yet if it was to liven or discourage the market the Bank must be free to change its rate of interest. There was also the unwillingness of the shareholders and directors of the Bank to sacrifice immediate for distant profit. This they must do if they were to detach themselves even a little from the rush of the City for profits in a boom, when they were accustomed to play their part, albeit with circumspection. They must also learn not to withdraw too early from the scene for fear of loss, in time of financial panic. There were signs before the end of the eighteenth century that the men in control of the Bank were beginning to take seriously the responsibilities of their position. They restricted their advances as Samuel Bosanquet a Director of the Bank tells us, at times when, as in 1783, the foreign exchanges became unfavourable and their gold stock was consequently threatened by the export of gold. In this way, they conserved the indispensable reserve, upon which their own safety and that of the money market depended. The crisis of 1793, which good judges felt had been worsened by the Bank's refusal of assistance even to sound houses, strengthened

the case for leadership by the Bank, as the only institution
which was able to give it, if it would.

The development by the Bank of its leadership in the money
market was interrupted by the long war with France between
1793 and 1815 and the unexpected effects which this had upon
the conditions of currency and credit.[1] One of the first effects
of the war was to replace gold currency by paper. This
happened early in 1797. In that year the country's overseas
balance of payments was seriously disorganized owing to the
need to make large payments for imports of corn and naval
stores from the Baltic and remittances to governments and
armies abroad. Violent changes had also occurred in the value
of French currency during the early years of the Revolution,
which caused wealthy men to send large sums in gold to
London and then to withdraw it again as French conditions
altered. These foreign payments, combined with an attempted
French invasion at Fishguard, a panic and a run on the banks,
produced one of those demands for immediate cash which the
Bank of England had had to face before. It now found itself
unable to meet the demand for gold. With the consent of
William Pitt's government, by Order in Council, dated 27 Feb-
ruary 1797, the Bank was released from the obligation to pay
cash against its notes. This was the famous suspension of cash
payments, confirmed by act of Parliament in May of the same
year and renewed at intervals throughout the war and after it
until 1821.

During these years the country depended on a paper
currency to an extent never experienced before. At the same
time there occurred a steep upward movement of British prices
which affected her competitive position on world markets and
the interests of merchant-bankers, export merchants and
export manufacturers. It also had serious consequences, as will
later be seen, upon retail prices, the cost of living and wages.
During the later years of the war the pound tended to fluctuate
in value upon the exchanges of such trading cities as Hamburg
and Amsterdam. The price of gold bullion in London rose,
among that small but important band of men who were
dealers in gold.

[1] One of the best descriptions of the money market during the wars is to
be found in the book of the London banker Henry Thornton on *The
Paper Credit of Great Britain* (1802); reprinted in 1939 with introduction by
F. A. Hayek). Thornton held strong views about the Bank's duty to lead the
market.

Much dispute raged from 1809 onwards about the parts played by the country banks and the Bank of England in producing, so it was alleged, this state of affairs. By an over-issue of paper money in the form of bank-notes, so ran the argument accepted by many, they had brought about the price rise by creating a quantity of money and hence of money incomes out of proportion to the quantity of goods available for purchase. The over-issue of paper money and the decline of its internal purchasing power was held to have led to the fall in the international estimate of the pound on the European exchanges and the rise in the value of gold compared with that of the paper pound. This, most briefly, was the gist of a famous report on the high price of gold bullion, issued by a select committee of the House of Commons in August 1810.[1] The committee, which fastened responsibility upon the issues of the Bank of England rather than upon those of the country banks, recommended a speedy return to cash payments by the Bank and a rigid proportioning of its note issues to its gold reserves by the re-establishment of the convertibility of paper into gold at the option of the holder. These were said to be the only means to bring the inflation of prices and the fluctuation of the exchanges to an end.

The 'Bullion Report' represented the opinion of able men, and of one man who was not on the committee at all, David Ricardo, a successful jobber on the London Stock Exchange, who was to become known as the best economic thinker since Adam Smith.[2] Wisdom may be held to have lain with the majority in Parliament and with the government, who refused to act upon the report. From a broad political point of view, it was clear that to abandon the paper pound, even to escape inflation, and return to a gold basis for the currency without regard to the issue of the war, would have increased the risks to public credit at a time of grave national danger, when the struggle with Napoleon was reaching its height. It would have made that credit depend upon a given quantity of gold, which

---

[1] Reprinted as *The Paper Pound of 1797–1821*, ed. E. Cannan (1919); but see also the comments of N. J. Silberling, 'Financial and Monetary Policy of Great Britain during the Napoleonic Wars', *Quart. J. Econ.* vol. xxxviii (1924).

[2] David Ricardo (1772–1823), with his acquaintance and friend Malthus, was the founder of the classical school of political economy. He published his *Principles of Political Economy and Taxation* in 1817; but much of his influence was personal and political.

might at any time be diminished by alarms and hoarding at home, by the violent fluctuations of wartime trade or sudden military need abroad. The practical case for suspension was that public spending must go on until the war was over, that suspension had become a part of the system of war finance, and that the evils of inflation must be put up with in the interests of national security.

The men of 1810 won their victory after the war. After a partial resumption of cash payments and further Parliamentary inquiry, a free gold basis to the currency was restored in 1821, to be maintained as standard monetary policy until 1914. But the influence of the controversy over the wartime policy of the Bank of England did not cease with the resumption of cash payments. The report of 1810 became the fountain-head of monetary thinking in Great Britain for many years. This authority it scarcely perhaps deserved. The problem to which it was addressed, the cause of the rise of prices, was most important; but its analysis of the great war inflation, although able and clear-headed, was no more than superficial. Too much was blamed upon the Bank. The Bank's role in the wartime expansion of currency and credit, although over-complacent, appears to have been mainly a passive one.[1] The chief responsibility lay with the war budgets of government, the behaviour of the country banks, the state of harvests, overseas payments and other circumstances noticed in the next chapter. These were not matters which could be much affected by central bank action, for the effect of war, then as in modern times, was to make government, not the Bank, the real controller of credit and currency.

The legislation which followed the war, when the Bank returned to gold payments, had effects upon its policy and its attitude towards the money market which were not happy. The impression seems to have prevailed among those who directed the Bank that the remarks of the critics upon its conduct during the war had been amply met by the abolition of the unrestricted paper currency. Nothing more was now required of them, they seem to have thought, than the caution of an ordinary prudent banker.

This belief was unfortunate because the violent ups and downs of trade and employment, accompanied by financial

---

[1] E. Victor Morgan, *Theory and Practice of Central Banking, 1797–1913* (1943), pp. 46–8.

speculation and crisis, which had been known before the war continued during its course. The whole period of the suspension of cash payments, including both the long war inflation and the period of falling prices which followed it from 1814 onwards until 1830 were marked by strong fluctuations in prices and heavy disturbances to trade from time to time. The war years 1797 and 1809–10 had been times of depression and, in 1797, of financial panic. After the war, the years 1816 and 1819 were years of acute distress, felt not only in prices but also in the volume of economic activity and employment and in personal incomes.

During years of rising and falling trade, the course of events in the provinces and in the City of London were by no means always identical, but the money market tended, broadly speaking, to exhibit in dramatic form the phases which were passing over the economy as a whole. It showed periods of prosperity, which from time to time reached heights of wild speculation, followed by financial stringency, even panic, and depression which lasted until a new spell of activity began.

One of these tremendous bursts of speculation, followed by despairing reaction, recalling the South Sea Bubble affair of a century before, took place in the years 1823–5. The foundation of the boom was the recovery of economic activity after the depression of the immediate post-war years and the opening up of new opportunities for trade and investment in Central and South America. The conduct of the banks, not least of the Bank of England, came in for severe criticism by intelligent men in the controversial inquest which followed. The Bank was accused, wrongly it seems, of having led the City in reckless lending,[1] but justly, of a timorous and unhelpful attitude when the crisis arrived. It could fairly be agreed that the Bank's Directors had not given the money market, either in the time of unwise speculation or in that of panic fear, the firm guidance which might properly have been expected from so powerful an institution.

The events of 1825 proved that a convertible currency did not free the Bank of England from the obligation to produce what were later to be known as the lines of sound central banking, that is, central bank leadership, as the nineteenth century came to understand them. Important changes took place, after 1827, both in the policy of the State and in that of

[1] Sir John Clapham, *The Bank of England*, vol. II (1944), p. 96.

the Bank, directed to making such disasters less likely in the future.

These changes took the shape, over the next two decades, of (1) further legislation, designed to concentrate the issue of paper money, that is, bank-notes, in the hands of a single institution and to enforce its convertibility with gold on the lines first laid down by the authors of the 'Bullion Report'; (2) other changes in the law, in 1826 and 1833, to make possible a type of joint stock banking organization and management, new in England although not in Scotland; and (3) more obscure and slow, but no less important, the gradual renunciation by the Bank of England of the profits of the discount market (which still left the Bank a highly profitable institution) and the development of the use of its discount rate to give a lead to short-term interest rates in London, and therefore throughout the world, since London was in those days the chief financial city. In these ways, a banking system was built up in mid-Victorian days as coherent and stable as that of late Georgian and early Victorian times had been disconnected and unreliable. But until these things happened, mostly after 1830, it was possible to argue with some force that the organization of credit in Great Britain was inferior to the organization of production. Certainly, production and employment both suffered severely from time to time from crises connected with the organization of the money market.

THE TRADE CYCLE

Informed opinion was justifiably severe in the early years of the nineteenth century upon the shortcomings of the banks, despite their great services to agriculture and industry. There was less reason in the belief that the organization of credit was all that was necessary to stabilize the economy as a whole. It is fair to say, however, that this view did not hold the field in isolation among economic thinkers, but had to share it with the grimmer conviction that the recurrent inflations and collapses of bank credit merely exaggerated and made more harmful an instability in production and demand which was inherent and probably incurable.

Periods of speculative banking, followed by panics among the bankers and their clients, had always tended to accompany the major ups and downs of trade. They tended to be found, that is, in association with booms and slumps which represented substantial changes in the employment of the national resources and in the real income of society—its income, that is, in terms of goods and services. These fluctuations in the economy as a whole came to be known in the nineteenth century as the trade cycle, because of their recurrent and similar character.

In the eighteenth century these fluctuations had no name, but they existed. Regular movements of trade of this kind may be traced in the first half of the century, perhaps even in the century before. After 1763, as we have already seen, they were well-marked, an expansion followed by a crisis of the economy following one another, with varying degrees of intensity, on an average about every nine or ten years. They continued to form a striking feature of British economic history throughout the whole of the nineteenth century, including the years before the First World War.

The classical period of the trade cycle, so far as Great Britain was concerned—these fluctuations in the course of the nineteenth century made themselves felt in every industrial country —undoubtedly fell within the century between the crisis of 1763 and the country bankers' crisis of 1866. During these hundred years the recurrent expansion and contraction can be traced very clearly and obviously over the whole field of production, credit and trade, sometimes in memorable and almost terrifying form. The most important of these movements have already been mentioned; they form the major events in the banking history of the time.

This was also the age, however, of a vast building up of the national economy in all its branches, agriculture, industry, transport, trade at home and abroad, by a process of private investment of capital. Modern economic theory would lead us to look for the causes of boom and slump in this expansion, which took place irregularly, certainly without plan, often along paths which were unforeseen until the moment when men began to tread them, as in the development of the steam engine and the railway. Surrounded by wars, rumour, ignorance, greed, fraud and inexperience, the process of investment was exposed to every possibility of error and accident. The broken rhythm in the economic life of society is to be traced to the successive waves of human optimism and pessimism among the varied groups of men responsible for new investment. The bankers are to be numbered among them, for not only did the supply of short-term capital tend to rise and fall along with long-term investment, but short-term loans were sometimes made to do duty in industrial enterprises for money which was not to be had at long term. In times of immense optimism and speculation, when the schemes of business men calling for capital outran available savings, as they seem to have done in the railway building boom of the 1840's, bank credit was strained to fill the gap.

The bankers tended to act in response to an environment much wider than their own. There were therefore strict limits to the banking policy of the State and to the policy of the central bank in their attempts, genuine but confused, to introduce more order into general economic life through a strengthened banking system. The instability of the new economy was rooted in its nature and would have required far different measures to deal with.it, even if its causes had been understood.

The lack of stability in the process of economic growth, the tendency not only of credit, but also of production and incomes to fluctuate wildly and unpredictably, was to form one of the gravest social evils of the nineteenth century. It was particularly serious for the mass of people living by small incomes. These found their bread and the security of their families threatened by a recurrent dearth of work, all the more painful because it took place in a country not exempt, until the century was half over, from the pressure of harvest shortages. In such spells of unemployment, with the penury they brought, wage-earners paid their part of the price of economic progress in the eighty years between 1750 and 1830. That progress, so much valued by the business and the governing classes, had been largely created by a minority who stood to gain greatly. But it was almost against the will of a majority of the nation, who were chiefly interested, because of their poverty and the lowness of their incomes, in economic stability. Out of this collision of interests, much bitterness was to flow.

Chapter VI

The State and the Foreign Balance

THE HISTORICAL ROOTS OF 'LAISSEZ-FAIRE'

The centuries-old monopoly by the State of the issue of money and the implied responsibility for the value of the currency, together with its duty to defend the realm, had compelled Parliament and the governments of the day to intervene in monetary events after 1793. Both the decision in 1797 to suspend and in 1819 to resume cash payments at the Bank of England were made by the State. They stood out all the more conspicuously because educated men were coming round to the view that the less the State intervened in economic affairs, the better.

How did this view of economic policy arise? Upon what principles was it based? For it was in some ways an innovation. Ancient tradition had assigned to English governments important powers, both in respect of the allocation of capital and labour between one employment and another and in the management of the external economic affairs of the kingdom. To understand the change of mood and conviction, it is necessary to go back well beyond 1750. Englishmen, being men of an empirical nation, had begun to adopt and practise the views which later came to be called 'laissez-faire' long before French and Scottish philosophers gave them systematic formulation. In doing so they were influenced by facts not only economic, but also political and religious, which had done much to create the atmosphere of English public life as it existed after the revolution of 1688.

The greatest of the changes since medieval times which had moulded men's interpretation of their own activities and altered the scale of values they applied to them had taken place in the sixteenth and seventeenth centuries. The profound secularization of human interests in the Renaissance, the driving of a sharp line of distinction in Protestant countries such as England, after the religious conflicts of Reformation and counter-Reformation, between the functions of the Church and those of the State, prepared the way for further movements which were felt generally in Western lands but with peculiar force in Great Britain. One such development, particularly marked after the incorporation of the Royal Society in 1662 and Newton's publication of his *Principia* in 1687, was the rise of habits of scientific investigation, especially in the fields of physics and mechanics. This was a growth of new intellectual interests which strongly affected, in the course of the next century, the mental life of men of the educated classes. It was to mix itself deeply and subtly with economic development in the England and the Scotland of the scientist-inventor James Watt.

Another development no less important was the rise of the State, in the shape of the monarchy, superior to both feudal and ecclesiastical influence. Religion as a function of society continued to be a great power, and the history of its relations to the economic changes of the eighteenth century and the growing industrialization of British society is both interesting and important. The French scholar, Elie Halévy, pointed out forty years ago the influence of the Wesleyan and Evangelical movements upon the industrialization of society and of this economic process upon the life of the churches and chapels.[1] The role he was inclined to assign to religion, as a stabilizer of society in an age of economic revolution, was perhaps only one-half of the whole; it was also a source of reform and of vigorous fighting personalities, as the early history of trade unionism and factory law bears witness.

Meanwhile, the social functions of religion became increasingly private as the doctrinal controversies of the seventeenth century were succeeded by the toleration and indifference of the next age, the natural expression of a more secular, more sceptical type of man. The State rather than the Church was becoming the pacemaker in society. The State did not create social values and was not their sole custodian; but it was one of their main guardians and in some ways the most powerful of them all. Through its action, existing values were assisted to form themselves, for good or for ill, into a kind of public pattern or scheme, which was enforced by law. This helped to establish the social structure and the beliefs and habits of the day.

It would be a great mistake to suppose however that, even in the highly secular society which eighteenth-century England

---

[1] In his *Histoire du Peuple Anglais au XIXième Siècle*, which began to appear in 1912; still, in its incomplete state, the best history of this country in the nineteenth century.

was becoming, the State enjoyed the same powers over its subjects as were commonly exercised by the public servants of other great European states, such as the Prussia of Frederick the Great or the France of the Old Régime before 1789. On the contrary, the executive ability of English governments was notably weak, and this was as conspicuous in the economic sphere as in any other, perhaps more so.

The explanation is to be found in the constitutional and social history of the previous age. In Tudor and early Stuart times, economic duties and policies became attached to the central government which had once been left to the towns and the cities, the parish and the local landowner. This was part of the expanding popularity and power of the monarchy at that date. How far new duties created new machinery of government or new machinery new duties, we need not stop to inquire. With the rise of its expenses, both military and administrative, brought about by the growth of its functions, the State had good reasons for interesting itself in the incomes which were being made by its subjects and which might be made to serve, by taxation or requisition, the purposes of government. To this fiscal preoccupation of the Crown was added the strengthening interests of merchants and moneyed men, not least in the City of London. Their support was equally necessary to Tudor kings and Stuart parliaments. Add the strong, even violent, national sentiment which was becoming marked among Englishmen in the sixteenth and seventeenth centuries, as the result particularly of the long conflict with Spain, and it may be understood that there were in the air of those times strong encouragements to the active use of the legislative powers of Crown and Parliament. In the economic sphere, they served what were regarded as the reasonable interests of the State, of the merchants and other organized groups, and of the nation.

The eighty years running from the accession of Elizabeth I in 1558 to the Scottish rising of 1639–40 and the opening of the Civil Wars had been notable in the history of English economic and social policy. The legislation passed, while often confused or self-contradictory, was so comprehensive and detailed that it might fairly be described as a system of industrial and social law. Parts of it, such as the Statute of Artificers of 1563 governing conditions of employment, and the Statute of 1601 codifying the Poor Law remained on the statute book until they were repealed in the first half of the nineteenth century.

This body of law was hammered out at a time when the instruments of conciliar government and jurisdiction were still available to help frame and enforce it. The vigour of the central government at that time had much to do with the activity of the local administration, that is, the justices of the peace and parish officers, in enforcing legislation which was often against their personal interests or did not obviously assist them.

The monarchy successfully advanced its right to decide many important matters affecting the internal use of the country's resources, its land, its capital and its labour. At a time when economic resources were beginning to be developed upon a larger scale, it strove hard, by legislation and administrative means, to make those resources more mobile, to bring them together in new ways and to increase the nation's wealth, largely for the sake of revenue. Whatever may be thought of the results of the policy, a sound general defence for it could be found in the conditions of the time, in the scarcity and timidity of capital, the want of industrial skill, and the need for exploration of existing resources, such as metallic ores.

The Crown, through Parliament, also claimed the right to control the foreign trade of the country. It had done this for centuries in the interests of revenue. But the State claimed to act for another interest besides its own. It declared the duty to be laid upon it to control trade in the interests of the nation in its rivalry with other countries. The national interest tended to be interpreted in terms of the distribution of political power and of economic interests within the nation at any given time, but a concern for it was an indispensable part of economic thinking and policy down to and even past the days of Adam Smith.

These claims made the English State a partner, often ill-informed, stupid and neglectful, in the main decisions of the national economy. The economic policies based upon it, such as they were, were inherited by Parliament when it became the supreme organ of government after 1688. But in the century between the Civil Wars and the middle of the eighteenth century, many changes had taken place in the national affairs which went far to alter both the methods and principles of economic policy. The English State had turned away after 1660 from the Continental model.[1]

[1] On the main developments and variations of economic policy in Europe before 1789, see Eli Heckscher's *Mercantilism* (translated from the Swedish), 2 vols. (1935).

One important change was administrative. In the early days of its conflict with the king, the Long Parliament had destroyed the machinery of conciliar government, which had been much used by statesmen like Laud and Strafford, on the ground that it had become an instrument of personal tyranny. Administration and jurisdiction acting through the king's privy council had never been restored, and Parliament had ever since jealously limited the executive power of the Crown. This impairment of the authority of the executive was not to be permanent. It was part of the work of Jeremy Bentham (1748–1832) to persuade his countrymen that a civilized community requires strong central administrative organs and that these were not inconsistent with political and civil freedom; but the day of Bentham's influence was mainly after 1832. In the eighteenth century, the country had to get along with a civil service which, although not lacking in ability, was filled by spoilsmen and aristocratic patrons, a local administration which in town and country was subject to few rules, good or bad, and a conspicuous lack of administrative machinery in the central government. British government was not well placed either to acquire reliable knowledge of what was happening economically in the country or to do much about it, even if it had known. Time was needed to build a new administrative machinery, wholly unlike that of the Tudors and Stuarts.

Even more important than the administrative weakness of government was the character of the political interests which controlled Parliament and the administration between 1688 and 1832, and the world of political and social sentiment in which they flourished. An eighteenth-century Parliament was a mixed assemblage. The men who gathered there were landowners and country gentlemen, lawyers, soldiers, sailors, bankers, government contractors, merchants and, under the conditions of those days, civil servants. They possessed a variety of information, but they looked at the nation's affairs from the point of view of their own experience and interests. On conditions in industry and in the new towns they were ill-informed and open to interested representations. The leadership of the aristocracy and the country gentlemen served the country badly in the transition to industrialism. The English aristocracy and gentry, although it had its town houses, especially in London, had never been an urban aristocracy or gentry. It lived on and cared for its country estates and in its country houses. There its

influence was, within limits, progressive, as the state of agriculture showed. The reverse side of its partiality for the country
was its neglect of the towns; not of the county and the market
towns, which had their social traditions, but of the newer
industrial and commercial centres. In an age when the old
balance of town and country was rapidly changing, the ruling
classes' indifference towards and even contempt for manufacture and the towns was a calamity. The failure to grasp firmly
the problems of town and city development was all the more
unfortunate, because a well-thought-out policy towards it might
have provided, by a judicious use of taxation and public investment at selected times, an answer to three separate problems:
the social condition of the industrial population, the fluctuations
of employment, and the enmity provoked by the feeling that
the rich did not make their fair contribution to the common life.

In the handling of economic questions in Parliament, the
country gentlemen were not acting alone. Some of the
industrialists of the day, such as the clothiers, were represented
there; the trading companies, wealthy merchants and financiers. The bias which these men gave to the actions of Parliament in the direction of their mercantile interests caused Adam
Smith, who disapproved of their influence and wrote to confute
it in the second half of the eighteenth century, to christen the
economy policy of the British State as it existed in his day 'the
mercantile system'. He believed that it grossly and deliberately
exaggerated the importance of foreign trade as other men and
systems exaggerated the wealth-producing capacities of agriculture. On the whole, the power of commercial and industrial
interests to make themselves felt in Parliament increased as the
century went on. The last quarter of the century saw a movement
towards the foundation of commercial societies in the larger
towns, which were the beginnings of the modern Chambers of
Commerce. There was even a short-lived General Chamber
of Manufacturers, in 1785, representative of the iron, pottery
and cotton interests.[1] Of these bodies few were permanent but
most developed political interests at some time or other, in connection with legislation proposed or impending, wars and treaties
and other events relevant to trade and industry.

The urban and agricultural wage-earner was neither represented in Parliament nor expected to be until the next century.

---

[1] Witt Bowden, *Industrial Society in England towards the end of the Eighteenth
Century* (1925), chapter III.

It was when radical middle-class opinion began to make itself felt in politics after the Reform Bill of 1832 that the working man's interests began to stand some chance of a hearing. He then found himself most unexpectedly a beneficiary by the centuries-old animosity between land and trade.

Meanwhile, Parliament had to legislate for a wider and more complex world than the Tudor and Stuart kings had known. English economic and social policy was British from 1707 onwards, when the Union with Scotland was effected. The English reconquest of Ireland in the seventeenth century, confirmed at the battle of the Boyne, widened its scope to include that country. After the Union of the Parliaments in 1800, British and Irish affairs were both handled, often most unsuccessfully, at Westminster. Just as important as the creation of the United Kingdom, with its internal stresses and strains, was the gradual building up of a trading and colonial empire, in India, the West Indies and on the mainland of North America. This took place mainly in the century between the end of the Civil Wars in 1660 and the revolt of the American colonists in 1776. British economic policy became an imperial economic policy, acting and acted upon in all parts of the world.

THE COLONIAL SYSTEM

One result of colonial expansion was the creation of a legislative code regulating the colonial trade and, to a less extent, colonial economic development. This grew out of regulations passed by the governments of James I, Charles I and the Interregnum. It was intended to settle relations between the mother country and the colonies and to exclude a third party, the Dutch, who were the main carriers of trade in the seventeenth century and the holders themselves of colonies in the New World. The Navigation Acts of 1651 and 1660 were both regulative and protective. They came to form the base of a colonial system resembling in its economic outlines the imperial system of other European powers. The colonial trade was reserved (to the exclusion of the Dutch and others) for the ships of the mother country and the colonists themselves. The most important colonial products—West Indian sugar, Virginian tobacco, rice, cotton, indigo, dye-woods—could only be sent to European markets through Great Britain. Taken together with the Staple Act of 1663, the Navigation Acts made Great

Britain not only the centre of colonial sales but also the centre of colonial supply in the way of manufactured goods.

There was a real element of monopoly and exploitation in the old colonial system, springing largely from the advanced state of economic development of the mother country compared with the colonies. But there was also a genuine element of mutuality, founded in the same disparity and in the imperfection of world markets. The colonists were to begin with farmers, fishermen, fur-traders, dealers in raw products, almost to a man. They were prepared to see important advantages given to English merchants and shipowners in return for the privileges given to their raw products in the English market (where they enjoyed preference under the tariff) and to the colonial ship-builders. They were relatively indifferent to industry in the early days of colonization, although important industries, such as ironmaking in Pennsylvania, had taken root in the colonies on the North American mainland, before they broke away from the mother country.

The colonial code was thus conceived as a kind of pact between Great Britain, supplying men, capital and defence, and the primary producers of the West Indies and the mainland colonies, particularly the wealthy settlements south of Maryland, exchanging primary products, partly of a tropical sort, against English manufactures. It could not have survived unaltered the rapid economic development of the colonies. The laws worked well enough so long as they were rather laxly administered. The attempt to stiffen the administration of colonial policy after 1688, still more the attempt to tax the colonies after 1764, first produced serious questioning of the right of Parliament at Westminster, in which the colonists were not represented, to settle their destiny wholly for them. Even so, the political dispute and the American war after 1775 was something larger than a quarrel over economic policy. It was a conflict between Great Britain and colonies which, by the middle of the eighteenth century, after a hundred years of growth, were no longer British men living beyond the seas but members of a growing American society with interests and standards of its own. Between the metropolis of the empire and such colonies, all the old relations, political, economic and social, were beginning to fall out of date. Only prescience and wise policy and good fortune out of the ordinary could have adjusted them. Between 1775 and 1823, the whole New

World, including the Spanish and Portuguese settlements in South and Central America, was growing up and away from European control.

The Navigation Acts remained on the statute book after the American war came to an end and the independence of the United States had been acknowledged. Framed for particular purposes, even particular commodities, they had little relevance to the economic life of the new empire which Great Britain was gathering together as a result partly of the wars against France after 1793. But the outbreak of those wars and their long duration prevented any overhaul of colonial economic policy. They also had the effect of vastly extending the tariff, which was the other part of the system of control over overseas trade.

Meanwhile, fundamental circumstances were altering and the bases of traditional economic policy were subject to intellectual attack. Within the country, a new stage of economic development had been reached. Resources had been made mobile and available for the purposes of society to a degree that had never existed before. The monarchy in the days of Elizabeth I had been forced to resort to Germany for capital and technical experts to initiate such industries as copper-mining. The huge metallurgical developments of the eighteenth century in Great Britain took place upon a wholly native basis and placed her well ahead of Continental countries. Externally, Great Britain faced and played her part in a trading world greatly expanded since the sixteenth and seventeenth centuries, when the foundations of her foreign economic policy had been laid in common with that of other European powers. The sources of supply and the centres of demand had multiplied themselves many times over. World markets were less limited, less isolated, less monopolized than they used to be. They had become wider, more interconnected and more perfectly competitive than ever before.

New conditions raised the question how far policies largely devised to meet the circumstances of an early time served any longer a rational purpose. Had they indeed ever done so; had purposes once thought to be rational deserved the name, or had they been the work of interested parties, perhaps contrary to the national interest?

These are matters on which conflicting judgements are still possible. It may be, for example, that the old insistence on controlling trade in such a way as to bring the maximum amount of gold and silver into the country had a certain justification in ages when English trade in some parts of Europe such as the Baltic and the Levant still went on under such primitive and one-sided conditions that it was necessary to export bullion to buy goods.[1]

What is certain is that such conditions were now ceasing to exist and that doubts concerning traditional trading policies were beginning to be expressed throughout Europe, after the middle of the eighteenth century.[2] They found their strongest expression in Great Britain, for there were to be heard the chief exponents of the new science of political economy.

THE NEW POLITICAL ECONOMY

The steady growth of manufacture, commerce and finance had important effects upon economic thinking. The daily life of the counting-house and the market led men to ponder economic questions, as they were also persuaded to do by the financial operations of the State, the growth of the National Debt, the rise of banking and the use of paper money. The middle years of the eighteenth century saw a new literature of economics growing up and an advance over earlier generations in the capacity to analyse economic problems. This was most marked in a small country where the pace of social change was swifter than in most parts of the British Isles, in Scotland. David Hume (1711–76), and above all Hume's friend, Adam Smith (1723–90), were among the men to whom a new and more systematic mode of thought was due. These men, living in a century much influenced by the memory of Sir Isaac Newton, were ambitious to see a science of human nature take its place side by side with the natural sciences. The task they had undertaken was perhaps more difficult than they or their contem-

---

[1] See Charles Wilson, 'Treasure and Trade Balances: the Mercantilist Problem', *Econ. Hist. Rev.*, 2nd series, vol. II (1949), pp. 152–61 and 'Treasure and Trade Balances: Further Evidence', ibid., 2nd series, vol. IV (1951), pp. 231–42 and the criticisms of E. Heckscher, 'Multilateralism, Baltic Trade and the Mercantilists', ibid., 2nd series, vol. III (1950), pp. 219–28.

[2] Anders Chydenius, a Swede, wrote in this strain, in his little book, *The National Gain* (1765, translated into English in 1931). So too, in France, did the Physiocrats, the followers of the economist Quesnay (1694–1774) in the years of self-criticism which followed the unsuccessful issue of the Seven Years War.

poraries supposed. But at least they raised the discussion of economic affairs on to a new plane, far above the old.[1] They united keen practical interests with theoretical. With them, a new and important point of view entered the discussion of economics and found its full expression in Smith's *Wealth of Nations*, first published in 1776.

The social order, to thinkers of Tudor and early Stuart times, had been something of which the king was the guardian; it was for him to maintain and correct, even guide it, when change was desirable. This had been the intellectual justification of economic intervention by the monarchy. Experience since those days seemed to show that it was too naïve an opinion to be a safe foundation for action, whether by Crown or Parliament. There could be no doubt that the wealth of the country had increased. But the growth of wealth, equally clearly, had owed comparatively little to the government. Adam Smith indicated the true source of economic development in the investment of capital and the growth of specialized skills and occupations which went with it. This made further investment possible out of the profits of the old. The mobility of the nation's economic resources which the monarchy in old times had unsuccessfully striven for now existed. Capital, labour and goods moved more easily than ever before, when and where they were most in demand, in response to market rates of interest, wages and prices. The new social economy in Great Britain, it appeared, was the creation not of the State, the obsolete laws of which were still on the statute book, but of the private citizen as he followed his personal advantage, in search of employment or profit. No one pretended that this process was altogether harmless or benevolent; its motives were often doubtful, its methods often cruel and unscrupulous.. It was judged in a utilitarian way by its results and these were held to be beneficial.

The new political economy reposed upon a profound faith in the practical achievements of English life after the Revolution and of Scotland since the Jacobite rising of 1745. But it was also a programme of criticism and reform. The new school challenged the older economic policy in two essential particulars: the desirability of the State having a say in the allocation

---

[1] Those who doubt this should compare the economic parts of Hume's *Essays* (1741–42) or *The Wealth of Nations* with a well-known publication of its day, King's *The British Merchant*, which went into a second edition, in three volumes, in 1743.

of resources between employments, and the need to regulate the balance of foreign payments. Neither, it was now
argued, was necessary. Both should be left to the decision of
the private capitalist and the workman. The action of the State
was superfluous even if it had not proved itself to be in number-
less cases misguided or corrupt.

This might be interpreted as a simple proposal to throw the
reins upon the back of capital; but it is only fair to add that
Adam Smith and his immediate disciples did not hold these
views in absolute form. He made important exceptions; he
thought that defence was of more importance than opulence;
he held that the State had other important duties besides
defence and police, such as education. He spoke for the
interests of capital rather than those of labour. But he did not
share the view, common in his time, that the wealth of the
nation could only be secured by the poverty of the great mass
of its citizens and that Britain's interests in export markets
required that the workman should submit to the lowest wages
and the longest hours that he could be compelled to accept.[1]

While well-intentioned towards labour, in that it genuinely
sought the wealth of the nation as a whole, the Smithian
doctrine is properly described as a system of economic indi-
vidualism. Its strength lay in its analytical understanding of
the new economic strength of Great Britain and the workings
of a market economy, although this was the work not only of
Adam Smith but of many able minds since the seventeenth
century. The results of analysis seemed to indicate that the
competition of the market could be trusted to distribute resources best and to maintain the economic system of the country
in a rough equilibrium, although not without stresses and
strains which might perhaps be severe. The responsibility
which an earlier age tended to put upon the State was now
placed upon the decisions of the private capitalist, checked and
controlled by competition. Competition would tend to cancel
out individual mistakes and excesses so long as it was left to
work freely. Competition was to control what law, it seemed,
could not.

Important political consequences seemed to follow. One
was that old industrial and social laws which obstructed or

[1] For an exposition of these views, gathered from the scattered writings
of the eighteenth century, see Edgar Furniss, *The Position of the Laborer in
a System of Nationalism* (1920).

which might hinder the free working of the economy, ought to be repealed. More important were the recommendations for commercial and colonial policy. Past generations had tended to look at international trade as a kind of war, waged for exclusive gains. Trade had been the brother of piracy and war. This attitude had directed a large part of the trade policy of Europe, although much else in that policy had been determined by private and sectional interests. Commercial policy in the seventeenth and eighteenth centuries, even in peacetime, has been compared to a system of mutual blockades. The British system shared this prohibitive character in trade with a country such as France, where the balance of commodity trade tended to be against Britain. The severity of the tariff was mitigated here and there by commercial treaty, such as the once famous 'Methuen treaty' with Portugal of 1703 which gave a preference to Portuguese wines over French in return for the admission of English manufactures. The British tariff in Adam Smith's day could hardly be described either as a cheap and convenient way of raising revenue or as justifiable protection. It contained within itself too many survivals of temporary expediency.

The conception of an exclusive national interest in trade had been applied by Parliament, assisted by sectional interests, with particular rigour to certain branches of trade. The East India Company maintained a monopoly of the trade to India until 1813, and to China until 1833. The Hudson's Bay Company held exclusive rights to trade to a later date in Canada. Many survivals of company organization holding exclusive rights from the Crown remained in the eighteenth century, although the business of dismantling them had begun before Adam Smith and many were no longer effective.

Colonial policy itself had some of the character of a survival, for on the economic side it was based upon the Navigation Acts of 1651 and 1660 and subsequent legislation. Enough has been said, however, of the history of colonial economic policy and of the difficulties and the dangers that policy was running into, just about the time when Adam Smith was putting the finishing touches to *The Wealth of Nations*.

The old commercial policy of Great Britain needs to be looked at from the point of view of the economic, political and social conditions of the time. It represented an attempt, often wholly mistaken or distorted from the start, to reach what

5   CEH

appeared rational ends. Historical understanding is not to be found in the writings of Adam Smith and those others who were bringing a new point of view to bear. They were far more conscious that conditions had changed and were changing; that a more forceful and flexible economy had come into being and that laws which assumed that markets were highly imperfect, that effective demand was limited, and that capital, enterprise and skill were forthcoming only in severely limited quantities, no longer applied. It is only by a sense of changing horizons and altering possibilities which was already active in his contemporaries that one can account for the immediate respect, although far from universal acceptance, which the ideas of *The Wealth of Nations* received. For its author looked forward to a drastic revision of existing trade and colonial policy; not to the complete abstention by the State from intervention, but to a policy conceding far more to the freedom of the merchant and the colonist.

TOWARDS A NEW COMMERCIAL POLICY

The economic thought of Adam Smith, published to the world in the same year as Bentham's *Fragment on Government* and only a few months before the Declaration of American Independence, was equal to the events of a stirring age and correctly divined its fundamental movement. The immediate period of influence of the new economic philosophy was, however, limited and its effects trifling. In less than twenty years, the effects of a new European war succeeding the outbreak of revolution in France in 1789 became a far greater influence upon British economic policy than the ideas of any economic school whatever.

Before Great Britain entered the war against France in 1793, the influence of Adam Smith appeared in certain aspects of the work of William Pitt, who had become Prime Minister in 1783. Pitt's consolidation of the customs, his financial reforms, his unsuccessful attempt in 1784-5 to moderate the tariffs between the United Kingdom and Ireland and his response to Vergennes's suggestion of a commercial agreement with France, which led to a mutual reduction of tariffs in 1786, marked him out as the first British statesman to accept the need for a reconstruction of economic policy. What lines that might have taken, if peace had lasted, we do not know. When the outbreak of war with France altered all his plans, the old commercial, colonial and financial policies remained substantially intact, and remained so for many years after his death in 1806.

Meanwhile, the ideas for which Adam Smith had stood were slowly becoming a part of the mental furniture of the upper-class Englishman. This was becoming obvious during the long years of Lord Liverpool's administration (1812–27) which bridged the transition from war back again to peace. Indeed, at this time they were so much more the property of rising young politicians and civil servants than of the mercantile community that in 1820, when certain London merchants petitioned the government for a reform of commercial policy in the hope of expanding trade, the merchant Thomas Tooke, who drafted the petition, had some difficulty in obtaining signatures. Towards the end of Liverpool's life, William Huskisson, then member of Parliament for Liverpool, who became President of the Board of Trade in 1823 and who continued in the same position in the cabinet of Liverpool's successor, Canning, carried out important changes in colonial economic policy and in the tariff. They belong, however, to the history of the nineteenth century and to the developments of policy which reached a climax with the economic reforms of Sir Robert Peel's government between 1841 and 1846.

The victory of Adam Smith's ideas, if the elaborate interplay of personalities and interests in those post-Napoleonic years can be so construed, was deferred into a society different from any which the economist could have foreseen. His views had been addressed to a Great Britain which was already a commercial state but was not yet in any true sense an industrial state. Fifty years later, industrialization was well advanced. The influence of the economists Adam Smith and David Ricardo upon British public life has sometimes been exaggerated. It is an important fact, however, that so far as public policy in this critical transition was based upon economic principles at all and so far as the principles were new, they tended to be those of the new school of political economists. They formulated ideas upon money and foreign trade which were to influence and in some real sense control national policies for the next hundred years.

During and after the Napoleonic Wars, the growth of the manufacturing interests, who had proved decidedly conservative in their views of commercial policy in Pitt's day, brought a powerful reinforcement to the new views. The repeated failures of trade during the thirty years of peace that followed, together with the known rise in the productivity of British labour, did much to persuade the industrialist that existing commercial policies hindered the expansion of trade and that he had less to fear from foreign competition than he had supposed, owing to the late start of Continental countries in the new methods of production. The more he reflected upon these things, the more he was inclined to see one of his principal enemies in the landowning and agricultural interest, and in the agricultural protection which stood in the way of profitable exchanges with the primary producers of Central and Eastern Europe.

The labourer's interest he saw as coinciding with his own. Did not capital give employment? And how could the accumulation of capital proceed, unless markets were thrown open? The influence of Malthus and his population theory, although Malthus was no free-trader himself, strengthened at this point the views upon commercial policy of Smith and Ricardo and of those who thought with them. For it was at the back of men's minds that the number of labourers to be given employment was increasing.

These were the arguments which began to tell in political and commercial circles. And given the conditions of the years between Waterloo and the Reform Bill, with the fall in manufacturing costs and the rise in population, with Great Britain's increasing need for imports and the growth of supply in other parts of the world, there can be no doubt that judicious investment abroad and a more liberal trade policy were correct policies to be pursued by a country which already enjoyed a healthy balance of payments and stood to strengthen, not weaken it, by importing more. The liberal trade policy was an employment policy in the long run. It did not, however, protect employment in the short run, and this became clear, after Huskisson's day, as the tariff was reduced while the trade cycle continued to operate with undiminished force. Indeed, the financial policy which emerged after the war, placing the emphasis as it did on the need to maintain an exchange rate fixed by the price of gold and to protect the gold reserve of the country, exposed the national economy to periodical bouts of severe deflation, accompanied by unemployment, in the interests of financial stability and a balanced external account. Smooth passage through the stormy waters of international trade was hardly to be expected; but the working men and their families, who formed the bulk of the passengers in the ship, were spared none of the severities of the voyage. These implications of the new financial and commercial policies were to become clearer as the policies themselves were worked out after 1830.

A relative indifference to the interests of labour in setting the course for the nineteenth century was to be expected. The working man did not enjoy the vote and was not consulted in politics, until that century was more than half over. At its beginning, Great Britain was a country ruled by aristocratic influences, increasingly tempered by the power of wealth. There were other circumstances favourable to the new ideas, of no less importance than the interests of class. When the free-trade policy came to be expounded in the Victorian era, it found some of its ablest and best-known exponents among the comparatively small group of political radicals such as Richard Cobden and John Bright. Partly because of association with their ideas it came to be denounced by Continental critics and even by some Englishmen as the product of cosmopolitan and pacifist motives. Whatever may have been the case then—and there is reason to believe that some of the Continental critics were ill-informed about the British political scene—there is little sign of any such motives in the first stage of the revolution in commercial policy, between 1776 and 1832. A liberal trade policy was then taught and it began to win acceptance as a national interest, independently of what other nations might do. Adam Smith's system of thought made room for moral sentiment and law as checks upon untutored self-interest. But these things were thought of by him and by others chiefly as applying within the nation and within the State. They meant little even in that sphere to many a man who would have agreed with the Scottish economist that free competition was the correct economic policy. They seemed to mean still less in the international sphere. As a national interest, conceived without reference to what practical men thought mere dreams of peace and international law, the new views of foreign economic policy commended themselves. They were congenial to the mood of vigorous and self-confident nationalism which succeeded the anxious time of the Napoleonic Wars. Their persuasiveness owed something to the successful issue of those wars, especially to the sea war and the victory at Trafalgar, which gave to Great Britain a new and undisputed power at sea.

Chapter VII

The Social Setting and the
Influence of War

THE STATE AND THE NEW SOCIETY

The counterpart of the doctrine that the State had no useful
function to perform in controlling the foreign trade of the
country and that any attempt to do so would harmfully direct
its capital and labour into artificial channels was the belief that
the State had no duties in the internal distribution of resources,
between the many purposes for which they might be used. The
competition of individuals in the markets for capital, labour,
commodities or land, and the unchecked variation of prices,
would do all that was required, whether in guiding supplies
where they were most wanted and the prices were highest or in
encouraging demand where supplies were most liberal and the
prices were lowest.

In absolute form, the doctrine of the liberty of commerce or,
as it came to be called, of 'laissez-faire'[1] was never accepted or
given effect in this country. There were important elements in
public opinion, including not only working-class but also
middle- and upper-class opinion, which disputed it in principle
or accepted it subject to qualifications the range and significance of which became apparent as time went on. In Parliament, between 1802 and 1831, the business of repealing the old
laws which were held to be inconsistent with free contract
between individuals and the slow building up of new codes of
social conduct and law, for example, in factory legislation, went
on side by side. This method of proceeding was congenial to
the empirical habits of the English mind and the balance of
interests in the country at the time.

The liberty of commerce was, in Great Britain more so
perhaps than on the Continent, less a doctrine and a policy
than a climate of opinion, in which new doctrines and policies

[1] The phrase 'Laissez nous faire' is said to have been the retort of a French
merchant, M. Legendre, to the dictatorial Colbert, minister of Louis XIV,
perhaps in Lyons about 1680. The French economist, Turgot, gave it
currency seventy years later. Adam Smith never used it; see D. H. Macgregor, *Economic Thought and Policy* (1949), pp. 56–60.

flourished. This climate set in and departed through a long series of gradations of thought and feeling among those who formed political opinion. In its origins it was a product of the discredit of the old regime in state and society in Western Europe before the French Revolution, but it was given a specific form in this country by the influences of British history and life, many of which had no parallel upon the Continent. They were the obsolescence, since the seventeenth century, of much of the machinery of central and local government; the negligence of the aristocratic parties in control of the State, preoccupied with their private estates and local magistracies, with party politics, war and foreign policy; the growth of a strong manufacturing interest, proud of its achievements and impatient of even the most modest control; finally, the growth of a body of economic analysis, given expression by Adam Smith, which seemed to show that the economic system was in some sort automatic or self-regulating, with its own methods of preserving balance, given freedom of competition.

The state of politics and society had long ago set a wide and easy stage for private economic activity by those who were in a position to seize its opportunities. The conclusions of the economists represented the reasoning of men upon conditions some of which had been long-established, even if others, such as the drift towards massive industrial production, were new. Hardly less important, in shaping the new views of economic policy, was the influence of Jeremy Bentham, the legal and political reformer, whose long life lasted until 1832, but whose influence remained strong among educated men for another thirty years or more.[1] Bentham was best known to his contemporaries, in the later years of his life, as a strong democrat when democratic doctrines were still new, who applied the test of the greatest happiness of the greatest number to the laws and political institutions of the Britain of his day and found them wanting. He was not a mere individualist; on the contrary, his thought provided for an expansion of the traditional duties of the State and prepared the way for important developments, for example, in the care of public health. But on the main economic point, the superfluousness of the State's old concern

[1] Strong testimony to the rising power of Benthamism is to be found in a book well known in its day, E. Bulwer Lytton's *England and the English* (1833). For Bentham's influence on legislation, see A. V. Dicey's *Law and Opinion in England*, 2nd ed. (1914), chapter vi.

with the employment of national resources, he was at one with Adam Smith and David Ricardo. These two economists and their circles of friends and disciples were responsible for much of the intellectual criticism of the older policies in the early years of the nineteenth century.[1] Their negative influence was reinforced by that of Malthus. He was temperamentally conservative and not averse from State action in education; but his doctrines on population seemed to suggest that there was little which public policy could do, in face of natural instincts and forces.

The economists were not the mere spokesmen of the manufacturers. Among the forces which were tearing the heart out of the old order of society, they represented an element of reason. In social conscience they were, if anything, above the average; there were men among them who were anxious that education and housing should be regarded as matters of public policy, while they also gave the early factory laws their somewhat reluctant support.[2] The country owed them a debt for their critical work, for they at least faced the fact that the greater part of existing social and industrial law was out of date. Even in the most negative aspect of their philosophy, there was something admirable in their respect for the complexity of great social forces, which earlier generations had imagined to serve the will of their rulers. A man such as Adam Smith combined this kind of scientific perception with an appreciation of the social functions of morals and law. His disciples, while zealous and even pre-eminent, as in Ricardo's case, as economists were less able as social philosophers. Respect for hidden forces gave way to dogmatism; values tended to be conventional. So it came about that, while the influence of the new science helped to clear away mistaken views and the ancient lumber of the statute book, it also dangerously weakened the content of social and economic law. Great Britain entered upon an age of swift transition, under the handicap of an

[1] The economic writings of both Ricardo and Bentham have now been published in critical editions by the Royal Economic Society, and make the study of thought and policy in this period much easier than it used to be; see *The Works and Correspondence of David Ricardo*, edited by P. Sraffa and M. H. Dobb (1951–4), and *Jeremy Bentham's Economic Writings*, edited by W. Stark (1952).

[2] The record of Nassau Senior, who became the first professor of Political Economy at Oxford, 1825–30, and a kind of economic adviser to the Whigs, is instructive; M. Bowley, *Nassau Senior and the Classical Economists* (1937).

inadequate, in some respects a mean and ignoble, conception of the State.

The detachment of the State from economic affairs at this time deprives the historian of much needed information about the processes of industrialization. The practice of official inquiry by Select Committee of the House of Commons or by Royal Commission became common in the first half of the nineteenth century when Parliament took up particular problems, often enough with little result; but the social records of the previous century are scattered and defective.

The want of evidence is the more unfortunate because the consequences of these economic events in their effects upon the delicate and complicated tissue of an old society must obviously have been far-reaching and profound. If investment on a comparable scale took place in an undeveloped community today, everyone would expect extraordinary social results; and the effects of industrial investment in Britain in the eighteenth century can hardly have been less revolutionary, in their own way, than the consequences of mining investment in South Africa a century later. Much ordinary human happiness, and with it many of the strongest loyalties and incentives of men, depend upon being a member of a group and aware of one's part in it. The gradual displacement of multitudes of men and women from the old kind of society, often comparatively stable and small, where their position, with its rights and obligations, had been fixed by slow-moving tradition, into urban and industrial life must have been an experience of the first order for them, however little they reasoned about it. The quality of the new industrial and communal relations they entered into were as important for them and for the well-being of society as the incomes they earned.

There was no precedent for industrial communities, on the scale of those which were now arising. The growth of civic pride and self-respect in the new towns was pitiably slow, and neither the Englishman nor the Scot learned easily to handle their problems. Serious recognition of the prerequisites of civilized life in industrial towns can hardly be said to have been given by public legislation (as distinct from private acts of Parliament, affecting individuals and corporations only and procured at their cost and initiative) before the Corporations Act of 1835 and the Public Health Act of 1848. By that time, a new type of town life had been growing vigorously for the

better part of a hundred years. This does not mean that nothing
was done during this long period. The use of statutory authority
for special purposes, under private act, was a device widely
employed towards the end of the eighteenth century. Between
1785 and 1800, over two hundred Improvement Acts were
passed by Parliament to give powers to particular towns to
levy rates and undertake the necessary work of paving, cleaning,
drainage, street-lighting, police organization and so forth,
following the example of London.[1] But the want of common
standards, even in matters so vital as sanitation, was severely
felt. Its consequences were suffered by all classes, but most of
all in working-class quarters with their higher death-rate.

The spectacle presented by industrial relations was similar
to that in the field of public health and town life. The nation
which tolerated the severe, often brutal discipline, of the fleet
and the army in Napoleonic days had, it must be confessed, no
fine sense for a moral any more than for a physical smell.
Industrial management varied enormously in its intelligence
and energy, then as now, and there were wide differences in the
handling of industrial relations. Exceptionally well-managed
works in the eighteenth century, such as the Crowley ironworks
by Newcastle, the Boulton and Watt engineering shop at
Birmingham, Oldknow's cotton-spinning mill in Derbyshire,
or Owen's cotton-spinning works at New Lanark on the Clyde,
were as experimental in the field of industrial relations as they
were in everything else, providing education, insurance against
sickness, pensions in old age, decent housing, and other amenities
for their workpeople.[2] The inspiration might be religious, as
with the Darbys of Coalbrookdale, or, as with Robert Owen,
secular. Enlightened self-interest, simple common sense and
good nature played their part. But throughout much of the
growing network of industrial relations those good qualities
were not to be found and others far less amicable ruled the
shop or the mine. The efforts of the better employers were left
unsupported by the law, which ought to have made some of
their standards general. The development of factory legislation
was notably slow. It was in 1784 and 1796 that the condition
of parish apprentices in the Lancashire cotton-mills was first

[1] Conrad Gill and Asa Briggs, *History of Birmingham*, vol. 1 (1952), p. 155.
[2] See, for example, George Unwin, *Samuel Oldknow and the Arkwrights*
(1924). Robert Owen's work is well known; see G. D. H. Cole, *Robert
Owen* (1925).

reported upon by competent doctors, it was in 1802 that the Health and Morals of Apprentices Act was passed at the instigation of the employer, Sir Robert Peel, to control the conditions of their employment. But it was not until 1833 that the first effective factory law was passed. The earlier measures of 1802, of 1819 and of 1831 were of little account, because there was no adequate machinery of enforcement.

The laws to control the hours of employment of children in the Lancashire cotton industry—which was the prime purpose of all the factory laws down to and including that of 1833—were passed to meet a new problem. The industrial employment of young children for long hours had long been known. But the children in many of the cotton-mills were working a twelve-hour day and longer. This was longer than the day commonly worked by adults in industry in those days, including the men who made the cotton-mill machines, who worked ten and a half hours. The failure to correct this gross anomaly by law was a serious failure. Workpeople and others noted it, although the organized agitation for a shorter working day in the factories, which led to the law of 1833, did not begin until towards the end of the 1820's.

The swift transformation of social and industrial relations and the slow, painful readjustment enforced upon men and women as new relationships took the place of an old, familiar world must be judged to have been, together with rural overpopulation, the loss of land and the want of it in a society still largely land-living, among the major causes of social tension and strain in Britain between 1780 and 1830. Such things have been in other countries enduring the first onset of industrialism. They might perhaps have been more successfully coped with if so many of those years—from 1793 to 1815—had not been marked by war and the fear of revolution, arising from the spectacle of France after 1789. Foreign events helped to distract attention and confuse the issues when a vigorous home policy was particularly necessary. It may appear, too, that there was something faulty about the scheme of values of a society which habitually rated its happiness in terms of personal money-income, to the exclusion of less tangible but not less important things. So some contemporaries thought, including a man of genius, Thomas Carlyle, coming south of the Scottish Border when the French wars were over, in the 1820's. He compared the simple society in which he was born with the men, money-mad he believed, whom he now met and felt that he was dealing with a society that had lost something of traditional wisdom.

Possibly he was correct in thinking that its reliance upon money incentives was to some extent abnormal. It would be a long story to explain how English social thinking had come to be so dominated by considerations of the market. That habit of mind was not so new as some who took notice of it supposed, although recent economic developments had strengthened it. Meanwhile, in a society where most men tested the efficiency of the economic system by its ability to churn out money-income according to a conventionally received scale of what money-incomes ought to be—a natural attitude considering that they lived by money transactions and not by barter—the creation of money-incomes had become the main drive behind the system itself.

It is of considerable importance therefore to be able to trace the incomes generated by the economic system at this time, even if it were our purpose merely to understand how that system kept going. In point of fact, one can scarcely separate the efficiency of the system from the welfare it created, if that welfare is conceived of in terms of income. What constitutes the efficiency of any economic system it is hard to say; but if it is to put the correct amounts of income in the correct hands at the correct time, and to go on doing this under varying conditions, it is clear that value-judgements must enter into our estimates of efficiency, which becomes to some extent therefore a matter of public policy. This may vary according to the needs of war and peace, or to the common estimation of needs—for example, the needs of those who play little part in the processes of working and saving, such as children and old people.

THE DISTRIBUTION OF INCOMES

The distribution of income in eighteenth-century Britain is not well known. Little official information, of the sort which is to be gained from tax records, exists for the years before the income tax was introduced in 1799. Nor does it do to approach the subject with modern equalitarian standards in mind. The dominant ideals of society were patrician, to an extent we can hardly realize now. The aristocrat and the country gentleman formed the pattern of those who aspired to the highest wealth and position. The social ambition of the manufacturer and the merchant at its most intense was to enjoy an income and a place in society comparable with theirs. In 1750 this was still a novel ambition for manufacturers, if not for merchants. A hundred years later, when John Guest, as manager and proprietor of the Dowlais ironworks, could marry the daughter of an earl,[1] and when Sir Robert Peel, the son of a manufacturer, could head the government, the highest worldly ambitions of the new industrial and mercantile middle classes may be said to have been realized. These men represented the topmost layers of a vast social movement, most of it innocent of aristocratic or political ambitions. But the social setting of the making of incomes needs to be remembered, especially if we are to understand the tolerance of enormous inequalities of wealth and the use men made of their money. Whether they were out to carve a way into the families of the county or simply to achieve what the early Victorians knew as 'a sufficiency' or 'a competence', the men who directed and managed the main economic activities of the country sought not so much the maximum economic, as the main social, advantage. This implied that, as personal social ambitions came to be satisfied, the system depended for its movement upon the constant inflow into the higher ranks of industry and trade of men who had their position to make.

The absence of any attempt by the State to influence by taxation or other means the distribution of incomes was an important factor in building up the new economic system. It is a striking fact that there was no tax which attempted to touch the increasing wealth of the country before the income tax was introduced, as a war measure, in 1799. It did not become effective until a few years later and was abolished when the Napoleonic Wars were over, in 1816. From then until the tax was reintroduced by Sir Robert Peel in 1841, there was no income tax, nor any system of death or succession duties. Considering the new wealth which improved methods were creating in both industry and agriculture, the relative lightness of taxation goes far to account for the rapid expansion of invested capital during the years 1780–1830 and for the activity in the building and the rebuilding of large private houses in

[1] Guest married a daughter of the ninth Earl of Lindsey, and she managed his ironworks for some time after his death. Her diaries have recently been published.

town and country at the same time. To do them justice, the classes which were making money, by rent, profit, fee or commission, did not keep the whole of their growing income for their private consumption or for the estate, the farm, the business or the partnership. They were not proud of the new cities they were creating and they left little good public building; but they were builders of churches and chapels, hospitals, dispensaries and schools, and a proportion of their income, unknown but considerable and perhaps growing with the influence of the Wesleyan and Evangelical religious movements, found its way through innumerable charities, sometimes most ill-managed, into the hands of the sick, the aged, orphan children, disabled soldiers and sailors and others who were held to deserve it by the judgement or whim of those who gave. The money, the clothes, the schooling or whatever it might be did not always reach those most in need or do so when they most needed it. But private charity, while sometimes most uncharitable, did something to discharge functions not carried out by the State, except by the inadequate device of the Poor Law.

The mass of the nation, in 1750 as long before, depended for its living upon a wage. The history of incomes until the end of the century is largely a record of what happened to wage-earnings. It was only at particular times of his or her life that the working man or woman came into touch, if they ever did, with the Poor Law or private charity. Most of this great class depended at every season of life upon what they could earn or from time to time put by to save them from severe hardship and perhaps from unimaginable distress. The history of wages is therefore of first-rate social importance.

The record is unfortunately extremely defective. In large sections of working-class life in the eighteenth century we have very little idea of what was happening, for men and women of this class left few written records behind them and could often enough neither read nor write, so that the documentary evidence of their history is almost in inverse proportion to their numbers and their importance in the national life. Some previous attempts, such as those of Thorold Rogers,[1] to

---

[1] Thorold Rogers, *Six Centuries of Work and Wages*, 8th ed. (1906), chapter xvii. The view briefly summarized here was hardly Thorold Rogers's sole creation. It was the view created by many writers, from Rogers and Toynbee to the Hammonds.

generalize about wages in the eighteenth century have proved unreliable in the light of evidence which has been examined since.

Broadly speaking, the older view was that the conditions of the early eighteenth century although hard, were easier than its later years; this was because of the tendency of wheat prices and consequently of the cost of living, to fall before 1760, and of real wages to rise. After 1760, wheat prices rose gradually to an extreme height at the end of the century. At the same time, the agricultural labourer lost part of his income by enclosure, another part by the decline of cottage industry, while the labourer in the towns suffered not only by the disappearance of old occupations but also by the badness of conditions in the new industries.

There are obvious elements of truth in this description. The movement of wheat prices and the cost of living cannot be left out of any picture of what was happening to real wages, that is, wages in terms not merely of money but also of what money will buy. The agricultural labourer in many parts of the country did suffer by enclosure and loss of bye-employments, while no one can dispute the evil conditions of employment, the truck, fines and deductions used to reduce the level of wages in many factories and workshops, although these were not new but old practices.

Further work on the puzzling wage and price records of the eighteenth century suggests many amendments to the old view. Its main weakness was that it was a general view. It paid too little attention to variations in conditions between one part of the country and another or between times of prosperity and times of depression. It also underrated the effect of war in producing a state of price and income inflation, with all the subtle and complicated play of group motive and interest which that implies.

Regional and local variations in wage and also in living standards were most important in a country of defective communications, where both the knowledge of districts other than one's own and the ability to move were severely limited. These variations bore little or no relation to grain prices and the cost of living.

Thus London, where many large incomes were spent, perpetually attracted men and women, some of them very highly skilled, who were relatively highly paid compared with labour elsewhere. This did not make London labour in general prosperous; there were vast stretches of poverty, especially in the riverside parishes, where the business of a great port encouraged the settlement of unskilled and casual labour. Samuel Johnson, a man of letters who had himself wanted for bread and shelter in London, once attempted to compute the annual rate of death by starvation in the city. Among those who lived hardest in London were the new Irish immigrants. Some of the poorest and worst quarters in the city were old and had been well known for their poverty and crime for a century past. But economically and politically the presence in London of the best-paid skilled labour in the country was important. There seems good reason to suppose that London wages improved in the course of the century.

In the old and well-settled agricultural and cloth-producing district of the West of England, stretching from Oxfordshire across the Cotswolds to Devon, different conditions prevailed. Old centres of textile industry were in decay there by the end of the century and new industry did not grow fast enough to absorb population or to compete effectually with agricultural wages. For a growing population, farm employment was the main employment. Wages and earnings tended to be stationary, particularly for the unskilled man, and living conditions, as in Dorset, might be wretched.

Wages tended to correspond, in a word, with the state of economic growth of a region. In the West of England's successful competitor in the cloth trade, the North of England, where many other industries besides textiles were developing, wages rose markedly during the century, not least for the ordinary labourer. The competition between industry and agriculture, while it left the conditions of life in counties north of the Trent still very hard, was on its way to make one of the best-paid parts of the country out of a region which in earlier times had been one of the poorest and roughest.

Much depended on where a man or woman was born and where he or she worked. The same occupations were differently paid in different parts of the kingdom. If we widen our view to take in Ireland, the difference in earnings for like occupations must appear immense. The poverty and overcrowding of Ireland were highly relevant to English and Scottish conditions. Just as Scottish Highlanders moved into the Lowlands, particularly Glasgow, in search of work, and Scots people into

England, so an even greater stream of Irish moved into both Scotland and England in the late eighteenth and early nineteenth century, especially after 1822. Much of this was seasonal agricultural labour, which returned to Ireland. Lancashire, Glasgow and London were the main centres of permanent settlement. The competition in wage-rates and living conditions was bitter, for the Irish families brought the standards of a deeply depressed community with them. The Irish took mainly unskilled jobs, in building, agriculture and the like; but they also flowed in numbers into the cotton industry. The height of the migration was still to come, in early Victorian days, following the potato famine of 1845–6.[1]

If much depended on place, much also depended on time. Fluctuations in employment were of many types; all affected earnings and the bigger fluctuations helped to determine current wage-rates. Much labour was seasonal, in the towns as well as on the farms, but especially in agriculture. Much was casual, as at the docks and wharves of the ports. There were variations due to war in an age of many wars. Finally, there were the rhythmic fluctuations of employment, due to alterations in the rate of investment from time to time, whether these were due to changes in export demand or at home. These were the most important of all, for they might affect the incomes of a large part of the nation for long periods. Bad harvests tended to be adverse to investment and employment in industry. At such times, the town labourer and his family suffered from the high price of bread, as well as from reduced earnings. Then the condition of affairs operated which has been described in our first chapter, when want brought disease and the death-rate rose, until the cycle of idleness and activity completed itself and easier times came round again.

Throughout the eighteenth century, wage-bargains were mainly individual bargains between employer and employed, which must have meant that they were largely based upon conventional wage-rates. Collective bargaining already existed in some trades. But the position of trade unions at law was extremely difficult and became more so as time went on. This must appear remarkable when one considers how imperfect the labour market was, how many advantages it threw into the hands of the employer, especially the unscrupulous employer, and consequently how much need there was for protection.

[1] A. Redford, *Labour Migration in England*, 1800–1850 (1926) chs. VIII and IX.

There were some sorts of associations of working men which were encouraged by law. These were the benefit or friendly societies, formed to accumulate savings against such contingencies as sickness and burial. They were becoming numerous in the towns, as a result among other things of rising real wages in the Midlands and the North of England. The funds of these societies were protected by law after 1793 and the numbers enrolled in the societies were astonishingly large—nearly a million persons in 1815.[1]

The existence of the friendly societies amply disproved the idea that working men did not know how to save. It also favoured the rise of collective bargaining, for the early trade unions, as a rule, ran benefit funds as well as entering into contracts with employers upon wages, hours and conditions of work. It was at this point that Parliament began to draw the line; not, at first, against all trade unions but against the activities of particular unions.

Trade unions of a sort had existed, in some of the London trades, since the seventeenth century, and strong combinations of working men sprang up in important trades, such as the West of England cloth industry, within the next fifty years. The skilled men, curriers, hatters, shipwrights, printers' compositors and so forth, were the pioneers of the trade unionism of the eighteenth century, as they were of so much in the century that followed. Their fortunes were various, but all tended to fall foul of the law. There were many statutes prohibiting combinations in particular trades before 1799, when a move in Parliament to legislate against the London millwrights led for the first time to a general law against all trade unions, in the Combination Acts of 1799 and 1800.

The explanation of the change in policy is to be found in the impact of the French Revolution in 1789, the beginning of the war with France in 1793 and the fear of political subversive activity. The result was long-lasting. For a quarter of a century until 1824, trade unions as such were under the ban of the law and even to found or to take part in one was a criminal offence.

While the Combination Laws put powers into the hands of the magistrates which were freely used against trade unions, it has often been pointed out that the year 1799 did not represent a break in the development of trade unionism. Collective

[1] Sir John Clapham, *Economic History of Modern Britain*. vol. 1, 2nd ed. (1930), p. 211.

bargaining was the natural form for wage-bargaining to take as the scale of industry grew. There were employers who recognized or accepted this and trade union activity continued, with or without the consent of the employer. The Combination Acts were not the only obstacle. Old parts of the common law, relating to criminal conspiracy in restraint of trade and to breach of contract, could be and were invoked against the unions. There were many prosecutions and some extremely savage sentences. But by the 1820's a new generation was coming into public life. It did not any longer fear Jacobinism, and, while generally hostile to trade unionism, was doubtful whether prohibitory laws did anything but make worse relations in industry which were already often bad enough. Hence the repeal of the law against combinations in 1824–5. The law relating to breach of contract and criminal conspiracy, which carried heavy sentences, still remained; so too did other legislation, which was to be used against country labourers in the South of England within the next ten years. But the trade unions, as such, were no longer criminal associations. Their regular contributing members were few, perhaps not more than 100,000, as late as the 1840's.[1] Holding as they did that the correct form for the wage-bargain to take was the collective agreement, they had a long and hard way to go before they could be said to have carried their point against those who controlled industry. They had also much to learn themselves. The anxiety of the early Victorian trade unionist leaders to make their unions respectable did not proceed solely out of a desire to stand well with a middle-class political public. It was based also upon memories of fraud, disloyalty and even violence in the unions, deeply offensive to these men, often of strong character and religious convictions, not a few of them Methodists and lay preachers, who were trying to pull order out of the confusion of the early trade union movements.

The trade unionist with sufficient regular earnings to meet the subscription to his trade club or society occupied the top-most tiers of the labour world of the eighteenth century. Such was the insecurity of working-class life, however, that prolonged unemployment, accident or death of the chief wage-earner might plunge the most careful family into deep poverty. Below the ranks of the skilled craftsmen lay many circles of occupation and income, stretching downwards through many kinds of

[1] S. and B. Webb, *History of Trade Unionism*, ed. (1920), p. 748.

casual work or service to the lowest depths of unemployment and destitution. There was the inevitable contingency of old age to be faced, even on the assumption that the children, if there were any, would help the parents. There were sickness and disease, which not all could guard against through friendly or benefit clubs. When death came, children might be left un-cared for and untrained to make a living. These were the natural and institutional contingencies of working-class life and owing to the slenderness, often the irregularity, of income at the best of times, they carried the risk of destitution with them. The first and strongest line of defence against this was the strict family sense of most working-class people; the second and the weaker, the help of other families. Both lines were often and completely broken.

A century and a half before our period opens, the govern-ment of the Tudors had come reluctantly to the conclusion that destitution was a matter for the State to deal with. Its final decisions, arrived at during a dearth in the last years of the sixteenth century, had been expressed in the Poor Laws of 1597 and 1601. These laws underlay the distribution of public assistance in eighteenth-century England. Ireland had no public system of relief until 1838, while the old Scottish Poor Law relied heavily on voluntary contributions.

The English Poor Law levied taxation, in the form of a rate, administered by the parish, which in the sixteenth and seven-teenth centuries had been the natural unit and the local administrative organ of a still largely rural society. During the next century this unit was being outgrown as large towns and cities developed. The parish was still trying to carry out, under fast-changing conditions, the tasks set for it by the Elizabethan law; to relieve the sick, old, lunatic and impotent, to maintain unemployed men or women over short periods in return for work done to the parish account, and to provide some sort of occupational training for children who had no one to care for them. It exercised wide powers over a large part of the popula-tion. Perhaps a quarter of the population at one time or another in their lives received relief. Until 1795 the parish officers had authority to move out of their bounds, not only any stranger to the parish who became chargeable to the poor rate, but also any stranger who might become chargeable.

The justice of the old Poor Law, where it was just, was rough. The central direction of the Poor Law, once provided by the

Privy Council, had not survived the Civil War. The parishes and their officers, the constable and the overseer of the poor, were a law to themselves after 1660. What they did best was the distribution of the forms of public assistance known as out-relief, because it was given to people in their own homes, outside of the poorhouse.[1] It took many forms: the provision of a cottage or house-rent; free clothing, boots and shoes, or fuel; medical attendance and maintenance during illness or small doles of cash, such as were not infrequently given to married labourers with many children, who could not maintain their family on their wages. Children were boarded out or apprenticed to some trade; both of these activities were subject to gross abuse.

Where the parishes failed badly, perhaps because they were unfitted for the task from the beginning, was in handling the problems of the men or women in want of work. The original idea of the Tudor law, that such people should be maintained in return for labour done, implied some form of public investment. Neither the finances of the parish nor the ability of its officers were equal to such work. The early laying in of parish stocks of raw material had soon ceased. The contracting out of the workhouse to private employers, who set up their own industry in it and made what profit they could out of the inmates in return for taking them off the hands of the parish, had been tried in the first half of the eighteenth century and was fortunately abandoned in the second. The workhouse tended to become a mere poorhouse, the sordid place to which the parish officers sent all those whom they could not dispose of elsewhere, including from time to time unemployed persons. The children, the diseased, the lame, the insane and the dissolute, might be found under one roof and even in one room, for the attempt to sort out the classes of destitute people and treat them separately, according to need, was beyond the resources or the intention of most parishes. This

> ...prison, with a milder name,
> Which few inhabit without dread or shame,

as George Crabbe described it,[2] not without conceding its better intentions, was the general mixed workhouse. It had

---

[1] On this side of the law, see Dorothy Marshall, *The English Poor in the Eighteenth Century* (1926), chapter III.
[2] In his poem, *The Borough*, published in 1810.

emerged from two centuries of Poor Law history and it was to be denounced by Poor Law reformers of many types for another hundred years. It is a mistake to think that its unpopularity dated from the severe discipline introduced into public assistance by the Poor Law Amendment Act of 1834. The causes of the 'dread and shame' were the break with the known and the familiar, the loss of social status, with its circle of small rights and duties, the defeat of hope and self-respect, which relief in the workhouse had always represented to most working men and women. There were of course some who did not suffer from these feelings or who had never known anything better, such as the parish children.

The workhouse therefore did not live up to its name nor could perhaps, since the original intention of this part of the Poor Law seems to have been to assist individuals to effect the transition from agriculture to textile industry at a particular juncture in English history.[1] Now, on the eve of a vaster economic change and a far greater transfer of labour than in Tudor times, Poor Law reform was in the air. It took the half hearted form of the act of 1782, introduced to Parliament by Thomas Gilbert. This law, which was permissive and did not compel the parishes to do anything, acknowledged the passing of the parish as a suitable unit for administration, especially in the towns, by allowing parishes to combine into Poor Law unions. It expressed a proper mistrust of the parish officer, by making it possible to place him under the control of a new kind of official, the guardians of the poor, appointed by the justices of the peace. The workhouse, it was hoped, would become a true poorhouse, kept for the old, sick, mothers of illegitimate offspring, and children. The unemployed man or woman under the new law could be given work outside the poorhouse and wages might be made up out of the rates.

Out of some fifteen thousand parishes in England and Wales, not more than 924 had been incorporated in Gilbert Unions by 1834. The poorhouse remained much what it had always been, to be condemned anew by official inquiry seventy years later. Unintelligent work on the roads and an equally easy and unintelligent, if indispensable, grant of out-relief in money became the current means of dealing with the workless man. Two Kentish parishes, which successfully ran, in one case for eighty years at a stretch, Poor Law farms for those capable of work but

[1] Gilbert Slater, *Poverty and the State* (1930), p. 336.

locally unemployed, were evidently felt to have taken their duties too seriously. They found no imitators.[1]

Such was the state of social law at the end of the eighteenth century. Within a few years of the act of 1782, revolution broke out in France; four years later, war began between France and Great Britain; and almost immediately the beginnings of a rapid inflation of prices began to alter the relations between wages and the cost of living and to prepare the way for a new distribution of incomes. For twenty years the transfer of labour from occupation to occupation was stimulated by the war expenditures of government, which assisted to bring the nation's resources into a state of high employment. Important problems of economic change seemed to solve themselves, while the eyes of the governing classes, never deeply interested in economic and social questions, were fixed upon the events of war and diplomacy in Napoleon Bonaparte's Europe.

THE ECONOMIC EFFORT OF THE WAR WITH FRANCE

From 1793 to 1815, except for the brief interlude of the Peace of Amiens, Great Britain was at war with France, under the governments of the Revolution and Napoleon. These twenty-two years of war, extending over the active life of a whole generation, may be regarded as closing the eighteenth century or opening the nineteenth. They did both, since they saw much transition in social, economic and political affairs. For Europe as a whole, the Revolution and the war formed a gateway to a new age; they introduced the great themes of nineteenth-century history—the politics of nationality and the politics of democracy. But the wars also represented a time of economic effort and stress, coinciding with the remarkable phase of population growth and economic development in Britain which has been described.

The economic task which the French wars set Great Britain was sufficiently hard to draw out all her powers, without being so heavy as to overwhelm her. A large number of men were under arms. Towards the end of the war there were about 140,000 in the navy and about 350,000 in the army, not counting the militia, volunteers, yeomanry and East India Company forces. In 1804, Lord Hawkesbury declared in

[1] A local historian seems to be the only source of information; see Slater, op. cit. pp. 65–6.

Parliament that the armed forces, including militia but not volunteers, represented rather more than one in ten of the population of military age in Great Britain and Ireland.[1] These men had to be fed and provided with arms, clothing and equipment, or the means for paying for these things abroad had to be found; for the British armies on the Continent footed their bills instead of living on the country. The working population had also to find the means to pay Britain's allies abroad. Pitt's subsidies to the Allies were met by the export of goods.

War in those times did not call for the enormous mass of equipment which is required by modern mechanized warfare. Mass slaughter requires mass weapons. But whereas in the Second World War, statisticians reckoned that three war-workers were needed to keep one fighting man in the field, under the less intense conditions of the Napoleonic Wars one war-worker, it was supposed, could maintain two fighting men.[2]

Against a people more numerous than her own and economically progressive, Great Britain enjoyed the general advantage of a productivity in agriculture and industry which was markedly rising. This rising national income was the economic fund out of which the war was fought. The change was perhaps most clearly perceptible in the field where Britain, with her rising population and limited area, might have appeared weakest, in food supply. As the war extended and the greater part of the Continent of Europe fell subject to French arms, Britain was cut off from the lands which at that date formed her chief source of imported food. The most important item was corn. The transition from being, on balance, a corn exporter to becoming an importer of corn, had preceded by about a generation the outbreak of the war. After the decade 1765–74, Britain became a considerable although irregular purchaser of corn abroad. How much she took in any one year depended on the state of the harvest. A diversity of ports in Northern and North-eastern Europe shared in the trade, especially those towns such as Danzig and Hamburg whose position gave them access by river to the grain lands of East Prussia and Poland. A new source of supply was opening up beyond the Atlantic,

[1] Joseph Lowe, *The Present State of England in regard to Agriculture, Trade and Finance*, 2nd ed. (1823), p. 46.
[2] For the modern statisticians see W. K. Hancock and M. M. Gowing, *British War Economy* (1949), p. 14; the contemporary writer was Joseph Lowe, op. cit. p. 48.

in the United States of America and Canada, but North America was a mere resort of emergency in those days and was closed for some time by the war of 1812. There did not then exist the surplus of supplies and the organization of international transport to handle them which would have been required to feed Britain annually with any high proportion of her supplies. Imports during the latter years of the Napoleonic Wars averaged no more than one-sixth of her annual consumption. But as the numbers of her people rose, the time came when any serious deficiency in the normal yield of her harvests produced panic prices. In 1800 and 1801 the annual average price of wheat reached 113s. 10d. and 119s. 6d. a quarter; in 1810, the price again exceeded 106s. a quarter. These were famine prices and the prices of all other grain foods rose in sympathy. It was in 1799 and 1800 that James Carlyle, the Scottish stonemason who was father of Thomas Carlyle, saw his fellow-labourers in a field going down, each alone and unwilling to confess his hunger, to a brook at the end of the field to drink, because they had no dinner.

After the victory of Trafalgar in 1805, British naval supremacy remained unchallenged for the rest of the war. This made possible the collection of American and Irish grain supplies as they became available. Ireland became a granary during the war, to her own ultimate misfortune. In so far as French military power could be brought to bear, British grain imports from Europe could be and were stopped with a respectable measure of success, especially during the height of the French military ascendancy, between 1807 and 1813, although the policy of Napoleon was not consistent. In 1809 and 1810, for reasons of internal politics, he permitted the export of grain to Britain under licence, excusing himself by the outdated economic argument that thereby he would drain her of gold. In these circumstances, a considerable effort was called for from British agriculture. The extension of the cultivable area and the improvement of agricultural method formed the heart of it. The attack on the waste lands by enclosure became vigorous after 1802, when the war recommenced. Better farming and higher yields were of even more importance than the extension of the margin of cultivation of wheat. A contemporary thought that the output of tillage crops had been raised by 50 per cent during the war and that less than 15 per cent of this was due to an extension of plough-land, the greater part being the result of better and more intensive cultivation.[1] It would appear that, during the later part of the war, conditions even in the worst years were better than they had been in earlier years of crisis. The agricultural advance did not protect the poorest part of the nation from extreme suffering from time to time, caused by the recurrence of dearth and high prices. But without the rise in agricultural production, the problem of subsistence must have been even greater.

The other economic resource which Great Britain possessed was the power of increasing productivity in manufacturing industry. This was important for all kinds of equipment and munitions of war. The bearing of the development of British resources in coal and iron upon the manufacture of weapons of war had been seen long before by intelligent observers. During the Seven Years War (1756–63), French naval officers noticed that British naval cannon were becoming superior to their own. Hence the visit of French metallurgists to Britain in the peace which followed, before Britain became embroiled with France again in the war with the American colonies. Investigation was not difficult, under the easy-going conditions of eighteenth-century Europe, and it is to Frenchmen who inspected English metallurgical works in the 1760's and 1770's that we owe much of our knowledge of the gap which was opening up between the British and Continental technical methods, especially in the smelting of iron-ore with coke and the casting and boring of cannon. The visit of one officer led the French government to invite William Wilkinson, the brother of the ironmaster John Wilkinson, to cross the Channel in 1776 and become part founder of the Le Creusot ironworks, which was the beginning of a new kind of heavy industry and munitions manufacture in France. Britain fought the war of 1793–1815 with an iron industry which used the new techniques as its basis, in contrast to the industry of the Continent, which had only just begun to change over to them. Upon this foundation of iron she expanded the finishing industries which were required for many war goods, such as gun-making, chain- and anchor-making and other industries, which flourished in the Midlands.

The war had its effect too on the textile industries, especially the woollen industry of the West Riding. In 1800, it was reckoned that under the old methods 101 workers were required

[1] Joseph Lowe, *The Present State of England*, 2nd ed. (1823), Appendix, pp. 36–7.

to make a pack of wool into yarn; given the new machinery only twenty-two were needed.[1] Such an industry was invaluable to the Commissary-General in London, whose business it was to make purchases for the army. Hence the enormous business done by such a man as Benjamin Gott of Leeds, of whom it has been said that he dressed and blanketed for many years a large part of the armies of England, Russia, Prussia and Sweden, as well as becoming one of the great exporters of broadcloth.

The introduction of power into industry was a development that would have taken place in any event. It was certainly helped by the war, perhaps because, although expensive, it formed one of the certain means towards a speedy increase of production. In the metal trades of Birmingham and the Black Country, the process of change can be watched with some precision. Visitors to that district from the Continent, such as the Swiss engineer J. G. Bodmer in 1816–17, were impressed by the penetration of steam and machinery into all kinds of manufacture, from the forging of gun-barrels to the drawing of wire, which had taken place during the wars. The development of the Soho Foundry at Birmingham after 1795, under the able management of Matthew Robinson Boulton and James Watt, junior, from which steam engines were supplied to men such as Gott and others working on war contracts, formed an economic asset in the naval and Continental war.

Rising productivity in agriculture and industry was the key to such success as Britain enjoyed in meeting both the needs of an exceptionally swift-growing population and the demands of the longest and most exhausting war she had yet fought. It must not be thought that her productive effort sufficed of itself for the successful economic conduct of the war. To bring much of this effort to bear in the changing theatres of the war, the world-wide mercantile and financial connections of her merchants were necessary. Barings, the merchant bankers, with other financial houses, are said to have remitted £57,000,000 between 1792 and 1816 to the Continental allies of Great Britain.[2] The remittances would not have been possible without a large export trade and the manufactures to support it. Britain was fortunate in the rapid rise of the cotton industry,

---

[1] H. Heaton, 'Benjamin Gott and the Industrial Revolution in Yorkshire', *Econ. Hist. Rev.* vol. III (1931), p. 61.
[2] R. Hidy, *House of Baring* (1949), p. 28.

which in the war years outstripped the woollen trade as an exporting industry and brought an accession of strength to her international economic position when it was most needed. The favourable position of the British manufacturer and export merchant during the war was also due to the attack on French trade by the fleet and the cutting off of competition in many markets with the changing fortunes of the war. This relative immunity from competition Great Britain could hardly be expected to keep as the new industrial processes and organization gained ground upon the European continent after the war. Meanwhile, it enabled her to fight the war as a creditor and to lend substantial economic assistance to her allies without piling up debts abroad.

If the nation's economic system showed no signs of breaking down under the strain of so long a war, this was because the changes which had been taking place in that system for some time before the war enabled it to carry the burden. There was no imperative need, as there was to be during the World Wars a century later, to replace the free markets by rationing and controls in the interests of an economical use of resources. The allocation of resources between many conflicting claims was not an easy matter. The high prices of the war period were an unmistakable sign of strain. But it was safe, given the social and political conditions of the time, to leave high prices to settle the matter. High prices drew towards the war sector of the economy what was needed for the economic conduct of the war. They also cut off, mainly by driving the poorest and weakest customers out of the market and inflicting severe suffering on those least able to bargain, part of the demand for civilian supplies and so set them free for war purposes. To compel a sacrifice of civilian consumption equal to war production, inflation was thus used as a weapon of war.

The main price of the war effort was paid during the war. The level of employment was high and earnings were often good by the standards of the time, once wages became adjusted to prices, but the cost of living was throughout high. The wage-earner's difficulties in the first upward surge of prices during the 1790's were acute. We have already seen something of this in relation to the country labourer and the decision of the justices of the peace in Berkshire in 1795 to supplement the wages of the local agricultural labourers out of the rates, according to size of family and the price of bread. The so-called 'Berkshire bread-scale' or 'Speenhamland system' was widely adopted during the war throughout the South of England as a kind of protection for the labourers in the country against war prices. Continued after the war, it was to become one of the main problems of economic policy in the next generation.

It was not food only that was dear and sometimes scarce. Shortage of timber, bricks and glass affected the building of houses. In middle-class districts this might mean no more than a slimmer banister in the stair-well, but it may account for, although it does not excuse, some of the jerry-built cottages and working-class streets of the time. Building tended not to keep pace with population; rents rose in the towns. Increased overcrowding may account, together with the fall of employment and earnings, for the rise in the death-rate in the towns after the war. The maintenance of public health during the war had been, by the standards of the time, remarkably good; even the return of the sick men from Walcheren led to no outbreak of malaria in the old centres of that disease in east and south-east England.

The rapid rise of prices compared with wages favoured the business man. The profits of farmers, merchants, bankers and manufacturers were increased by a windfall element, as well as by their own labours. Agricultural rents rose by 40 per cent in the corn-growing eastern counties. Is it surprising that some men suffered from the idea that the war was the main source of the national wealth? Lenders to government, William Cobbett's hated loan-mongers, did well. The income tax skimmed some of the cream from the higher incomes, but taxation, by the measure of a later age, was light. The general picture of British incomes during the war is that of a series of transfers of income over long years to the pockets of landlords, farmers, houseowners, bondholders and entrepreneurs. The wage-earner and the fixed annuitant suffered the transfer.[1]

This transfer of purchasing power was the rough mechanism by which the national economy was brought to bear on the war. It was the natural consequence of the unrestricted rise of money prices and incomes, that is of monetary inflation, and of the inequality with which inflation bore upon the different groups and classes within the nation. For the economic effort of the war brought inflation in its train. The inflation was due

[1] T. S. Ashton, 'The Standard of Life of the Workers in England, 1790–1830', *J. Econ. Hist.* Supplement IX (1949), p. 23.

to the failure of additional output to keep pace with the growth of money incomes and the competition of these incomes, including the income of government, for the supplies of goods and the services that were available. To understand how this came about, it is necessary to know something about the finance of the war.

In considering this, we find ourselves at once surveying the policy of William Pitt. From 1783 to 1801, the financial record of Great Britain is the record of Pitt's eighteen consecutive budgets. He was not only the political leader of the nation during the war, so long as he lived, but also the framer of the financial policy with which the war was fought. He was the most important figure in the history of British public finance since Sir Robert Walpole in the first half of the eighteenth century, and had no comparable successor until Sir Robert Peel and Gladstone.

The immediate financial burden was great, for a population and national income such as Great Britain then possessed. In 1793, the United Kingdom contained a population of perhaps 14 or 15 millions. The National Debt stood at £240 million. The annual expenses of government, exclusive of contributions to the sinking fund, were some £18–19 million. The Debt charges absorbed £9½ million of this, the army and navy about £6 million. As the normal revenue amounted to about £20 million, government was budgeting, at peacetime levels of expenditure, for a small surplus. All this was changed by 1815. The population of the United Kingdom had by then risen to some 20 millions. The National Debt, largely as a consequence of the war, was up to £900 million and the Debt charges had reached £32 million a year. The annual expenditure of government was running at £100 million, of which £56 million was being spent on the army and navy. Annual revenue, at almost £80 million, was high above that of pre-war days, but much lower than expenditure.[1] Government was meeting the deficits between taxation and expenses by borrowing from the wealthier classes.

The war largely increased the National Debt and unbalanced the budget, and in its financial aspects resembled the great wars of the present century. Vast government spendings in the conduct of the war created personal incomes, in the form of

[1] S. Buxton, *Finance and Politics, An Historical Study, 1783-1885*, vol. 1 (1888), pp. 7-8.

wages, interest, salary, profit and commission which outran the increase in goods and services available for purchase. Prices therefore rose. Average opinion was less interested, however, in the mechanism of inflation which it found impossible to understand than in some of the specific financial measures which were adopted to fight the war. These had a direct bearing on the timing and the extent of the inflation.

Pitt began badly, as finance ministers who have gone into war unprepared usually do. The period of hesitant, ineffectual or even inept finance was in the first part of the war, during the years 1793–1802. From 1802 onwards, taxation was both rigorous and fruitful, although it was not sufficient to prevent considerable additions to the National Debt. The Chancellors of the Exchequer who financed the war against France compared favourably with their successors of 1914–18, during the war against the Central Powers, in their willingness to meet the expenses of the war out of taxes. Over the whole period of the war, revenue from taxes amounted to 35 per cent of the addition to the country's annual average expenditure brought about by the war. During the First World War the proportion was 17 per cent.[1]

One of the means by which this revenue was obtained was the introduction of a new tax. This was the income-tax, introduced by Pitt in 1799, removed in 1802 on the conclusion of the Peace of Amiens and at once renewed when that peace broke down. So strong was the feeling against the tax, especially in the City of London, that as soon as the war was over Parliament was persuaded, in March 1816, to vote its repeal and the destruction of the tax records. Duplicates of the records were, however, preserved, and they enable us to watch the building up, under the direction of two able civil servants, Matthew Winter and Richard Gray, of an organization for collection of the tax in London and the provinces. Through the records we can survey the serious effects of the break with the United States after 1811 upon the trade of Lancashire, the prosperity of wartime agriculture in Cambridgeshire, Norfolk and the West Riding, the rising industrial and commercial incomes of Birmingham and the Midlands, the activity of tin- and copper-mining in remote Cornwall, and the concentration of wealth drawn from many sources in the City of London. The income-

[1] N. J. Silberling, 'Financial and Monetary Policy of Great Britain during the Napoleonic Wars', *Quart. J. Econ.* vol. XXXVIII (1924), p. 221.

tax was the first tax which successfully tapped the annual
increase in the wealth of the country, and the first British tax
reasonably proportioned to means. Paying at the rate of two
shillings in the pound, the taxpaying classes contributed
between April 1806, when the tax received its final form, and
April 1816 nearly £142 million to the State.[1] Both the
efficiency and the equity of the tax were sufficient causes of its
unpopularity.

Income-tax was not the major source of revenue during the
war. Customs and excise duties brought in nearly half the war
supplies from taxation in 1811. Direct taxation never brought
in more than a third of the tax income, even when the income-
tax was at its height. Taxation of all kinds may have taken one-
sixth of the national income annually, towards the end of the
war.[2]

The economic significance of the expansion of taxes during
the war was that, by withdrawing in the form of taxation much
of the money which it disbursed in war contracts, the government prevented—without intending to do so—private purchases from competing with its own purchases of war requirements. It facilitated to that extent the steady direction of a
large proportion of the national economic resources towards
purposes of war. At the same time, by checking through taxes
the inflation of prices which would otherwise have come about
as war-created incomes competed for goods, the government
forestalled some of the discontent arising from a rapidly
increasing cost of living which is the natural consequence of
inflation. War inflation was, however, not avoided, nor was the
prevention of it the object of national finance. This was
dominated almost entirely by political expediency and administrative convenience, to the exclusion of considerations of the
stability of the national economy. Few expected that economy
to be stable at any time, while some benefited directly by the
violent rise of prices, which was the main symptom of inflation.

The first steep ascent of prices took place during the years
1793–1802, when large government spendings were creating
new incomes and before heavy taxation had been imposed.
A further violent rise took place in the later years of the war,
after 1809. A selected group of thirty-five commodities doubled
their prices between 1790 and 1814. These were wholesale, not

[1] A. Hope-Jones, *Income Tax in the Napoleonic Wars* (1939), p. 124.
[2] Hope Jones, op. cit. p. 112.

retail prices; but it was the rise of wholesale prices and the problems created for commercial people and bankers, rather than the complaints of the consumer, which formed the background of the public controversy over prices and currency after 1809. As we have seen, the inflation was blamed upon the Bank of England; but it was in its essential character the result of the economic policies pursued by British governments during the war. Once the war was over and the State ceased its demands upon the economy, prices fell. A long and painful period of deflation followed. Prices dropped sharply in 1816 and 1819; they continued to fall in the 1820's, until by the end of the decade they were back to the level of 1790.[1] They did not rise again until the international boom of the late 1830's and then to nothing comparable with their wartime height. The Napoleonic level of prices was not reached again until after another and greater general European war had broken out in 1914.

The great war inflations of the present century have taken place amid circumstances far different from those of the period 1793–1815. Not only the nature of the British economy, but the powers and even the conception of the State, to say nothing of the weapons and processes of war, have been altered in an intervening century of huge economic, political and military developments. The most striking difference between the two ages is that the economic burden of the wars with France, while it strained the national economy, proved well within its capacity to bear. Relying upon the rising productivity of the country and its trading surplus abroad, British governments were never forced to guard against war scarcities by control, as they have had to do in recent times.

The war was to this extent a victory not only for British arms but also for that free market economy which Adam Smith and other eighteenth-century thinkers had analysed as growing up around them. It was to provide the material foundations of British power in the century which followed Waterloo. What course economic development and policy would have taken, if the issue of the war had been different, who can tell? They could hardly have been the same; Adam Smith's words, that defence is of more importance than opulence, would have rung differently in the ear if the day had gone to the French at

[1] N. J. Silberling, 'British Prices and Business Cycles, 1779–1850', *Review of Economic Statistics*, Supplement II (1923), pp. 232–3, table 3.

Trafalgar or Waterloo. As things happened, private and public investment and commercial policy went on throughout the century under conditions of security laid down by British supremacy at sea after 1805, which remained without a serious threat until the building up of the German fleet after 1898.

The economic policies pursued by British governments in Napoleon's day throw light in other ways upon the character of the economy which had been growing up in the eighteenth century and the economic policies which seemed appropriate to it, in relation to the balance of social and political interests. If the economy remained substantially without control during the war, this was partly due to its growing strength but also because eighteenth-century Parliaments were not particularly concerned to hold the balance evenly between the various classes of the nation. It would have been foreign to the outlook of the age to do so. The wars with France were fought partly in the age-old interest of national security, partly in resistance to the democratic ideas then issuing from France. The strictly controlled war economies of a later Britain have been the product not only of the war-created scarcities, but also of the revolution brought about by the democratizing of British political institutions in the nineteenth century. In the wars of the earlier period, the economic cost of the struggle was borne by all classes in higher prices, but chiefly by those whose incomes could least stand the strain, so that they were driven out of the market. The additional employment which the wars created was regarded as sufficient compensation to them for the inconvenience and discomfort of unregulated prices.

AFTER THE WAR

The period of transition after the war brought other problems. The national economy had then to be redirected. The depressing effects of the close of the war upon the investments and activity of such big capitalists as the Shropshire ironmasters and the Yorkshire clothiers, who had worked to war contracts, were obvious. There was much to be done during the next few years in redistributing the country's resources so as to serve the purposes of peace. Great Britain in the decade that followed the war, with its complaints of falling profits, unpaid rents and unemployment, with its severe depression in agriculture, acute as late as the early 1830's, and in the heavy industries of iron and coal, gave every appearance of a country engaged, amid social distress and political discontent, upon such a task. In so far as new markets were gradually found at home and abroad, the waste of invested capital in manufactures was perhaps not great, although the story in agriculture may be different. The chief economic waste seems to have taken the form of unemployment among soldiers and sailors discharged from the services after the war, half-pay officers temporarily without an occupation, and those displaced from jobs in agriculture and industry by changes directly due to the war.

The owners of agricultural capital, finding themselves in difficulties both acute and prolonged, and being better represented and more powerful in Parliament than most people, took steps to protect themselves. In 1815, foreign wheat was excluded until the British price reached 80s. a quarter, a price based on the experience of the war generation. But corn could not be kept at that price or anything like it by law, and corn protection, although it was stiffly maintained, had to be modified in 1822 and 1828. When one part of the nation was suffering from loss of employment and reduced wages, while another part was under the necessity of finding new markets at home and abroad for its industrial and commercial products, the action of the agricultural interest, which both maintained the cost of living and added to the difficulties of exporting, was an added burden and an irritant. But the bitterness of the middle classes against landowners, which led to the foundation of an Anti-Corn Law League in Manchester in 1838, was only one aspect of the heightened class and sectional feeling characteristic of the two decades which followed the war.

Agricultural capital was not the only interest protected by the tariff and fearful of trusting itself to the unknown waters of the post-war world. The reconstruction of commercial and financial policy which had been urgent in Pitt's day was over-due twenty years after his death. Industrial and commercial interests, looking for markets after the war, were beginning to reconcile themselves to the proposition that Britain must buy more if she was going to sell more abroad. In response to their pressure and sometimes a little ahead of it, Huskisson and other members of the administrations of the 1820's and 1830's had undertaken to modify the tariff and the colonial system. But down to 1830 and even ten years later, the spokesmen of commerce and industry upon the Continent could reproach

Britain with some justice that, while she sought markets and disapproved of protection in Continental states, her own market remained hidden behind the barrier of a high and confusing tariff.

The position of the labouring man was very different. The man without capital except in his hands remained without protection in what he regarded as his proper economic interests. Old legislation which might conceivably have been used for the purpose had just been repealed. The clauses of the Elizabethan Statute of Artificers of 1563, which provided for the enforcement of apprenticeship in many trades and for the settling of wages by the justice of the peace, had been repealed towards the end of the war in 1813–14. A law which gave binding force to wage-rates agreed in the London silk-weavers' trade, the Spitalfields Act of 1773, was abolished in 1824. From that date onwards until 1909, no attempt was made to establish wage-rates in any industry by law.

The Elizabethan social code was unsuited to the economic and administrative conditions of the early nineteenth century. Its disappearance would have mattered little, if any vigorous extension of collective bargaining had been going forward in agriculture and industry or if Parliament had provided any remedy for the evils in industrial employment. But these things were slow in coming. Meanwhile, the contrast between the attention given by the State to the interests of the owners of capital and its neglect of those of labour forced itself on the notice of thoughtful working men.

These years between 1815 and 1832 were marked by the beginnings of the long agitation for Parliamentary reform and a widened franchise, which aroused the political interests of many wage-earners for the first time. They were also years of recurrent and severe trade depression and much social unrest. Economic and political conditions worked together to produce a generation of debate, when men struck out the leading themes of later economic policy and social politics, as well as some ideas which were not to receive the attention they deserved.

Men of the educated and the commercial classes raised most of the difficult problems connected with the cause and the cure of trade depression just after the war and in the 1820's, when the contrast with the active employment of wartime was too striking to be overlooked. It was then that Thomas Attwood the Birmingham banker campaigned against the resumption of cash payments after 1821 and taught with misleading simplicity the virtues of paper money as a stimulator of effective demand. A much better economist, T. R. Malthus, took issue with David Ricardo on this question of effective demand and posed more strongly than anyone the question why employment should be falling while needs remained unfilled. But he neither solved the theoretical problem nor had anything to suggest, beyond the maintenance of consumption by the spending of the country gentlemen. Educated opinion was more influenced by his doctrine about the tendency of population to outrun subsistence. Men argued, loosely enough, that the country was cursed by surplus population, which they supposed might be dealt with by the reform of the Poor Law. But if population appeared surplus in those years so too did capital. Edward Gibbon Wakefield, the most systematic British thinker of the nineteenth century on colonization as a field of employment for both men and money, began to write his *Letter from Sydney* in Newgate prison in the late 1820's, urging a new kind of organized colonization. A Liverpool merchant and Quaker, James Cropper,[1] in a letter to the statesman George Canning, in 1817, spoke for another school. He denied that either capital or population were redundant or that colonization could correct the matter, and sketched out a programme of public works in roads and other matters to revive demand and through demand investment by private capitalists.[2]

Such men were in the minority. The majority in business and professional circles trusted to the enterprise, the savings, the organizing ability, the manual skill which had carried the country so far, and to the expansion of markets at home and abroad, without asking too closely how resources and demand were to be brought together. Indeed, they were beginning to think they had the answer, for they had dropped some of the economic policy of the past and they were getting ready to drop more, especially in the field of commercial policy, to obtain outlets for their products abroad. They did not conceive that they owed anything to the working man, whom they rather thought of as owing to them what employment and income he possessed. They regarded as a dangerous fellow the popular

---

[1] James Cropper (1773–1840), founder of the Liverpool mercantile house, Cropper, Benson and Co., was a noted business man and philanthropist of his day.

[2] C. R. Fay, *Huskisson and his Age* (1951), pp. 252–3.

Radical, William Cobbett, who was riding about the country from 1821, publishing in his *Political Register* denunciations of the return to cash payments and the Corn Laws as injurious to working people; much of it mere abuse, but much good social politics, of a commonsensical kind. They must have thought more dangerous, if they had ever heard of him, Robert Owen, the Lanarkshire cotton-spinner, who in the bad year 1817, proposed to match consumption with production in small planned communities, which were intended to become a model for the world. He became an organizer and forerunner of some of the most important socialist and co-operative movements of the next twenty years.

There were other writers and thinkers of interest in the 1820's, although so little known at the time that they have had to be rediscovered by the historians of social thought. These men, arguing from Ricardo's economics, especially the labour theory of value which he had inherited from Adam Smith, reasoned that what was wrong was the distribution of wealth. Give the worker, they asserted, the whole value of the product which he made and no more would be heard of demand being wanting or resources left unused. These men, the so-called Ricardian Socialists, William Thompson, John Gray and Thomas Hodgskin, were predecessors of Karl Marx. They had some influence on him and through him upon the later social democracy of the Continent. None of them was a profound or systematic thinker, neither did their ideas spread beyond the narrowest circles, but they reflected the unrest of the time.[1]

These revolutionary doctrines sprang out of the heart of the school of economic and social thought which was now coming to dominate and which taught that social and economic forces should be allowed to work themselves out, subject to the elementary political needs of public order and defence. They suggest how little power resided in the new economic philosophy and policies to reconcile interests and hopes which in those gloomy post-war years seemed far apart and almost irreconcilable.

[1] These men were rediscovered for English readers by H. S. Foxwell, in his introduction to the English edition of Anton Menger's *Right to the Whole Produce of Labour* (1899).

Book II

THE VICTORIAN ECONOMY AND AFTER

1837 TO 1939

Chapter VIII

Economic Life in the Victorian Age to 1880

THE CONDITIONS OF ECONOMIC EXPANSION

The economic problem facing Great Britain in the years after Waterloo was whether she could employ all her people. The population of England and Wales had included perhaps $7\frac{1}{2}$ million people in 1780. By the census of 1821 it was up to 12 millions. Between that year and 1871 it was to rise to $22\frac{3}{4}$ millions. This was more than the whole population of the United Kingdom had been in 1821. It then stood at a little under 21 millions, including 2 million for Scotland and between 6 and 7 millions for Ireland.[1]

Much of the economic thought of the nineteenth century took it for granted that Great Britain could and would employ her population, under any circumstances short of a disastrous war or great natural calamity. The discussions which surrounded the reform of the Poor Law in 1834 reflected this belief. Many supporters of reform held that if any sane and healthy man or woman stood in need of public relief, it was because of some physical or moral defect, not because of genuine lack of employment. The free-traders of the mid-century believed that the labour and capital of the country would be employed, if only the State would not try to direct them.

Malthus had taught, however, that there was no guarantee in nature or history that an increasing population would always be fed. An important element in educated opinion, well schooled by him, remained doubtful. The state of Ireland for many years before the potato famine and the course of the subsequent events appeared to such men a terrible demonstration of the truth of Malthus's doctrine. There, for decade after decade following the famine, the population fell by emigration, until Ireland, which had possessed in 1841 more than three times the population of Scotland, had at the end of the century a smaller population than Scotland.[2] But Englishmen did not

[1] Figures from G. T. Griffith, *Population Problems of the Age of Malthus* (1926), pp. 18 and 21, and G. R. Porter, *Progress of the Nation* (1912), pp. 3, 4.   [2] Porter, op. cit. p. 4.

regard Irish lessons as applying to them and in the prosperous decades which followed the Great Exhibition of 1851 Malthusianism lost much of its hold. It is certain, however, that Great Britain was fortunate in being able to match a swift and long-continued increase of population with an ample employment of her resources and a rising if modest standard of life. It is the object of the present chapter to consider some of the conditions which made this possible.

The favouring conditions were not all of them economic. One of the most important was the long immunity from major war which followed the Congress of Vienna in 1815. Great Britain was not engaged in another European conflict until the war with Russia (1854–6) and operations then were distant. She stood aloof from the wars of nationality during the mid-century, which engaged France, Austria, Prussia and Piedmont. This was an exceptionally peaceful period of her history, which lasted almost without a break to 1914; for the Boer War (1899–1901) was no more than the greatest of colonial wars. Throughout the century, Great Britain was free from invasion and even from the need to make any first-rate exertion in war. Her immunity she owed partly to the condition of European politics, partly to the superiority of her sea power. This last had a bearing upon the economic policies she pursued; for example, in the freeing of import and export trade from all control and the maintenance of the 'open door' in the colonies.

During this peaceful age, she was also one of the most stable of European states. Between 1832 and the First World War her political structure broadened down into political democracy, without revolution or serious disorder. Her legal system was successfully adapted to the needs of an industrial and commercial society. What was more important, the structure of her society proved amenable to change in an age when change of many kinds, economic, intellectual, political, was swifter and deeper than at any other period of her modern history.

Peace and order, though favourable to economic development, will not of themselves account for it or for its rate of progress. These are to be explained in terms of the investment of capital in agriculture, manufactures and transport; the extension of credit; the management of business; the productivity of labour; the character, the talent and the education, social and formal, of the men and women who form the working population.

The course of investment, which was fundamental to the employment of resources, was much influenced by what happened to prices, both those which the merchant and the manufacturer had to pay upon commodity markets and retail prices. To trace prices in detail is often a difficult matter, but between the close of the French wars and the last quarter of the nineteenth century, when very different economic conditions set in, two distinct phases were passed through by commodity prices, which did much to determine the tone of business.

The first was the tendency of prices to fall from the height of the Napoleonic inflation. War finance, as we have seen, had the effect of putting a great deal of money into circulation between 1793 and 1815. A liberal creation of credit by the country banks and the Bank of England, for use in commerce, industry and agriculture, helped to keep the level of business activity high and inflate prices and incomes. Heavy payments abroad for corn and naval stores, remittances to governments and armies, and the violent fluctuations in the value of French currency during the Revolution strained the balance of payments and brought about heavy falls from time to time in the value of the pound on the foreign exchanges, so that the price of imports rose. The peak of the first upward movement of prices was reached in 1801, when they stood, compared with those of 1790, as 166 to 100. After a moderate fall, prices began to rise again rapidly after 1808, to reach their height in 1814, when for a brief period they were more than twice the prices of 1790. Thereafter they fell, violently at first, and the fall continued for many years. In 1820 they were still above the prewar level, which they did not reach until eight or nine years later.[1]

The tendency of prices to decline persisted, with many ups and downs, throughout the 1830's and 1840's, reaching its lowest point at the end of the latter decade. After 1850 they rose. The middle nineteenth century is represented in the history of prices not by the downward slope of a hill but by a kind of upland plateau, broken by low hills. The plateau represents the broad upward movement of commodity prices, the low broken hills the ups and downs of trade, which earned the name of the trade cycle. During this period, with the

[1] N. J. Silberling, 'British Prices and Business Cycles, 1779–1850', *Rev. Econ. Statist.* Supplement II (1923), pp. 232–3, table 3.

important exception of the years of great price fluctuation, such as 1857–8, the manufacturer and the merchant experienced the exhilaration of selling upon a rising market, even if they were paying more for materials and labour. Behind this buoyancy of markets lay the pressure of effective demand, coming from many sources both at home and abroad; from new gold discoveries in Australia and California, and the settlement and opening up of new lands in the area of the Pacific; from wars in Europe; from the vast investments of the mid-century in many lands, including Britain herself. The last great burst of activity around this level of prices took place from 1868 to 1873. Then came not only a sharp financial crisis but a general and long-continued fall of prices, which opened what was to be a new chapter in the economic history of Great Britain and of the world.

The course of prices was enormously important, because it was upon prices that men's eyes were set. Prices indicated what the producer should produce, whether in the factory or on the farm; they helped to decide what the consumer would buy, whether the purchase was a ship or a machine or the family's food for the week. Prices entered into all economic decisions and expectations. They assisted to produce an atmosphere of optimism or pessimism, characteristic of the age.

The movements of prices looked, however, perhaps more important to contemporaries than they do to us. The course of economic development depended upon the investment of new capital, bringing new employment of resources and new efficiency of labour with it. But the motive to investment was profit and this was far from depending wholly upon general trends of prices, which few men watched steadily. A vast variety of other circumstances bore upon the prospect of profit and the productivity of capital. Prices often appear to have been less the prime mover in economic events than the consequence of more fundamental movements, such as the settlement of a new country, the exploitation of a new invention, or the expenditure of a government at war. These conditions which influenced the distribution of the national resources between one employment and another are central to Victorian economic history, and they are perhaps best understood by following the development of some branches of production in detail.

AGRICULTURE

The pace of industrialization was headlong, the expansion of foreign trade hardly less so during the early and middle Victorian period. Agriculture, the ancient source of national income, declined in relative importance. We have seen, however, that it was the rising output of British farms which had made possible industrialization, by feeding the towns, and it continued to do so far down into the century. Until the international trade in foodstuffs developed after 1873, Great Britain was reasonably self-sufficient, although not wholly so, in meat and wheat. She could have stood a siege, not of course without danger or inconvenience. Agriculture was an industry which absorbed a great part of the nation's labour—roughly a quarter of the grown men in Britain at the census of 1851.[1] Then, and for some time 'after, agriculture was still, judged by numbers employed, the largest industry in Britain.

By the early 1850's, agriculture had undergone considerable changes. The Napoleonic Wars had over-expanded the industry, compared with peacetime requirements. Rents and the personal expenditure of farmers had gone up; many farmers had bought land at high prices, often on mortgage. The fall of prices as the wars drew to a close produced a severe agricultural depression in the years 1814–16. The adaptation to new conditions was long and difficult, partly owing to the mistaken hopes which were placed by landowners and farmers in the Corn Laws, by which they strove to keep corn prices up to a level to which they had become accustomed. Protection neither succeeded in keeping prices high nor in making them stable. The complaints of the agriculturists continued to come in to Parliament down to 1836. Two classes of men suffered much. The small owner-occupiers or yeomen were often heavily mortgaged and many were sold up. The labourers endured reduction of wages, partly alleviated by public relief, and in the South of England they found alternative employment hard to come by. The early 1830's were years of much dark distress and discontent among the southern labourers, as the affair[2] among the Dorsetshire labourers at Tolpuddle in 1834 showed.

[1] Sir John Clapham, *Economic History of Modern Britain*, vol. III (1938), p. 1.
[2] The transportation of George Loveless and others for forming an agricultural union with oaths of initiation is a part of trade union history. See *The Book of the Martyrs of Tolpuddle, 1834–94*, published by the Trades Union Congress (1934).

The recovery of agricultural profits and enterprise began in the same decade. The conditions of it were a readjustment of costs, brought about by the fall of rents and wages, the improvement of agricultural technique, the Tithe Commutation Act of 1836 which reduced the farmers' liabilities and the maintenance of demand in the towns. The 1840's, however, saw a panic among many landlords and farmers, caused by the repeal in 1846 of the Corn Laws so as to rush corn into Ireland during the famine. There was also a fall of prices and abrupt decline of demand caused by the industrial depression of 1847. Then came a revival of prices and activity in the mid-1850's. This proved to be the beginning of a long period of agricultural prosperity. It lasted, with ups and downs inevitable in an industry controlled by an uncertain climate and the fluctuations of town demand, until the disastrous agricultural depression of the 1870's. The economic position of the industry, from being weak, became strong. Standards of farming practice were raised substantially. British farming became, for the kind of products on which it was based, a leader in the world.

How was this transformation brought about? The foundation of the situation was the slow but successful adaptation of commercial farming to special conditions. The 1840's had been marked by the abolition of agricultural protection, for meat and cattle as well as for corn, as part of the movement towards free trade. But after the effects of the legislative panic and the depression of 1847 had worn off, the decline of prices which landowners and farmers had feared from foreign competition did not arrive. On the contrary, the price of agricultural products, including wool, which was an important product of many farms, was well maintained. The price of wheat was more steady than under the Corn Laws. There was a growth of incomes in the towns as industry expanded. Population was growing fast and consumption, as Peel had noted even in the unfavourable 1840's, was rising faster. The new purchasing power and the new consumption were most unequally distributed between different classes and sections of the nation, but they created a market for agricultural products greater than had yet been seen.

Until new centres of food production were created abroad and new systems of transport linked them with Great Britain, she had to be fed for the most part off her own fields. Down to the late 1860's, this country produced one-half of the wheat and all but one-seventh of the meat she required in any one year. Imports were growing, but the British farmer enjoyed a privileged position in the supply of the towns. Farming was organized towards the necessities of the Victorian family table: wheat, beef and mutton. Wheat was the single most valuable product on British farms in 1867. Milk and dairy products were in demand, but they did not secure the same attention from farmers as meat and corn.

The farmer's beef and corn factory was linked to the towns by the railways after the railway-building booms of the late 1830's and the 1840's. The railways not only brought him into touch with his market; they also carried his supplies; the agricultural machinery, the fertilizers, oil-cake, tested seeds, and other apparatus of specialized farming. How large the new investment of capital in agriculture was during these years of good profit there is no means of telling, but it must have been considerable on the landlord's side, judging by the advance of rents. The landowners as a class invested widely in the land, in the buildings and roads of the farms, and they expected to be remunerated for doing so. The financial strength of mid-Victorian farming derived, however, from the investments of the tenant-farmer, as well as from the landowner. Bold investment by both indicated a confident age.

Both were becoming instructed in new methods of farming, as the opportunities for profit opened up. James Caird's *High Farming, the Substitute for Protection* (1848) suggested by its title as well as its argument the drift of men's fears and hopes after the repeal of the Corn Laws. It was in the 1840's that 'high farming' as a movement began. The scientific side of it was represented by the work of the agricultural chemist, Justus von Liebig, whom Sir Robert Peel once took down to visit his estate at Drayton Manor, and, more permanently, by the foundation of the Rothamsted Experimental Station for agricultural research in 1842 by John Lawes and Joseph Henry Gilbert, a pupil of Liebig. What 'improvement' had been for the eighteenth century, 'high farming' was for the nineteenth century. Both movements owed much to private initiative, little to official encouragement. There was no Ministry of Agriculture before 1889. The presiding institution, so far as there was one, was the Royal Agricultural Society, founded in 1838, with a membership chiefly of landowners and farmers. Some of the main lines of advance were in drainage and deep ploughing, initiated by

James Smith of Deanston, and indispensable to the full exploita-
of heavy soils in a damp climate. Artificial fertilizers and
manures were becoming available with the advance of chemical
science and manufacture, as were oil-cake and meal for feeding
stock. Agricultural machinery had been coming in increasingly
since 1830 and was making liberal use of steam power by the
1860's.

The effect of this activity was marked upon many of the
larger farms. Under the existing system of landownership and
tenancy, farms containing from 100 to 300 acres, often much
larger, accounted for nearly one-half of the cultivated area of
England and Wales. There were many small farms, but the
medium- and large-sized holdings were responsible for the
greater part of the country's agricultural production. The drive
towards a higher output from the land came from a highly
individualist and wealthy landowning class and its chief
tenants, before they suffered the disappointments of later years
of the century. The outline of their achievements down to the
1870's was impressive. Agricultural statistics only began to be
collected officially in 1866, but they showed in 1870 a total
area under the plough in England of 13,646,000 acres. This
was the greatest extent the tillage area had yet reached and has
not since been exceeded. The area under wheat a year or two
before, in 1869, was the greatest ever known, 3,417,054 acres.
This compares with a little under two million acres in 1949.
As conspicuous as the wheat were the root crops which the old
improvers had made famous as rotation crops and food for
stock—mangolds, swedes and turnips. Their English acreage
in 1871 was 1,944,000 acres, compared with less than three-
quarters of a million acres today. The figures reflected the long-
standing success of the rotation and cropping systems in which
they played their part, directed towards profit upon wheat and
cattle in mid-Victorian markets.

The profitability of farming and the revenues derived from
agricultural land were reflected in the farmhouse, the manor
house and the country house, and the dwelling houses of the
professional men and traders, clergy, doctors, solicitors,
auctioneers and factors associated with them. It cannot be
said that much improvement of conditions was felt in the
cottages of the labourers. The eastern counties, the home of
some of the best farming in the country, were the scene of a
bitter contest between the farmers and the new National

Agricultural Labourer's Union, within a few years of the statistics of 1871 being collected. Agriculture's prosperity, at a time when so much of the nation's resources were locked up in farming and when the rural element in British society was still strong, did much to create the stability and the special character of mid-Victorian life. The social atmosphere among the middle and upper classes in country and country town is well preserved in the novels of Anthony Trollope, who died in 1882. The other, less comfortable, side of Victorian rural life is to be found in the vigorously written memoirs of Joseph Arch, the dissenter and agricultural worker who had founded the Warwickshire Agricultural Labourers' Union ten years before.[1]

THE RAILWAYS

The railways represented a new and most important form of employment for the nation's resources of men and capital. Their indirect as well as their direct economic influence was immense. Thomas Tooke, the Victorian economist, observed that during the years 1847 and 1848 probably not less than one million persons, including the families of men preparing the materials as well as those of the navvies engaged on railway construction, depended on the wages arising from the building of the railways. On the average of the five years 1846–50, he thought that not less than 600,000 persons were so dependent, or a number roughly equal to the total population engaged in the factories of the United Kingdom at that time. In his opinion, the volume of wages and employment provided by the railways was part cause of the comparative ease with which Great Britain passed through the economic and political crisis of the years 1848–51, which was so severely felt upon the Continent.[2]

The level of economic activity in Great Britain during the middle period of the nineteenth century is certainly unintelligible without reference to the railways. By increasing the prospects of profit and the fruitfulness of investments in a multitude of directions, they induced outlays of capital of huge if indeterminate extent, as well as forming a major investment in themselves. They were important as a source of employment,

---

[1] Joseph Arch, *The Story of his Life Told by Himself*, 2nd ed. (1898).
[2] T. Tooke and W. Newmarch, *A History of Prices*, vol. v (1857; reprinted 1928), pp. 368, 370.

both directly and indirectly. They expanded the national economy and they helped to make it a different kind of economy from what it had once been, by linking the country to the town, the towns to one another and inland industrial regions to the sea, in an entirely new system of communications.

The experimental period of the railways may be said to have come to an end by 1830. Once James Watt had perfected the steam engine, it was perhaps only a question of time before its powers were turned to traction. In the opening years of the nineteenth century, the first successful experiments were made. Richard Trevithick (1771–1833) produced a working steam carriage in 1801 and a locomotive to run on rails in 1804. The effective presiding genius in the development of the steam locomotive was George Stephenson (1781–1848). It was he who built the successful engines for the line at Killingworth colliery in 1814 and was engineer for the Stockton and Darlington line, opened in 1825. Finally, it was he who proved the possibilities of fast travel by winning the Rainhill trials on the Liverpool and Manchester railway in 1829.

By this time, the idea that the railway, making use of the horse-drawn tram or the steam engine, was nothing more than a means to move coal away from the pit-head was already dead. The railway as a general conveyor of goods and passengers was coming to be a familiar conception, and the success of the fast locomotive opened new possibilities. The investor and good managing heads became interested in the railway. There followed the railway-building boom which began in 1836; it ended when the effects of the American banking crisis of the next year were felt in this country, after creating about 1000 miles of line, though there were as yet no lines in Wales and no through communication between London and Scotland. A second and much larger construction boom came in the 1840's, following a period of cheap money in the depressed early years of that decade. Reaching its height in 1846, it finished in 1847, although the dangerous financial crisis of that year was not due solely to the railway speculation, but was also connected with bad harvests, the Irish famine, and the need to pay for abnormal imports of grain from the Continent. The railway construction of the 1840's laid down the skeleton of the later main-line railway system of the United Kingdom—about 5000 miles of line, including some 400 miles in Ireland. There was much still to be done before the finished railway network of 16,700 miles in 1886 was reached, but the foundation had been laid. This prodigious burst of activity placed Great Britain far ahead of other countries in railway services. By the test of territorial area compared with railway mileage, Great Britain possessed by the middle 1850's a mileage three times as great as that of Belgium or the states of New York and Pennsylvania in America and seven times greater than France and Germany. The economic advantages so gained help to explain the competitive force of Great Britain in the world of the mid-nineteenth century, before other countries had had the chance to catch up.[1]

At £40,000 a mile, the British railways were not cheap to build. They were much dearer in initial outlay than the French, German or United States lines. This was due to many things; to the high price paid for land, in bargaining between the railway companies and the landowners, since there was no system of public arbitration; to the hilly and difficult nature of much of the country, as in Wales and the Pennines; and to the wide margin of safety adopted by British engineers, finding their way through unknown problems of railway construction. On the other hand, no other railway system in the world at that date made use of double-track working or attained such high average speeds.

The expense of railway construction was an incentive to the railway companies to make the most of their investments. The building of lines, which was done at first to serve local interests, was followed by the amalgamations of companies to reap the maximum profit from the traffic and to secure economies of working. The creation of regional amalgamations out of local companies lent significance in the 1840's to the career of George Hudson (1800–71), the banker and linen draper from York who became known as the 'Railway King'. Hudson directed the unification of companies in the Midlands and might have spread his empire further, if he had not broken himself by falsifying the accounts of the Midland Counties Railway. Lease and amalgamation were the instruments of railway consolidation. It was largely through them that more than a thousand railway companies authorized by Parliament in private acts were reduced by 1914 to eleven comparatively large systems.

Railway consolidation raised important questions of public policy. Competition was understood by early nineteenth-

[1] Figures from Tooke and Newmarch, op. cit. vol. v, p. 387.

century Parliaments to be the means by which the efficiency of producers was maintained and the interests of the consumer were preserved. What was to happen to either if the railways became a monopoly? Transport tends towards monopoly, and the country had had a good deal of experience of the incompetence and the unscrupulousness of turnpike trusts and canal companies. The road and canal interests fought the railway bills hard and the pickings made by the barristers, such as Macaulay's old college friend Charles Austin, while the battle was on were large. But the road and canal interests were ill-fitted to survive. The canal companies had spent too little thought and money on providing facilities for through traffic. Many turnpike trusts were already bankrupt or in debt before the railways arrived to complete their discomfiture. They went down and the railways had it all their own way, until mechanical road transport came to transform the situation between the two World Wars.

Some men, including good practical railwaymen such as James Morrison, who in the 1830's was M.P. for Ipswich, held from the start that the State ought to exercise a firm control over the railways. This school of thought found a spokesman at the height of the railway boom in W. E. Gladstone, then President of the Board of Trade under Peel. Gladstone's Railway Act of 1844, as it was passed, did not represent his original ideas. He had proposed to give the government the right, in the case of new railway companies, to revise their fares and charges at the end of fifteen years or, if it thought fit, to purchase the lines. This was far too strong meat for a Parliament in which the railway interests were already strongly represented. Peel was persuaded to throw over his subordinate. The bill as passed gave the Board of Trade important powers in the interests of public safety and helped to settle railway passenger fares by requiring the companies to put on the so-called 'parliamentary train', of Gilbert and Sullivan's later joke, which stopped at every station and charged 1*d*. a mile to third-class passengers. This was to prevent the companies excluding third-class passengers in the interests of those who could pay higher fares. But there was no more talk of taking over the companies, although Walter Bagehot (1826–77), an economist of a later generation, favoured that course. The classical political economy which he represented had never favoured monopoly and saw in public ownership the only effective means of control.

The railways, stimulating an enormous new traffic, had assumed since the mid-century the carriage of goods throughout the country, with little more control than the sketchy maximum rates imposed by the original railway acts. There was much discussion of railway amalgamation and rate policy, and legislation followed in 1854, 1873 and 1888.[1] Through all those years, Parliament assumed some degree of competition still to exist, despite consolidation, and endeavoured to preserve and strengthen it. The railway traffic acts of 1894 and 1913, which curtailed the powers of a railway company to alter its rates at will, even within the maxima laid down by the railway acts and even if no 'undue preference' was being given, and which made an increase in railway rates dependent upon Parliamentary sanction, marked the end of the Victorian assumption. But by 1914 no adequate alternative policy had been found.

The building of the railways had immense consequences, both social and economic. Bagehot argued that by democratizing travel they were among the levellers of the age. No doubt they were, especially when the distinction involved in second-class passenger fare was abolished in the 1870's. In the economic sphere they forced down transport costs, broke down or widened many imperfect or monopolized markets and inaugurated a new and highly competitive period in production and merchanting. The middle nineteenth century was wedded to the open market not only in theory but also in practice, more firmly than any previous age. The swift collapse of old monopolies or semi-monopolies in inland transport was immensely important for almost all branches of industry and trade in the mid-century. Its effects were reinforced by the contemporary application of steam to coastal shipping, which also competed with road and canal interests. By a process of 'creative destruction', in some ways extremely wasteful, steam transport worked a revolution in the costs of industry and trade at the mid-century.

The competitive breeze produced by the railways would no doubt have been less congenial to producers but for the simultaneous growth of demand, much of which was also produced by railway construction. This was all the more welcome, because it followed the slack times and depression of the years

[1] E. Cleveland-Stevens, *English Railways, their Development and their Relations to the State* (1915).

1839–42. A growth in demand was due in the first instance to outlay upon the railways themselves. The railways formed a major constructional job. The contractors employed many navvies—for the term navigator, which had been applied to the men who built the canals, because inland navigation was their business, was transferred to the workers on the new railways. The amount of employment offered was large, as Tooke's estimates show, and particularly important in parts of the country, such as the south and west of England, where industrial employment was rare. The conditions of employment in the camps run by the railway contractors were another matter. They werę so bad as to call for public inquiry in 1846. The sanitary reformer Edwin Chadwick failed, however, to persuade Parliament to adopt a system of government inspection and a change in the law regarding the liability of employers for accident.[1] Once the railways were built, there came the recruiting and training of railway staffs—a long and interesting story, for a domestic servant might turn signalman or a man who had deserted his ship and fought in distant wars in South America might end his days peacefully on an English country station. Here again the employment which was provided and its conditions in terms of hours and pay were different matters; the latter were to be a source of much dispute later between the railway companies and the railway servants' trade unions.

Railway construction at home was soon followed by the construction, by British equipment and management and often British labour, of railways abroad. This development began early, with railway-building by Englishmen in France and Belgium in the 1840's. It soon reached far beyond Europe. Scottish engineers helped to build the first standard-gauge railway in South America, from Callao to Lima in Peru, which was opened to traffic as early as May 1851.[2] The large organizations built up by such leading contractors as Thomas Brassey and Samuel Morton Peto, which could not find scope at home after the main railway building was over, were turned in the 1850's to build railways elsewhere. Brassey is said at one time to have had railways and docks under construction in five continents. John Brunton, an engineer who wrote the story of his life and travels for his children, spent many years in India,

---

[1] R. A. Lewis, 'Edwin Chadwick and the Railway Labourers', *Econ. Hist. Rev.*, 2nd series, vol. III (1950), p. 115.
[2] *The Times*, 29 December 1951.

planning and superintending the construction of the railways and public works which distinguished British rule in that part of the world during the mid-Victorian era.[1] He was only one among many such men who passed the best part of their lives abroad. The construction firms were partly, not wholly, responsible for another great development—the growth of an export trade in railway material. Railway iron became one of the main products of the large South Wales ironworks in the first half of the century, such as the Guest works at Dowlais. The building of locomotives and rolling stock on foreign account became a branch of British engineering.

The effects of the railway investments were not confined to employment in railway building and operation. Given the existence of entrepreneurs prepared to push new forms of production, investors prepared to allow their money to be employed, and a working population prepared to adopt new occupations, the coming of rapid communications tended to raise the expectations of profit and the flow of capital for investment generally. The railways must be regarded as an expansive force of considerable magnitude in the economic world of the middle nineteenth century. The construction of new railway systems down to the 1870's, when other countries were becoming as well equipped as Great Britain, was an important cause of the world-wide economic activity of that period. Railways helped to shape a new world economy of which Great Britain became for many years the centre, just as at home they helped to build up and maintain the peculiar structure of industry which was hers.

THE FORMS OF INVESTMENT AND ENTERPRISE

The State took no measures to precipitate, although it did grant legal facilities to, the great rush of capital seeking a profitable outlet in British railways. There was no need to encourage or to draw out investment; the doubt among public-spirited men such as Gladstone and Dalhousie, when they were working together on railway problems in the 1840's, was rather, whether authority ought not to do more to regulate it, to prevent waste and fraud and disregard of the public interest. Three hundred millions of capital were flung into the railways before 1855, of which one-half, or £150 million, was raised in the five years

[1] *John Brunton's Book, being the memories of John Brunton, Engineer*, ed. Sir John Clapham (1939).

1846–50.[1] This enormous burst of investment by private capital, much of it both blind and greedy, was owing to the prevailing conditions in the capital market, where money was cheap in the early 1840's. The ultimate foundation of it was a commercial view of property and income, which regards the former as something to be perpetually increased by the judicious outlay of the latter and is, therefore, distinct from the feudal or the military views. Already well established in British society, it was stronger than ever after half a century in which the opportunities of profitable investment had multiplied rapidly and had been studied by wide circles of men intently and with success.

The picture which presented itself to the man with some hundreds or thousands of pounds to spare and to the government watching his actions was complicated, thanks to the fleet, by no fears of invasion or strategic considerations. When the Crimean War first showed the part which railways might play in war and led to the building of strategic railways in Central and Eastern Europe, the initiative often came from governments interested mainly in the military possibilities of the new means of transport. Special measures might have to be taken, as in Russia, to encourage private investors, where the chances of commercial profit appeared slender. In other lands, where there was a sound commercial basis for railway building, the investor had to be officially coaxed to take what appeared the extraordinary risks. This happened in the early days of railway building in British India. The investors of capital there were British, the guarantor of dividends was the government of British India. This occurred at the height of the 'laissez-faire' age in Great Britain.

No such encouragement was required by the investor in British railways. The greater part of the railway capital is said to have been raised in relatively small sums, from two hundred to two thousand pounds, mainly from middle-class people, most of them living not in London but in the provinces, who found in the building of the lines an opening, in some years, for the whole of their available savings. The new railway companies raised the money they required by public subscription; in December 1845, the London Stock Exchange quoted no fewer than 260 different kinds of railway shares. Much money was borrowed on debenture; much on shares enjoying a pre-

[1] Tooke and Newmarch, op. cit. vol. v, p. 352.

ference; but the larger part of it was ordinary stock, which took the full risk of the market.[1]

These proceedings opened a new chapter in the history of investment and the Stock Exchange. The latter had done much of its business in government stocks and the shares of well-known and exclusive companies, such as the East India Company. Now the foundation of the new banking and railway enterprises was forcing it to open its doors to a much wider range of dealings. The railways by their huge flotations diffused the investment habit beyond the narrow circle of a few rich people living or having connections in London.

The new investment was an upper- and middle-class habit, although it might go deep and even enlist working-class savings, according to district and industry, as it did with the cotton operatives around Oldham after 1850. It could never have taken root, however, but for changes in the law relating to joint-stock companies. The relaxation and simplification of the law by Parliament not only helped the railway companies, but encouraged joint-stock enterprise in fields where it had previously not been seen.

Before 1825 the public joint-stock company had been a rare and privileged form of enterprise, mainly confined to commerce and finance. It invaded transport in order to finance canals in the 1780's and 1790's and to build the railways in the 1830's and 1840's. But the experience gained, much of it at great cost to the public, in the flotation of railway companies suggested that here was an invaluable method of obtaining the additional capital required by expanding industry. Even before 1825 the need for some form of collective enterprise in industry other than the private partnership had been met, as we have already seen, by the foundation of unincorporate joint-stock associations, with transferable shares. But the unincorporate company occupied an unsatisfactory position under the law. It enjoyed the economic advantages of combined capitals; but the protection of its capital was uncertain. The law of partnership, not the law of corporations, applied to it. Thus its members' liabilities for the debts of the concern was unlimited, as in the partnership. It could not sue one of its members or be sued, as if it was a person, in a court of law. This made for laborious and intricate litigation. From the point of view of the investor, there could be no doubt that the

---

[1] Tooke and Newmarch, op. cit. vol. v, pp. 353, 371.

incorporated joint-stock company, possessing limited liability and, under the law of corporations, the status of a corporate person in a court of law, was the more desirable form of joint-stock enterprise.

The history of the nineteenth-century alterations in the law is the history of the gradual breaking down of the idea that corporateness and limited liability were privileges to be reserved for the few. This occurred as Parliament became convinced that fraud and recklessness, common though they were, were not the most important aspects of joint-stock enterprise. The provision by law in 1837 of a third way of obtaining the privileges of corporateness by letters patent, besides crown charter and private act of Parliament, showed which way the wind was blowing. The first big overhaul of the law came during the reviving economic activity of the 1840's in the Registration Act of 1844. This permitted any company to register by a simple process and in so doing to become incorporated. Liability remained unlimited and the law did not apply to banks. The act of registration was further simplified in 1856, when limited liability was extended to all registered companies. Banks were again excluded from these privileges, which were only opened to them in 1858. A consolidating act in 1862 extended the new legal facilities to insurance companies, hitherto omitted, and was useful in codifying the law. But the substantial work of revising company law had already been done in 1844 and 1856.

A rapid, in some respects too rapid, growth of public companies, affecting a wide variety of business, followed the alterations of the law. In the 1850's and 1860's, private companies in industry, especially in coal, iron and engineering, began to convert themselves into public companies. The movement became more marked as time went on; many of the firms concerned, however, were family firms and the family interest remained strong after conversion. It was in the Lancashire cotton industry, among the spinning firms of the Oldham district, that the first extended and deliberate use was made in manufacturing of the borrowing powers of the public limited joint stock company. This was in the decade 1875–85. The day of the public joint-stock limited company in manufacture did not come until after that date. There was a rapid growth in the paid-up capital of such concerns in Great Britain between 1885 and 1905, although the private limited companies continued to outnumber them. Large tracts of enterprise were never financed by joint stock, whether in the public or private form, at any time in the nineteenth century—for example, agriculture, building and much small retail shopkeeping.

The spread of joint-stock finance in the first three-quarters of the century, while it was restricted and slow, was of immense significance for the future. It marked the beginning of the end of the forms of enterprise and financing known to the founders of political economy, Adam Smith and Ricardo, in the classical age of industrial revolution before 1830. The time had been when the prime mover of the economic world had been the man who, as sole owner or partner, financed and managed his own business, assuming the full risks without limitation of his liability. His claims to profit and reward, often urged without moderation or restraint, had been based partly upon the risks to his capital, partly to his having 'mixed his labour' in the form of active management with the products he disposed of. Under the new regime now slowly coming in, capital tended to be blind, in the sense that the investor had often no practical experience of the industry he put his money into, and anonymous, since the shareholder did not appear at the works and was unknown to the workers. Investment and management were functions which became divided, with the main decisions of the firm being increasingly taken by salaried managers, whose relations to the shareholders were not always easy to define. Joint-stock finance made possible a different form of economic world, built to a different scale and organized in a different way, where great concentrations of capital and labour moved uneasily together to execute tasks and policies increasingly worked out for them by professional managers.

The change from the older form of private enterprise to the new was only beginning in the first half of the century. Mid-Victorian England was nearer to Matthew Boulton and his partner James Watt than to the men and the methods of 1914. This state of industrial organization was connected with the self-made character of many of the men in control of business at that time. The Victorian economist, Alfred Marshall, believed that 'perhaps nearly half' of the older men among them in 1850 had been born in a cottage and had worked their way up with the expansion of industry during the first half of the century.[1] Such men had learned to live hard; they drove themselves and others hard in the pursuit of wealth and position.

[1] A. Marshall, *Industry and Trade*, 3rd ed. (1927), p. 87.

At the same time they were the most complete individualists, owing nothing, so they supposed, either to society or to education.

The Midland industrialist, Josiah Mason, would be a good example of an entrepreneur of the highest ability at the mid-century. He was born in 1795, the son of a carpet weaver in Kidderminster, therefore low down on a social ladder which in his day was formidably steep. He died in 1881, and it might be said that his long life had been spent in the search for the maximum return. Never having been apprenticed, he moved about restlessly, after his few years at a dame's school, looking for occupation. His attempts to turn himself into a skilled man were vain. He found his feet in Birmingham, where he was taken up by an old Unitarian and friend of Joseph Priestley, Samuel Harrison. The making of split-steel rings for keys formed Mason's first introduction to the world of manufacturing, but his fortune was made in machine-made steel pens, at a time when the quill was becoming obsolete in offices and counting-houses. He entered the electro-plating trade, in partnership with George Elkington, and copper-smelting in South Wales with the same man. Late in life, he engaged, at first with heavy losses, later with characteristic success, in nickel-refining from New Caledonian ores. His powers lay in a good head for and a deep experience in mechanical problems, although he was without engineering training, together with most unusual abilities in finance and in the business of organizing and negotiating. Says his biographer: 'He was good at a bargain and liked it, both for the negotiation and the profit. He was not easily taken in; nor did he readily allow an advantage to pass out of his hands.'[1]

In one respect, Josiah Mason was not the characteristic man of business of his age. His long experience of the metal trades had taught him what help science might give to industry, although he was not a scientist and hardly an educated man. A generation before other men were prepared to accept the idea, he decided that an era of competition was opening in which no nation could safely trust to anything but science as a foundation for its industry. Acting on this conviction, he built and opened a Science College in 1880. The typical business man of the mid-Victorian age in the Midlands or elsewhere, whatever his abilities, had little understanding of the possibilities of organized research or technical training.

[1] J. Bunce, *Life of Josiah Mason* (1882), p. 152.

INDUSTRIAL OUTPUT AND EMPLOYMENT

The coming-of-age of Great Britain as an industrial state may be said to have dated from the Prince Consort's Great Exhibition of 1851, when the manufactures of the nations were exhibited at the Crystal Palace in order to demonstrate Britain's supremacy. The years between 1815 and 1847 have been described, probably with truth, as the period of the swiftest development of domestic resources in the whole of Great Britain's economic history.[1]

A decline in the proportion of people living upon the land and a rise in the productivity of agriculture cleared the way for a great concentration upon manufactures and mining. G. R. Porter, the contemporary statistician, pointed out that the proportion of the families of the nation engaged in agriculture fell from 35·2 to 25·9 per cent between 1811 and 1841. The quantity of food previously grown by seven families was now produced by five families; 'A fact of considerable importance in reference to the capability of this country to continue its present onward course with respect to manufactures....'[2]

Throughout the century, the rate of increase of British industrial production kept well ahead of population. Down to 1873, the rate of growth of industrial output grew little less fast than it had between 1815 and 1847, being 3·2 per cent per annum in the later period and 3·5 per cent in the earlier. The figures refer to physical production in groups of industries covering between one-half and three-quarters of British industrial production, but they probably represent with approximate accuracy the rate of growth of the whole.[3] The rate of growth of population between 1815 and 1873 never rose much above 1 per cent per annum.

While industrial growth much exceeded the growth of population, the modification of the occupations of the nation was slower and more patchy than is sometimes imagined. The census of 1851 gives us the self-portrait of a society which was still in process of industrializing itself. The stage which had been reached resembled that of Japan between the two World Wars, eighty years later. Old and new flourished side by side,

---

[1] W. W. Rostow, *British Economy of the Nineteenth Century* (1948), p. 19.

[2] G. R. Porter, *Progress of the Nation* (1912), p. 36.

[3] W. Hoffmann, 'Ein Index der industriellen Produktion für Grossbritannien seit dem 18ten Jahrhundert', *Weltwirtschaftliches Arch.* vol. XL (1934), p. 387.

the newest, most highly organized and most elaborately mechanical industries check by jowl with the personal services, the agriculture and the handicrafts of ancient tradition. Out of between fifteen and sixteen million persons aged more than ten years, over one and three-quarter millions worked in agriculture, as employer or employed, while over one million were domestic servants, excluding servants on farms. Among the occupations which people followed, more men worked in building than in cotton, more men made shoes than raised coal, more men laboured as blacksmiths than in ironworks and foundries, and more women sewed by hand as milliners, dressmakers and seamstresses than tended the machines in the cotton mills.[1]

This was not the machine age, but the machine age had begun. Mechanical production had started most easily in the textile industries. The simplicity of the processes, given power, made possible the use of the labour of untrained women and children. The role of the cotton industry has since declined so greatly in the national life that we may easily forget the extraordinary weight which attached to the development of the textile industries by the middle of the century. The textile industries, cotton, wool, silk, linen and hemp, employed in 1851 no less than one in every nineteen persons in the occupied population of Great Britain.[2] This dominating position, which they were to lose before the end of the century, was largely due to the expansion of the cotton industry. In 1851 the cotton industry already employed 527,000 workers of all kinds, not so very many fewer than the 544,000 of the year 1901. Handlooms still worked in the industry, but by far the greater part of the output in 1851 came from power-looms.

The effect of the cotton industry's growth upon the external economic relations of the country had been as swift and profound as were to be those of the rise of the Japanese cotton industry upon the foreign trade of Japan a century later. It was during the French wars that cotton cloth began to outstrip the old woollen cloth as the leading export commodity. A few years later, in 1827–30, the industry accounted for about one-half of the value of British exports. Lancashire depended wholly upon imports for its raw material. Both before and after

---

[1] See the table in Sir John Clapham, *Economic History of Modern Britain*, vol. II (1932), p. 24.

[2] Sir John Clapham, op. cit. vol. II, p. 29.

the years 1861-4, when the American Civil War produced severe distress in Lancashire by cutting off supplies, the bulk of the cotton used came from the United States. The experience of the 'Cotton Famine' during that war led to attempts to encourage cotton-growing in other parts of the world. The dependence of Lancashire upon the Southern States and of those states upon her remained, however, an abiding feature of international trade in the nineteenth century.

When we consider the swift growth of the cotton industry in scores of Lancashire towns and villages, the huge expansion of Manchester and Liverpool, the activity of the Anti-Corn Law League and of Chartism in the North-West counties, and the aspirations of men such as Cobden and Bright to mould not only Britain's commercial policy but also her foreign policy, it is hardly surprising that the Lancashire cotton men came to be looked upon as uniquely representative of the new industrial life, both by those who admired it and by those who hated and feared it. The weight and the momentum of the development of the cotton industry were very great, and the recovery from the severe distress of the 'Cotton Famine' seemed to demonstrate its impregnable strength. Old markets declined, but they were replaced by new and larger ones. The industry had begun to export staple yarns to Europe for working up there just after the French wars. When the European cotton textile mills rose, this trade ceased to grow. It was supplemented, however, by a new and profitable trade in yarn to the East, to India, the East Indies, China and Japan. Europe and the United States formed the first big market for cotton piece-goods. But as the weaving industry grew there and came to be protected by tariff, the exports of Lancashire found their way, from the second quarter of the century onwards, in increasing quantity to other markets, especially in the East. By 1860, Eastern and Far Eastern, Near Eastern and African consumers took one-half of the exports.[1] They were to take more as time went on.

The stamp which the Lancashire cotton industry was setting on the face of the world was deep and obvious. Its meaning was pondered and interpreted by some of those who influenced most the economic thought and policies of the century: by Friedrich Engels, the young German who observed it from the windows of the office of Ermen and Engels at Manchester and

[1] G. C. Allen, *British Industries and their Organisation* (1933), p. 214.

expressed his detestation of what he saw in his *Conditions of the Working Classes in England* (1844); by the son of a great cotton manufacturer who became Prime Minister of Britain in the 1840's, Sir Robert Peel; and by Richard Cobden, who more than any other man spoke for Lancashire in national politics between 1841 and 1860.

But the influence of the cotton industry on the world may be deemed transient compared with the influence of certain other industries. Through the Lancashire industry, Britain brought the products of the Industrial Revolution to the doors of remote populations. She carried the Industrial Revolution itself to other lands, or much hastened their economic development, by the exports of her capital goods industries.

The growth of the heavy industries, coal, iron and engineering had begun by the end of the previous century to influence the whole British industrial structure, owing to the rise of steam-power and the metal-made machine. Machine-making formed slowly its own professional and industrial circles in the early years of the nineteenth century. The first engineers had to find their way through their problems without the aid of profes-sional training. The most important product of their workshop was the trained engineer. Thus Henry Maudslay (1771–1831), the London engineer and inventor of the screw-cutting lathe, who set new standards of accuracy in engineering work, learned his craft under Joseph Bramah (1748–1814) whose mechanic and foreman he had been. Bramah, a Yorkshireman who migrated to London, had been a universal inventor, who had devised the lock that goes by his name; the water-closet, that important contribution to sanitation and public health; and the publican's pull-over beer-tap. Maudslay, in his turn, trained Joseph Whitworth (1803–87) and James Nasmyth (1808–90). Out of their shops came a steady stream of mechanics and foremen, who carried the art and science of engineering far and wide.

By the 1840's there were several distinct branches of mechanical engineering. There were, for example, the machine-tool making of the London shops; the textile machinery making of Richard Roberts (1789–1864) and other men at Manchester, and the new and important industry of railway locomotive and rolling stock construction and repair, which led to the founda-tion of the railway colonies at Crewe and Swindon in that decade.

The expansion of the production of capital goods, that is, of articles for use by other producers, not by the ultimate consumer, was fundamental to industrial development. The flow of goods to consumers, at home and overseas, could not have continued without it. Throughout the nineteenth century, the output of producer's goods in Great Britain, in the way of machinery and equipment of all kinds, rose faster than the output of consumer's goods, the rate being 2·3 per cent per annum for the former and 1·6 per cent for the latter.[1] Out of this increasing production of capital goods came not only the maintenance of existing production, but also the machines for new industries and the possibility of expanded industrial production.

The extent of the backing of power and mechanical equipment which the Victorian working man possessed can of course be exaggerated. The measurement of it is imperfect, for there was no official survey of capital equipment, apart from the government-inspected textile industries. Returns of the size of establishments are not a sure guide. Large numbers might be employed where mechanization had not gone far. In the coal industry, upon which most of the rest of industry was built, there were some very large business undertakings and many pits of considerable size. But while power was used at the pit-head for winding and other purposes, coal-getting at the face of the seam remained a handicraft. It is clear that conditions varied enormously from industry to industry; within industries they varied from unit to unit. There were parts of the kingdom, as in the South Staffordshire Black Country and in Birmingham, where many trades flourished down to the last quarter of the nineteenth century with little more capital to the worker, in the form of machines and equipment of any kind, than had been customary there in the reign of George III. Outwork, put out by the piece in the worker's home, varied in its conditions from the comparatively mild textile industrialism of the Stroud Valley to the barbarous ill-paid domestic trades of East London. But it was generally carried on in ways which, so far as concerned the amount of capital employed for every worker, was old and traditional. The same was true of the country crafts of the wheelwright and blacksmith; of building; of many trades which served the household, such as baking; and of domestic service.

[1] Hoffmann, op. cit. p. 397.

Small quantities of equipment represented perhaps by nothing larger than a sewing-machine, could, however, make a remarkable difference to the productivity of the worker. Additions to capital of less modest kind, an application of power here, a new machine or a range of machines or other equipment there, went on year by year during these decades over wide ranges of industry. Unimpressive in detail, their cumulative effects gave to industrial production as a whole that mechanical nature which it increasingly bore in the third quarter of the century. There was no break in the gradation between these many industries of growing mechanization and those where equipment was used upon the largest scale. These were the metal shipbuilding of Clydeside and the North of England, Lancashire cotton, iron and steel production, and the engineering shops. The coal, iron, cotton and wool textile, iron shipbuilding and engineering trades, in the scale of their organization and equipment, were rare in the world. These industries, technically and administratively the most advanced in the country, showed the productivity of labour at its highest.

Industrial occupations meanwhile were becoming dominant. The change dated from the first half of the century. The census of 1851 showed that one-half of the population of Britain, excluding Ireland, was urban for the first time. In the next twenty years, industrial employment rose formidably. The numbers employed in agriculture, which had been 1,904,687 at the census of 1851, fell to 1,423,854 in 1871. In coal-mining, to take an industry towards which agricultural labourers tended to drift, the numbers rose over the same census years from 193,111 to 315,398; in iron and steel, including foundry work, from 95,350 to 191,291; in machinery making and ship-building, from 80,528 to 172,948; in cotton textiles, where numbers were already large, from 414,998 to 508,715.[1] These were four only among many groups of industrial occupations. Some few, such as lace and silk, showed a decline in employment, but many more showed an increase. The British people had become, since Waterloo and largely within the reign of Victoria, what they had never been in the eighteenth century, a thoroughly industrial nation.

Industrial output rose faster than industrial employment. Late in the 1850's, the annual import of raw cotton into the

[1] *Memoranda, Statistical Tables and Charts on British and Foreign Trade and Industrial Conditions*, Cd. 1761 (1903), p. 362.

United Kingdom had been a little over 9 million hundredweight, of which something over 1 million hundredweight were re-exported in a raw state, leaving nearly 8 million hundredweight to be worked up by the textile industries. Early in the 1870's, both the quantity exported and that retained had gone up substantially. Retained imports now stood at over 11 million hundredweight, representing an annual consumption of raw cotton equal to over 37 pounds for every person in the United Kingdom. The output of coal rose from an annual average of 66 million tons in 1855–9 to over 120 million tons in 1870–4. This represented an enlargement of the scale of output from 2·34 tons a year for every person in the United Kingdom to 3·79 tons, at a time when the population was increasing rapidly. The production of pig-iron rose from about 3½ million tons every year, in 1855–9, to nearly 6½ million tons in 1870–4, an increase from 0·12 ton a year for every person in the United Kingdom to 0·20 ton.[1] The list might be multiplied, but it must be enough to say that upon this productivity and upon this trained industrial population was based Britain's economic position in the world.

It was a position in which she was still alone. The British throughout the first three-quarters of the nineteenth century were the leading manufacturers in the world. The industrialization of the Continent had begun with the generation which grew up after Napoleon's final defeat. It proceeded apace in Belgium, Switzerland, Germany and France during the middle years of the century. The spread of railways, telegraphs and banking systems after 1851 promoted the growth of industry and of occupations remote from agriculture. Under the Second Empire (1851–71) in France and in Prussia during the same period, industrial growth was marked. But economic change was disturbed and hindered by political events, especially by wars from 1859 onwards. It had also to make headway against adverse social conditions. When after 1871 Western and Central Europe emerged from a series of sharp conflicts between warring nationalities into a generation of uneasy peace, the process of industrialization had still a long way to go. The France and the Germany which fought the war of 1870–1 were still mainly agricultural in their pursuits, France very much so. The United States which endured the conflict

[1] Above figures in *Statistical Tables relating to British and Foreign Trade and Industry (1854–1908)*, Cd. 4954 (1909), section VI, pp. 152, 166, 167.

between North and South in 1861–5 was even more strongly agricultural, although signs of economic change were strong.

The world which heard that the French army had been defeated, and Napoleon III taken a prisoner by his enemies in September 1870, regarded Great Britain as still the first industrial power, although the primacy in military power had passed in a single day from France to Germany. She was stronger than the strongest of her competitors, pre-eminent in economic strength, as she had been for many years.

THE STRUCTURE OF CREDIT

One further element in her economic power has still to be described. This was the organized use of credit. Credit had become so essential to production that both now appeared as the two sides of a single activity. It so happened that in this age when the chief nations of the Continent and North America were still searching for a system of banking and credit appropriate to their rapid economic development, Great Britain possessed a credit system which was as far in advance of others as her railways were ahead of their systems of communications.

The banking history of the nineteenth century began before Victoria came to the throne, with the commercial crisis of the autumn of 1825. This crisis and panic, one of the most memorable of the century, profoundly affected public and Parliamentary opinion. It took place some years after the banks had resumed the obligation to pay gold for notes, when they were therefore vulnerable to a panic. The run followed a period of rising trade, which had come to form the foundation for a speculative boom. When the crack came, over seventy English banks disappeared while many others stopped payment temporarily.[1] The Bank of England itself had been hard pressed. The joint-stock Scottish banks weathered the storm. The annulment outside of London of the monopoly of the Bank of England in joint-stock banking or banking by more than six partners followed, as we have seen, in 1826. It was intended to be Parliament's contribution towards a more stable banking system, by opening the way to banking upon the Scottish principle. The Bank clung to its monopoly of joint-stock banking in London until 1833.

By that time, several score of joint-stock banks had established themselves in the provinces. Not only the Bank but also the

[1] Sir John Clapham, *The Bank of England*, vol. II (1944), p. 102.

hundred-odd private banks in London looked forward with distaste to the new competition. They fought hard the first of the joint stocks to open its doors in the capital, the London and Westminster, established in 1834. This was the beginning of a London battle which continued for some years. The London private banks and the Bank of England did all in their power to make life difficult for their new competitors. The newcomers were debarred until 1844 from acceptance business, that is, the earning of commission by underwriting bills of exchange, and were excluded from the London Bankers' Clearing House until ten years later.

The number of London joint-stock banks was only five in 1844. Though few, they were successful, despite the opposition which they had had to meet. The causes of their success were significant, for they showed some important superiorities in the management of joint-stock compared with private banks. The joint stocks probably drew most of their business from hitherto untapped sources; but they also offered more favourable terms than the old banks. They possessed great reserves of capital, managements which contained much talent, and they were less secretive than the private bankers, printing and circulating (though reluctantly) annual statements of accounts. These advantages of the joint-stock banks were perhaps more marked in competition with the provincial than with the London private bankers. Provincial private banking and the market for credit had been marked by much local monopoly and only too often by inadequate reserves and weak management. Furthermore, the facilities extended for deposit and loan by the private banks were becoming unequal to the growing needs of the country, especially in the industrial towns.

For all these reasons, the growth of joint-stock banking was rapid, particularly in the middle decades of the century. The joint-stock banks were for long reluctant to give themselves the cover of limited liability, even after the law permitted it, partly from thinking that their goodwill depended on the unlimited liability of their partners, partly from unwillingness to publish balance sheets. Hence the wide ruin spread by the failure of the joint-stock but unlimited City of Glasgow Bank in 1878. But as time passed, the ultimate victory of the joint-stock banks was assured. The greater part of the huge new banking business created by the industrial and commercial activity of the middle years of the nineteenth century fell to them. In the provinces,

by the early 1880's, the number of private banks had fallen to
172. While they still outnumbered the 91 joint-stock banks, the
deposit business of the latter far exceeded theirs. The average
size of the banking concern had increased.[1] The progress of
banking amalgamations and the development of branch
banking was bringing into being a far more unified national
system of banking than had been seen before. Much banking
was still locally controlled, but there was now a powerful group
of banks operating both in London and the provinces and con-
ducting a considerable proportion of the total banking business
of the country. This process of consolidation was to be carried
much further at a later date, until the 800 banks of 1825 gave
place to the overwhelming supremacy in 1918 of five large
banks, combining London with provincial business and controlling nearly two-thirds of the banking resources of the
country.

Banking stability was slow in following, however, the introduction of joint-stock banking. The new joint-stock banks were
severely blamed for their conduct in 1836–9. The structure of
credit was roughly shaken in those years, partly by internal
events, partly by the collapse of a lively inflation in France,
Belgium and the United States. Stable credit, it seemed, was
not only a matter of the organization of the banks. It was also
a question of their policy and especially that of the largest and
strongest of them all, the Bank of England.

The conditions of bank policy altered with the changing
organization of the banks themselves as they grew larger and
more national. But the point of policy affected the functions
of the banks. It could not be solved by amalgamation and the
growth of larger units. The fundamental problem was whether
the bankers should be left free to create as much credit as they
thought fit, acting as they did usually with local and immediate
conditions in mind. At first, this appeared to be a question of
the liberty of note issue, for bank loans in the early years of the
century were made in the notes of the bank giving credit.

The issuing of its own notes was generally regarded as one of
the vital functions of a bank, without which no banker could
carry on his business or make his profit. There had been for
many years one conspicuous exception to this state of affairs.
The London private bankers had got into a habit of issuing no

[1] W. F. Crick and J. E. Wadsworth, *A Hundred Years of Joint Stock Banking*
(1936), p. 34.

notes of their own, because they used Bank of England notes. They suffered no grave inconvenience in doing so and were many of them wealthy and powerful bankers. The country bankers, on the contrary, had built up the issue of notes upon a great scale. Their creation from time to time of credit upon a shaky foundation, appeared in the form of an over-issue of notes in relation to the cash reserves which they needed to keep in hand if they were to retain the confidence of their customers. This went with an expansion of loans in notes against inadequate security. The optimistic action of the banks themselves in times of boom, by increasing the number of industrial and commercial enterprises which lived upon the margin of credit, helped to provoke an ultimate loss of confidence. Financial panic was the consequence, when sound as well as unsound banks went down.

An unstable banking system, cursed by bank failures upon a considerable scale and by frequent and widespread crises of credit, stood in need of reform. Many men over-simplified the problem of the control of credit, however, by supposing that only bank-notes mattered. They neglected the importance of the overdraft and the cheque, which were becoming the chief means by which the banks extended credit. They were reducing the importance of the bank-note even before 1844 and driving out by the early 1870's the old freely circulating bill of exchange.

Under the influence of this deceptive view, that too free a use of their note-issuing powers was the main source of the instability of the banks, Parliament began to curb the right of note issue. After the banking crash of 1825, it was the small bank-note which seemed to be the enemy. Down to 1797, the pound note had been known in Scotland for about a century and was the denomination of paper money in most use there. But south of the Border its place was taken in the provinces by the notes for five pounds and more of the country bankers and in the City of London by the notes for ten and twenty pounds and larger sums issued by the Bank of England. The one-pound note came into use in England after 1797, during the period of the restriction on cash payments, and was the usual means of payment during and just after the French war. But it was criticized as giving the small depositor a temptation to make panic runs upon the banks for gold and the events of 1825 were held to have proved its dangers. Therefore in 1826 it was abolished by law in England, although not in Scotland; it did not return until the First World War. In 1833, the new joint-stock banks were made to conform to the practice of the London private banks in using Bank of England notes, since they were denied in that year the right of note-issue. Then came the disillusioning failures among banks and merchant houses of the late 1830's, much criticism and public inquiry, and the Bank Charter Act of 1844.

This measure carried to a logical conclusion the movement towards a unification of all note-issues in a single hand. It stopped the creation of new banks of issue and provided for the gradual extinction of private note-issues of all kinds and the concentration of the business of issuing paper money for England and Wales in the hands of the Bank of England. The process by which this was done went on into the next century, Fox, Fowler and Co., absorbed in 1921 by Lloyds Bank, being the last English bank with an independent right of note-issue.

Bank of England notes had been convertible into gold, at the will of the holder, ever since the cash payments of the Bank had been resumed in 1821. It now became the duty of the Bank to hold at all times a reserve of gold adequate to cover notes in use all over the country, if confidence in the currency was to be maintained. Since London was at that time the largest market for gold in the world, this might not appear a particularly difficult thing to do. In point of fact, the management by the Bank of a reserve upon which the banking system as a whole depended and which constituted it a central bank, proved no easier after the Act than before. Three times within the next quarter of a century the Bank had to be released from its legal obligation to pay cash, in order to weather a general financial storm. This happened in 1847, 1857 and 1866. The shaking of credit in all three years was severe. The belief, which some had held too easily, that the unification of control over the issue of notes would prevent bank failures and create a stable world of credit and production, was proved illusory.

Nevertheless, the panic occasioned by the collapse of one of the largest financial houses in London, the discount firm of Overend, Gurney and Co., in 1866 was the last of the regular crises which had visited the money market periodically for so many years. The crisis of 1873 in the United States and in Central Europe passed relatively quietly in London. The money market was not without its ups and downs or its bankruptcies, sometimes of important firms. But events in 1890, when the house of Baring, which had committed itself beyond the limits of prudence, some said of honour, in the underwriting of loans to South America, and was pulled out of its troubles by a consortium in the City, headed by the Bank of England, indicated that the structure of credit had reached a strength previously unknown.

Forces had been quietly gathering which made for stability, although they were often concealed behind or even delayed by the more spectacular events of the banking and Parliamentary world. One of these new influences was the building up of larger banks, which did not depend upon the fortunes of a particular community or industry for their stability; another was the growing experience and skill of the managements of the banks and other financial houses. But this in itself would not have been enough, if the management of the most important of them all, the Bank of England, had not been willing to use its knowledge to give a lead to all those engaged in the business of lending and borrowing money in London. This it did by taking advantage of its powerful position in the discount market.

The advancing of money against bills of exchange, otherwise known as the discounting of bills, was a general function of bankers in the first half of the nineteenth century, as we have seen. The bill of exchange continued to be issued in the course of provincial trade and to be a common form of currency until the 1870's, when the cheque replaced it. To advance money against sound bills was a most useful form of credit, and the rate of interest charged was known as the discount rate. The Bank of England, like other London banks, had always done a great business in bills. The policy was now adopted, however, of retiring from the profitable competition with other London banks for bills, as this was held to risk lending the Bank's countenance to speculation. The Bank withdrew gradually from competing in the discount market, and at the same time employed its powerful position as lender of last resort in that market to establish a separate rate for the assistance it was prepared to give to other banks and institutions. At one time, the market rate had tended to become the Bank's rate. Now, the Bank's rate tended to lead the market. By moving its rate up and down, as the Bank was free to do after the legal maximum on rates of interest had been removed in 1833, it not only gave a lead to the market, but protected its reserve, since if it raised its rate sufficiently high, it drew gold to London. The signifi-cance of the Bank's actions lay in the extreme importance of the discount market in the City of London, where it found pro-fitable employment for great quantities of money which individuals and institutions wished to hold at call or at short notice. The discount market looked after their liquid assets. The Bank of England's discount rate thus came to set the rate for short-term loans throughout the country and, as London became a cosmopolitan money centre, throughout the world.

The emergence of this policy on the part of the Bank of England began as early as the years following the crisis of 1825. It was clearly stated by the Governor of the Bank, John Horsley Palmer, in 1832, but its development was retarded by the influence of the Bank Charter Act of 1844, which had laid the emphasis upon the Bank's control over the issue of notes. It was resumed with growing decision when that act had clearly failed to work as a stabilizing force. In 1878 the Bank formally renounced competitive bill business, even when its reserves were ample. This marks the full and conscious development of the policy.

The Bank of England had recognized that, given the constant pressure for funds on the London money market and its own strong position there, the price it charged for money was the most significant factor in the supply of credit. In undertaking to give a lead to the market by the manipulation of that price, the Bank had assumed a public duty to keep credit, as far as possible, stable. Since production depended upon credit, this policy was of great importance to the national economy as a whole. The discretion of the Bank, together with the growing organization and experience of the London money market, certainly contributed towards that quieter phase in the develop-ment of the national economy which succeeded the disorderly fluctuations of the early years of the century.

But the special conditions of the Bank's success in pursuing its attempt to control the creation of credit must be borne in mind; it would be unwise to be dazzled by so much success. London was throughout the century, even until 1914, the head-quarters of the world's finance. It was unnecessary for the Bank to co-operate with other centres or to consider facts other than those which for the most part were under its eyes in the City of London. It was operating also in an age which for Great Britain was free from major war or civil disturbance.

These things apart, there was an economic circumstance which was of great significance for the money market and appears on retrospect of more importance than the doings of the country bankers or the Bank of England. In the first three-quarters of the century, Great Britain was equipping herself with the fixed capital of a modern industrial State. By the early 1880's, this process had been carried far. The value of the capital sunk in railways by that time much exceeded the whole value of agricultural capital. The value of capital in industry and trade exceeded the railway and farmers' capitals put together.[1] A great part of this capital growth had taken place within fifty years, much of it since the first railway-building. The process of installing this great mass of factories, mines, warehouses and lines of communications had not been a constant one. On the contrary, it had moved in a series of violent fluctuations. Railway and industrial investment had come in like a stormy tide and the growth of bank credit had done little more than reflect and aggravate the flow and ebb of new capital investment at home and abroad. The later nineteenth century was for various reasons, partly because the British investor had eggs in many baskets in many parts of the world, partly perhaps because of a slower rate of growth of the British economy itself, a quieter period. It is doubtful, to say the least, whether the wisest and strongest of bankers could have pulled order out of the violent economic movements of the early railway age.

Nothing could have been further removed, however, from the economic ideas of the nineteenth century than a degree of control over the volume and direction of private investment or the use of State expenditures to correct the unevenness of private outlay, although modern communities have experimented with both in the effort to deal with the problems of an inflated or deflated economy. On the contrary, the trend of the development of British public finance in the second and third quarters of the century was towards the reduction to a minimum of the economic control of the State, towards rigorous balancing of the public budget, and the reduction of public expenditure to the least amount compatible with the provision of defence and police. This was the tradition established by Sir Robert Peel in the 1840's, and by Peel's disciple, W. E. Gladstone, in the long series of budgets introduced by him, beginning with that of 1853. There was so little disposition to

[1] G. R. Porter, *Progress of the Nation* (1912), p. 701.

magnify the functions of the State and to provide it with the revenue required by ambitious policies that the highly important income tax, which had been re-introduced by Peel in 1842 to correct a persistent deficit in the public accounts, was treated throughout the whole of this period as a temporary device. Its ultimate repeal was promised by the heads of both political parties, Disraeli and Gladstone, in the general election of 1874.

In the minds of the men at the head of the great political parties and the increasingly middle-class administrations of the mid-nineteenth century, this attitude towards the State and its duties was directly linked with the importance of leaving money to fructify, as it was said, in the pockets of the taxpayer and with their faith in the ability of the private capitalist to maintain investment and employment at any level which might be required by the national interest. The economic wastes and the personal suffering involved in heavy trade depression from time to time were set off, in their calculations, by the immense progress which the economy had made in their lifetime and were assumed to be inseparable from its working.

The State was profoundly, even ostentatiously, withdrawn from any responsibility for the employment of the national resources. Never had the pursuit of private interest seemed to lead so obviously and automatically to the general good. The consequent power of the existing system over men's minds was immense.

Chapter IX

The Vicissitudes of an Industrial State
1880–1939

THE GENERAL CHARACTER OF THE PERIOD

The years between 1880 and the outbreak in 1914 of the First
World War closed one great chapter in the employment of
national resources and opened a new one. The period would
be remarkable, if for no other thing, because of a profound
change in the position of agriculture. The proportions and
balance of the Victorian industrial state, as it had stood in the
middle of the nineteenth century, were destroyed by the
agricultural depression of the years 1873–1900. For many
years there was a relative neglect of the land as an important
source of national income. This indifference was brought to an
end by the sharp demands of two wars and the recent falling
off in Great Britain's ability to import and to pay for all the
food she wants—the consequence of deep changes in her
economic relations with the rest of the world.

Farming and the land apart, the years after 1880 saw the
beginnings of new and sweeping changes in the field of manufacturing technique. The foundations of Victorian industrial
success had lain in the national priority in the exploitation of
steam, iron and coal. The time at last arrived, with the growing
industrialization of the West, when the main advantages to be
derived from having been first in the use of these slipped away.
About the same time, in the 1880's and 1890's, the signs appeared
of new and momentous scientific applications, which had to do
mainly with electricity, the internal combustion engine and
the application of industrial chemistry in the manufacture of
such things as rayon and plastics.

The new industrial techniques made possible what was really
a new kind of industrial state. They did not, however, establish
themselves at once. It was not until after 1900 that they began
to develop strongly. Meanwhile, the main structure of industry
stood in nineteenth-century style. The fall of large parts of the
older fabric did not take place until after the First World War
was over. In the 1920's the same fate overtook the industrial

capitalist and the wage-earner in the staple manufactures—
coal, cotton and pig-iron—that had crushed and wounded the
capitalist farmer and the country labourer thirty years before.
Then, Great Britain had to meet the competition of new
agrarian states. Now she lost ground heavily to new industrial
states, some of which had been among the new agrarian producers little more than a generation before.

These painful events did not of course mark the beginning
of the end of Great Britain as an industrial state, although they
were the end of a particular system of industry and of a particular type of industrial society. The period of industrial
development from 1919 to 1939 strongly resembled in its
general character a period almost exactly a century before,
from 1815 to 1830, when the old decayed and the new developed
with peculiar intensity. Both periods were marked by great
suffering and by the introduction of new industrial technique
and capacity on the large scale. As a result of these processes of
decay and growth in the 1920's and 1930's, the economic
structure which carried Great Britain through the economic
effort of the Second World War was more ample in its product
than the structure which had carried her through the effort of
the First World War; it was also a substantially different
structure.

The successive phases by which the industrial nineteenth
century was absorbed and transformed into the twentieth form
the subject of the present chapter. Their history is the record of
how the different groups in industry, but especially its managing
and directing classes, adjusted themselves to changes in their
opportunities and conditions. It is also the history of what they
thought they were doing and what they thought might be done.
Much of Victorian economic philosophy dissolved with the
world which it had been designed to explain. Late Victorian
times saw the beginnings of a revolt, coming from several sides
at once, against views of economic policy which had appeared
justified by the increase of wealth in the mid-century. From
the 1880's onward, Socialism, a revived Protectionism and a
self-conscious Imperialism all came to be powerful influences
over economic and social thought. By their operation, and
after 1914 by the circumstances of war, the relation of the State
to society and the economic system came into debate as it had
never done since the days of Adam Smith.

THE COURSE OF PRICES

We may begin with the history of prices, on which the eyes of the markets and the men who crowded them were set. Prices offer us a key to the ante-rooms of recent economic history, from which a journey of exploration may fitly begin.

The mid-Victorian era, between 1851 and 1873, had been a time of rising and relatively high commodity prices, favourable to profit margins and to the expansion of business of all kinds based upon them. It ended in the tremendous boom of 1868–73, when prices rose higher than they were to be again until the First World War.

When the succeeding depression and the liquidations of the 1870's were over, the next wave of activity did not restore prices to their old level. From 1873, a fall of commodity prices, prolonged, broken and uneven, but distinct and impressive, was experienced throughout the Western world, and it continued down to the end of the century. These twenty-three years of falling prices, which have come to be known, somewhat misleadingly, as 'the Great Depression', contrast strongly in the history of the last century with the rising prices of its middle years. To some contemporaries they were reminiscent of the long price fall after Waterloo, when the century was still young. Wholesale commodity prices, as measured by the statistician, fell nearly 40 per cent. This was lower than prices had gone in the earlier fall between 1814 and 1851.

The fall was neither uniform nor continuous. This period spanned three trade slumps and two recoveries of trade. The trough of the first slump fell in 1879, of the second in 1886, of the third in 1894. The top of the first recovery of industry was reached in 1883, the second in 1890. The recoveries or booms were associated with rising prices, the slumps with falls. The falls tended to go a little lower each time.

Trade depression, while far from continuous, was sufficiently prevalent to give rise to much grumbling and discontent among the property-owning and business classes. Those who lived by profits, interest and rents were the most articulate classes in press and Parliament, and their complaints gave rise to the term 'Great Depression'. There was much official activity and inquiry into prices and trade, including two Royal Commissions (reporting in 1886 and in 1888) on the depression in trade and industry and on its possible causes in changes in the value of the precious metals. There were also important government inquiries into agricultural depression in 1882 and 1897.

The economist, Alfred Marshall, who lived through these years, was fond of pointing out that, whatever the grievances of the business world, national material welfare, measured by real wages and industrial output, was rising substantially. Wages rose in terms of what they would buy in the shops by an amount roughly proportional to the fall in prices. It was rates of interest and profits and agricultural rents which were down from the high levels that men had grown used to in the previous twenty years. The depression was in the nature of a depression of expectations among capital-holders, although unemployment was also severe among wage-earners in certain years, particularly in certain trades.[1]

This episode in the history of prices came to an end after 1896. Then commodity prices—that is, the prices of the chief commodities in international trade—began to rise again, gently at first, but after 1905 swiftly and powerfully. As the fall of prices had been world-wide, so was the rise; both were irregular. There were marked flowings and ebbings of economic activity. The period 1896–1914 included three booms, reaching their peak in 1900, in 1907 and 1913. Trade receded in 1904 and again in 1908, after a memorable financial crisis in the United States. In 1914 it was once more ceasing to flow after the astonishing boom of the years 1909–13. By that time, prices had recovered much but not all of the ground lost since 1873. Prices before the First World War were roughly comparable with those of the early 1880's.

As falling prices had depressed the expectations of capital-owners, so rising prices roused them. Statisticians have since pointed out that economic conditions were fundamentally adverse to this country after 1900. For the first time for many years, the real national income, that is, incomes in terms of what they would buy, ceased to grow.[2] Wage-earners felt the check severely as prices rose and the cost of living with it. Complaints about the cost of living and about foreign competition replaced the controversies of the years before 1900 over

[1] For some of the leading statistics of the period, see Layton and Crowther, *A Study of Prices*, 3rd ed. (1938). For more detailed and recent studies, see W. W. Rostow, *British Economy of the Nineteenth Century* (1948) and A. K. Cairncross, *Home and Foreign Investment, 1870–1913* (1953).
[2] A. L. Bowley, *Wages and Income in the United Kingdom since 1860* (1937), pp. xiv, 93–5; see also Colin Clark, *National Income and Outlay* (1937), pp. 270–2.

depression in trade and agriculture. But as agricultural rents and the rates of profit and interest rose, the views of those who had capital to trade with brightened, despite mounting industrial costs and higher prices in the shops. The revolution in expectations and not any substantial improvement in incomes accounts for the nostalgia with which business men of that generation looked back upon this prosperity in the years just after the First World War.

The suggestion was heard at the time that mounting world prices after 1900 had something to do with the rapid increase of gold-mining in South Africa and with the passage of the gold into other countries in the course of international trade. It was certainly hardly an accident that the turn of the tide in business activity coincided with the beginning of large investments in gold-mining in South Africa and of a spectacular gold output from 1896. So had the rising prices and production of the 1850's coincided with the gold discoveries of 1849–52 and the settlement of Australia and the Pacific coast of the United States. This is, however, another way of saying that in the nineteenth century gold discoveries acted as a form of international public works. They created new incomes, beginning with those of the gold-diggers, and got demand moving, without unbalancing public budgets or discouraging the private capitalist.[1]

The gold discoveries were real causes of economic expansion. They were not the only or the most important causes. It is in the many other influences affecting the course of massive new investments of capital that the main origins not only of the rise of prices but also of the active employment of resources in many countries, including Great Britain, are to be found. They must be sought in the export of capital from Great Britain herself to new countries in need of development, which was upon an extraordinarily large scale after 1905; in the economic growth of the United States, already by 1900 the largest and most active economy in the world; in that of Canada, the Argentine and many similar lands. Together with the rise of new techniques in Western countries, which demanded industrial investment on the great scale, these developments among the new primary producing countries of the world are probably sufficient to account for the rising prices and demands of the years 1900–14.

[1] J. R. Hicks, 'The History of Economic Doctrine', *Econ. Hist. Rev.* vol. XIII (1943), p. 113.

In the course of world investments, too, we may expect to find the origins of the main features of the preceding 'Great Depression'. The long fall of prices, like the later rise, was put down by many men at the time to the account of gold. They postulated a scarcity of it, or rather a relative scarcity, after 1871, owing to, they said, the growth of economic transactions outstripping gold supplies, and so either cutting off demand or forcing up interest rates against the business man; the exact nature of the relationship between cause and effect was never satisfactorily explained. We would probably be wiser to give full weight—while admitting that the influence of the gold-digging boom of 1849–50 had long ago worn out—to the enormous investments in many countries, between 1840 and 1870, in railway systems and steamships, in settlement and in the opening up of new agricultural land and mineral resources. These investments and the demands they made upon the world's real resources produced the long secular boom and the high prices of the middle nineteenth century. They bore their full harvest after 1870. Slow to develop their full potentialities, they were forcing down in the 1880's and 1890's the costs of production of all sorts of commodities and services, bringing in masses of new consumption goods at low prices to raise the working man's standard of living and at the same time to depress the profit-earning prospects of capital and to create idle resources and unemployment. British investments abroad slackened; primary producing countries themselves were often depressed. Meanwhile, new industrial techniques, such as helped to raise the prospect of unusual profits on investment after 1900, were slow in developing. Deflationary influences were at work in the world economy, forcing down prices, halting activity from time to time and forcing capital to work at a lower return. These developments were more important than the behaviour of gold or of silver (the subject of enormous agitation in those days in the United States) or the shortcomings of the banks.[1]

---

[1] The interpretation of late nineteenth-century economic history is still in the making. For the theories fashionable at the time and until 1912, see W. T. Layton, *Introduction to the Study of Prices* (1912). The more recent line of interpretation, accepted above, may be followed in W. W. Rostow, *British Economy of the Nineteenth Century* (1948); W. A. Lewis, *Economic Survey, 1919–1939* (1949); A. K. Cairncross, *Home and Foreign Investment, 1870–1913* (1953) and E. H. Phelps Brown and S. J. Handfield Jones, 'The Climacteric of the Nineties', *Oxford Economic Papers* (1952).

Whatever the explanation of world economic events may be, it is against the background of the declining prices and the altering economic fortunes of the late nineteenth century, especially the heavy fall in the prices of farm goods, and the rise of prices after 1900, including those of many industrial products in which Great Britain was by tradition interested, such as coal, steel and ships, that we can best view her modern industrial history before 1914. For much that happened within her industrial system was by way of response to mighty changes in the world outside.

Stirrings and trends in the outside world again account for much in her more recent development. After the gigantic events of the First World War, the world experienced again from 1925 onwards a time of falling prices. Dropping first slowly, they sank after 1929 to immense depths in the world slump of 1930–2, carrying with them not only agricultural prices but also the price of the older industrial staples, such as cotton piece-goods, in which Great Britain customarily dealt, until the pace became too hot and the strain too prolonged for some of those industries to bear. Yet some industries, such as rayon manufacture, throve among the falling prices which ruined others. When prices began to rise once more in the late 1930's, the users of new techniques had obviously improved their position while some older trades had lost for ever the status which they had enjoyed before 1914.

Much of the industrial history of Britain over the last seventy years is therefore the history of an incessant mutual adjustment between her economic system and that of other nations in a world which has been in a state of incessant and often violent change. The Victorian industrial state of the middle years of last century had no doubt been built up by a similar process. But then the tides of fortune flowed strongly in Britain's favour. Those of more recent times have sometimes been fatally adverse and in the course of their working treated the once firm structure of nineteenth-century industry unceremoniously, as the waves of the sea overwhelm a sandcastle proudly and laboriously raised by children on the shore.

AGRICULTURE

An economic movement began soon after 1870 which was comparable in scale and importance with anything which happened in the later age of violent transformations between 1919 and 1939. This was the decline of agriculture as a major source of employment and income. Suffered not as a slow decline but as a sudden catastrophe, it carried away many apparently solid and reliable elements in Victorian social and economic life. The event followed a period of prolonged agricultural prosperity, and just for that reason it gave a deep shock to public opinion, not only on the farms.

The underlying causes of the crisis in agriculture were to be found in the rise of new sources of world food supply and of a new system of communications by railway and steamship. The new centres of supply were sometimes countries of old agriculture, such as Russia and India, which were becoming linked to the world's markets for the first time and were using grain exports to make interest payments upon foreign debts. Others were countries of new settlement, such as Argentine, Australia and the United States, where the mid-century development of communications and population had produced new types of extensive farming in the staple products most in demand in Western Europe, such as wool, cattle and meat, and wheat. These new producers often worked at low cost and upon a vast scale.

Whether the rest of the world was able to draw upon the new supplies depended upon communications and the ability to command foreign exchange. In Western Europe, where industrial production and exports were expanding and the new systems of communication by railway and steamship originated, these difficulties did not arise; industrial exports and commercial services footed the food bill and supplied the transport. Great Britain, as the headquarters of the world's shipping and manufacturing, was better placed than any other European country to take advantage of the shift in the comparative costs and prices of foodstuffs and agricultural raw materials which now began.

The growth of the new imports cannot easily be traced, but it does not appear that the first effects upon British agriculture were adverse. Mid-Victorian farming had made considerable use of Russian linseed and North American meals as cattle food and made money out of them. But in the last quarter of the century there was a world-wide fall of agricultural prices and the importation of foodstuffs into Great Britain rose swiftly. The British export manufacturer became a competitor of the British farmer in an altogether new sense.

The decline of prices was particularly heavy for certain commodities such as wheat which, being easily stored and transported, as well as grown upon a great scale and at low cost in temperate lands now being opened for settlement, were peculiarly suitable for the long-distance trade of the world. But the fall of prices was general. Thus British wheat prices, which had averaged 52s. a quarter in the twenty years 1848–68, became for a few years at the end of the century, between 1893 and 1902, as low as 27s. a quarter. The prices of animal products fell more slowly than those of cereals, until the spread of refrigerated transport in the 1880's, but it was decisive when it came. The value of beef fell 29 per cent between 1871–5 and 1894–8; of mutton, 25 per cent and of bacon, 26 per cent over the same years.[1] The fall extended even to such products as butter, now coming in from Denmark and to potatoes, brought in from Holland.

The decline of prices, not steady but persistent, was accompanied by a revolution in the British trade in foodstuffs. This took place with surprising suddenness. In ten years, between 1868 and 1878, the United Kingdom ceased to grow the greater part of the wheat she consumed and began to take from abroad nearly one-half instead of one-seventh of the meat which she needed. This was the beginning of a bulk importation of foodstuffs, upon which the national standard of living was to depend in future, even during two world wars. On the eve of the first of those wars, in 1913, the United Kingdom was importing annually £220 million worth of food, including tropical or semi-tropical commodities such as sugar, and producing £190 million worth of food. In bread-corn, the British had become a nation of 'week-enders', that is to say, requirements could be satisfied from British fields for one-fifth of the week, from Saturday afternoon to Monday morning.

For the townsman, especially the ill-paid townsman, the great price fall at the end of the century was very satisfactory. The cost of living had never been so low at any time in the century, and the price fall gave material assistance to the

[1] R. R. Enfield, *The Agricultural Crisis, 1920–23* (1924), p. 136.

poorest part of the population. This was remembered by both political parties in the next few years when complaints of agricultural distress began to come in and protectionist sentiment to revive among farmers and landowners. Throughout Western Europe, the competition of the New World in foodstuffs posed a difficult problem for the agriculturist, whether peasant or great estate owner, and anxiety was shown early about its extent and permanence.[1] A great political debate followed and most parts of the Continent, led by France and Germany, resorted to subsidy and protection to maintain the existing structure of their agriculture. In Great Britain, the controversy between town and country over the price of food appeared to have been settled for good in 1846 by the repeal of the Corn Laws, when agricultural protection had ceased to exist. Neither Conservative nor Liberal was prepared to upset the free-trade policy, now a generation old, for the sake of rural interests. They might possibly have been prepared to do so, if military needs had seemed to demand it. When later Great Britain was abandoning her old confidence in isolated power, at the time of the Japanese alliance (1902) and the Anglo-French understanding (1904), a Royal Commission sat upon the question of food supply and raw materials in time of war. The report of that inquiry in 1905 advised that if war came, the main hope must lie in the ability of the fleet to preserve the ocean lines of communication. The fundamental change in the conditions of Great Britain's food supplies had already occurred. It took place at a time when her absolute supremacy at sea made war-like considerations seem irrelevant.

The agricultural depression which followed the great price fall was felt differently in different parts of the United Kingdom, according not only to product and natural conditions, but also variety of tenure and land system. By far the most important effects were experienced in Ireland. The decline even of the scanty well-being which some sections of Irish agriculture had managed to achieve, with the help of the English market, in the mid-century, led straight to a formidable agrarian war between the landowners and the tenants, organized in the Land League by Davitt and Parnell; and to the dissolution of the existing Irish land system under legislation between 1881 and 1903. The thorough-going reconstruction of the Irish land

[1] See, for example, Max Sering's book, *Die Landwirtschaftliche Konkurrenz Nordamerikas* (1887).

system by British governments, both Conservative and Liberal, was one of the most dramatic events in modern British economic history. No sweeping action of this kind was provoked by the agricultural distress on the other side of the Irish Channel. In the Highlands and Islands of Scotland, where conditions among the poor crofters resembled Irish conditions upon a very much smaller scale, similar special legislation followed an inquiry in 1884. In England, the working partnership of landlord and capitalist tenant was unbroken by depression, although the trend of legislation under the Agricultural Holdings Acts was to protect the rights of the tenant in bad times.

The times were indeed bad, from the point of view of English farmers and landlords. Many men on the land were in a strong financial position, following a long period of relatively high prices and good returns. But many farmers had bought land and bid up rents on the strength of the good times lasting. They now found themselves with debts and outgoings beyond their strength. Wages at first tended to follow prices down. The labourer's wage had risen slowly with the reviving prosperity of farming, from the 1850's onwards. It was at its highest, although still low compared with the labourer's necessities, in 1872 and just after, partly owing to the work of the new Agricultural Labourers' Union. There followed a fall in the next decade; then relative stability; in the 1890's, a slight rise.[1] Many a farmer found himself losing heavily, between falling prices and receipts and his money costs. These included not only wages, but also rents, which were held for some years at a point which would only have been justified by a continuance of high prices. This was unjustifiable but hardly surprising, for under Victorian conditions a great mass of family settlements among the aristocracy and country gentlemen depended upon them.

There had been no such volume of complaint in agriculture since the depression which followed the Napoleonic Wars. Important official inquiries were held for England and Wales by Royal Commissions in 1879–82 and in 1893–7, and there was endless debate. The Parliamentary remedies for agricultural depression were palliatives and did not for the most part pretend to be more, although some of them were useful measures. The most important legislative outcome of the

[1] Figures in Lord Ernle, *English Farming, Past and Present*, 4th ed. (1927), appendix IX.

agricultural crisis was the setting up in 1889 of a separate department of government, the beginnings of the present Ministry of Agriculture, devoted to agricultural questions. Its functions were for long confined to crop and animal disease and agricultural education, but it was to find more work to do in the First World War. The relief extended to agriculture by the Agricultural Rates Act (1896) resembled the relief from rates given thirty years later to manufacturing industry in depressed parts of the country by the Derating Act (1929). Further afield, the operations of the Congested Districts Board in the poorest parts of Ireland and of the Crofter Commission in Scotland, in the 1890's and early 1900's, anticipated the kind of duties which were loaded on to the Commissioners for the Special Areas of England and Wales in the industrial depression after 1934.

Agriculture was the first of the great staple industries of modern Britain to be hard hit by economic development abroad. The redistribution of farm resources which the new competition demanded turned out, however, not to be beyond the powers of farmer and landowner. The belief that this was so accounts for the relative inaction of the State, party political considerations apart. A particular type of farming and a particular use of the land were being driven out of existence. The man who lost heavily, and his labourers with him, was the farmer who had concentrated on the staple foods of the Victorian table, wheat bread and the family joint. Wheat had been in 1867 the most valuable single product upon English farms. Wheat-farming now ceased to pay on any except the most favourable soils. While this lesson was being learned, great losses were made on heavy or poor soils, as in parts of Essex, Wiltshire and the North Cotswolds. The cultivation of wheat upon such soils had been profitable in the mid-century only with the aid of lavish capital and a partial monopoly of the market. Arable farming as a whole entered upon a swift decline. With it fell much of that mixed farming which had fed corn and green crops to beasts and returned their manure to the fields. This type of arable farming had paid well while good prices were to be had for wheat and meat. Much of it had been rather poor farming, but it had been widespread. Its going left a great gap in the life of the countryside and had important consequences for many people, including some, such as the country clergy, who were not engaged in agriculture but whose tithes depended upon it. The total cultivated area in England and Wales changed very little, although the growth of the cities was taking away bits of it. But the area under plough fell rapidly, the acreage under wheat falling from its maximum, 3,417,054 acres in 1869 to 1,302,404 acres in 1904. It took the First World War to bring the figure back for a brief period to over 2 million acres. With the decline in wheat went a fall in the number of the sheep whose annual folding had played such a part in arable farming. The number of cattle, on the other hand, rose as former ploughland went down to grass, especially in the north and the western counties.[1]

Arable farming had been a great employer of farm-labour. The number of men required for every arable acre, under mid-Victorian conditions, was sometimes conventionally described as four. A substantial reduction of the working force of agriculture and with it of the rural population was inevitable. Perhaps the agricultural worker sometimes gained by the enforced change of employment. Farm-labour had often been wasted and badly organized; it was certainly ill-paid. But the labourer was immediately a heavy loser, for he lost his job. If it had not been for the contemporary growth of employment in the cities, his fate must have been hard. The movement of men off the land was not new; it had begun to take place during the 1860's, as alternative employment to farm work opened up. Now it became a flood, moving quietly, because the country labourer was not organized to resist his fate, but with impressive volume. Between 1871 and 1901, the number of agricultural workers of all classes in England and Wales fell from 962,348 to 620,986. There was to be no such movement as this out of any industry, until the decline of coal-mining after the First World War.

A redistribution of the resources of farming accompanied and followed the movement of men. The new farming after 1900 owed something to the modest personal needs and the different technical traditions of Scottish Lowland agriculturists, numbers of whom had come south of the Border as rents fell. By whosoever or however it was done, British agriculture succeeded in pulling itself out of the lines which had ceased to pay, and pursued the products and the methods of farming which did pay. Dairy-farming, cattle-grazing, market- and

[1] Figures in R. Trow-Smith, *English Husbandry* (1951), p. 187 and in Lord Ernle, *English Farming, Past and Present*, 4th ed. (1927), appendix VIII.

flower-gardening, poultry-farming, especially in the neigh-
bourhood of the cities, or in the good pasture country of the
West of England and Wales, paid even in the depths of depression. The gradual diversification of product, including a welcome concentration on milk and the more dubious spread of
an inferior type of grazing; the fall of rents; a different, sometimes a more intelligent use of labour; the rise of prices in the
new century—all these things helped to pull agriculture out of
debt and make it a paying industry again. The revival of prices,
profits and rents started in the early 1900's, but the reduction
of costs and the redistribution of resources in the pursuit of new
lines of production had begun before that. After 1910, agriculture was again a reasonably prosperous industry, even upon
arable land. Wages had followed prices and profits up and the
number of agricultural workers had increased, although men
were still leaving the land for the towns or to go to the Dominions
or the United States.

A fundamental alteration had taken place in the national
economy. In the early and middle years of Victoria's reign,
agriculture had been not only the greatest single industry of
the United Kingdom, including Ireland, but the largest
industry in the more limited and more industrial area of
Britain. It occupied, in 1851, the year of the Great Exhibition,
about one-quarter of the grown men in the population, if we
include landowners, farmers, crofters and labourers of every
sort. Of the males over ten years old, one in six was an agricultural labourer in 1851, nearly one in ten still in 1881. By the
time the census came to be taken in 1911, the proportion of
agricultural workers had sunk to less than one in twenty and
the agricultural part of the occupied population was now only
8 per cent of the whole.[1] By that year, there were many more
coal-miners than agricultural workers. Coal exports helped to
pay for the annual import of foodstuffs.

There was a change in the quantitative importance of the
farming industry, and a change in its quality. The value of the
produce of agriculture did not exceed again the level of the
late 1860's and early 1870's, even when farm prices began to
rise again between 1900 and 1914. The standards of the best
farming of the earlier period were maintained upon the best
farms, but the capitalistic farming of Great Britain ceased to

[1] Figures from Sir John Clapham, *Economic History of Modern Britain*,
vol. II (1932), p. 22, and vol. III (1938), p. 1.

be the model for the rest of the world, as it had for a brief time been. The farmers of other countries had caught or were catching up in their standards, as the agriculture of Western Europe and North America became highly capitalized in its turn. Great Britain maintained a high standard, but not her lead.

Agricultural economists pointed out that, while the farming industry had stood up to rough weather, it had sustained damage. The farmer, even when highly skilled as such, was still too often an indifferent manager; a poor keeper of accounts, without method in marketing; indifferent to science and agricultural education, although there had been advance in both since 1880; short of capital and dependent for credit and advice upon landowners, auctioneers and solicitors, whose views of the future of farming were coloured by memories of the depression and apprehension over the proposed land taxes of 1909. Moreover, the depression had taught men, so a good judge and generous critic believed, to be satisfied with small earnings, obtained by the least outlay of capital and energy; enterprise was lacking, farming was an industry without much fight or push, and the passage to poor permanent pasture was a sign of it despite Great Britain's eminence in stock-breeding.[1] More capital, more knowledge and more willingness to take risks were wanted. There was a significant demand for protection among landowners and farmers, which did not disappear when rents and profits recovered and there was a sense of grievance, which spoke of lost confidence.

Rural social life had suffered, although it was to show great powers of new growth later. The landed gentry and the country clergy had suffered in income from the long years of depression and forfeited something of their old social eminence; more was to go with the high taxation of a later age. Labouring life lost many vigorous personalities into the towns or abroad. Wages had risen, and the agricultural worker was materially a little better off, but he was not satisfied with his prospects of employment, with his cottage or with his access to land. The justified sense of discontent expressed itself in a revived trade unionism, or sometimes in a determination to get away.

Some observers thought the State might be about to replace the great landlord in his economic functions, others that when the labourer got the vote in 1884 the initiative in rural life

[1] The views of A. D. Hall, *Agriculture after the War* (1916).

had passed to him. These were but speculations. If anything substantially different from the nineteenth-century economic organization of British agriculture was on its way, it was not yet in sight when the First World War broke out.

INDUSTRIAL PRODUCTION

The large owners of agricultural land, aristocrats or plain country gentlemen, had been since 1688 the undisputed political and social leaders of Great Britain. From among such men, distinguished statesmen and Prime Ministers had been drawn, from Sir Robert Walpole onwards. Under Salisbury, Rosebery and Balfour, between 1895 and 1906, the country houses entered upon a long and brilliant spell of political power, before a new type of middle-class leadership came into office, in the persons of Campbell-Bannerman and Asquith, after 1906. The authority of landed property was living on, however, into an age which economically and politically was unfavourable to it. The heavy loss of rents between 1875 and 1900 was one of the earlier features of this relative decline in the influence of land values; Harcourt's revision of the death duties in 1894, the first step towards heavy taxation at a later date, was another. But even more decisive was the constant growth of industrial employments and capital. The nation was coming to depend upon industry for its daily bread to an extent which would have appeared impossible even to those men who, earlier in the century, had joined Cobden and Bright in advocating the repeal of the Corn Laws.

Population had continued to rise, although influences were already at work, in the generation before the First World War, which were to bring the rapid increase of the past hundred years to an end. The last census before the war, that of 1911, showed a total population for the United Kingdom of 45,220,000, of whom 14,300,000 men and boys and 5,850,000 women and girls described themselves as occupied, although a number of them were at the time unemployed. But of all these people normally employed, no fewer than 6,520,000 men and boys and 2,155,000 women and girls were employed in industry and mining. These figures excluded the transport industries such as railways, but included Ireland, which was still mainly a farming country. Even so, the number of persons engaged in agriculture and fishing, mainly in agriculture, a total of 2,320,000, was far fewer than those in industry. And while agriculture provided in that year 8 per cent of incomes in the United Kingdom, industry accounted for nearly 40 per cent.[1] A further substantial proportion of the national income arose from transporting and distributing the products of industry. A population which owed so much to industry, both for occupation and income, as that of Great Britain in those years just before the war was irrevocably industrial.

The structure and the output of industry had continued to grow rapidly. The volume of industrial production was rising between the early 1870's and the years immediately before the First World War at an average rate of 1·7 per cent per annum.[2] This kept it ahead of population, then advancing at a rate of somewhat less than 1 per cent. The rate of growth was less swift than in the early years of the nineteenth century. The period of the highest annual rate of growth in industrial production had been in the sixty years between the end of the Napoleonic Wars and the early 1870's. Over this whole period, down to 1871–5, it was 3·4 per cent per annum. This was very high expansion indeed. But much of the growth of output reflected little more than the growth of the working population. There are far too few satisfactory measurements of output per head before 1914 to be able to generalize easily about changes in efficiency. Nor can the question of industrial efficiency be divorced from important changes which were going on at the time in the character of the product.

The average size of business undertaking had increased. An inquiry into the Lancashire cotton industry in 1914 showed that the average number of spindles in each spinning mill had more than doubled between 1884 and 1911, although the average number of looms in a weaving shed rose by much less. In the pig-iron producing industry, taking into account both the size of blast-furnaces and the number of them owned by each firm, average output capacity more than doubled between 1882 and 1913.[3]

[1] A. L. Bowley, *Division of the Product of Industry* (1919), table II and C. Clark, *National Income and Outlay* (1937), p. 238.

[2] W. Hoffmann, 'Ein Index der industriellen Produktion für Grossbritannien seit dem 18ten Jahrhundert', *Weltwirtschaftliches Arch.* XL (1934), p. 395.

[3] *Factors in Industrial and Commercial Efficiency; Balfour Committee on Industry and Trade* (1924–7), Introduction, pp. 3, 4.

There were many reasons for this building up of larger concerns. The representative firm, as Marshall called it, grew with changing technical conditions; with the advantages to be obtained by larger and more specialized forms of organization; and the widening of demand at home and abroad. But much could be put down to joint-stock company finance and its results. The main achievements of joint-stock in the first three-quarters of the nineteenth century were in banking and transport, not in manufacturing industry. After 1880 the joint-stock company promoter became far more active in industry. British business men came to be the greatest users of the joint-stock company device in Europe, the paid-up capital of such public companies quadrupling in Great Britain in the twenty years before 1905.[1] The new public companies tended to be larger than the old private firm. In the textile industries, for example, in 1914, the average size of the public companies tended to be about five times that of the private firms.

The joint-stock company had many interesting features. Not the least was that it provided the financial and legal resources by which large-scale consolidation was made possible. The spread of joint-stock organization and the emergence of large concerns pursuing monopoly or quasi-monopoly policies was simultaneous. The contrast between the growing mass of capital invested in manufacturing and mining and the fall in prices after 1873 encouraged men to consider the ways and means by which prices might be held or costs reduced and protection secured for their capital outlays and for the outlays of their shareholders. The movement was international in scope, as were industrial investment and the price fall. The form it took depended upon national economic and legal conditions and national legislation. In the United States this was the age, not exactly of the trust, for the strict trust was declared illegal in the State of New York in 1890 and was thereafter generally abandoned, but of powerful corporations such as the Standard Oil Company and the United States Steel Corporation and their organizers and legal advisers. These large industrial organizations were popularly called trusts. As they were suspected, sometimes very properly, of monopolistic leanings and practices, they became the object between the Sherman Act of 1890 and the Clayton Act of 1914 of an important body of what

[1] *Factors in Industrial and Commercial Efficiency; Balfour Committee on Industry and Trade* (1924–7), Introduction, p. 4.

came to be called anti-trust legislation. In the other great industrial State of the day, Germany, the trust was unknown. It was replaced by the legally recognized organization of independent producers for particular purposes, especially for the control of prices, sales and output, known as the cartel, which was congenial to German temperament and business traditions. The activities of the German cartels, with their different prices for export and for home market, became painfully familiar to some British business men, for example those interested in the steel market after 1902. Trust and cartel sprang from economic tendencies too deeply rooted to pass away with the fall of prices, whatever their rise may have owed to it. They might appear when economic opportunities were narrowing, but they could also be, as among the German steel producers, the servants of vigorous and aggressive economic expansion.

In this country, no practical problems of monopoly and control of monopoly arose between 1870 and 1914 comparable with those presented by North America and Central Europe. There was no such theoretical discussion or public debate here as in the United States or Germany. But there were interesting developments, which aroused comment at the time and were to appear significant in the light of later experience. There were powerful reasons in British conditions why the trust and cartel movements found no parallel here. One effective limit lay in the relative scarcity of British raw materials or products for which there was an important demand and which were not easily produced elsewhere. Coal was the only raw material in which the British output was an important part of the world supply; but the coal industry happened to be peculiarly competitive in the form of its organization. A coal combine was proposed more than once in times of depression, including a famous scheme by Sir George Elliot in 1893. But conditions were against such plans until 1930. Other products existed in which a working monopoly was possible, but they were not for the most part products which carried great weight in the national economy. Neither did there seem to be, from a national point of view, any advantage to be gained by closing the British market to manufactured imports from abroad, or restricting such imports, equal to the advantages to be gained from importing the cheapest food and raw materials in the world and from the flexibility of costs and export prices which the free-trade policy forced upon the British manufacturer.

The time was to come in 1931 when heavy and intractable unemployment was to alter the basis of economic calculation and break the free-trade policy. The maintenance of that policy before 1914 gave the exponent of industrial combination conditions different to work under from those of the German and American manufacturer. Industrial combination in Germany and the United States operated, as was often pointed out at the time, behind tariffs which in the last quarter of the nineteenth century were rising and which did not substantially fall in the years before the First World War. How much industrial combination owed to the tariff was a matter in dispute but it certainly owed something. The short railway haul from the ports to all the home markets increased the competition which prevailed in Great Britain.

Precisely because conditions were in so many ways unfavourable to combination, the reaction before 1914 against a willing acceptance of competitive conditions is interesting. Perhaps this acceptance had never been much more than the making of a virtue out of a necessity, as technical invention and the railways broke down old markets after 1840. The older traditions of industry had been moulded as much by monopoly as by competition. There had been formidable combinations among producers in the eighteenth century in the coal and the copper industries, as well as many local monopolies in trade and transport. Then the conditions of many generations were swept away. Men came to persuade themselves that some natural law was at work in the supersession of monopoly by competition, as they watched institutions so majestic and politically powerful as the Corn Law monopoly destroyed in 1846, the Bank of England's preserve in joint-stock banking destroyed in 1826 and 1833, and the venerable monopoly of the East India Company of the trade to India and China taken away by Parliament in 1813 and 1833. The institutions and traditions of centuries had been swept away in little more than a long lifetime. The effect on men's thinking and on their emotions was profound and in some ways exaggerated.

The new, even bitter, winds of competition had been tempered between 1851 and 1875 by the expansion of demand at home and abroad. A marked rise of prices accompanying an increase in transactions made those years memorable and settled many a man's notions of what was normal and desirable. The depression of the late 1870's and the novel and often disappointing experiences of the years of falling prices from 1874 to 1896 prepared the way for a new climate of opinion. One aspect of it was the revival of protectionist thought and sentiment, although this did not become politically strong until the early 1900's. Another, less noticeable at the time but perhaps no less significant, was the alteration of accepted views on combination.

Falling prices and the alteration in the tone of business suggested that perhaps there was something to be said for the combination of firms to control prices and competition. The industrial movement towards combination continued, however, in the period of rising prices after 1900. Its dynamics lay deeper than the long downward and upward swings of price, although these had an effect upon its momentum. Justifications of industrial combination tended to harp upon at least three different and sometimes contradictory themes. First, the economies to be made by the large-scale organization in transport and raw materials, for example, the purchase of coal or iron, and in dealing with organized labour. Secondly, the elimination of what was described as cut-throat competition. The business man's dislike of competition sometimes met the working man's fear for his job half-way, as in the curious episode of the Birmingham Alliances in the 1890's, which were price-fixing arrangements among the makers of metal bedsteads and other articles, to which the local unions were parties, in return for a closed shop. Finally, there was the argument that the large concern or the combination, by its superior scale and planning, might lessen trade fluctuations or ride out the storm better than the small firm and the unassociated trade.

How far these arguments told in each particular case, only the detailed histories of firms and industries can tell us. The first of the new industrial combines appears to have been the ineffective Salt Union, formed in 1888 to put an end to competition between old saltworks in Cheshire and new ones on the Tees. British companies had participated from 1886 in the Nobel Dynamite Trust Company, which was an international combine and perhaps the first true holding company. But the first set of industrial amalgamations to make a deep impression on commercial opinion came between 1894 and 1896, when interest rates were extremely low and finance for the new concerns could easily be arranged. There emerged the Scottish tube-making combine, Stewart and Menzies, which united with English firms in 1902 to form Stewarts and Lloyds; a series of amalgamations in the heavy chemical industry, which formed the basis of Brunner, Mond and Co., and later of Imperial Chemical Industries; the coal-merchanting concern, William Cory and Son; and the sewing thread combine, known as J. and P. Coats. These were powerful amalgamations in important industries. They were followed by others during the trade boom of the next few years, especially in the textile finishing trades. Perhaps the nearest to true monopolistic organizations were those in cement and wallpaper.

The burst of amalgamation in the 1890's was not maintained. Amalgamations took place at a slower rate henceforward. But by 1914 they were coming to be accepted by careful thinkers as representing an important movement in industrial organization,[1] even in a country where economic changes were less revolutionary in scope and nature than in the United States or Germany. They were no longer regarded as strange variants from the Victorian norm. But the area they covered in industry was not great. They were perhaps no more significant of ruling trends than was the growth, less noticed and infinitely unsensational, of the trade association. Trade associations among employers had been well known in the mid-Victorian age. They tended to grow side by side with the trade unions, handling questions of wages and hours, collecting statistics and representing the interests of the trade to Parliament. They were not always active, but they had been known in some industries for many years. Perhaps they had never quite left prices alone, but as long as markets were good and prices high, there was little temptation for the organized trade to do much about output or price. One result of the fall of prices in the 1870's was to put new life into schemes to control both, especially in the heavy industries, which suffered severely in the reaction from the great boom. The Scottish and the Cleveland ironmasters tried unsuccessfully in the next decade to regulate output. The British railmakers formed, with Belgian and German railmakers, an international cartel which broke down in 1886. It was only forty years since the coal cartel of the North of England had disappeared. The age of belief in unfettered competition had not lasted for long.

[1] D. H. Macgregor, *Industrial Combination* (1906) is a good example of contemporary discussion.

Apart from the heavy industries, trade associations were at first not strong. But while the amalgamation movement slowed down after the 1890's, the trade association continued to grow in response to the need for organization in an age of collective bargaining and in face of the growing activity of the State in relation to things industrial. Association was becoming powerful in the early 1900's in the light-castings trades, supplying fitments of all sorts for houses and buildings and in the new electrical trades, for example, cablemaking. Some of these were industries of high technical efficiency, and the associations might take an interest in standard specifications and design. But it was also notable that their price-fixing activities were beginning to cover a wide range of commodities. The range might have become wider, if the electorate had plumped in 1906 for protection and the cutting off of a certain amount of foreign competition. The encouragement the trade associations failed to get from a tariff came their way during the war of 1914–18, when shortages of finished products and raw materials and increasing government control made industrial organization prudent, if not inevitable. The day of power of the trade association came after the introduction of the general tariff in 1931, amid trade depression more serious than anything that had been seen in the nineteenth century. What happened before 1914 in the sphere of amalgamation and association was by way of preparation for these later developments and was pitched in a quiet key.

The increase in the scale of the firm; joint-stock finance and company management and organization; the amalgamation and association movements—these were creating between 1880 and the First World War an industrial society very different from that which the classical economists had known. The direct personal relations, friendly or hostile or simply indifferent, between master and servant, to use the old terms which English law still applied to cases of industrial contract in the first three-quarters of the century, were by no means extinguished; they remained strong in many firms and in many industries, particularly in some parts of the country. But over a large part of the field they were beginning to be replaced by corporate and associate life in many forms, not only among the business men but also among the industrial workers as trade unions grew. In this larger and more complicated world, personality, except that of the strongest, seemed to be submerged; collective and

sectional loyalty to shareholders or directors or the trade association or the union tended to replace personal loyalty. The significance of the growth of corporateness was recognized as early
as 1900 by a deep legal thinker who was also sensitive to the
atmosphere of his time, F. W. Maitland.[1] This was within
twenty-five years of the death in 1877 of Walter Bagehot, the
West Country banker and editor of the *Economist* newspaper,
a wise commentator on the economic affairs of mid-Victorian
England, who had sometimes described himself as the last of
the direct disciples of Ricardo.

Out of this new industrial world of large and even nation-
wide organization, much that was best in industry, in the way
of research and administration, emerged in the next thirty
years. Out of it and out of the contemporary and related
movement towards larger organization in the world of labour,
also arose a long series of great industrial conflicts, from the
lock-out in the engineering industry in 1897 to the general
strike of 1926. The significance of the new types of industrial
organization was therefore more than economic; they contributed towards the increasing sectionalization of society and
the growth of sectional interests and conflicts, which was one
of the marked features of the period just before the First World
War. At their worst, these disputes seemed to threaten the
unity of the nation and the authority of the State, which were
beginning to be menaced in different fashion by developments
in the world outside.

INNOVATION AND THE EFFICIENCY OF INDUSTRY

New industries and new methods were increasingly evident in
Britain from the 1890's onwards, partly as a result of the
growing pressure of foreign competition, partly because a new
generation was coming into business which was not satisfied
with the Victorian industrial structure. The introduction of
new products and new ways of producing old ones is most
apparent in the history of particular districts. The rapid
building up of the shipbuilding industry, using the new raw
material steel on Clydeside and the Tyne would be a good
example. Electricity and oil were beginning to come into use

[1] In the introduction to his translation of Otto Gierke's *Political Theories
of the Middle Age* (1900). Maitland's inspiration, however, was neither
wholly German nor wholly medieval. He was a keen observer of the contemporary scene.

in the 1880's and 1890's, although they were far from being ready to challenge coal and steam-power. Artificial silk was beginning to roll off the loom after 1900, although it had many handicaps to overcome. The internal combustion engine had begun to compete with the horse on the roads by 1914, as the bicycle had long done. The first radio equipment and plastics were being manufactured. These two decades before the First World War were the seed-time of our present industrial technique.

A remarkable instance of change of industrial structure occurred in the Midlands, the district of Joseph Chamberlain. For over two centuries, the industrial life of this district had been associated with the exploitation of coal and iron-ore. Around the coal and iron industries had been developed the great mass of the hardware trades of the Black Country; hand-wrought nails, locks, chains, nuts and bolts, saddlers' iron-mongery, hollow-ware and many other articles, most of them produced with the minimum of power and machinery, by concerns often of the smallest, including many which continued the traditions of the domestic industry of an earlier day. Birmingham, described as 'the toyshop of Europe' in the eighteenth century, had become a city of many industries, mostly based on metal. The most important of them were the brass and copper trades, the making of small arms, metal buttons and jewellery, which included all sorts of metal knick-knacks. The West Midland trades flourished exceedingly in mid-Victorian times. The old foundations in coal and iron were undermined, however, for the mineral reserves of the district were approaching exhaustion. When prices fell violently after the boom of 1868–73, the high costs of some of the most characteristic of the local industries began to tell heavily against them. Their difficulties were the greater because of an industrial transition taking place from the use as raw material of wrought-iron, which was a South Staffordshire speciality, to steel, in which the Midlands had no economic advantage.

The Black Country declined as a centre of coal and iron production in the decade 1876–86 and a transformation began among the Midland trades. Heavy structural engineering, pursued there since the days of the Darbys and the Wilkinsons, followed the new steel industry to the North of England. The Birmingham district, especially Birmingham itself, from being the centre of a multitude of hardware trades based on iron or brass took on the aspect of a light engineering centre based mainly on steel, much of it imported into the district. New industries came into the city, including some which were new, or relatively new, to Britain, such as electrical engineering and the motor-car, motor-cycle, cycle and rubber industries. The food and drink trades, such as cocoa- and chocolate-making and brewing, grew with changing tastes and with an expanding market. The industrial structure which had existed in the West Midlands during mid-Victorian times was replaced by another, turning out new products, making more use of power and machinery and complicated techniques, organized often on a joint-stock basis and sometimes upon a very large scale.

The development of the Midland trades between 1876 and 1914, with their strong interest in the home market, are sometimes said to have changed the balance of social and political interests in the country. In some ways they did. Birmingham looked more to the home market than did Manchester, and in the days of Joseph Chamberlain, between 1895 and 1906, the making of industrial and commercial policy no longer lay so indisputably in the North of England as it had done in the days of Richard Cobden, Robert Peel and John Bright.

These and similar changes elsewhere were not without relevance to a question which began to be debated politically towards the end of the century and in the early 1900's; 'How efficient is British industry?' The problem was usually discussed in terms of a comparison with the German and American industrial systems.

The question 'How efficient is British industry?' was deceptively easy to put. It led to a maze of considerations upon the relevance of the standards to be applied and the exactness of methods of statistical measurement. Later experience has shown that international comparisons of industrial productivity and its conditions are rarely profitable, unless limited to a particular product or a particular size of firm and even then are far from easy to answer. Some of the wisest discussion at this time concentrated upon the qualitative aspects.[1] The question asked was not how far superior was the foreigner in this or that branch of production, but what were the underlying conditions of a superiority which in certain branches was already incontestable.

[1] See Alfred Marshall's *Industry and Trade*, published in 1919, but based upon experience before the First World War.

The answer as regarded Germany, one of the most successful of competitors in world markets, seemed to be that she owed much to the State and to her universities. Her political authorities paid attention to technical and commercial training, and a specifically German type of educated business administration successfully linked the work of the scientific laboratory with the practical life of the factory. British traditional skill and empirical resource were not meeting on equal terms the trained management and the advanced technique for which the German chemical and electricity industries had become famous. These were lessons slowly learned in the years before the First World War. As for government encouragement of scientific research in relation to industry, outside of agriculture, this did not come until the war with the foundation in 1916 of the Department of Scientific and Industrial Research.

The advantages of American industry lay, like the German, in methods and organization which were the creation of broad conditions of the national life. The size of the American home market and the relative scarcity and expensiveness of American labour were already causing the industry of the United States to be known for large-scale, highly modernized and standardized production. But the day of American competition on world markets upon the great scale had not yet arrived, although it was sometimes feared to be not far off. Meanwhile, there was a considerable interchange of engineering ideas and adaptation of American inventions.

It could still be reasonably argued that the signs for British industry were broadly favourable. They certainly varied from industry to industry. Thus, the progress of the world's textile industries was potentially of the utmost significance to Lancashire, which just before the First World War sold abroad three-quarters of the yarn it made and an even higher proportion of its cotton piece-goods. World textile industries were growing rapidly just because the skill required was relatively low and the making of coarse cloth by machine became everywhere the first easy stage in industrialization. Lancashire had already been largely excluded from her old markets in Europe and the United States. Yet Lancashire skill appeared unchallengeable, and the large business in the export of textile machinery to the East and Far East seemed of little moment compared with the wide and profitable field of existing trade in those parts of the world.

More fundamental to the industrialization of the world was the development of the heavy industries, coal, iron and structural engineering. Here also a double-faced prosperity prevailed. The rising costs in the coal industry which a Victorian economist, Stanley Jevons, had foreseen as early as 1865,[1] and which he supposed must come as a result of the exhaustion of the easier seams, appeared before the end of the century. It needed more men, material and organization to raise a ton of coal to the surface after 1891 than before; output for every man employed began to fall. But so long as a coal-hungry world continued to raise its demand at the rate of 4 per cent per annum and the value of coal rose faster than its production, it was possible to put the higher costs on to the consumer. There were some signs that this was ceasing to be possible before 1914; proceeds per ton were beginning to fall. But they were still good, and the quantity sold never better. Sweeping technical changes in the industry were still far off and productivity per head, though falling, was as high as anywhere in Europe. There seemed little to alarm men who took the current rate of profit for their main guide.

The rise of steel production and branches of heavy engineering abroad was more severely felt. The chief technical steps toward the use of steel as a principal industrial raw material had been taken in Britain and the first effects were favourable to the competitive power of British industry. The trade revolution produced by Henry Bessemer's converter (1856) and by Sir William Siemens's open hearth (1866) was a genuine revolution. The old trade at home and abroad in iron rails, so important to the ironworks, was killed off and replaced by one in steel rails within less than ten years (1873–9), and by the 1890's steel had displaced iron for shipbuilding. British works were to the fore in supplying the new demand for steel. Even the Gilchrist-Thomas steelmaking process, applicable to phosphoric ores, announced in 1879, had as one of its earliest consequences the opening of a great new centre of steelmaking around Middlesbrough.

But from the 1880's onwards, immense strides were taken in building up the steel industries of the United States and of Germany, where after 1871 the coal of the Ruhr was being brought together with the iron-ore of Lorraine in a joint exploitation. By 1901, each of these countries had in its steel

[1] W. S. Jevons, *The Coal Question* (1865).

production outstripped Great Britain, which thirty years before had been the largest producer of iron and steel in the world. With the increase in world production went a rapid growth of steel exports. The British share of the international trade in steel fell sharply between 1909 and 1912 from 40 to 34 per cent, while imports of iron and steel, both semi-manufactured and finished, into the United Kingdom had multiplied themselves by between three and four times since 1896. General figures do not tell the whole story, which can only be elicited by an analysis of particular products and particular markets. Much of the trade was complementary rather than competitive. But if these trends of exchange continued, the British steel industry might conceivably find itself losing some of its export markets, while being forced at the same time to meet heavy competition at home. This happened between the two World Wars.

Between 1900 and 1913 the main advances in the technique of steel production were being made chiefly in German and American works. A well-known inquiry by G. T. Jones[1] into the making of pig-iron in the largest steel centre in Great Britain, the Cleveland district of Yorkshire, disclosed no important economy of technique, no reorganization of the first class which might have made capital and labour more effective, between 1885 and 1910. The explanation of the contrast is not simple. Many of the American economies were economies of scale. A large-scale structure for the industry was possible in that country partly because of a uniform demand and the high rate of growth of that uniform demand. The structure of the British industry was connected by many links with the multitude of comparatively small special markets which it served. Still, the contrast was there.

The same inquiry showed somewhat similar results for two other leading industries over the same period, the Lancashire cotton industry and the coal industry. No one of these three great staple industries of Great Britain showed any deep change in technical method or business organization of a sort to bring about a radical fall in costs or any substantial improvement in economic efficiency between 1880 and 1913. In the coal industry, the tendency of costs was, if anything, the other way about.

There was thus a paradox at the heart of the industrial life of late-Victorian and Edwardian Britain. The great industries of the Industrial Revolution of the late eighteenth and early

[1] G. T. Jones, *Increasing Return* (1933).

nineteenth century, iron, cotton and coal, were ceasing to be the theatres of innovation in technique and organization which they had once been, and were ceasing to produce the increasing returns to human labour on which their great start in the world had depended. They remained, however, fundamental to the British industrial structure, and they were growing exceptionally fast. In the decade before the First World War, coalmining, iron and steel, engineering and shipbuilding, and the textile industries in Lancashire and Yorkshire formed the dominant industries of the country. Their predominance seemed to increase as trade picked up after 1905 and the world entered a phase of boom. Smartly checked by the financial crisis of 1907, this boom became prodigious after 1909, largely owing to high prosperity in the United States, but amid good trading signs from almost every country. In 1911, during years of flourishing exports, the census disclosed that the numbers engaged in the coal-mining, metal and machinery and textile trades, together with those in clothing and chemicals, had risen by nearly 20 per cent since 1901, at a time when the whole occupied population of the country increased by only 12–13 per cent. The next census, in 1921, showed that this high rate of growth had been maintained, even increased, since these industrial groups had recruited their numbers by a further 20 per cent, while the rate of growth of the occupied population had fallen to 5–6 per cent over the decade.[1] The groups referred to included some industries, such as rayon, motor-car manufacture and the electrical trades, which were new and which were to be among the fastest-growing industries of the next twenty years. But they were as yet small. The main growth of industrial employment had taken place in such large and well-established industries as coal-mining (which by 1913 employed more men in Great Britain than any other industry except agriculture) shipbuilding and engineering.

The conservative shape of the British industrial structure just before and after the First World War is thus partly to be explained in terms of the character of the boom between 1909 and 1913 and the encouragement it gave to traditional exports.

The boom, with the high rate of return on foreign investments which it brought, may also have discouraged investment

[1] G. C. Allen, *British Industries* (1933), p. 23, quoting *Further Factors in Industrial and Commercial Efficiency*; *Balfour Committee on Industry and Trade* (1924–7), pp. 24, 253.

in new industries at home. This is debatable; it seems more certain that the rage for investment abroad was unfavourable to new building and the holding of mortgages on house property.

The influence of the First World War worked in the same general direction as the pre-war boom. While it did not encourage cotton textiles, the demands of war production fell heavily on such industries as coal, steel and iron, and ship-building. The question whether these were the best industries for peacetime did not arise; short-term considerations ruled, as they had in the boom, although for different reasons.

While British agriculture had suffered acutely between 1870 and 1914 from developments among the world's primary producers and had been forced to carry out, amid heavy losses, a large-scale redistribution of its resources, not always at much profit either to private owners or the nation, no such general redistribution of resources had taken place, despite important changes, in manufacturing industry. From the force and range of the world's industrial growth before the First World War, some such industrial change in Great Britain might perhaps have been expected. The change, as events proved, had been postponed rather than avoided. The general redistribution of industrial resources required by an altered world came after the war, with something of the catastrophic violence of the war itself.

INDUSTRIAL TRENDS BETWEEN THE TWO WORLD WARS

The boom of the period 1909–13 left on the memories of the propertied and business classes an image of high prosperity and of what came to be called normality. Long years of depression and unemployment printed an impression of universal decay between the two World Wars equally firmly upon the minds of many working men. Both were subjective beliefs, not wholly justified by the facts.

Great Britain was economically active before 1914, but the currents of the world were running against her; she was not progressing, judged by the real incomes enjoyed by her people. She had ceased to enjoy her early nineteenth-century industrial monopoly in ways of making new things and in new ways of making old things. That advantage had been lost to her before 1900, but the fall in the price of imported foodstuffs and raw materials had fortunately permitted the nineteenth-century rise of real incomes to continue. The prices of primary commodities between 1900 and 1914, were, however, high and rising and they helped to bring the advance of real incomes to an end, notwithstanding the revival of foreign lending and the boom in trade.

What the unemployed man between the wars did not know was that the nation's income, in terms of the aggregate commodities and services earned by it over the year, had begun to rise again. It was perhaps 30 per cent higher in 1938 than in 1911. The foundations of this gradual improvement lay in the declining prices of foodstuffs and raw materials after 1925, spelling ruin to primary producers but bringing down the cost of living in Britain; and in a marked rise in the productivity of labour in British industry. Favoured by these circumstances, Great Britain was able to rise above the wreck of some of her largest and oldest trades and occupations and to afford out of her rising income the melancholy dole of the unemployed man and his family. The working man's impression of enormous disaster had, however, its own measure of truth. Oral tradition will probably preserve for many years the memory of the decline of great staple industries such as coal and cotton textiles in the 1920's and 1930's.

The main export trades of Victorian and Edwardian times never regained their position after the First World War. The events of the war itself were in some degree responsible for the decline. They disrupted old trading connections and ran down the capital equipment and impaired the efficiency of mining and manufacturing industry. The war also hastened the industrialization of countries which had once depended on the West and particularly on Great Britain for supplies of capital goods and for elementary consumer goods. New competition had to be met in old markets. The greater part of this came from the rise of new indigenous manufactures as in India, but much was now coming from third parties, such as the Japanese textile exporters. In circumstances remarkably similar to those of Great Britain herself a century before they were striving to establish themselves as suppliers of cheap industrial goods to other and especially to poorer peoples.

No doubt British monetary policy after 1925 did not help. It temporarily overvalued the pound and so raised selling prices abroad. But this condition did not last beyond 1931, when the pound sterling was devalued in the financial crisis of that year. Once the offending gold standard had been removed, industry found that it had to meet for the rest of the 1930's the growing pressure of a world in which the output of manufactures of all kinds was by 1937 probably twice what it had been in 1913.

The battle for markets went unfavourably. The year 1929 was the best for exports since 1913; but the volume of exports, measured in terms of money at constant prices, was below that of the pre-war years. The export trade of the next few years was exceptionally depressed because of the world fall in prices, incomes and demand in the years of slump between 1929 and 1931. The volume of exports in 1937, the best year of the 1930's, was below that of 1929, as that had been below the high level of the immediate pre-war years.

The inter-war period therefore was marked by prolonged depression among large export trades and in all the industries affected by their decline, such as shipping. The effects on a national economy deeply penetrated by foreign trade and normally exporting, before 1913, between one-third and two-fifths of its industrial output, were immense and the economic waste and the social suffering in proportion. Continued over the lifetime of a generation, they did more than the catastrophic events of 1929–31 to mould for good and for ill the lasting attitudes of labour and management in industry, and to promote industrial and labour policies which might be briefly described as protective and defensive.

One of the first trades to be learned by a people anxious to mechanize its industrial activities is usually cotton textiles. Great Britain had been herself the first learner. How well the lesson was being digested in other countries between the two World Wars may be judged from the fact that in 1938 British exports of cotton piece-goods were the lowest for ninety years past. The year 1938 was particularly bad; but even in 1937, a year of relatively good trade, the heavy loss of foreign markets since 1913 by the cotton industry and by other industries such as coal and iron and steel was obvious. British industry depended in 1939 upon the home market to an extent that it had not done for many decades, exporting no more than 15 per cent of its product.

The drift of change was evident in commercial policy. After 1931, British industry was protected by tariff. An alteration in the mood of political opinion and in public policy towards the restraint of competition was another consequence of adversity. The building up among business men of organizations for the control of prices and production, often with State encouragement or acquiescence, and the development by trades unions of restrictive practices, not wholly new by any means, designed to prevent unemployment in the short period and to spread what employment there was, were striking features of these years, for example, in the coal, iron and steel and ship-building industries. Industrial relations suffered immeasurably, for the large exporting industries of the past were also the industries with well-organized trade unions. However hopeless their cause, some of these men were not disposed to take a beating from economic circumstance quietly, especially when it came to them through managements whom they did not trust. The social life and the industrial future of the whole nation suffered by the antagonism, suspicion, anger and re-crimination and the abiding lack of confidence produced by the long-drawn-out contraction of great industries such as coal-mining at this time.

Whether the loss of economic place and power by old staples need have been as great as it was, and how far, even where it was inescapable, different behaviour and policies might have avoided some of the deplorable social and economic conse-quences, are questions that do not admit of a general answer; they could only be answered industry by industry, firm by firm, town by town. The industrial historian may, however, recall the comment of an economist and statistician of those days, Sir Josiah Stamp, that society had still to invent a civilized technique of economic and social change. He may even wonder whether in this respect Britain between the wars had a record to show much better than that of the Britain of a century before in the first age of industrialization.

Nothing did more than the decline of the old staples to dis-credit the fundamental axiom of nineteenth-century economic policy that the allocation of the country's resources to their different uses was best left to the decision of the private capitalist and that the less the State had to do with it the better. For it was precisely the proper allocation of resources, with respect to the time and place and character of their employment, which was brought into question by the experience of those years and by the tendency of idle resources and men to be concentrated in particular parts of the country such as industrial South

Wales and Lowland Scotland and in particular industries, such as the Lancashire cotton textile trade.

As confidence in the wisdom and foresight of the private investor of capital declined, the State assumed new powers. The Special Areas Act of 1934 was, for example, although a limited and piecemeal law in itself, the beginnings of a permanent policy of control over the location of industry which found expression after the Second World War in the Distribution of Industry Act of 1945 and in the Town and Country Planning Act of 1947. The interest of the inter-war years lies, however, neither in particular measures nor in the attainment of a general policy, for this never existed, but in the swift dissolution of Victorian social philosophy, already attacked theoretically by critics before 1914, and in the confused attempt to think out once more, for the first time since the eighteenth century, the exact nature of the relations which join or sever the economic system and the State. This effort, sometimes pursued on fruitful and original, sometimes on highly retrograde lines, under the pressure of immediate circumstance, cannot, however, be discussed in detail here.

While these fierce tides of economic change were running, a new structure of industry was building itself up in Britain under their impulse, as a line of coast which has long been altering slowly will under the influence of gale and tide take a shape in a short time which it may hold for years. Aggregate figures tend to conceal the varied nature of the changes which were taking place. Over British industry as a whole, the volume of industrial production was larger by about a quarter in 1937 than in 1929 and much larger again than in 1907, the year of the first census of production. This increase in general industrial production brought with it a national real income substantially above that of pre-1914 days. It made possible, taken together with the falling prices of the imports for which part of it was exchanged, the relative prosperity of those years, despite a level of unemployment which would have been regarded as catastrophic before the First World War. It also formed the foundation of the economic effort of the war years 1939–45. The rise in aggregate production, at a time of persistent unemployment, owed much to a remarkable rise in productivity, both per man and per man-hour, between 1913 and 1937. Real costs were being forced down over important sections of industry.

But not over all sections, by any means, nor were all industries expanding their total output. The increase in production was most unevenly distributed and the fortunes of particular industries and particular towns were widely different. A wide range of industries, including some of those which had been the most important in the Victorian and Edwardian eras, were losing labour almost continuously throughout the 1920's and the 1930's, not because they were changing their technical methods fast and could achieve the same output with fewer workers, but because of lack of prosperity and of prospects of employment. Coal-mining, pig-iron making and iron-ore mining, steel smelting and rolling, marine engineering, ship-building and repairing, cotton and woollen textiles, the linen, jute and lace industries, boots and shoes and leather goods, all employed fewer people in 1939 than in 1923 and many of them fewer in 1939 than in 1929, having experienced an almost continuous decline.

One result of industrial contraction was unemployment. The average annual rate of unemployment between the wars was much higher than in the early 1900's. The comparison is not easy to make, but 'the indications are', says the authority on the subject,[1] 'that if general unemployment insurance had been in force and unemployment had been recorded from 1883 to 1913 in the same way as from 1921 to 1938', it would have shown a mean unemployment rate before the First World War of about 6 per cent of the insured working population. The actual rate among the great mass of workers covered by the scheme in the eighteen years from 1921 to 1938 was 14·2 per cent.

The average rate of the statisticians was built up, however, from all types of unemployment, seasonal, cyclical and structural; short- and long-term. The slump of 1929–32 was marked by terrible lack of work; but what distinguished the interwar period of industrial history as it had another period a century before was widespread structural unemployment persisting over many years. Once the curse of the hand-loom weaver, now of the miner and the shipbuilder, it provided that 'hard core' of unemployment, of people unemployed for long periods, both old and young, who in August 1939 still numbered nearly a quarter of a million men and women.[2] Round these

[1] Lord Beveridge, *Full Employment in a Free Society* (1944), pp. 72–3. His earlier book, *Unemployment* (1930) compares the situation in 1909 and in the 1920's.
[2] Beveridge, *Full Employment in a Free Society* (1944), p. 66.

and the other unemployed at various periods raged many of the chief economic and political controversies of the inter-war years.

While whole districts sank into stagnation, to become the 'Special Areas' of Parliament's legislation, immense advances in population and production were being made elsewhere. This almost reversed the distribution of unemployment before 1914; for in those days London and the South of England had suffered relatively high rates of unemployment, while Scotland, Wales and the North of England were districts of low rates. Now, it was in Greater London, the South of England and the Midlands that industry was tending to grow.

Part of this new industrial growth was not traditional, but due to the rise of new industries. The building boom of the 1930's was responsible for much of what is described here as traditional growth, in furniture-making, the carpet industry and the provision of builders' materials, as well as in the building industry itself. But side by side with these grew a number of industries which had been rooted in the technical development of the early 1900's or earlier but which only now were coming to full stature. Chemicals, electrical engineering, motor vehicles, cycles and aircraft, silk and rayon, the plastics, scientific and photographic instruments—a familiar list of industries, very much part of our present world, offered many of the new opportunities of employment, particularly in the 1930's when the slump of 1929–32 was over. But not all those who had lost jobs in contracting industries were in a position to take new ones in expanding ones. Moreover, to prevent unemployment appearing, industry must provide new jobs equal in number not only to the old jobs lost but also to the additions which every year makes to the population in a growing community. Industry failed to do this, so that heavy unemployment persisted down to the outbreak of the Second World War. At the same time, the slackening rate of capital accumulation in industries, some of which had become unfavourable fields for the outside investor or which no longer produced the profits out of which their old rate of self-investment had been supplied, raised serious doubts about their ability to improve in the future upon their performance in the recent past. Some answer to these great questions of labour and capital had still to be found when the outbreak of war in September 1939 put a hasty end to an inconclusive chapter in British industrial history.

Chapter X

Industry and the Social Order in early and middle Victorian Times

THE GROWTH OF INDUSTRIAL OCCUPATIONS AND TOWNS

The secret of Great Britain's economic development in the nineteenth century lay in a process of capital investment and accumulation which, compared with the experience of past times, was enormous. But to be economically effective this required to be matched with a no less important process of social adaptation. If society had to accustom itself to industrialism, industrialism had also to make its way with circumspection into a society which was both old and complicated. Concessions had to be exchanged between the new conception of the economic functions of society and the other purposes for which society exists. Out of the marriage of economic development with sharp social change arose a struggle not only of interests but also of values, which lends dignity and worth to the social history of that age.

The alteration in the scale of society was one of the most important facts of nineteenth-century history. Many special features of the rate of growth and the character of the economy were related to the swift growth of population. A large part of the population was at any given time either not occupied, being too young or too old, or it was engaged upon duties, which although necessary and arduous, such as house-keeping, were unpaid and therefore not classified by the census-takers among occupations for gain. Even so, the population recorded as gainfully employed in Great Britain rose from 4,216,000 in 1801 to 18,351,000 in 1911, the last census before the First World War.[1] The rise in population made England (not Britain) the most densely populated State in the world and formed the foundation, given employment, of increased national income. Within a few years of the census of 1911, when the long peace of the nineteenth century was over, that popula-

[1] *Report of the Royal Commission on the Distribution of the Industrial Population,* Cmd. 6153 (1940), p. 23, table 2.

tion manned the armies of French and Haig and the munitions factories and the mines which stood behind them. The steady forward sweep of population—the greatest decennial increase came between 1891 and 1901, and but for emigration the following decade to 1911 would have shown a still greater addition[1]—conditioned every side of economic history in the nineteenth century.

As the population grew, it became more mobile. This was extremely important for economic development, granted that this was also a society in which the habits of saving and investing and the zeal of accumulation were firmly planted among the classes with income to save and that their activities created new opportunities for employment of various kinds. Great Britain became in the course of the century a country of large-scale emigration and even of considerable immigration. But her growth in economic stature owed most to an enormous internal migration. This was in effect the colonization of an old country. It appeared particularly in the emergence of new regions of economic importance and in the building up of town life upon a new scale.

In 1801, seven large districts already held nearly one-half (45 per cent) of the occupied population. Over a hundred years later, between the two World Wars, in 1931, they appear to have held nearly three-quarters (73 per cent) of the population, so defined.[2] These seven districts were London and the Home Counties; Lancashire; the West Riding of Yorkshire, Nottinghamshire and Derbyshire; the Midland counties of Staffordshire, Warwickshire, Worcestershire, Leicestershire and Northamptonshire; Northumberland and Durham; Central Scotland; Glamorganshire and Monmouth. The gathering together of people in these districts began well before 1801 and continued throughout the nineteenth century, with many changes of pace and relative position. Between 1901 and 1911, Lancashire and Central Scotland were both losing a little of their position, relative to the country as a whole. Far greater shifts took place after the First World War, when the proportion of the occupied population in Lancashire, Northumberland and Durham, Central Scotland, Glamorganshire and Monmouth generally declined, while it rose heavily in London and the Home Counties. But by that time the specifically nineteenth-century conditions of British industry

[1] Ibid. p. 138.　　　　[2] Ibid. p. 24.

and social life were at an end. Meanwhile, in the hundred years that followed the first census, the growth of these seven districts, even making allowance for the fact that they excluded large and fast-growing towns, such as the ports and naval centres of Bristol, Southampton, Hull, Portsmouth and Plymouth, provided the regional and local setting for the larger part of the economic and social life of the country.

The concentration of population in these regions was mainly due to an efflorescence of town life, growing from roots both old and new. This did not lack vitality and power, although it wanted much in beauty and grace. The nineteenth century was a great age of city and town building. But while in recent times much town growth has been the result of movement from one town to another, the urban life of the nineteenth century was fed mainly by immigration from the countryside and by the fertility of the town populations themselves.

The towns did not depopulate the countryside—the rural population of England and Wales was larger in 1911 than in 1841—but they did receive its overflow, in an age of multiplying rural families. This migration seems to have been at its height in the 1840's, when English and Scottish town life was also absorbing a mass of immigrants driven from Ireland by the famine. London, Liverpool and Manchester—all three favoured by Irish immigrants—grew with particular speed, as did the textile towns generally in the North of England. After 1851 there came a change, when Irish immigration ceased to be important. The movement into the towns remained vigorous. Much of it came from short distances, but with the aid of the railways men might travel long distances in search of work, as they did to Swindon. Town recruitment from the countryside, which had been growing throughout mid-Victorian times, reached its height during the agricultural depression of the 1870's and 1880's, although during the latter decade heavy emigration to the United States and elsewhere was simultaneously taking away an unusual proportion of the town population. Emigration fell away in the 1890's and early 1900's to recommence on the large scale after 1906. Meanwhile, the movement from country to town began to fall sharply from 1900 onwards; but town growth remained strong, from the fertility of the town population itself.

The same century which saw the representative man turn town-dweller witnessed also the settlement of the coal-fields with a dense population, which was an important part of the whole. Many of the new coal-miners were immigrant country labourers; but the colliery population grew also by its own natural increase, which for many years was the highest of any section of the population.[1]

Great Britain in the early years of the nineteenth century was a country with a population in which agricultural pursuits and rural traditions were still strong, but where the towns, with their special preoccupations and interests, were unmistakably gaining the upper hand. By the mid-century, the population was about equally balanced between country and town. Then the balance tilted, to come down heavily in favour of the towns by 1871. In the next forty years, agriculture and rural economy fell into the background of the national life. In 1911, out of every thousand males employed in England and Wales, 99 were occupied in agriculture; but there were 85 occupied, in one way or another, with coal-mining, 124 with metals, engineering, vehicles or metal products, 97 with transport, mainly railways. Out of every thousand women and girls occupied, 20 were still in agriculture; but 136 worked at textiles, 145 in the clothing trades and 96 in finance, commerce and dealing. Industry, shop and office did not absorb everybody; the number of 386 females in personal service showed the hold which traditional occupations still possessed.[2] Over the century, there had also been a notable growth in the professions, among both men and women.

The enormous character of the drift towards urban life and new occupations, which the Victorians had come to regard as natural, is obvious. At no earlier period in British history had so many people been on the move from one residence to another, from one occupation to another, for what seemed to them good and sufficient reasons. The occasion of the change was often, in part at least, non-economic. There were reasons which had little or nothing to do with income: the wish to be near relatives or to keep away from them; the desire to maintain affiliations with a church or a chapel; the longing to avoid the dullness of the country or to pursue the social life and the glamour of the town. But most moves were undoubtedly intended to better

[1] A. K. Cairncross, 'Internal Migration in Victorian England', *The Manchester School*, January 1949.
[2] A. L. Bowley, *Wages and Income in the United Kingdom since 1860* (1937), p. 12, table III.

men's conditions or prospects in the way of income, whatever other advantages were arrived at. Whether they did always improve them or whether they did this without injury to the incomes and prospects of others is another matter. Not everyone sought an income rationally, or honestly, or even lawfully. Indeed, much of the history of that century was a kind of debate, about what a rational honest and lawful income was or ought to be. It does little to illuminate the world of human motive which lay behind the great migration to assume that men followed their interests; we need to know also how they conceived their interests, including that part of them which was non-economic, and what they supposed was the relation between their interests and those of other men. This is the inner history of economic thought and policy in the nineteenth century.

THE SOCIAL POLITICS OF TOWN LIFE

We left the development of opinion on economic and social matters in the distressed years just after the Napoleonic Wars. At that time, the cohesion given to the nation by war against a dangerous enemy had relaxed. Domestic problems were coming to the fore and sectional interests and animosities with them. A form of government which in the days of Liverpool and Grey was still intensely aristocratic was finding its way uneasily, sometimes halting altogether, among new conditions and rival claims. Both within the governing circles of the day and outside them a slow crystallization of views was going forward which was to issue in a series of radical alterations of national policy, especially after 1832. The gradual character of the process was natural considering the variety of conditions in the country and the multiplicity of issues which seemed important to one powerful interest or another. The future was a landscape seen confusedly through cloud and much depended on the locality of the observer.

One great rift within the nation was classical and had been apparent to keen students of the social scene long before the nineteenth century. This was the opposition between the country and the town, which had provided Adam Smith with much of his philosophy of history. In a country such as Great Britain, with her peculiar structure of landownership and agriculture, this tended to be an opposition between the country gentleman and the town population, and it turned increasingly after 1815 upon the Corn Laws and the general question of protection for agriculture.

During the public discussion which surrounded the passage of the Corn Law in that year, the economist David Ricardo, in the course of an essay[1] which analysed the economic effects of the law, opened the problems, little discussed by earlier writers, of the distribution of the national income. He declared that as a nation increases in wealth and population, the price of corn will rise, in the absence of agricultural improvement. This development favours the farmer, but even more the landowner. Where agricultural profits and rents pass into different hands, the landowners become the chief beneficiaries of economic progress. They derive from it an increment in the value of their property, which depends upon no efforts of theirs. Behind the increase of wealth and population lay, however, the accumulation of capital, which gave industrial employment to the nation. As the price of corn rises, not only do rents rise but the real wages of the town labourer, his wages in terms of what they would buy, must tend to be depressed towards the level of a mere subsistence. Since a rising proportion of the national income falls to the landowner, and since the wage-earners must in any case receive enough to propagate their kind, the amount available for accumulation in the form of capital must decline and prosperity and employment with it. Ricardo drew the conclusion that 'the interest of the landlord is always opposed to the interest of every other class in the community'.[2]

This thesis was belied at many points by subsequent history. The wages of the workman did not fall to subsistence, neither did the accumulation of capital halt nor the price of corn rise again above the level it reached in the Napoleonic Wars, as long as Great Britain depended upon her agriculture for the bulk of her food supplies. Ricardo's essay reflected the facts and the potentialities of a certain moment in the process of industrialization rather than the shape of the things which were to come. But his words were an opening shot in the long contest between the landowner and the manufacturer on the question of agricultural protection, which governed much of British politics for many years.

[1] David Ricardo, 'Essay on the Influence of a Low Price of Corn on the Profits of Stock,' *The Works and Correspondence of David Ricardo*, ed. P. Sraffa and M. H. Dobb (1951–4), vol. IV, pp. 9–41.
[2] Ibid.

The argument that these laws constituted an unjust diversion of part of the national income towards farmers and landowners was most easily accepted in a manufacturing and mercantile centre such as Manchester, where they were also seen as an obstacle to the exchange of Lancashire textiles with the corn of the Continent. The association between the rising industry of the north-west and the campaign against agricultural protection began early and became close in the period of depressed trade towards the end of the 1830's, which led to the foundation of the Anti-Corn Law League in 1838. At this point, a dispute over the distribution of wealth touched major issues of commercial policy and transformed it with the help of Peel, who abolished the Corn Laws in 1846—an episode in the history of external economic policy which we shall later have to examine.[1]

The agitation against protection to corn and to agricultural capital never occupied the whole stage of Manchester's social politics. That part of the country was distinguished, as John Bright and others who knew it well observed, by the wide division between employer and employed in the textile industries and the bitterness of class feeling, which is reflected in the observant pages of Friedrich Engels's *Condition of the Working Classes in England* (1845), a book conceived during Engels's years in Manchester. Cobden and Bright, who led the Anti-Corn Law League to victory against the agricultural interests in the 1840's, were not open to the charge that they hoped to get the cost of living down in order to reduce wages. They saw no reason why the workman should not share in the increased prosperity brought by export manufacture. Not all of their followers were equally clear-headed or sympathetic to working-class claims. The agitation against the Corn Laws was mainly a middle-class movement. But the typical working-class radical in the towns became a free-trader, with a long memory for dear and poor bread—which had not, however, always been due to the Corn Laws—and a deep suspicion of the squire, parson and farmer in the countryside.

Working-class people did not feel they could be content with a victory of manufacturer over landowner. They had a bone or two of their own to pick with the manufacturer. Some, especially among those who were too old to take up new employment, found that in hand-loom weaving they had committed themselves to a trade which was dying. Its decay, and the

---

[1] See below, chapter XII.

under-employment and deterioration of incomes which went with it, was a major cause of social unrest, particularly in those parts of the country, such as Lancashire and the South of Scotland, where domestic weaving had once been strong and had attracted Irish immigration. The misery of these unfortunate people was twice the subject of official inquiry in 1834–5 and 1837–40; but it lay beyond the reach of Corn Law repeal or any other measure which Parliament was willing to contemplate. The cotton-weavers, whose state was the worst, were left— like the framework knitters of stockings in Derby, Nottingham and Leicester, whose troubles were much older than the competition of machinery—to their own desperate shifts and the Poor Law.

The domestic cotton-weavers of the north-west were a small group in Lancashire's industrial population—perhaps 60,000 or 70,000 out of a million and a quarter people in 1838[1] — but significant because the hopelessness of their state, combined with the education which some of them possessed, made them willing recruits for the Chartist cause. That movement, demanding a vote and entry to Parliament for working men, had begun with the London Working Men's Association in 1836. Much more was to be heard of Chartism in the next ten years, when it ran side by side and competed for the attention of the country with the Anti-Corn Law League.

The larger part of the working population of Lancashire stood apart from Chartism. This did not mean that it had no conception of its own interests and no programme. On the contrary, wages and hours were coming to be a subject of controversy between employer and employed throughout the cotton textile area. Trade unionism and the demand for a shorter working day grew together. It was after the repeal of the Combination Act in 1825 that considerable union organizations were built up among the cotton-workers by such men as the Ulster catholic, John Doherty, and that the ten-hour day first began to be demanded for children, for women and for men.

The short-time movement among working people found strong leadership and formidable expression in Yorkshire, at Leeds. An organized agitation for the ten-hour day, which owed something to the example of the contemporary agitation for the abolition of negro slavery in the West Indies, had begun

[1] M. Hovell, *The Chartist Movement* (1925), p. 14.

in that county, among the woollen textile workers, with a letter by Richard Oastler,[1] Tory and High Churchman, and steward of the Fixby estates by Huddersfield, to the *Leeds Mercury* in September 1830. The sense of sharp opposition between employer and employed which marked the factory life of Lancashire had entered deep into the social life of Yorkshire too and it provided the cutting edge of the agitation. This enjoyed the blessing of the local country gentlemen, only too glad to see factory-owners who were hostile to the Corn Laws in trouble. The votes of the landed interest as a whole in Parliament were cast for the Ten Hours Bill, when it became law in 1847. This was their revenge for the loss of agricultural protection the year before. There also survived among them perhaps some traces of the paternal or authoritarian view of the State which had once created the Elizabethan social code, but which was going out of favour in the age of Cobden and Bright.

Social and economic conditions in the Midlands differed markedly from those in the North of England.[2] This was especially so in its biggest town, Birmingham, where there was a large population of skilled men and small masters, whose tendency was to come together rather than to fly apart in depressed times. Their sense of common interest provided the basis of Thomas Attwood's agitation for monetary and Parliamentary reform in the 1830's. This part of the country, having much less of a factory system than the north, was less interested in short-time and factory reform. It was concerned, however, over bad trade and unemployment and took an interest for many years in schemes of currency and banking reform intended to influence the level of employment. Much less preoccupied with import and export than the north-west, it turned its eyes to the home market and showed a disposition to think in terms less of the foreign than of home demand.

The domestic industries of the Midlands played a minor role in the agitation for the ten-hour day, but had their own grievances over conditions of employment among the hardware trades of the Black Country, the Coventry silkweavers and the framework knitters of Nottingham and Leicester. These problems of child-employment, debt, underpayment and

[1] For Oastler's strange career, see C. H. Driver, *Tory Radical: the Life of Richard Oastler* (1946).
[2] A. Briggs, 'The Background of the Parliamentary Reform Movement in Three English Cities, 1830–2,' *Camb. Hist. J.* vol. x (1952), pp. 297–302.

overwork were old, but they were persistent and sometimes worsening. They helped to feed the agitations of the first half of the century—for Parliamentary reform in 1830–2 and for the Charter in 1839–48—which were concerned with the control of government and the protection of labour by law. The employment of children, women and men in the coal-mines, from Fife to Somerset, could show evils equally old and dreadful. But though some small part of the mining popula-tion shared in the Chartism of the 1840's, the miners stood apart, owing to the isolation of their life and employment, from many of the currents which agitated the social politics of the rest of the kingdom. They witnessed important developments among themselves in the beginnings of coal-mining trade unionism between 1825 and 1841.

Out of this variegation of interests and ideals as it existed in and about the year 1830 arose the agitation for Parliamentary reform which led to the widening of the franchise and the re-distribution of seats in 1832. The main issue that year was not economic, since it concerned the whole position of the middle class in the State. But there was an important economic side to it, not least for those sections of the working class which supported the demand for reform in the hope of winning a measure of political power for themselves. A confused period followed, marked, among other things, by a number of attempts to use the law-making power of the State to influence, in one direction or another, the conditions under which in-comes were made and the distribution of wealth. Temporarily, the advantage lay with the middle class or rather with the upper reaches of that class who were admitted in 1832 by the aristocracy and the country gentlemen to share a political power which they had no intention of abdicating. There was no victory of the middle class over the old governing elements; but there was an immediate strengthening of middle-class influence and values in Parliament.

At the same time there was a great agitation outside Parlia-ment by the disappointed and the excluded, both among the middle class and the working class. This took the form of Chartism or the demand for universal manhood suffrage. Chartism ran through several phases between 1839 and 1848 and was connected in its time with a variety of schemes of social reform, from the currency plans of the Birmingham banker Attwood to the land settlement for poor weavers of the later

Chartist leader Fergus O'Connor. Chartism declined after a series of rebuffs by Parliament. It was replaced in the middle years of the century by the different but more successful middle- and working-class pressure for further Parliamentary reform. This led to the working man in the towns getting the vote in 1867 and the country labourer and the coal-miner receiving it in 1884. The line of continuity between all these movements was direct.

The period of political change after 1832 saw much economic and social legislation. The practical importance of it can be overrated, compared with the magnitude of the changes which were coming over society. Its scope was limited, its administrative effectiveness often deficient. It was the final result, however, of changes going on in the deeps of public opinion and in the relations between the various sections and groups of which society was composed. As an index to social change extending far outside of Parliament the economic and social policy of the age is interesting even when the law corresponded ill with reality.

One of the first changes to take place after the shift of political power in 1832 was a reform of the Poor Law. This occurred in 1834 under the new Poor Law Amendment Act. The reform of the law fell about midway in the difficult period of transition when industrial occupations, between 1815 and 1851, were rapidly growing, but before they proved themselves capable of absorbing the surplus of a rapidly growing rural population. The railways, which did so much to promote employment later, were not yet laid down. It was at this time, when there was unrest among the country labourers, that the law was passed.

The new law aimed at a reform of the relations between wages and public assistance among the agricultural labourers in the South of England, where the failure of employment to grow had been most marked and where the practice of making an allowance out of the poor rates in aid of wages, to men whose wages were inadequate to the needs of their family, had become most widespread. The relations of the labourer and the workman to the Poor Law in the North of England, where industrial employments were growing fastest, were on a slightly different basis. There the competition for labour tended to raise wages, even in the country districts, compared with the South of England. The wages paid were often most inadequate for the labourer's needs, but as a consequence of the high state of employment from time to time, the northern labourer was in want of public assistance not continually, as in the south, but mainly during times of bad trade. This difference of conditions —there was a distinction to be drawn also between conditions of employment in London and in the rural south of England— was insufficiently appreciated by the men, principally Nassau Senior, the economist, and Edwin Chadwick, the Benthamite lawyer, following whose official inquiry and report the new law was passed. They were chiefly concerned to deny, not the southern labourer's rights to relief, but his right to relief in aid of wages. But the measures they recommended to this end, which passed into law, were cast in general form and applied to the whole of England and Wales.

The Poor Law reform of 1834 was one of the most notable social and administrative measures of the nineteenth century. The new law marked a break with English traditions in local government. For if the existing system of poor relief was to be discontinued and a new one put in its place, uniformity of practice must be enforced by a central authority. The law restored to the local administration of relief a national and central supervision which it had not known since the days of Charles I, in the form of the Poor Law Commission. This non-political body—an attempt to take the Poor Law out of politics, which failed—was replaced in 1847 by the Poor Law Board with its responsible head in Parliament. The Board in turn handed over in 1871 to the Local Government Board, a new government department which controlled both poor relief and public health until its functions were taken over by the Ministry of Health in 1919.

If the old system was to be abolished, a change was necessary in the local administration itself. The argument was that the parish overseers of the poor, working under the distant, perhaps the drooping eyes of the justices of the peace, were not independent in face of local feeling. More independence might, it was thought, be obtained by abolishing the parochial basis of relief and the old parish workhouse, substituting a union of parishes and a new union workhouse for it, and giving charge of the union to an elected board of guardians of the poor, drawn from the ratepayers.

The modifications introduced into local government by these changes represented a break with the traditions of centuries in the government of county and parish. The country gentlemen, in their capacity of justices of the peace, and the parish officers, whether constable, or overseer, or surveyor, had performed the functions since Tudor times. A beginning was made in 1834 with the introduction of a measure of centralization and elected representation. The change of direction was to be carried much further before the century was over.

The intention of these changes was to enable the distributors of relief to resist local pressure, whether from employer or workman. The rate in aid of wages, the reformers contended, corrupted the employer by encouraging him not to pay the market rate of wage, and the labourer, by making him satisfied with casual labour, instead of a regular job. Both men had an interest in maintaining the existing system. This circle it was intended to break by refusing all relief outside of the workhouse except to those destitute sick and old people, children and infirm persons whose right to relief had never been denied. Relief outside or inside the workhouse was to continue to be given to these, even perhaps some improvement in treatment, for the reformers urged the abandonment of the general mixed workhouse and the use of more specialized institutions and policies. The real innovation in 1834 was the refusal of relief, except inside the workhouse, to the unemployed person, and the principle of making the circumstances of the men there in receipt of relief less eligible, in the phrase of the law, than those of the poorest-paid labourers outside it. For this reason, the new workhouses were made as harsh as the Poor Law Commissioners, who laid down the general rules of their administration, dared allow them to be.

The Poor Law Amendment Act of 1834 was regarded in its day, by ruling political opinion, as a revolutionary measure. What it failed to accomplish appears now more obvious than what it achieved. The financial basis of the Poor Law, which was essential to radical reform of its administration, remained unchanged. It was not until 1865, as a result of severe distress in Lancashire following the 'Cotton Famine', that the union, not the parish, became the financial unit of the Poor Law; not until then was the way clear to abolish the old disputes about financial liability between the parishes by the adoption of a new law of settlements in 1876.

The act of 1834 did not bring any great improvement in the management of that part of the work of the Poor Law which

consisted in the relief of those who were unfitted to earn income
for themselves. The old people and children, sick, insane, blind
or lame formed at all times the majority of those relieved
publicly. Their relief continued in their homes or it was done
in the new workhouses on the old lines. It was not the law of
1834 but the growth of rateable wealth, of medical and other
professional knowledge, and of local government initiative,
especially after 1888, which helped these unfortunates. London
was a leader among the big towns, after the passage of the
Metropolitan Poor Act of 1867, in providing specialized treatment in fever hospitals, Poor Law schools, training ships,
mental asylums and so forth. But the old mixed workhouse, so
sharply condemned in 1834, generally persisted, with its
plentiful provision of stench and unhappiness, for the rest of the
century, to be condemned once more in 1909.

The Poor Law inquiry and the law of 1834 concentrated on
the problem of the unemployed or underemployed working man
or woman, and of the use of rates to supplement their inadequate wages, because recent events in the South of England had
brought it to the front.[1] The men who devised the new system
were better intentioned than many landowners and farmers.
They genuinely respected the independence and the personality
of the working man, although they were not prepared to give
him the right to combine against his employer to obtain a fair
day's wage for a fair day's work, which was necessary for the
success of the reform they aimed at in his condition. They were,
however, too deeply affected by the harsh conventionality of
current upper- and middle-class opinion not to fail in compre-
hension and administrative wisdom. They had set out to
abolish out-relief to those who were able to work at a job. In
the South of England, in the 1830's, they could show much
success, owing to good harvests and employment on the farm
and the beginnings of railway-building. But conditions in the
North of England were different. When industrial depression
returned in 1836–7 and unemployment spread there, the Poor
Law Commissioners were at once in trouble. Over the next
few years, the enforcement of the law provoked much resent-
ment, and an immense agitation against the new Poor Law
overflowed into Chartism. Distress was again widespread in

[1] The events of the winter of 1830–1 showed the deep discontent existing;
see J. L. and B. Hammond, *The Village Labourer, 1760–1832* (1920), chapters
x–xi.

the North of England in the 1860's, during the trade difficulties of the American Civil War; it occurred in London too, for different reasons, and the administration of the law had to be relaxed. By 1870, the effective prohibition of out-relief was confined to rural unions and was not universal even there. It was the agricultural labourer who had paid for the victories of the Poor Law reformer.

The shape of national employment had been altered by the coming of the railways and the long secular boom of the mid-Victorian era and the success of the law was beholden to events which the men of 1834 could hardly have been said to have foreseen. The mid-century course of investment and employment did much to free the country from the difficult economic conditions which had caused the old practices of the Poor Law to flourish. If this had not happened and if Britain had turned out to be the country cursed with overpopulation that so many of those who voted for the law feared, the law of 1834 would have appeared less of a success than it did to mid-Victorian politicians.

Buoyed up and assisted by the rising prosperity of the country, the new Poor Law maintained itself, and carried on to the century's end the economic thinking and the social values of its earlier years. Yet the law had been imperfect from the start and it did much to sharpen ill-feeling between the classes. What should have been at best a limited and severe device, to break undesirable employment practices in a particular part of the country at a particular time, was allowed to set the tone of public assistance as a whole for many years. In the new Poor Law institutions, every type of man, woman and child in need of relief came under the stringent discipline which had been invented to deter men from seeking relief in aid of their wages. To many of these people, the principle of deterrence, on which the law was founded, had little if any relevance; yet the man genuinely unemployed found himself subject to the workhouse-test, along with the vagrant and the idler. A stigma was placed by the law on all these people, deserving as well as undeserving. By its creation of the pauper status, which subjected the man or woman in receipt of relief under the Poor Law to a special discipline, and to civil and political disabilities, such as loss of voting rights, and by its use of such odious symbols as pauper uniform, the Poor Law went far to treat mere poverty as an offence, even a crime. Its maintenance in the severest form during the middle years of the century trespassed against the sound rule that a law, to work well, still more to become permanent, needs the assent of those to whom it applies. It is not surprising that, once the franchise was widened, particularly after 1884, a move began away from 'the principles of 1834'.

The new Poor Law was one of the most characteristic creations of the early nineteenth century. It was one of the first pieces of legislation to be passed after the Reform Act of 1832, and it played a great part in the politics of the next few years. Working-class political consciousness was beginning to awake, under the stress of many forces, including the spread of the newspapers, the organized agitation which had helped to pass the Reform Act itself, and the excitement of the French revolutions of 1789 and 1830. The character of the new Parliament, as it seemed to reveal itself in the Poor Law, provoked the leaders of radical working-class politics, such men as Richard Oastler, John Fielden of Todmorden and Joseph Rayner Stephens to a high pitch of activity in the years 1834–8. The working-class agitation against the new Poor Law became a main root of Chartism in the provinces.

The advantage lay, however, with the middle classes, or rather with such part of them as the country gentlemen were prepared to take into political partnership. The early years of Victoria's reign saw the long, dragging movement towards Free Trade and the blow delivered to the prestige, even more than the interests, of landed property by the repeal of the Corn Laws in 1846. These events were an important part of the social history of the time. The struggle over Free Trade was a real struggle and did much to give the social development of Britain in the late 1830's and early 1840's the temporary but formidable character of a rebellion of commercial and industrial capital against land. The disappearance, by 1853, of the protective tariff, both for agriculture and industry together with the continued operation of the new Poor Law, reflected the new faith in the power of private capital to supply employment and income to the nation and the consequent belief that it was important to free the market, whether for capital or for goods or for labour, from any trace of State direction or control. It also signified the strengthening in society and in politics of the men and the values, mainly those of the high urban middle class, driving these policies forward.

9

Meanwhile, other interests were organizing themselves on the stage of social politics. When working-class opinion came into conflict with the new Poor Law in the northern counties, it was the Yorkshire and Lancashire Ten-Hour Committees which turned aside from their original purpose to organize the campaign. The short-time agitation had its strength among the textile workers of the North of England. Its leadership was varied. John Doherty, one of the earliest of those who worked for factory reform, was a working-man, an Ulsterman and a Catholic, living in Manchester. Richard Oastler and Michael Sadler, of whom the latter chaired a Select Committee of the House of Commons to inquire into the labour of factory children in 1831–2, were middle-class men and Tories. Lord Ashley, who assumed the Parliamentary leadership of the movement after Sadler, was an aristocrat and a devout Evangelical. John Wood and John Fielden were great employers in the textile trades, the one in Yorkshire, the other in Lancashire.

The first effective factory law to pass the jealous scrutiny of Parliament was that of 1833, and it was the reluctant reply of Earl Grey's government to the agitation. Like the other laws which had been passed since 1802, it was limited in its scope. It applied to children up to the age of 13 and to young persons up to the age of 18, and it established not a ten-hour day but two different sets of hours, nine and twelve respectively. The employment of children below the age of 9 was prohibited, as it had been in law but not in practice since 1819. The significance of the act of 1833 lay not in the hours it laid down, which applied to textile mills only and disappointed the workers by not regulating the time of adults, but in the provision, included at the request of some employers, of a factory inspectorate reporting regularly to a Secretary of State. The inspectors secured the enforcement of the law, despite opposition and apathy from employers and employed. The ten-hour day which the short-time committees had asked for did not come until the legislation of the years 1847–53, which established a working day running from 6 a.m. to 6 p.m., with an hour and a half off for meals; that is, a ten and a half hour day. An act of 1850, which shut the mills on Saturday afternoons, was the beginning of the free week-end. By 1844, something else had arrived— the enforced fencing of machinery, long before carried out by the more careful employers and neglected by the unscrupulous.

Factory legislation, which owed a good deal after 1846 to the Parliamentary vote of the country gentlemen, getting their own back for the repeal of the Corn Laws, had been piecemeal and limited. It dealt with the employment of the women and the children; the hours of men were never touched, except indirectly, through the control of others in the mill; and the law was not extended to factories and workshops generally outside of the textile trades, until 1867.

The control of labour in mines began in the same concern with the employment of women and children and the same sense that normal social relations had been distorted by industrial growth. It was again Lord Ashley who put through Parliament the act of 1842, forbidding the employment of women and of boys younger than ten below ground. But the Coal Mines Act of 1850 first listed coal-mining as a dangerous trade and became the foundation, late in the day and for many years defective, of a regular code of coal-mining law.

The abuse of conditions of employment spread far beyond manufacturing and mining, as the records of domestic service could show, to say nothing of the poor chimney sweeps' boys whom Charles Kingsley had in mind when he wrote *The Water Babies* in 1863. Much of it was traditional, although much had been created by the spread of industrial occupations in the previous hundred years. And much of it, not only in the provinces but also in London, remained untouched by the legislation of the first half of the nineteenth century. The beginnings of factory law are nevertheless memorable. The law's effects on the range of employments to which it applied was important and even more the awakening of a public opinion formerly indifferent or calloused.

The legal regulation of hours affected the few; the legal regulation of wages did not exist, although it was sometimes suggested as a remedy for the evils of declining domestic trades such as hand-loom weaving. The conditions under which incomes were made and spent and the amount of the income itself were left to be settled by free contract between individuals, although the bargaining strength of the parties was often most unequal. Out of these hard industrial facts arose some of the most characteristic social developments of Victorian Britain, including trade unionism and consumers' co-operation.

The formation of workmen's associations to promote collective bargaining had ceased to be prohibited when the

Combination Laws were repealed in 1824–5. A lively but un-certain growth began in the 1830's, led by the cotton-spinners' operatives, the builders, the shipwrights, the millwrights and other skilled men. Robert Owen was a power among the trade unionists of those days, although his influence may have been exaggerated. It was after his day, in the middle decades of the century, that trade unionism began to take firm root and to affect the conditions of employment even outside the organized trades.

The legal position of trade unions remained in some respects obscure. They were no longer prohibited bodies, but their activities, especially at times of dispute between employer and employed, might be judged to come within the scope of the criminal law as it then stood, and this so seriously as to make some good lawyers, who were not always friends of the trade unions, doubt whether trade unions as such were not criminal associations in restraint of trade. Throughout these years, the trade unions were liable to be prosecuted for acts of their members both under the common law doctrine of restraint of trade and under the law relating to breach of contract. The latter branch of the law was decidedly unequal in its incidence, since it made breach of contract a civil offence in the employer, criminal in the employee. The law was unequal in other ways, notably in the collection of evidence on oath from workmen. Trade union funds were inadequately protected under the law, although they got into a habit of claiming protection under the Friendly Societies Act of 1855—a right of which they found themselves suddenly deprived in 1867 by a decision in the Court of Queen's Bench against the Boilermakers' Society, who had proceeded against their Bradford secretary for wrongful withholding of funds.

Important steps to clear up the law dealing with trade unions were taken by the Gladstone and Disraeli administrations in 1871–5. This was a time of public debate about the unions. It began partly with the legal decision of 1867, partly from activities which were indisputably criminal among men in the cutlers' unions in Sheffield and the consequent inquiries carried out by a Royal Commission on Trade Unions. It was no accident, however, that the change in the law coincided with the obtaining of the vote by working men in the towns in 1867 and with the holding of the first Trades Union Congress in 1868. There was a strong case to be made out for the unions,

which the well-known and able 'Junta' of trade union secre-
taries—William Allan of the engineers, Robert Applegarth of
the carpenters, Daniel Guile of the ironfounders and the others
—together with their middle-class friends and advisers, such
men as Frederic Harrison the Positivist and Thomas Hughes
the Christian Socialist, showed that they knew how to make.
The trade unions obtained in 1871 an explicit legitimation of
their status at law. The most vital of their activities in pur-
suance of trade disputes, such as picketing, were freed in 1875
from the application of the doctrine of criminal conspiracy.
A reform of the law relating to the finishing of contracts put
employer and employed upon an equal footing in the courts
for the first time. Trade union funds were given legal protection,
like those of friendly societies and other associations and clubs.

These changes in the law helped to open a new chapter in
the history of the trade unions, during the last quarter of the
century. The legislation of 1871–5, together with the later and
swift expansion of the unions, were the result of the well-
founded authority which the trade unions had slowly won for
themselves in industry, as well as of the shifting political circumstances of those years. The historians of trade unionism
doubt whether there had been in 1842 as many as 100,000
enrolled and contributing trade union members. The years of
booming trade after 1871 may have produced a million members,
a number which fell off heavily in the ensuing slump, to rise
again to the same figure in 1885.[1] The number of manual wage-
earners in 1880 was between twelve and thirteen millions.[2]

Trade unionists had increased in numbers from a negligible
minority of wage-earners to a substantial and well-organized
group. Their leaders varied as widely as any class of men
could. Men of developed character and religious convictions,
who had learned something of organized social life from the
Methodist chapel as well as the union lodge, quoters of the
Bible, stubborn negotiators and fighters in the hard industrial
world of the mid-century were strong among them. Such men
as Joseph Arch, who organized the agricultural workers at the
end of this period, and John Wilson[3] and Thomas Burt, among

[1] S. and B. Webb, *History of Trade Unionism* (1920), appendix VI, p. 749.
[2] A. L. Bowley, *Change in the Distribution of the National Income, 1880–1913*
(1920), p. 13.
[3] Wilson, like Arch, wrote his autobiography, an exceedingly interesting
document of a working man's life in Victorian times: *Memories of a Labour
Leader* (1910).

the miners of Durham and Northumberland, would have been remarkable in almost any society.

The main lead came from the skilled, that is, the apprenticed men, and their unions, such as the engineers, the ironfounders, the boilermakers and shipwrights, the bricklayers and carpenters. They evolved a type of stable and business-like trade unionism, dependent on registered membership and regular subscription, which rode out the industrial storms of the time and made collective bargaining permanent. Their influence was thrown into the scale against the employers during the 1868–73 boom, when they managed to obtain not only substantial advances of money-wages, but also the first large reduction of hours in industry for many years. This made the 54-hour week, extended by overtime in periods of brisk trade, representative of important trades, but not of all, in the last quarter of the century.

The growing power and stability of the unions was a cause both of the public discussion and the changes in the law in the early 1870's. At the same time, their membership was limited and their functions contained many relics of past times. Trade unions among agricultural workers, among women, among men who were not members of a craft, remained weak or non-existent. The day of general union power was still far off. In its functions, the union retained some of the activities of the friendly society or the benefit club, from which it had been in the past sometimes almost indistinguishable. It was first and foremost a collective bargaining body, to maintain and improve the working conditions of its members; but it might also pay out sick and burial funds or unemployment pay or pensions in old age, even emigration money. These seemed appropriate functions for the trade union and the friendly society at a time when the state maintained no social service except the Poor Law. By the 1880's, some men were beginning to argue that it was for the State to look after these things, leaving the union to concentrate on industrial affairs.

The co-operative movement, which grew rapidly in Victorian times side by side with the unions, was concerned, like the friendly society and the savings bank, mainly with making working-class incomes go as far as possible. Originally, co-operation had been preached for other purposes. Robert Owen and others too had dreamed of working men co-operating in production, owning factories, mines and workshops of their own, winning a new prosperity for themselves by cutting out the profits of the employer and the middlemen and learning how to live without competition. But the early experiments in co-operative production were unsuccessful. The old ethical and productive ideals were not lost, but attention came to be more and more directed to a different form of co-operation. Truck, or the payment of wages in the form of goods, often bad, adulteration and deterioration of quality and short measure in retail shops were all too widely known in working-class districts in the early nineteenth century. It was with the limited and practical purpose of checking these things and to secure value for money, with the bait of the dividend to bring members in, that consumers' co-operation began in the North of England. From the foundation of the Rochdale shop by flannel-weavers in 1844—not the first co-operative store but the first to be such a success that it came to be a model for others—consumers' co-operation began to take on in the industrial towns. The 1860's saw the foundation of the English and Scottish Whole-sale Societies to supply the existing stores and by the end of the century the co-operative movement was being studied by middle-class inquirers[1] as a new force which had quietly built itself into the national life. It was not until the years just before the First World War that the ideals of ethical and productive co-operation, which had meant so much to Robert Owen and to Christian Socialists such as Thomas Hughes, had another innings in the Gild Socialist movement of Orage, Penty and G. D. H. Cole.

The legislation and the institutions which have been de-scribed modified, but did not materially alter, the vast system by which private income was distributed in money form through a multitude of private contracts, subject only to the safeguards which the law provided against fraud and violence. There had been men, such as Robert Owen, who had hoped that one day the current system of making and distributing income might be abolished and replaced by something better. The best-known if not the ablest of mid-Victorian economists, John Stuart Mill, approaching these problems with a different training and in a different spirit, proved to have been less far from Owen in ultimate ends than contemporaries supposed, who had been brought up on his *Principles of Political Economy* (1848). For in

[1] Beatrice Potter, later Beatrice Webb, wrote her well-known study, *The Co-operative Movement in Great Britain*, in 1891.

his autobiography, published after his death in 1873, he wrote: 'We yet looked forward to a time when society will no longer be divided into the idle and the industrious; when the rule that they who do not work shall not eat, will be applied not to paupers only, but impartially to all; when the division of the produce of labour, instead of depending, as in so great a degree it now does, on the accident of birth, will be made by concert on an acknowledged principle of justice....'[1]

There was far more social heresy among the mid-Victorians than at first sight appears, and it was far from being confined to the working class. But the influence of Socialist ideas, whether French or English, although perceptible, did not become powerful until the end of the century and they only slowly affected social values and law.

Meanwhile, the system which Adam Smith and the classical economists had analysed but not created held sway. They had pitched their expectations of the State low and expected more, sometimes everything, from the working of the market.

About the mid-century, men were altering the balance of emphasis. Two great forces in the spiritual and intellectual life of that time, Evangelical Christianity and Benthamite Utilitarianism, which was not Christian at all, found themselves unable to accept the view that there was nothing which the State could or ought to do in the economic sphere. The one, in common with other branches of Christianity such as Quakerism, engaged in the work of social reform and set out to preserve human rights which were an essential part of its system. The Benthamites, while they adopted happiness as their test of utility and the individual judgement as their measuring rod, did not think this inconsistent with State action designed to increase the number of those capable of seeking happiness for themselves.[2]

These great streams of thought, working through many social groups and intellectual traditions, were slowly modifying in many ways the accepted relationship between the State and the economic system in current political thought. The turning-point may be reckoned to have been reached about 1882, with

[1] J. S. Mill, *Autobiography*, World's Classics ed. (1924), p. 196. It is well known that the development of Mill's thought in this direction owed much to the influence of Harriet Taylor, who became his wife. Hence the 'we' in this quotation.
[2] The debt of collectivism to Benthamism was pointed out many years ago by A. V. Dicey, *Law and Opinion in England*, 2nd ed. (1914), Lecture IX.

a little book by the economist Stanley Jevons. 'The all-important point', he observed, 'is to explain if possible why, in general, we uphold the rule of laissez faire, and yet in large classes of cases invoke the interference of local or central authorities...the outcome of the inquiry is that we can lay down no hard-and-fast rules, but must treat every case in detail upon its merits.'[1] This was a marked relaxation on the view of an earlier generation, which held that there was a general presumption against all intervention and in favour of un-restricted competition.

THE RISE IN PRIVATE INCOMES

The chief reason why, despite these changes in thought, the State in Victorian times intervened seldom in the ways in which income was made was that existing economic institutions seemed to the political classes to be working well. Incomes were growing fast. One striking feature of the prosperity of the nation after 1851 was that it seemed to extend to all classes. Agriculture was making money. The landed interest no longer enjoyed protection or exclusive political power, but it had never been so prosperous. Rents had risen, between 1850 and 1870, on selected agricultural land widely scattered in England and Wales, from their previous average level of 20s. 6d. to 24s. an acre; the national average may even have been higher.[2] Many landowners gained as much or more by mineral rights or the expansion of the towns as they did from agriculture. The picture presented by the rural and urban middle classes, in their upper ranges, was one of great wealth and power, although the evidence about the rate of growth of profits and interest is very defective. The rapid accumulation of capital, in industry, railways and many forms of private investment coincided with equally striking private spending, chiefly on houses, churches and chapels, which has left its mark on the older and wealthier quarters of many towns and cities.

However satisfied they might be by the contemplation of the riches of the rich, on which all employment was conceived as automatically depending, the improvement of conditions among

[1] Preface to W. S. Jevons, *The State in Relation to Labour* (1882).
[2] R. J. Thompson, 'Inquiry into the Rent of Agricultural Land in England and Wales', *J. R. Statist. Soc.* vol. LXX (1907), p. 613. These were gross rents, including interest on the landlords' outgoings, in the shape of land drainage and farm buildings, as well as payment for the use of the land.

wage-earners appeared even more significant to scrupulous contemporaries. The decline of poverty was in one sense relative only. An official inquiry of 1894 pointed out that fifty years before, the proportion of persons receiving extremely low wages to the whole working population had been much larger, but owing to the growth of population, the actual number of such very poorly paid persons was probably as large in the 1890's as it had been then.[1] Taking this into account, an improvement had taken place which was striking. First, a great mass of new and better-paid employment had come into existence, and many now found employment at the higher scales of wage or salary. Secondly, even when a man had not changed his job, his money-income in many employments had so increased and had risen so much faster than the cost of living, that his real earnings were above what a man of the same age would have earned forty or fifty years before. The rise of earnings was broken by periods of short-time or unemployment which might be severe. But the man who remained in the same occupation all his life had on the average lived to see a rise in his rate of pay between 1851 and 1886 of some thirty per cent.[2] The first rise of wages, in the 1850's, had been offset by the high prices of the Crimean War. But the average rate of wages and average prices for articles of common consumption showed a real gain between 1850 and the early 1870's, especially during the boom produced by the Franco-Prussian War. There was a further gain even more marked, for the man still in employment, when prices fell and living became cheaper between 1876 and 1886.[3]

This great turn for the better freed the mid-Victorian age from social quarrels to a degree rare in history; it also bred an unguarded mood of optimism. Robert Giffen, a well-known statistician of those times, reviewing the half-century of Victoria's reign in 1886, expressed the hopes of a sincere and well-meaning man in words often quoted, which may be quoted again because they were representative of opinion among the educated and political classes. 'The great rise of money-wages among labourers of every class, coupled with stationary or falling prices of commodities on the average, the

[1] *Royal Commission on Labour; Final Report*, C. 7421 (1894), p. 11.
[2] Sir John Clapham, *Economic History of Modern Britain*, vol. II (1932), p. 451.
[3] A. L. Bowley, *Wages and Income in the United Kingdom since 1860* (1937), p. xiii, quoting G. H. Wood.

all but universal shortening of hours of labour, the decline of pauperism [he meant by this the number of people in receipt of public assistance], the enormously increased consumption of the luxuries of the masses, the improvement in the rate of mortality—these and other facts combine to prove that there has been a great general advance in well-being among the masses of the community.... The new possibilities implied in changes which in fifty years have substituted for millions of people in the United Kingdom who were constantly on the brink of starvation, and who suffered untold privations, new millions of artisans and fairly well-paid labourers, ought indeed to excite the hopes of philanthropists and public men. From being a dependent class without future or hope, the masses of working-men have got into a position from which they may effectually advance to almost any degree of civilization.... The working men have the game in their own hands. Education and thrift, which they can achieve for themselves, will, if necessary, do all that remains to be done.'[1]

Why was it that men later came to regard these words as merely the dream of an expansive age? The facts of the rise of the national income, outstripping the growth of population, are not in dispute. They were limited, however as has been said, by the continuance of an immense mass of deep poverty and downright destitution. The existence of this submerged part of the nation had always been known. It was perhaps better known to a London journalist like Henry Mayhew,[2] who was writing vivid descriptions of it in the 1860's, than to Giffen. But its breadth and depth had not yet been measured and they were not exactly known until Charles Booth and others investigated them in the last quarter of the century. The new knowledge when it came had a profoundly chastening effect.

A different inference could be and was already being drawn from the facts which Giffen quoted. The main achievement of the industrial changes of the eighteenth century had been not so much to raise working-class incomes as to prevent them falling at a time of rapid population growth. There had been some improvement of wages in the North of England and elsewhere; but what was chiefly remarkable was the expansion of

---

[1] Sir Robert Giffen, *Essays in Finance*, vol. II (1887), pp. 409 and 473.
[2] Henry Mayhew, *London Labour and the London Poor* (1862), selections from which have been printed recently by Peter Quennell as *Mayhew's London* (1949).

employment and the disappearance of much of the chronic underemployment and underpayment of an earlier time. The nation carried into the next century much fatalistic acceptance of a traditionally low material standard of life; men and women were only too glad to be employed, without asking whether they earned a better income than those who went before them. The work of the expanding economy of Victorian times was to break down this habit of mind and to accustom vast masses of people to the idea, commonplace now but novel then, of a rising standard of life. How their personal income came, by what social process, they neither knew or inquired, but its mere growth widened their expectations and hopes. Whether it followed that 'education and thrift would do all that remained to be done' was a matter of opinion. Many thinking working men were coming at this very time to the conclusion that only the powerful aid of the State could give them the kind of life which they now perceived was within their reach. The altered ambitions which followed the rise of personal incomes, the mental comparisons and the spiritual ferment to which it gave rise, threw out of date the optimism of Giffen's generation and made it appear old-fashioned within the next twenty years.

A vast cultural change had preceded by two hundred years the Industrial Revolution of the eighteenth century; an equally vast cultural change was succeeding it. The mid-Victorian age represented a new stage in this process. After the violent tensions and the misgivings of the early years of the reign, an era of successful social adaptation had been reached. Solutions appeared to have been found for many of the problems which had troubled previous generations. The creation of wealth, power and comfort upon a scale altogether new, the justifiable pride of achievement in directing minds, during the years between the Great Exhibition of 1851 and the Franco-Prussian war of 1870–71, became the foundation of a new and often boastful optimism. That optimism later came to seem too slender a foundation for the hopes and expectations which had been based upon it. The successful removal of one set of problems brought into sight others equally intractable and sphinx-like. A society, like an individual, creates the problems which it solves and can only live by exchanging risks. The risks of grave social conflict following the economic successes of the mid-century were not, however, obvious to the men who witnessed the new extension of the franchise in 1867 and who saw the trade boom which followed the Continental war. It is only the hindsight of posterity which sees the expansion and the security of that age as directly related to later miseries and mishaps.

LOCAL GOVERNMENT AND ITS INCOME

What has been said so far of the social consequences of industrialization relates mainly to the effects on private incomes and the conditions under which they were earned and spent. Public expenditures formed, however, an important part of the history of incomes. Many of the most furious controversies of the time revolved upon public finance, not least of local authorities. It is of some importance to understand what had happened and how affairs stood down to the time when, towards the end of the century, public finance, both local and national, began to be revolutionized by popular demand, by the changing scale and technique of action, and by fears for national security.

The state of the towns in the hundred years of rapid town growth between 1750 and 1850 had been deeply unsatisfactory from almost any point of view, except perhaps that of the incomes which were made in them by the more substantial class of citizens. The flow of population into the towns and the spread of industrial occupations—the two by no means always corresponded, for there was much growth where there was little or no manufacture or nothing but the traditional crafts—have already been described. The new urban life, as it developed then and afterwards, supplied the Victorian age with its main social problems. For the values of the town became increasingly those of the nation, and all social institutions—the family, church and chapel, school and university, picture gallery and music room, national and local government and the law courts—bore with every passing decade the deepening stamp of city life.

This transformation of existing social ties as it affected countless lives formed the real inner history of the British people in the nineteenth century. It was the greatest social change which had taken place since town life first became vigorous in Britain seven or eight centuries before, and it brought with it what was virtually a new civilization. The towns and cities and the conurbations or town-clusters which became characteristic of Victorian life moulded public opinion and policy to a great degree, so that there would be real use in looking at the national history in terms of the contribution of this or that city or region to it. The towns also enjoyed, or developed, powers of self-government which raised important questions of economics and law.

Some of the activities which came to be supported by local rate before 1880 were paid for in that way rather than by national tax and were left to the discretion of local authorities because no agreement could be reached on the lines of a national policy. This was so with education. Education was a vital concern of the new manufacturing districts for two different reasons: first, because of the concentration of population there and the neglected state of the children, which made organized primary education a necessity; and secondly, because of the growing perception of the need for technical training, as industry progressed and foreign competition increased. No adequate handling of the problems of technology and technical instruction was possible without a foundation of primary education, but many men in the first half of the century were prepared to make the latter compulsory for social rather than for industrial reasons. The idea of national education arose out of the early Factory Acts and the Poor Law, with their requirements that factory children and Poor Law children should be educated. The proposals which Peel's government put before the country in 1843 were never executed, despite the volume of discussion upon educational matters and the importance which the government attached to them, because of the jealousy between the Established Church and Nonconformity. Each was determined either to control a national education system or not be controlled. When a primary school system was provided for the first time, a generation later, under the Education Act of 1870, it supplied a final answer to the old question of the exploitation of child-labour. But the management of the new schools which were to fill the gaps left by voluntary efforts was left in the hands of the local school boards and local rating for education was established as a corollary, because the dispute over religious teaching was still unhealed. From that time forward, the growth of rates for this purpose was rapid. In 1908–9 they came to equal in amount the Parliamentary vote in aid of education,[1] which had begun as far back as 1833, when schooling had been entirely a matter

[1] Edwin Cannan, *History of Local Rates in England*, 2nd ed. (1927), p. 156.

of voluntary effort. By that time much progress had been made, although late in the day, in the educational field.

Other matters came to the local authority and its budget at a much earlier date than education. Public health was not more important than primary education in the early nineteenth century. But the first great Parliamentary battle over health and the sanitation of the towns was won, not lost, by the reformers. This was just about the time when (in 1848) the contest over education was being relinquished, because, as Peel's Home Secretary, Sir James Graham, observed, 'religion, the keystone of education, is in this country the bar to its progress'.[1]

The state of public health had been a matter of deep concern to medical men, especially in the North of England, before the end of the eighteenth century. The men and women who moved into the towns brought with them the primitive sanitary standards of the countryside, where a good deal could be neglected with relative impunity which was fatal in the crowded and infectious conditions of urban life. The traditions of the towns themselves, judged by modern standards, were and had been for centuries exceedingly bad. Epidemic and endemic disease formed an extraordinarily important part of the history of almost all towns from their earliest days. The modest improvements in paving, lighting, cleansing and watering brought about during the eighteenth century and paid for out of local rates under special legislation were not equal to the needs of their rapid growth. The rate of deaths in the towns rose in the 1820's, although it may have been affected by unemployment and by diminished earnings among the very poor as well as by bad living conditions. The first outbreak of cholera—a disease of dirt, since it is intimately connected with bad sanitation and above all with drinking water contaminated by sewerage—was in 1831-2, when the outbreak spread from Russia. There were renewed outbreaks in 1848-9 and 1853-4; the last was in 1865-6. The first cholera visitation led to the creation of local boards of health and even the passage of an act of Parliament to make payment of the necessary rate compulsory. But the boards were suffered to lapse, when the worst was over. What brought permanent improvement and a change in policy was a rise in the rate of deaths from typhus in the poorer districts of London in 1838. This led to an official inquiry by the three

[1] C. S. Parker, *Life and Letters of Sir James Graham*, vol. 1 (1907), p. 339.

medical men, Drs Arnott, Kay and Southwood Smith, and a report by Edwin Chadwick, the Secretary to the Poor Law Commissioners. The Commissioners' immediate interest was narrow and financial; a high degree of destitution and persistent expenditure on public relief tended to go with a bad state of public health. It was Dr Blomfield, the Bishop of London, who suggested that the inquiry be extended to the whole country and so helped to bring to birth one of the memorable documents of the nineteenth century, Edwin Chadwick's *Report on the Sanitary Condition of the Labouring Population* of 1842. By this time, public health was coming to be a matter of public discussion and Chadwick's labours began to overlap with those of other men, notably Lord Ashley and Dr Southwood Smith.

The task in dealing with public opinion was twofold. In the first place, educated people had to be persuaded to accept ideas and knowledge which were as novel to them as to anyone else. The elements of sanitation were so neglected even in the houses of the great that a too-outspoken report upon Buckingham Palace by the scientist Lyon Playfair in the 1840's had to be suppressed.[1] Secondly, the known principles and methods of public sanitation had to be applied upon a scale which was bound to bring them into conflict with many individual and local interests. Edwin Chadwick's report of 1842 was an outspoken attack upon the interests, as well as a description and analysis of existing conditions. His main argument was clear, however, and needed no technical knowledge to understand. Disease was more fatal than war; it was the result, for the most part, of bad sanitation; and this was preventable by public action.

Nevertheless, action was deferred until after the Corn Law repeal. A first bill miscarried; the second formed the Public Health Act of 1848. The main purpose of this law was to impose common standards upon local authorities and private persons through the advice and supervision of a central authority, the General Board of Health. It was suitably small, consisting of Lord Morpeth, the First Commissioner of Woods and Forests, an amiable man of the world as president, with Lord Ashley and Chadwick; but it had no responsible minister in Parliament. The board could act only on the petition of the ratepayers or where the death-rate rose above a given figure, when it could establish a local public health authority.

[1] Wemyss Reid, *Memoirs of Lyon Playfair* (1899), chapter v, p. 94.

In municipalities, the town council became the health authority and might appoint a medical officer of health, although this was not obligatory. London's problems of sewage and water-supply were left to be dealt with by separate legislation.

Many towns, both corporate and unincorporate, had never sought powers to deal with health by private legislation, as the more enlightened districts had done. The effect of the Act was to widen the powers of the local authorities considerably, if they chose to take advantage of it. Between 1848 and 1853, 284 towns applied for the Board's intervention and 182 of them, with a population of 2,100,000, were brought under the provisions of the Act. Surveys of 126 towns had been completed or were in progress; schemes of public works, based on the surveys, had been drawn up for 70 towns. It was known that by suitable action, the death-rate even in working-class districts could be reduced from 30 to 13 a thousand; this set the aims of the more ardent reformers.[1]

At this point, political opinion wearied of well-doing. The second cholera epidemic was over; many men, landlords, undertakers, contractors, members of town corporations, found their peace and their interests disturbed; and the Board, particularly Chadwick, had not been tactful. The Board, which had been set up in the first place for five years, was wound up and its powers distributed between the Privy Council and the Home Office, acting through their Medical Officer, Sir John Simon. A long and lamentable absence of political interest followed until in 1871 the new Local Government Board took over these duties. The Public Health Act of 1875 was the beginning of the modern code of public health law. But no centralized authority charged solely with public health questions existed after 1854 until the Ministry of Health was set up in 1918. The duties of the Local Government Board included, appropriately enough according to mid-century opinion, the administration of the Poor Law and it treated this as more important.

Edwin Chadwick, despite many failings as a man, a politician and a colleague, probably had a better grasp of what organized administration could do for the community than any other Englishman of the first half of the century. His reward was that

[1] R. A. Lewis, *Edwin Chadwick and the Public Health Movement* (1952), pp. 339–40. But on the views of what was possible, see also Sir John Clapham, *Economic History of Modern Britain*, vol. II (1932), p. 440.

he had been put on the shelf by his countrymen, at the age of fifty-four. Yet it was mainly owing to him that 'the sanitary idea' took root in Victorian Britain and its modest achievement can be recorded. The crude death-rate in England and Wales fell between the 1850's and the 1880's, remaining slightly better than other Western European death-rates. It did not fall as fast as it might have done 'if administration had kept pace with knowledge and the law'[1] and the infant death-rate remained almost constant. But the towns had become habitable, in a sense that they had not been fifty or a hundred years before.

The policy of 'thorough', which was Chadwick's way, could not have been carried to a conclusion in public health without an attack at some time or other on low standards of housing. There was support for this in instructed opinion in the 1840's, among men so opposed in general outlook as Lord Ashley, the Tory peer, and Nassau Senior, the Whig economist. The building industry was one of the largest industries in the country and it succeeded in housing the enormous Victorian increase in population. But the scale of enterprise and the methods of many builders must bear their share of responsibility for the bad housing that was run up, not in working-class quarters only, but there above all, as the towns grew. The want of housing law to prevent or correct evils was serious. Parliament was slow to admit any public responsibility. The common lodging-house, which was of some importance in a society of mobile and insanitary habits, had come under regulation, thanks to Lord Shaftesbury, in 1851. Model dwellings, made to pay, were being put up in London by George Peabody and others in the 1860's. Octavia Hill, a grand-daughter of Southwood Smith, who did not accept the proposition that working-class housing must either be unprofitable or wretched, purchased her first houses for improvement, with John Ruskin's aid and blessing, in 1865. The housing laws of 1866 and 1875 first made it possible for local authorities to compel landlords to put insanitary property in order and to condemn, demolish and reconstruct whole sections of a town. Clearance schemes in the cities, such as Birmingham and Liverpool, were undertaken on a large scale. The growth of municipal financing and development of water, gas and electricity services after 1880 were opening new possibilities in the building of cities. Long

[1] Sir John Clapham, op. cit. vol. II, p. 440.

after the legislation of the 1870's, however, the towns remained unwilling to put up houses themselves even when they pulled old houses down; house-building became a municipal service between the two World Wars. The first town and country planning act was not passed until 1909 and then in almost useless form.

The history of housing in the nineteenth century was redeemed from complete failure by local energy and private initiative, especially among the wealthier classes. The failure to give shape and decency to the industrial town, especially in its working-class and lower middle-class quarters, was none the less a national disaster, as bad as losing a major war, and the consequences were visited far and wide upon society. The rapid growth of thoroughly bad housing conditions was particularly evident in such parts of the country as Scotland, Tyneside and London. The failure was the more dismal because the island was becoming crowded as other countries were not, and by contrast with the more successful policies of housing and urban development in other States such as Germany.

As late as the 1870's, Joseph Chamberlain in Birmingham could run a political campaign and a successful mayoralty (1871–3) on the need for a city to be paved and supplied with water and gas. The public which was so slow in reconciling itself to elementary sanitary requirements and expenditures was able to boast few compensations in the way of the amenities and the pleasures of life. Nothing is more remarkable in that age than the contrast between the houses and the gardens, the literature, the art and the science which well-to-do and educated men enjoyed privately, and the low standards of collective enjoyment. Legislation was required to give great cities the powers to provide the parks, libraries, museums and picture galleries which wealthy men had long collected and enjoyed for themselves. Until 1850 it was not possible to spend public money on these things, and it was not until the second half of the century that they came to form a regular part of the budget of the towns.

The awakening of civic pride and consciousness had been painfully slow, but it was abundant when it came. The reform of the municipalities in 1835 was less important than a widening and deepening of public interests among the middle classes. Town government lay in the hands of the ratepayers until 1867; after that date it rested upon household suffrage. It was not until 1888 that-elected county councils and county borough councils replaced the ancient government of the counties by the justices of the peace. Six years later, the urban and rural district councils and the parish councils were created. All were based upon direct popular election, so creating a wholly new structure of local government. Down to the last quarter of the century, local government had been seriously wanting in the machinery of administration to cope with big problems of health, education and such matters. From 1888 onwards, such machinery was beginning to grow.

The lack of institutions had been, however, no more serious than the want of will to use them. The reform of the municipalities in 1835 was far from bringing into public service an immediate flow of public-spirited and broad-minded men. The new middle classes had much to learn about the business of government and even the need for it. Incapable and stupid cliques dominated much of town life for years after 1835. It was not until late in the 1860's that a powerful school of municipal reformers arose in Birmingham, which taught that a city ought to be a civilizing force, not a mere place to sleep and work in.[1] Their ideas passed on to Joseph Chamberlain and the radicals of the 1870's. The lateness of development in the Midland city could be paralleled in many other towns. The middle classes of the late nineteenth century were different men from those of its early years. They had had to live down much indifference, corruption and narrow-mindedness and, of course, much still remained. The inflow of working-class votes and representatives into local government brought about striking changes, not least in the largest of cities, London. A great age of local government followed, in the years 1880–1913, the comparative indifference of early and mid-Victorian times.

CENTRAL GOVERNMENT AND ITS INCOME

Much has been said about the towns and cities because they mirrored faithfully the new state of social forces and ideas in the country. From them, too, were to come the great social movements of the next era. The rise in local authority revenues, whether from rates and taxes or from loans from £36 million in the year 1867–8 to £101 million in 1897–8[2] represented an

[1] For these men, see C. Gill and A. Briggs, *History of Birmingham*, vol. 1, (1952), pp. 377–82.
[2] G. R. Porter, *Progress of the Nation* (1912), p. 645.

important change in public finance, for no sums on this scale for local use had ever been raised before. Furthermore, now that local authority expenditures were becoming large for the first time, their effect on general economic activity began to deserve consideration. In 1886, as President of the Local Government Board, Joseph Chamberlain urged municipal relief work upon London and the other large towns, during the unemployment of that year. This was a return to the Elizabethan idea that relief should be provided to unemployed people in return for work provided at public expense. But to some it suggested that public works might also have a part to play in smoothing out those fluctuations of employment which were caused by the rise and fall of private investment. More was to be heard of this view later on, for it raised difficult questions of what the relations ought to be between private and public investment and between the state and its citizens.

The proportion of the national income withdrawn from private hands for local government use was of course always much smaller than the amount raised by the central government. The army and navy, civil service, National Debt payments, postal services, collection of customs and other traditional functions of the State required large national expenditures which increased throughout the nineteenth century. The State in Victorian times was economical. It kept its expenditure down to the minimum consistent with national safety and the slowly expanding expenses of administration. It had no economic functions, the direction of resources and the creation of incomes being left in private hands. It is hardly true that the State was made in the image of the middle classes, for those classes were conspicuously investing classes. On the other hand, its functions were very much what the country gentlemen had always felt they ought to be. Their conception of government was taken over by the middle classes when they came to share legislative and executive power after 1832, and it only gradually changed, partly as the result of a real and important change of values and ideas among the middle classes themselves, partly because of the increasing power of the working-class vote after the Reform Bills of 1867 and 1884. Down to 1865, the year of the death of Lord Palmerston, the influence of the old aristocracy and of the landed interest over government remained very powerful. It continued to be a great force for many years after that date, as was amply shown by the part played by the English landed interest in the dispute in the 1880's over the Irish land reforms, which helped to split the Liberal party. In that same decade, the new working-class interest displayed itself in Parliament for the first time, although within the limits of the existing party system, without independent representation. It depended not only on the reformed franchise, but also on the growth of literacy. The election of 1880 was the first in which the overwhelming majority of the votes were cast by literate men. From that time forward, new brands of social politics and public finance were in the making.

The public finance of the mid-Victorian years represented a compromise between the conceptions of the two groups sharing effective power, that is, the landed interest and the wealthier section of the urban middle class, influenced after 1867 by the popular vote. The streak of philistine anarchism and contempt for the State so characteristic of the upper-class Englishman of the day was brilliantly analysed by a contemporary, Matthew Arnold, and appears in its more favourable aspects in the pages of Walter Bagehot.[1] These qualities which made him so good a guide in all matters of politics requiring initiative and improvisation, but dilatory and neglectful in those which needed organization and a taste for detailed administration, settled the general shape of public policy and expenditure.

One other great influence upon the sphere of public finance is to be added. This was an age in which Great Britain stood aloof from Continental affairs, took part in no European war after the Crimea, and avoided alliances with other powers. This period in her foreign policy did not come to an end until the beginning of the rise of Germany as a naval power at the end of the century and the Anglo-Japanese alliance, which marked the passing of a deliberate policy of isolation, of 1902. Despite large additions to the Empire and to the trade which the fleet had to guard, the cost of the armed services throughout this period was relatively light and almost stationary. The Crimean War drove up the army estimates, but for years afterwards they hardly changed. The army cost £14,406,000 in 1857–8, and less than £20 million in 1897–8. Expenditure on the navy rose slightly faster, being £10,590,000 in 1857–8 and not quite double that sum in 1897–8. The civil estimates, which included the grants for education, poor law, roads and health,

---

[1] See Matthew Arnold, *Culture and Anarchy* (1869) and Walter Bagehot, *The English Constitution* (1867).

were less than half of the service estimates in 1857–8, standing at £10,147,000. They rose to £23,446,000 by 1897–8.[1]

Considering the expansion of military liabilities and the growth of the national income, State expenditure was remarkably low and taxation extraordinarily light. The entire national expenditure in 1857–8 had been £68,129,000; not until the very end of the century, in 1894–5, did it rise for the first time to over £100 million. This occurred when Sir William Harcourt was Chancellor of the Exchequer, and it led to a revision of the death duties or taxes on inherited property, which now began to become a more important part of direct taxation.

Throughout the middle years of the century, the record of the income-tax shows how little the State, under the political conditions of the time, found it necessary to collect from its subjects. The income-tax had been restored temporarily at 7d. in the pound, in 1842, by Sir Robert Peel, in order to balance the budget after a long series of deficits. It was continued in 1845, to make possible reductions in the tariff which reduced for the time being the receipts of the Exchequer. Gladstone renewed it in 1853 until 1860, and it helped to pay for the Crimean War. Its existence was essential to the drastic simplification of the tariff over the next few years. In 1860, Gladstone renewed the tax, once more in association with the achievement of a free trade policy. It stood at 4d. in the pound in the middle 1860's, although it rose to 6d. later in that decade. The great trade boom in 1869–73 revived hopes of a complete abolition of income-tax; both Disraeli and Gladstone held this out to the electorate in 1874. The depressed years which followed put the idea out of court, and in the 1880's and 1890's, with rising government expenditure, the income-tax became obviously irremovable. The rate of the tax did not rise to 1s. in the pound until the Boer War (1899–1901), and it was not categorically accepted by any Chancellor of the Exchequer as a permanent part of the machinery of taxation until Asquith's day, when the basis of the tax was revised. Gladstone had always refused to consider the reform of the income-tax on the ground of its temporary nature. This attitude, although perverse, had naturally been popular. The principle of differentiation between earned and unearned income was not introduced until 1907–8 and the graduated scale of tax, requiring the larger incomes to pay a higher rate of tax, not until 1909–10.

[1] Porter, op. cit. p. 641.

Victorian taxation had been regressive at the upper end; that is to say, owing to the avoidance of graduation the burden of direct taxation fell more lightly on the big than on medium and small incomes. There were men of the propertied classes who were sensitive to the charge that great wealth did not pay enough in taxation and were willing that it should pay more. Sir William Harcourt was one of these. His revised scheme of inheritance taxes, in 1894, marked the first radical change in direct taxation since Peel, fifty-two years before, had begged the gentlemen of England, assembled in Parliament, to suffer themselves to be assessed to pay income-tax in peacetime.

Direct taxes were not the most important source of tax revenue. Indirect taxes, that is, customs and excise, had produced two-thirds of the revenue of the State in the years 1816–42 and continued to supply the greater part of it for many years after that. Direct taxes, including not only the estate duties and income-tax, but also land-tax, stamp duties and certain other sources of revenue, produced rather less than half the total revenue down to the end of the century.[1] How did this come about, considering that so much of the old structure of the customs had been swept away by the Free-Traders after 1842? The explanation lies in the rise of imports as foreign trade grew and the practice adopted by successive Chancellors of the Exchequer of concentrating the main burden of customs and excise upon a few articles in popular demand, which had the effect of raising the maximum possible revenue from customs and excise. The greater part of this revenue came from the consumption of beer, spirits, tobacco, sugar and tea. Indirect taxation, when it is levied on necessaries or what are regarded as necessaries, falls more heavily on small incomes than on medium- or large-sized incomes. The working man made a contribution to the national finances which in the aggregate was substantial, although it would be difficult to say what proportion of his income he paid.

Victorian public finance did not profess, however, to hold the balance between the classes in any except an extremely rough and ready way, while it openly shunned the idea of using taxation to redistribute wealth. It was the finance of landowners and of wealthy professional and business people, anxious to limit their liabilities and confident that they could invest to good effect every penny of their income that the State

[1] Bernard Mallet, *British Budgets, 1887–1913* (1913), p. 493, table XIV.

did not take. Under their leadership, the State became a careful spender and even a considerable saver. National expenditure per head of population in 1887–8 was still almost exactly what it had been in 1857, and the amount of the National Debt fell almost without a break from the years following the Crimean War until the end of the century. The justification of this policy, whatever may be thought of the sense of social responsibility which it showed, was strictly economic. It lay in the high rate and volume of private savings and investment and the consequent growth of capital and employment. In a century of rapid population growth, the simultaneous increase of capital at home and abroad and of employment and incomes was unprecedented and extraordinary. These were encouraged by the consideration which the State showed for the pockets and the fears of wealthy men. On the other hand, since saving was so largely a function of income, and since the investment and income-making opportunities of the Victorian age were exceptional, it seems probable that a rapid rate of advance in the national economy might still have been hoped for, even with a greater burden of taxation than the State chose to inflict. Victorian public finance is thus open to the charge that it neglected the long-term interests of the nation in favour of strict attention to economy and the annual balancing of the budget. It is scarcely an answer to this, although it is an explanation of what was done, that the conception of public interest altered profoundly between the beginning and the end of the nineteenth century, largely as the result of the work of men and women born and brought up under Victoria.

If the State did little to build up with its financial aid social and economic assets, neither did it do much to fill the gaps left by private enterprise when this grew timid, as it did in slump and depression, or to prevent the huge waste of idle resources which went on at such times. On the contrary, it became the custom to reduce public spending as far as possible at such times, so making a bad situation worse. The age of Victorian finance was an era of great opportunities lost, as well as of great economic opportunities seized. It was the sense of this failure, not only among working men but also among middle-class people, which prepared the way for new brands of social politics. These and a shattering European war were to transform old views of what it was right and possible for the State to do and the taxpayer to pay for.

Chapter XI

The Origins of the Welfare State
1880–1939

Class relationships are not the most universally significant of human relations. Historians of Britain as she was in the late nineteenth and early twentieth century may one day regard the changes which took place in the relations between the sexes and the position of the family as more important in the long run than the disputes between social classes, critical though these were at the time. What is evident from all these changes is that a slow but deep transformation of the values by which men and women judged existing institutions and codes of behaviour and by which they framed their actions and lives was already removing society from its Victorian moorings before the 1914–18 war. The war simply and immensely accelerated that process. Many things contributed towards the transformation. They included the emancipation of women, the beginnings of family limitation, and the decline of the birth-rate after 1870, which was the product of important changes in contemporary thought and feeling. A complete picture of the alteration in current modes of life would have to take into account many other matters, not least the decline in the influence of organized religion. This began to make itself felt among educated men in the universities in the 1860's, but was apparent in far wider circles twenty and thirty years later. It had effects which cannot be ignored even by the economic historian. A kind of social Darwinism influenced social and economic thought in the age that followed the publication of *The Origin of Species* (1859) and *The Descent of Man* (1871), as Benthamism had passed current in intellectual circles many years before. If Socialism enjoyed the power of a new religion in the last quarter of the century, this was to some extent due to its success in filling the gap left in some lives by the decline of traditional belief. (With other men, Socialism was a direct outcome of religious conviction.) The mental climate in which social philosophies decay or flourish was on the change. One would also have to add the consequences of the revolution in the balance of military power after the Prussian victory over France in 1871. This re-established war as an instrument of policy in Europe. It struck a blow simultaneously at British hopes of universal peace based upon free trade and at the revolutionary ideas of liberty, equality and fraternity which had for so long been identified with France. The Imperialism of the last quarter of the century was the British reaction to the altered political and strategic aspect of the world as much as it was to economic events.

The transformation of social values in Britain was part of a profound change in the public spirit of Europe, which took place in the generation or the generation and a half before the First World War. As such, it largely concerns British relations with the outside world and, in so far as it influenced or was influenced by economic conditions, may be left to a consideration of Great Britain's external economic position. The purpose of the present chapter is to examine the shift in relation to internal economic arrangements and the development of policy. Some of the important movements of the time, not least in the field of public finance, could hardly be said to have been consummated before the period between the two World Wars, perhaps even later. It will be necessary to glance from time to time beyond 1914.

In the internal history of the nation the relations between social classes appear as powerful moulders of social thought and economic opinion, as they had been in the first half of the century. The moving forces at that time had been on the one side the growing wealth, education and social and political ambition of the urban middle class, led by its most active and thoughtful members and supported, as in 1832 and 1846, by the discontent of the working men; on the other, the readiness of members of the old aristocratic and professional classes to consider, with varying degrees of welcome or resignation, a reform of existing institutions and policies. The powers at work reshaping opinion between 1880 and 1914 arose out of the unstable equilibrium of social forces created by the political compromise of the mid-century. The most important were a disillusionment on the part of middle-class critics with the kind of economy and society which prevailed and the growing strength of working-class opinion in the State. The combined effect of the two was to establish new public ends, which were bound in the course of time to influence the way in which resources were used and income distributed.

The achievements of the mid-Victorian period had never been without disbelievers. It was one of the marks of that age that it produced and tolerated social sceptics. Of these only a few ventured to challenge directly economic ideas and institutions. The fiercest and in many respects the deepest critic, Karl Marx, who lived in London from 1849 to 1883, was not a product of that society at all, but of the wholly different intellectual and social order of Central Europe. Marxian influence, though sometimes underrated, was slender in Great Britain before 1914. H. M. Hyndman's Social Democratic Federation, founded in 1881, and the Socialist League, which split from it in 1884 and numbered the artist William Morris among its founders, were early bodies dedicated to the Marxian doctrine. They produced nothing, however, resembling the conflict for and against Marx on the Continent which made the 1890's and early 1900's a turning-point for good and for evil in European thought.

The explanation was not merely that Karl Marx's main work was written in German and not translated into English until 1886, but that the British field was already occupied by a variety of powerful influences. These gave the last years of the century the same critical importance as on the Continent, but in a wholly different way. The men and ideas at work defy easy classification. Some of the most important were not directly concerned with economics at all or they were not British and touched only indirectly upon British problems. It would be a great mistake, nevertheless, to underrate the influence of men of letters such as Thomas Carlyle (1795–1881) and Matthew Arnold (1822–88), and the men whom they had taught so thoroughly to suspect the optimism of the mid-Victorians; or of the clergymen and divines who were the late representatives of the spirit of F. D. Maurice's Christian Socialists, such men as Canon Barnett (1844–1913), co-founder of Toynbee Hall and the Whitechapel Art Gallery and Henry Scott-Holland (1847–1918); or of artists, art critics and dramatists, such as William Morris (1834–96) and John Ruskin (1819–1900) and the later Galsworthy and Shaw. What these men did in their various ways was to keep alive and to extend among educated men the reserves and discontents with the accepted values of society which had never been wholly silent at any time and which became much stronger once the long reign of Victoria was over. Their influence helped to alter political ideas.

Before the educated classes could be convinced, however, that wide measures of social and economic reform were necessary, criticism had to be concentrated and defined in the economic field. This was the work of men and movements far removed for the most part from the world of literature and art, and often far apart from one another. In the 1880's and 1890's, the failure of the Irish land system and the resulting land war was one such agent. Not only did the Irish Land League become linked, through the personality of its organizer Michael Davitt (1848–1906) with the labour movements on the other side of the Irish Channel, but the Irish agitation brought about the visits to Great Britain of the American writer Henry George (1839–97), a man whose views,[1] although they sprang out of the agrarian discontents of the United States, had an immediate and astonishing influence over industrial working-class opinion in this country, giving an immense stimulus to old radical ideas of the public ownership and taxation of land. Gladstone's final instalment of Irish land legislation failed to pass in 1886, but contemporaries were as quick to perceive wide implications in the drift of his thinking as he to deny them. If Irish rents could be fixed by law, why not Scottish or English? Why not house rents too? If the Irish tenant needed protection, what about the Irish labourer or the English labourer? Lord Acton described the land legislation of his friend Gladstone as socialist; he was not disapproving of it. It was not that, tested by the meaning many men were coming to give to Socialism; but it was a long step away from the belief in the automatic benefits of laissez-faire policy applied to the Irish economy which with too many Englishmen had too long done duty for economic thinking in relation to that country.

Money and monetary policy, which along with agrarian problems became in the United States towards the end of the century a subject of furious popular politics, never roused in this country one tithe of the interest of the Irish question. The big inquiry into monetary policy in the 1880's, the Gold and Silver Commission, left expert opinion unconvinced that any serious change was required. But while the controversies on

[1] George's *Progress and Poverty* had been published in the United States in 1879 and became one of the most widely read books of the next decade.

monetary policy here and in British India between 1880 and
1914 left in the minds of some of the men concerned with them
a keen sense of the artifice and the imperfections of existing
arrangements,[1] they did not break through the level of economic
discussion since Ricardo's day to grapple with the forces controlling the volume of employment and production as a whole,
as they were to do in a later period of violently falling prices,
in the 1930's. In this country after 1900, when prices began to
rise, the question of money ceased to interest. The bimetallism
of the previous twenty years made a limited appeal to special
interests in land and in trade to the silver-using East, but it
had no perceptible influence on public opinion at large.

The towns and their industrial problems were the great
forcing grounds of new social thought. The severe trade
fluctuations of the 1880's and 1890's, especially such years of
depression as 1885–6 and 1890–5, gave an edge to discontent,
owing to the formidable unemployment they created. Public
opinion was growing more intolerant of these periodical visita-
tions of worklessness, as political life became fully democratic. Middle- and upper-class opinion came across the problem of unemployment chiefly in the form of destitution and
the need for relief. But while unemployment and how to deal
with it were questions debated with increasing vigour as time
went on, the movement of thought at the beginning of the
present century is best studied in relation to the administration
of the Poor Law as a whole. There for thinking people the
question of the distribution of wealth came up in the most direct
and practical form. Was income, under the existing system of
society, coming into the hands which most needed it, in the
right places and times, and if not, what alternative arrangements could be adopted?

Mid-Victorian opinion had had little difficulty in answering
this question in its own way. The existing system, with all its
faults, did two things by the device of free competition. On the
one hand, it set in motion and distributed the resources of
society where they were most wanted, according to market
price; on the other, it put an income into the hands of those
who owned those resources, including the great mass of those
who had nothing to sell but their hands. The great trade

---

[1] Both Alfred Marshall and the young J. M. Keynes were involved in the
Indian discussions, which were very important in their time. See R. F.
Harrod, *Life of John Maynard Keynes* (1950), chapter IV.

fluctuations had suggested to the mid-Victorian economist, J. S. Mill, that to bring about such slumps there must be considerable maldistribution of resources in the boom, owing to errors of investment on the part of capitalists. But the catastrophe of trade depression apart, it appeared to contemporaries that failure to make an income was personal failure, a sign of want of public virtue, if not of private vice. This, if it was not the universal belief of the comfortable classes, was an inference which they had been quick to draw and it had become almost a part of conventional religion and morals.

THE DEBATE ON POVERTY AND THE POOR LAW

Among educated and leisured men, the first great doubt to be thrown upon this belief came not from the writings of socialists but from new inquiry into the extent and sources of urban poverty and destitution. The social survey of leading cities in Great Britain, carried out by men such as Charles Booth and Seebohm Rowntree between 1889 and 1901, was a new kind of work in this country, although it has been so often copied since as to become commonplace. The results were deeply disturbing to respectable opinion, which it appeared had been content to found its convictions on an extensive ignorance of the facts. Booth's survey of *Life and Labour of the People in London* was the first and the most impressive. London contained in 1881 nearer four than three million people and was used to being described as the largest and wealthiest city in the world. It staged at this very time, in 1887 and 1897, the magnificent celebrations of the golden and diamond jubilees of the queen's accession. Booth, living in an age when the name of the people was often invoked in politics, might be described as the man who first asked himself, who are the people of England?[1] The attempt to answer the question truthfully, by exact description and statistics, led him into quarters of London where the wealthy and the educated seldom or never went. He found himself obliged to try to answer the further question, how many of the people he met there might be described as living in poverty? Booth's test of poverty was low by modern standards as Victorian living standards were lower than those of today and it included two classes of person: those who lived under a constant struggle to obtain the necessities of life but who might,

[1] This was Beatrice Webb's phrase: *My Apprenticeship* (1926), p. 223.

so long as they could struggle, obtain them, and those many others who lived in a state of chronic want. The result of his elaborate inquiries was to show that about 30 per cent of the population lived below his poverty line, that is, on a standard well below that of the decent home of the relatively well-paid skilled man. Nearly 10 per cent of London's people fell into his lowest class, as labourers only occasionally employed, loafers and semi-criminals. Many of them the product of 'problem families', they could not be classified even with the casual labourer who endured severe want between spells of employment or with the regular labourer whose wages were low. Daily journalism was quick to attach to them the name of 'the submerged tenth'.

A decade later, Seebohm Rowntree published the results of a similar survey at York, the significance of which was that he treated York as a representative English city of its size. The results of his more refined statistical methods corresponded closely with those of Booth for London; 28 per cent of the population of York in 1901 either never earned income sufficient to maintain their physical effectiveness or they had incomes so small that by failing to apportion their expenditure properly they fell into want. Studies of four other towns, Reading, Northampton, Stanley and Warrington, carried out by Bowley and Burnett-Hurst in 1912–13, were not readily comparable with those of Booth and Seebohm Rowntree, because of the different methods employed by the investigators. They showed nevertheless about 10 per cent of the population living in a perpetual state of chronic want and a considerably larger proportion failing to earn a wage to bring up their family in elementary decency.

The broad result of nineteenth-century economic history was that a population far larger than that of preceding centuries had been provided with an income, that much underemployment and ill-paid employment had been swept away, and that, generation by generation, many people found their way to occupations better rewarded than those of their parents. The material standard of living in Great Britain in Booth's time was better than in any other country in Europe, and incomparably higher than in the lands of long-standing poverty, such as India and the Middle East. The shock to educated opinion administered by his findings was all the greater for this. It became

[1] Seebohm Rowntree, *Poverty: a Study of Town Life* (1900).

clear that the amount and degree of poverty and destitution still existing was far greater than had been supposed; that the number of people in Great Britain who still lived in a state of extreme want was probably not inferior to the number who had so lived a hundred years before; and that this great reservoir of poverty, destitution and crime, preserved at the base of a great, rich and civilized society, was fed by constant springs.

Much of British social politics, in the half-century after Charles Booth wrote, turned upon the question of the responsibility for this condition of affairs. An effort, coming from many quarters and enlisting men and women of various creeds and philosophies, was made to remedy evils which had come to be regarded as a reproach and a menace to society. The consequent effects on the distribution of wealth and the public finances, strikingly apparent after 1914, concern us here less than the beginnings of the revolution in men's ideas. This started in the 1880's and 1890's. For a new and measured sense of the amount of poverty existing was not the only result of the work of the Booth school of social investigators. A simultaneous change in men's ideas on the causes of poverty began to carry an important section of educated opinion far away from the assumptions of the social thinking of the first half of the nineteenth century.

Charles Booth himself was partly responsible for this. He had become impressed by the importance of old age, as a cause of destitution—the unavoidable growing beyond the capacity to earn an income and beyond the ability or the willingness of others to help. This had been so in every generation, and since Elizabethan times the Poor Law had been the last dreaded resort of helpless old people. In 1906 about one-third of those in receipt of public assistance were classified as old and infirm. Poor Law administrators, from the 1890's on, were beginning to alter their treatment of old people in the workhouse; but the increasing wealth of society suggested that there was an alternative to the workhouse. Booth's proposal, which was for old age pensions, was not finally put into law until 1908, when it applied to persons over seventy. The law was both important in itself and as a step towards new methods of dealing with other causes of poverty.

These new methods were already arising. They depended largely upon the sweeping changes which had come over

10   C E H

English local government since 1888. The significance of the
formation of the county councils and county boroughs in that
year and of the urban and rural district councils in 1894 was
not only that the new forms of local government were democratic and therefore open to popular influence. They were also,
from the administrative point of view, more effective than anything which had been seen since the reforms of local government
under the Tudors. The neglect to modernize local government
in step with the development of local problems had been one of
the most serious weaknesses of post-Reform Bill England. The
rise of a new type of local government in late Victorian and
Edwardian times made many things practically possible for the
first time. Among them was a diversification and improvement
of the common services of local government, especially in education and health. This corresponded with a simultaneous improvement and diversification in the administration of the Poor
Law, in relation to destitute children, sick and mentally unsound people. A kind of dovetailing and overlapping of Poor
Law and local government services was the result. Poor Law
infirmaries grew side by side with local hospitals and asylums,
Poor Law children were educated at local schools, underfed
schoolchildren were fed by local education committees, and
local medical officers of health tackled the conditions of ill-
health and disease which had always lain at the root of much
destitution.

The number of persons concerned was considerable—in 1906,
throughout the United Kingdom, there were 237,000 children
wholly or partly on the hands of the Poor Law authorities,
probably 160,000 people receiving medical treatment, and
nearly 200,000 mental defectives.[1] It was the variety and confusion of competing agencies and the mounting cost of Poor Law
expenditure which partly accounted for the political decision
in 1905 to appoint a Royal Commission to sit upon the Poor
Law, for the first time since 1834. There was another reason
too, in contemporary slack trade and the controversy over unemployment. The men of 1834, it had sometimes been remarked
said little about the relief of children, sick and mentally defec
tive people; the principles they had laid down did not give
much assistance in that direction. Neither did they help, it wa
now beginning to be contended, in dealing with industrial un

[1] Figures from *Report of the Royal Commission on the Poor Law*, vol. III (1909)
pp. 110, 170, 234.

employment. A new attitude to the unemployed man or woman had been growing up in the twenty years before 1905. The employment at wages of the temporarily workless by local authorities was older than the nineteenth century. After 1885, it was encouraged by the Local Government Board, whose chiefs tended increasingly to recognize that relief in the workhouse was not only no remedy, but an injury to the person relieved and to society at large. The Unemployed Workmen Act of 1905, passed in the depression after the South African War, went further along this line. It aimed at taking the victims of cyclical unemployment off the Poor Law by a system of municipal public works.

Systematic investigation was beginning to show[1] how many varieties of industrial employment there were and what were the causes of some of the failures to deal with it. For municipal employment before and after 1904 was not a great success. In many trades there was seasonal unemployment; in others, including occupations so widespread as the loading and unloading of ships, employment was casual and underemployment chronic. The existence at all times of serious underemployment in particular trades and districts nullified policies intended to deal only with cyclical unemployment. Different policies appeared to be required for different diseases—here, a permanently better organization of the labour market, perhaps State-aided; there, temporary public works. Whatever was done, it appeared that the person willing to work but out of a job for no fault of his own ought to be taken off the Poor Law.

The urgent need to define or to redefine first principles in public assistance lay behind the Poor Law inquiry of 1905–9. It now blazed up into a controversy which illumined the past and the future of social thought, although it did singularly little to assist the reform of the law. The Commission, appointed to inquire both into the working of the laws relating to relief and into methods of relieving distress arising from want of employment, was largely composed of those who had taken part in the administration of the Poor Law. It also included philanthropists and social investigators such as Charles Booth and Beatrice Webb, social workers and representatives of the Charity Organization Society such as Octavia Hill and a few

[1] See, for example, Lord Beveridge, *Unemployment, A Problem of Industry* (1909) and N. B. Dearle, *Problems of Unemployment in the London Building Trades* (1908).

experienced Poor Law guardians and labour men such as
George Lansbury and Francis Chandler, all sitting together
under the chairmanship of the aristocratic politician, Lord
George Hamilton. From the first dissension was evident. After
four years of work, which was hardly too long for the task in
hand, the commission produced two separate reports, the one
signed by a majority of the Commission the other by a small
minority consisting of Russell Wakefield, later Bishop of
Birmingham, Chandler, Lansbury and Beatrice Webb, the last
named being its effective author.

The two sections of the Commission had much in common,
and if they had put forward a unanimous series of recommendations the fate of the old law would have been sealed. Both
agreed that the time had come to wind up the elected boards
of guardians and the organization adopted in 1834; both
favoured the county and the county borough as the centre of
administration of public assistance, instead of the parish or the
union of parishes; both desired the abolition of the general
mixed workhouse and the proper classification of Poor Law
institutions. They also agreed that the indiscriminate application of the principle of deterrence and the fastening of a stigma
to the mere receipt of relief was a mistake. The change of view
in matters of principle was particularly noticeable in the
attitude towards unemployment. Both sections agreed that
relief to children and the sick could and ought to be given under
conditions which were not chiefly designed to frighten people
off public assistance. But they also went on to contemplate an
attack upon unemployment by a system of employment exchanges, where vacancies could be notified and qualifications
sifted, and by public works. The majority were prepared to
consider some sort of unemployment insurance.

Notwithstanding this wide measure of agreement, the Commission failed to submit unanimous advice. The reform of the
law was postponed in consequence for another twenty years.
Not until 1929, by the Local Government Act of that year,
were the boards of guardians abolished and their duties and
powers relating to the 'non-able-bodied poor' in need of relief
transferred to the counties and the county boroughs. These
authorities proceeded to deal with children and the sick on
lines which tended increasingly to remove them from the circle
of the Poor Law. Meanwhile, important changes in the public
handling of assistance to unemployed persons followed the

1914–18 war. In 1909, a beginning had been made with the system of employment exchanges. Because of the formidable amount of unemployment after 1919 they tended to become centres of unemployment relief, instead of bringing employer and the seeker for employment together as had been intended. When the Ministry of Labour was formed in 1916, it took over all labour questions and arrangements including the exchanges from the Board of Trade. The final step in detaching the unemployed from the Poor Law occurred as a result of the great trade depression of 1929–33. The Unemployment Act of 1934 established a central board under the general control of the Minister of Labour to give public assistance to unemployed persons not covered by national unemployment insurance, instead of throwing them on the local authorities and the Poor Law. It was in this way that the present system of public assistance came into being.

The long delay in reform was due to the refusal to act of John Burns, the head of the Local Government Board in 1909. It was also the result of the clash of personalities and ideas on the Commission. The underlying failure to agree arose, not on questions of organization or administrative structure, but on a deep sense of differing values. The minority, absorbing what appeared to be the teaching of social investigators such as Charles Booth, although he was not of their school, regarded the low incomes of the destitute as the product of social conditions, rather than of personal responsibility and failure. Poverty was its own chief cause. Their recommendations were framed accordingly. They aimed to establish, through education, pensions, public medical services and so forth, a minimum standard of living, a kind of grid or bottom to society, to prevent individuals falling, by no fault of their own, into a measureless pit of want and misery. They were prepared to abolish the Poor Law and dissolve it in what one of them called a policy of the national minimum. They aspired, that is to say, to correct one of the gravest weaknesses of nineteenth-century society, its failure to prevent destitution or relieve distress in a manner which seemed to the majority of people fair and equitable. They opposed themselves to the willingness of the wealthy and comfortable to look upon poverty and destitution as moral failure, if not a crime.

The policy of the national minimum arose out of the nascent social science and the local government activities of the time.

But it ran up against serious objections, by virtue of assumptions which it shared with its opponents. The object of the national minimum policy was to save human personality from being broken and crushed by forces too strong for it. But the personality worth saving is free, in the sense of freely choosing. Given a great extension of social and economic aid to prevent destitution arising, how was the free citizen to be preserved? Without the independent personality, must not the whole system of mutual obligations upon which the new kind of society would depend for its existence sooner or later decay?

Considerations of this kind lay in the background of the dispute over what in form was the Poor Law but in reality was the whole future of social policy.[1] Personal conflicts exaggerated the difference over principles. There was no practical philosopher on the Commission sufficiently comprehensive and profound to reconcile the differences and to clothe an agreed doctrine in systematic proposals; nor perhaps was political opinion ripe for them. It was a misfortune for Great Britain that in the next three decades, which were years of exceptionally fast and painful social change, she never enjoyed the substantial advantages which a thorough and thoughtful remodelling of her social policies before the First World War would have given her. Her social legislation, by tradition empirical, remained piecemeal, and she lost something as well as gained much in the result.

SOCIAL LEGISLATION AND THE IDEA OF A NATIONAL MINIMUM

Within a year or two of the Commission's reporting, legislation was introduced which aimed at the national minimum by a new road or at least one which had received only the moderate support of the Commission. This was the National Insurance Act of 1911. The idea of insuring the chief risks of working-class life had been preached in England as early as the 1880's by an amiable clergyman, Canon Blackley,[2] without success. It

---

[1] Beatrice Webb, *Our Partnership* (1948) and Una Cormack, *The Welfare State: Loch Memorial Lecture* (1953), give fruitfully contrasting views of the historic debate on the Poor Law.

[2] Blackley's compulsory state insurance scheme had been examined by a House of Commons committee in 1885-7 and turned down. The idea of compulsory insurance and of old age pensions was much older than his day and goes back to the eighteenth century.

owed its adoption in this country largely to German example and experience, for national insurance against sickness, accident, invalidity and old age had been introduced into the German Empire by Prince Bismarck between 1883 and 1888. Despite the jealousy between the two peoples, the pattern of German social and economic policies was influential in this country in the early 1900's. There was a foundation to build on in the mutual insurance run by a multitude of friendly and provident societies. What the State did in 1911 was to step in to the aid of a system of voluntary insurance against sickness and funeral expenses, which neither covered everybody nor worked perfectly, and subsidize it, to the extent that it could be made to fit in to a national health insurance scheme. This scheme, enlarged by later legislation, included by 1927 between fourteen and fifteen million people, organized in the societies approved under the act or contributing through the post office. By that time, several important developments in the field of public health policy had followed the original national health in- surance scheme of 1911. They included sanatorium treatment for tuberculosis and the growth, after 1921, of maternity and child welfare work.

The Pensions Act of 1908 and the national health scheme of 1911 represented a long step away, not only from the Poor Law system created in 1834, but from the traditions of many centuries. They were, however, in line with similar develop- ments in other countries both new and old about the same time; New Zealand, for example, had had public old age pensions since 1898. What was more original was the adoption of insurance against unemployment, under the same National Insurance Act of 1911. Here the State, instead of subsidizing the trade unions, which paid out-of-work money to their members and notified them of vacancies, began a new insurance scheme, to which the wage-earner, the employer and the State all contributed. The scheme covered at first only a small although important part of the working population; the two and a quarter million people engaged in the big fluctuating industries of building, engineering, shipbuilding, vehicle con- struction, iron-founding and saw-milling. In 1916 and 1920, it was extended to include all wage-earners except those engaged in agriculture, in domestic service and certain per- manent situations—about eleven million persons in all.

While the system of unemployment insurance was being

built up, a deep and long-lasting change was coming over the state of employment itself. This was the result largely of the special economic difficulties of the period between the First and the Second World Wars. We do not know what unemployment existed at any given time in the nineteenth century. Those trade unions—mainly of the highly skilled workers, such as the shipbuilders and engineers—who kept records of the men to whom they paid out-of-work money described about 5·3 per cent of their membership as unemployed in the difficult years of the 1880's, about 4·5 per cent in the more active period between 1900 and 1913. These were a relatively small group of trades. It may be that, taking all trades that were later insured against unemployment into account, there were about 6·5 per cent of workers out of work on the average in the 1880's and about 5·5 per cent in 1900–13. But unemployment in the 1920's, after 1922 and before the depression of 1929–32, was about twice as high as it had been in the early 1900's.[1] The effect on the unemployment insurance scheme was temporarily to deprive it of reality as thousands of men ran out of benefit in long years of unemployment. A scheme designed to meet cyclical and short-term unemployment had run full tilt into the severe problems created by changes in the structure of industry. Great staple industries contracted and new ones rose only slowly to take their place. The setting up of the Unemployment Assistance Board in 1930, referred to above, was the result of the effort to make the unemployment insurance fund solvent again after this dismal experience.

By 1930 the forces of fluctuation were making themselves felt, in addition to the evils of structural change. This terrible double experience opened a new chapter in the history of the attitude towards unemployment. Before 1914 it had appeared enough to prevent large masses of the population from being forced from time to time below the surface of things by the movement of economic forces. To do this some redistribution of incomes was necessary, but the provision of employment and income remained the business of private investment. In the 1930's a break with nineteenth-century economic thought began with the perception that the maintenance of a satisfactory volume of investment and employment might sometimes require vigorous action by the State. But it was not until the

[1] The estimates are those of Sir John Clapham, *Economic History of Modern Britain*, vol. III (1938), pp. 543–4.

next decade that government explicitly assumed a responsibility for the preservation of a 'high and stable level of employment',[1] and in doing so, a certain responsibility for incomes. This was the final unexpected chapter in the history of the idea of the national minimum, when it came to be recognized that the legislation of social security built up since 1911 required for its completion and safety an employment policy too.

The climate of the 1930's was very far from the atmosphere of the period just before the First World War. The booming trade of the years 1909–13, together with the long economic expansion of the past, made any concern with the provision of employment and income seem superfluous. In the early 1900's the return of a state of high industrial and trading activity encouraged the penetration of social policies by the idea of a national minimum of leisure, education and living conditions. Other examples of the trend might be picked out from the legislation of that era, besides the Insurance Act of 1911; for example, the Coal Mines (Eight Hours) Act of 1908, the Trade Boards Act of 1909, and the Miners' Minimum Wage Act of 1912. The first applied to the coal-mines only and it disappointed the miners, because it did not include within the eight-hour day the time spent in descending or ascending the shaft. It even had the effect of lengthening hours for some men, although it shortened the day for the industry as a whole. This was not the first law to limit the hours of male adult labour, for an Act of 1893 had given the Board of Trade certain restricted powers to deal with excessive overtime on the railways. But the demand for an eight-hour day had become a kind of test of advanced working-class thinking in the 1880's and 1890's, and legislation affecting so large a number of men as the miners, who themselves had found it difficult to agree[2] on the need for a limited day, was an impressive move. The Shops Act of 1911, securing a weekly half-holiday for shop assistants, was in its own way hardly less significant of an altered trend of thinking.

[1] The phrase comes from the White Paper on *Employment Policy* (Cmd. 6527), issued by the Coalition Government in May 1944, during the Second World War.

[2] A difference of opinion between the miners of Northumberland and Durham, where a shorter working day for adult males had already been secured by local agreement with the owners, and the rest of the miners' unions kept the former outside the Miners' Federation until 1908, when the passage of the Act closed the dispute.

The Trade Boards Act, like so many other things, arose out of Charles Booth's inquiries into poverty in London and the political campaign which followed against the 'sweat shops' of the East End, in such trades as tailoring. The out-work industries of London, where work was contracted out to workers in their own homes, were far from being the only such trades in the kingdom. The same evils tended to prevail in them all: low earnings; extremely long hours; primitive and dangerous sanitary conditions. Between the 1880's and 1909, political opinion had come round to the idea of public regulation of wages in these trades. It was over eighty years since Parliament had abolished, in 1824, the acts which authorized the London magistrates to fix the wages of the silk-weavers of Spitalfields. Now provision was made for the fixing of minimum wages in certain selected trades. The first to be taken in hand were the hand-forged chainmaking of the South Staffordshire Black Country; the paper and cardboard box trade of London; and the widespread and well-known ready-made and bespoke tailoring. Shirtmaking, the conditions of which had roused the protest of Thomas Hood's *Song of the Shirt* many years before, and some other trades were added later. The Trade Boards did a good deal to improve wages and hours and to remove cheating and oppression.

The circumstances under which minimum wages came to be fixed for the coal-miners were different. The workers in the out-work trades were unorganized; the miners, on the other hand, had been organized for years. Since 1888 their Federation had been striving to bring to an end the system by which wages were settled by the course of coal prices, irrespective of proceeds, and to replace it by a legal minimum wage ensuring to the miner a reasonable living income, independent of the fluctuations of the coal market. The issue came up in a local form in South Wales in 1912, but it led to a national strike. The Minimum Wage Act was passed to bring the strike to an end. The system which the Act brought into being resembled in general outlines the Trade Boards—minimum wages being settled for each coal-mining district by district boards, with independent chairmen, who in practice acted as arbitrators. A somewhat similar system of county wage tribunals came into existence in agriculture in 1924 after the First World War. The putting into effect of a system of minimum wages in these two large industries, which had been markedly intolerant, both of collective bargaining and State regulation of any kind, showed how fast and far the tide of Victorian and Edwardian social philosophy was ebbing under the pull of new forces.

These forces were not to be summed up wholly in the altering mood of what were still, despite the growing democratization of politics, the ruling classes. The change in tone among those classes was certainly remarkable between say the Liberalism of Gladstone, who left politics in 1894, and that of Asquith, who became Prime Minister in 1908. Important sections of upper-class opinion became divorced from Liberalism altogether after 1880 and accepted varieties of Socialist doctrine. The State Socialism of the Webbs and others in the Fabian Society, founded in 1889, and the Gild Socialism of A. R. Orage and the Coles after 1911, were both strands in the still rare Socialism of the educated classes. Both, particularly the first, had an influence upon a new political party, the Labour party. This entered politics in competition with the older Liberal and Conservative parties in the early years of the century and began to make itself felt as a small but active Parliamentary force after 1906. The rise of the Labour party about that time, however, is to be accounted for less in terms of middle-class Socialism than in the careers of two working-class politicians of remarkable personality, the Scotsman Keir Hardie and the Englishman George Lansbury.[1] They did the spadework and laid the foundations on which a party could be built. The work of these men gave organized political reality to the conviction, felt by many who did not share their specific beliefs, that the working man and his family and their material, intellectual and spiritual needs had become the supreme problem in the State.

The altered trend of economic and social policy was immediately a political phenomenon. But it was connected with important changes in industry and in the organization of the trade unions. The movements of Socialist thought and the legislative activity in Parliament were both related to industrial events. There was a reciprocity between the industrial and political spheres. Much of the pressure for legislation came from the unions; and it has been often pointed out that when the

[1] See H. M. Pelling, *The Origins of the Labour Party, 1880–1900* (1954), published since this was written.

reforming zeal of the Liberal government seemed to have spent itself after 1911, working-class hopes tended to be transferred to the unions which then opened a new chapter in their history.

The explanation is probably superficial which looks wholly either to Parliamentary developments or to industrial organization to account for the marked turning away from Victorian economic and social ideas in the years just before the First World War. The trend of opinion in the upper classes is perhaps best seen in the literature of the time, for example, in the plays of George Bernard Shaw and John Galsworthy and the novels of H. G. Wells rather than in the specific doctrines of the Fabians or the legislation of a Liberal Parliament. This literature was increasingly critical of conventional purposes and arrangements; so much so that one might say the thought of the age had stumbled against the injustice which lies at the root of all organized society. This was not the mere satiety of an age of immense material achievement; it was also the conclusion of a century which had seen great advances in human freedom and the thinking of men who had come to be profoundly impressed by what remained to be done.

The disillusionment and the discontent of educated men was matched by the restlessness of classes who were new upon the political scene. This dated back, like the discontent of the educated, to a time before 1900. As the first half of the nineteenth century had seen something like a revolt, in 1846, of capital against land, so its last quarter saw something that resembled the beginnings of an uprising of labour against capital. The main roots of this were to be found in the substantial improvement of working-class conditions in the middle and late Victorian age, particularly after 1880. The rise of real wages, especially as the cost of living declined in the long price fall; the shortened working day; the spread of primary education; the widened franchise; the growth of new loyalties in factory and mine and of a new sense of community in the towns—all combined to produce a working-class culture stronger and more independent than had existed before. There was a development of personalities and a flow of ideas, much of which found its way into industrial and national politics.

Industrially, this was the period of what came to be called the 'New Unionism'. This was marked by the organization of unskilled men, such as the London dockers, whose successful strike in 1889 was recognized at the time as opening a new era in industrial relations; the tendency, which went with the organization of the unapprenticed workers, to organize on lines of the industry rather than the craft in what came to be known as industrial unions; the penetration of Socialist ideas into the unions; a cultivation by trade union leaders of political interests; and a new type of leadership represented by the three organizers of the London dockers, John Burns, Ben Tillett and Tom Mann, and by Will Thorne of the London gasworkers, compared with the leadership of an earlier generation—that of a Henry Broadhurst, a John Wilson, or a Thomas Burt. The difference was as much a difference of generations as anything —the political interests of trade union leaders were old, it was the type of their politics which was new—and the foundations for a new advance of trade unionism had been laid in the earlier period. A rapid development was the result which created a larger, more highly organized, more political trade union world by 1900.

After 1901, the trade unions found themselves in serious difficulties with the law, owing to the Taff Vale judgement. The issue in that case, which arose out of a strike on a small South Wales railway, was the civil liability of a trade union for acts of its members carried out in furtherance of a trade dispute. The state of the law in this connection was believed by many, including sound lawyers, to have been settled in favour of the trade unions by the legislation of 1871–6. This assumption overlooked developments in the law since that date, especially the theory of the representative action, which had prepared the way for the Taff Vale decision by making it possible to call into court an unincorporated association, such as a trade union was.

The Taff Vale case stood in the way of trade union expansion for some years and stimulated the trade unionist's interest in current politics, until the judgement was reversed by the Trade Disputes Act, passed by the Liberal government in 1906. By that year, a new phase of economic development was on its way. The rising employment and incomes of 1906–13 were favourable to trade union growth, while the steep upward movement in the cost of living after 1911 and the relatively slow change in wage-rates made many a man eager for union, and for what the union could do for him, who had never been eager before. The period before the First World War, like the late 1880's and early 1890's, was a time of rapid trade union expansion, bringing membership up from under two millions in 1905 to just below four millions in 1913, the year of maximum trade boom. The war, which put a premium on organization, and the post-war boom which followed it doubled the 1913 figure by 1920.

The trade unions can be seen in these years climbing up to their present position as regards strength and universality of membership. It was after 1890 that the unions began to have a shaping effect on the wages structure of industry, especially by their preference for day-rates over piece-rates and their development of conventional practices and written agreements. These accessions of strength were not regarded otherwise than with deep distrust by industrial managements and by the State. The railway companies, for example, refused either to recognize or to negotiate with the railway unions down to 1914, and both before and after the First World War there was a disposition among many employers to regard the new-found power of the unions as an invitation to a trial of strength—a willingness to fight which was met half-way by some unions. The mistrust among politicians and lawyers was proved by a House of Lords' judgement on appeal in the Osborne case in 1909. This judgement, arising out of an action brought by W. V. Osborne, a railwayman, against the Amalgamated Society of Railway Servants, had the effect of barring the use of trade union funds for political purposes. The question of law turned upon the Trade Union Act of 1876 and the old question of the corporate or unincorporate status of trade unions. The new judgement had important political effects. It broke a practice which had grown up since the Reform Act of 1867 and had the immediate result of cutting off the new Labour party from its main source of funds. Not until the Trade Union Act of 1913 was the Osborne decision practically reversed by the provision that trade union funds could be so used except where trade union members definitely contracted out of political activities. So the law stood until the passage of the Trade Unions Act and Trade Disputes Act of 1927, just after the General Strike, and so it became again when that law was repealed in 1946.

If the trade unions were looked upon with suspicion by employers, politicians and men of law, so too did the trade union leaders mistrust the industrial, legal and political world they were growing up in. Perhaps they had good reason to do so, for they were often offered occasion. At any rate, it is only in the light of hostility between the industrial and political worlds which was deep and mutual, and the immediate discouragement to political action by the Osborne judgement, that we can understand the rapid spread among trade unionists in the years just before the First World War of doctrines for which the State, as well as the employer, was the enemy.

Syndicalism, which taught a vision of the world from which the State was to disappear after a General Strike, where successful revolutionary workers would administer their own affairs through the trade unions, was not solely or even mainly a British doctrine. It had its most distinguished exponents on the Continent, such as the Frenchman, Georges Sorel. But the theory of what came to be known as 'direct action' had its day in this country, under the favouring influence of many circumstances, not least the rapid progress of the trade unions in membership and authority between 1911 and 1926.

Doctrine of various brands and hues seems, however, to have had less to do than the day-to-day complexities and necessities of industrial politics with the emergence of an important alliance among trade unions in 1914. Experience seemed to suggest that men were stronger if they acted together. The coal-miners, the railwaymen and the transport workers came to a resolution just before the war broke out to negotiate their future wage agreements in association, terminating and renegotiating their agreements at the same times and holding in the background the threat of a joint strike. The 'Triple Alliance', as it came to be known, broke down in 1921 among post-war industrial disputes and was probably always less important for what it was than for what it was supposed to be, both by its friends and its enemies. But into the disturbed years before the First World War it cast the shadow of the coming General Strike of 1926.

The two decades before that event, from the Trade Disputes Act of 1906 onwards, hang together in trade union history. They formed a period of expansion and of growing conflict, the outcome of which was obscure. He would have been a bold prophet who had guessed, in 1914, the uneasy combination of trade unions, employers' associations and the State, by which industry has since come to be governed. The disputes between the unions and the employers in a long series of strikes after 1911, and the possibility of disputes between the unions and the State, suggested no peaceful settlement of outstanding problems. A kind of *stasis* or standstill, a long wasting struggle of embattled forces, seemed possible.

On this note of deep uncertainty a century closed which had seen greater material prosperity than any other in British history and which had trusted mainly to men's sense of their material advantage to reconcile them to the new order of society. A true spokesman of the age was the Polish seaman turned novelist, Joseph Conrad, who in the years 1903–4 was writing the imaginary history of the Gould concession in the state of Costaguana. He penned these disillusioning words of Dr Monygham to Mrs Gould: 'There is no peace and no rest in the development of material interests. They have their law and their justice. But it is founded on expediency... without the continuity and the force that can be found only in a moral principle.' His story of *Nostromo* was not only about South America.

BETWEEN THE TWO WORLD WARS

An historian may be excused from attempting, at a late stage in his book, a social history of the inter-war years, even in the sphere where social is related to economic development. Much of the history of the period is in the true sense unknown, in that the abundant evidence has never yet been subjected to scrutiny and judgement. The remarks which follow are merely by way of a pendant to what has already been said of pre-1914 events. They are chiefly intended to draw attention to some of the continuities between the years before and after the First World War.

History is, however, not all continuity and the slow growth of social character. It may be invaded from time to time by crises such as erupt into the lives both of individuals and nations. A crisis opened this period. Whether the First World War and the Russian Revolution of 1917 formed a single crisis or whether they should be regarded separately, whether the war introduced the revolution or whether the revolution was only a chapter in the history of the war, are questions which we fortunately do not need to consider. Whatever the relationship between them, it can hardly be denied that together they constituted an outburst of violence of unparalleled magnitude or that they introduced a new era in European history. A time of revolution and counter-revolution began on the Continent, such as had not been known since the wars of religious confession in the middle of the seventeenth century, and with few signs of an eighteenth century-like age of enlightenment and philosophy to follow.

British social development was not and could not be un-influenced by the currents flowing so strongly in Europe. It would be impossible to write the intellectual and spiritual history of the inter-war years without reference to them. Yet the course of her social life remained less broken and less effected by them than that of any other of the European great powers who had gone to war in 1914. It continued to develop to a very large extent under the directing energy of values and institutions which were native and traditional and of changes in these which require to be explained in terms of her past history and altering domestic conditions.

Among domestic conditions of which the economic historian can take cognizance, the revolution in the use of industrial resources, referred to in a previous chapter,[1] must take a high place. Great Britain was the oldest industrial State in Europe. Her social history a century before had been deeply marked by the early processes of industrialization, with all that that meant for her people in the countryside and the town, in the field and in the factory; and by the gradual assembling of the factors of industrial production over eighty years in a pattern which remained substantially unchanged over a large part of the nineteenth century. Now, when the economic development of the world was entering upon a new phase, her social life was deeply distressed and torn by the dissolution of that pattern and the need to reorganize her industrial resources upon new lines.

The spirit of change was felt in many small alterations in the organization of shop, office, workshop, factory and mine. These were far more important to many persons than the great changes in the alternative uses of labour and capital which were going on at the same time and which were often out of their sight, as they were out of their mind. But many individuals, as we have seen in discussing unemployment, were vitally affected by the huge shifts of aggregate resources from one industry to another and by the enormous economic and social wastes which attended the process.

These wastes were especially perceptible in the 1920's, when much in British politics and industrial relations becomes

[1] Above, chapter IX.

unintelligible without reference to the decline of the staple industries. The contraction of one of the largest, coal-mining, and the long-drawn-out conflict between the mine-owner and the miner, each struggling for position in a world which was shifting under his feet, fired the train of the General Strike in 1926. That ambiguous event owed much to the building up of trade union organization before 1914 and to the spread of the theory of direct action; something perhaps to fears created by the Russian Revolution; but much immediately to a shift in the economic conditions of the country of a kind which could not have been foreseen and which caught both the organized employers and the working classes off their guard, with their eyes fixed upon issues which had often ceased to be relevant.

The terrible corroding effects of long unemployment and the poisoning of industrial relations, often already bad, which were the consequences of the decline of the staple industries make much of the history of the 1920's a study in the pathology of society rather than in normal physiology. These influences were reinforced and complicated in the early 1930's by the effects of the years of deep slump between 1929 and 1932. As a result, the society which in the fourth decade of the century had to brace itself for the economic effort of the Second World War could not be complimented on the cleanness of its bill of health and the unimpaired vigour of its frame. A careful student of its condition must have detected many recent scars and unhealed wounds. There was a certain degree of sickness observable in society, just because there was a certain degree of sickness in industry.

During the 1920's the number of people officially registered as unemployed had never fallen below a million—about 8 per cent of the insured working population. The slump of 1929–32 drove the number up to over two millions for four years, 23 per cent of all insured workers being out of work when things were at their worst, in August 1932. Employment recovered far better in some regions than in others in the 1930's. For the country as a whole, the number of unemployed remained at over a million for the rest of the inter-war period. But while London and the South of England fared comparatively well, unemployment rates remained high in Wales, Scotland and the North of England.

Health can be callous towards sickness. Because parts of the body economic were flourishing and in process of growth, large sections of public opinion accepted with undesirable equanimity decay and disintegration elsewhere. No doubt this was faulty judgement. The decline of a community is not compensated for by the rise of a new one, which must be different in its essential character, or it would hardly be a new community. One cannot really set off the growth of an iron-ore town like Corby, or the expansion of a motor-car manufacturing centre like Coventry, or the strung-out population and factories of Slough and the Great West Road, against the decay of Merthyr Tydfil or Jarrow at that date, without doing some violence to human values. A town is not merely a place of work, and comparable volumes of employment and wage-rates were not alone at stake.

In economic terms, the growth of the new communities was nevertheless important. The mistake of balancing them, so to speak, against what was dying was easily made. There was a rift within the nation in those years, between those who knew nothing but the expanding works and spreading suburbs of prosperous centres of the new industrialism and those who lived with the disorder, the dirt and the gloom of the dying sections of the old. The sociology of a country in which the observer could pass within the day from the men without work[1] of the stricken mining towns of County Durham to the life of the new featureless suburbs of a thriving engineering centre like Birmingham was strange. But the line of descent from Victorian and Edwardian Britain to that society was direct, the continuity and the uniformity in many ways apparent.

One consequence of the rise of new industries and the expansion of production and real income over twenty years, despite unemployment, was that the social policies which originated before 1914 were permitted to develop, despite unbelievable changes in the economic landscape. From the economist's point of view it is a matter of considerable interest that it was during these years that social expenditure became for the first time a large item in the national budget and absorbed a substantial proportion of real national resources.

No doubt political changes accounted in part for this, the Franchise Act of 1918, at the end of the First World War, having completed the formal structure of democratic politics.

---

[1] *Men Without Work* was the title of a report on unemployment published by the Pilgrim Trust in 1938. It gives a vivid impression of this side of the history of the period.

But changes in fundamental social conditions and values accounted for more.

The social services may be roughly defined as all services provided by public authority for the purpose of improving welfare, health or education. They had been growing since the 1890's, as a result partly of private initiative and philanthropy and the transfer of voluntary services—the education of the blind for example—to the State when they had proved their worth; partly from the tendency to establish new forms of service, especially under local authority, independent of the Poor Law. The growth of social expenditure, together with the cost of armaments, had led to sharp political dispute before the First World War. This happened when, at the time of the Lloyd George budget of 1909, it became clear to the wealthy classes that the social services were becoming an instrument in the redistribution of wealth, involving new and, by contemporary standards, heavy taxes.

The war changed traditional views of what could be borne in the way of taxation, and it much enlarged men's conception of the power of the State. In the relatively prosperous years 1925–9 and 1936–7 considerable extensions to the social services took place. They now covered a wide range. Including education; public health and medical services; national health and unemployment insurance; old age, widow's and orphan's pensions; the work of employment exchanges, unemployment relief and public assistance, they touched in the middle 1930's the lives of from twenty to twenty-five million people. The total expenditure upon them was over £400 million—about one-tenth of the aggregate national income in the same year. If we include local as well as central services, social expenditure accounted for between one-quarter and one-third of the government expenditures in 1934.[1] The foundations of the later Welfare State could hardly be said to have been laid according to a plan; unifying principle was conspicuously lacking; neithei had the relations between social and economic policies been explored.[2] But the developments which had taken place since the beginning of the century were very striking. Compared with the Britain of 1834 and the first Poor Law Commissioners, they were revolutionary.

[1] (Political and Economic Planning) *Report on the British Social Services* (1937), p. 10.
[2] U. K. Hicks, *The Finance of British Government, 1920–1936* (1938), p. 60.

The financial basis for this un-Victorian conception of the State's duties, as well as for its great efforts in war and defence, had been provided by a series of tax reforms before 1914. These were aimed to solve piecemeal the pressing questions of public finance which arose on the annual budgets; but the result of much public discussion and a spirit of experiment on the part of Chancellors of the Exchequer from 1894 onwards had been to effect a radical change in the principles and machinery of public finance.

Victorian public finance had shunned the progressive principle—that is, the device of grading the rate of tax so as to make the rich man pay proportionately more than the poor—and had maintained that direct taxes—taxes on income and property—should be ungraduated. The income-tax, which was the main direct tax, had been left ungraduated and undifferentiated, as to source of income. The effect had been to give a considerable advantage to the owners of large incomes. At the same time, indirect taxes were still an important source of revenue and were so levied as to raise considerable sums from the working man. Down to 1913, he contributed to the State's revenue more than he benefited by its social expenditure.[1]

This was a position which could hardly be expected to last in an age of political democracy. It had been criticized by many from among the classes paying direct taxation themselves since the middle of the nineteenth century.[2] From 1885 an increase of direct taxation, which must almost certainly involve graduation, was part of the Radical programme. The first break with Gladstonian tradition came in the year of Gladstone's retirement. The effect of Harcourt's reform of the death duties in 1894 was not only to increase the rate of taxation on inherited property but to graduate the tax, making the larger estates pay more. In 1907, the principle of differentiation was brought into the income-tax by the introduction of the distinction between earned and unearned income. In 1909, the Lloyd George budget of that year, which was particularly directed at social reforms, graduated income-tax for the first time by levying a super-tax (now surtax) on the higher incomes. The budget in 1914, the last before the war, saw increases alike in the income-tax, in super-tax and in death duties.

[1] Hicks, op. cit. p. 58.
[2] The lines of argument then used both for and against reform have been summarized by F. Shehab, *Progressive Taxation* (1953).

The political issue of direct taxation, whether it might properly be used to redistribute the nation's wealth by financing elaborate schemes of social reform, had been settled after long struggles over the 1909 budget, which rent party life from top to bottom and led to important changes in the balance of power between the House of Commons and the House of Lords in the Parliament Act of 1911. The expansion of direct taxation after that date furnished much of the means, not only of war finance in the years 1914–18, but also of the larger budgets which followed the war. After making allowance for the fall in the value of money since 1914, public expenditure both local and central between the wars was running at a level well above what had once been regarded as high. In 1913 it had topped £300 million,[1] which would have been regarded by the Victorians as a formidable figure; but between the wars it was consistently above £1000 million. Social expenditure formed by the early 1930's an important part of this—more nearly £500 than £400 million, or getting on for the entire sum of public expenditure before the war. Part of this sum was raised by insurance contributions payable by the working man, part from taxes paid by him; the rest represented a transfer of wealth from rich to poor.

A society which arranged its finances in this way had departed far and on the whole properly from Victorian conceptions of the use of taxes. It was beginning to leave behind the image of what society is and what the relations between the classes ought to be which had supported the old scheme of public finance. As late as 1914 Britain, which had long ceased to be governed by her aristocracy, was still a country dominated politically by the well-born, the rich and the educated, while the social gulf between the classes struck good observers as both complete and unhealthy.[2] Disraeli's two nations governed by the queen, which he had distinguished when he was writing his political novels in the 1840's, existed still, thirty years after his death in 1881.

These things were, however, changing and the altered direction of public finance between the wars was a sure index of the force and intensity of the change. The deliberate use of taxation to redistribute income did not abolish great inequalities of

---

[1] Between £500 and £600 million, at 1930 prices: Hicks, op. cit. diagram I.

[2] Violet R. Markham, *Return Passage* (1953), p. 135.

property, such as had been strenuously defended in the past century on the plea—the rather unwise plea—that in no other way could economic progress possibly be secured. Public property of all types had, it is true, been on the increase since 1911, especially if we include the new public corporations created after 1919—the British Broadcasting Corporation, the Central Electricity Board and the London Passenger Transport Board. But outside of the sixth of it owned or directly administered by public bodies, property, which was the main source of private income, was privately owned. One half of this, in 1936, was in the hands of 1 per cent of the population aged over 25. This was a lower concentration of wealth than had existed in 1911–13 when 1 per cent of the adult population owned 70 per cent of all private property. Three quarters of all adults in 1936 owned between them little more than 5 per cent of all private property, the great majority being therefore unpropertied and dependent for income on the property in the hands of the remaining quarter of the nation.[1]

Thus Great Britain continued to present, as she had for long, the spectacle of a land of high civilization and genuine liberty precariously based upon exclusive class advantages,[2] although these were now diminishing, and a firm but slender basis of economic power. It remained to be seen after September 1939 whether such a society could withstand the onset of savage forces unloosed in the Western world by general war, by revolution and counter-revolution and by the less obvious but no less powerful pressure of long-term economic change.

[1] The figures refer to England and Wales only; see H. Campion, *Public and Private Property in Great Britain* (1939) pp. 109–10.
[2] Alfred Marshall's phrase, not mine; see his *Industry and Trade*, 3rd ed. (1927), title of chapter XIV.

Chapter XII

First of the Few: Great Britain as Leader of the World's Economy before 1880

THE EXPANSION OF TRADE

While sweeping changes came over British economy and society during the nineteenth century, the relations between that economy and the economic life of the rest of the world altered beyond recognition. With these transformations, caused by the movement of people, capital and goods on a new scale, went important changes in men's views of what was necessary and desirable in trade and in the external economic policy of the kingdom.

The British did not rise immediately and easily towards the position which they held in the nineteenth century as the most important of trading nations and the leader in the economic development of the world. Many factors entered into their ultimate success, including some which were not economic, such as the stability of government, the soundness of public credit and the ability of the fleet to protect the sea routes. It cost the political classes some painful changes in habit of mind and some striking innovations in economic policy to which considerable national risk attached. Since their new position in the trade of the world was bound up with manufacturing supremacy, it goes almost without saying that ascendancy was no sooner reached and enjoyed than it was sharply called in question by new developments in the world of the late nineteenth century. New moods and new movements of ideas entered. The consequent tension in the field of economic policy was still unresolved when the First World War broke out.

The rapid commercial development of Great Britain in the late eighteenth century after the American war (1776–83) at a time when mercantile activity was marked throughout Western Europe, from Hamburg to Bordeaux, has been mentioned.[1] This growth, stimulated by industrial progress at home as well as by the advance of production and incomes in other countries, represented the beginning of a new and important

[1] Above, chapter IV.

chapter in the history of trade. It also made urgent a recasting of national commercial policy. The old jealousy of trade with other European peoples, which had led to so many wars in the course of the eighteenth century, and the confusion of the tariff were becoming anachronisms which needed to be dealt with. This work was begun by William Pitt after 1784. He consolidated the customs, made in 1785 unsuccessful proposals to modify the restrictions upon trade with Ireland, and carried through the commercial treaty with France in 1786. Pitt also laid his hand, in the income-tax which he introduced in 1799, upon the financial tool which would be needed if there was ever to be an effective overhaul of commercial policy and public finance. But the relation between these things was not grasped at the time; the income-tax was regarded as merely a war tax; and the Napoleonic Wars not only introduced wholly new conditions for trade but also postponed for a generation any further consideration of the problems of peacetime commercial policy.

The long period of Continental war (1793–1815) was more injurious to other traders than to the British. It seriously affected, for example, the position of the Dutch and of their city of Amsterdam. Similarly, the war between Great Britain and the United States which began in 1812, arising out of the European conflict, damaged American more than British trade. It remains true, however, that the years of war temporarily halted the rapid advance in the foreign trade of the United Kingdom which had just begun; that this was further retarded by the slow recovery of economic activity after the war; and that, while trade began to grow again markedly in the 1820's, the huge increase of it which distinguished the middle of the nineteenth century did not begin until the 1840's.

Between the 1840's and the 1870's lay the long secular boom of the middle century, a period distinguished by improving prospects of profit and by rising investment, production and incomes in many countries. As incomes grew, the world or those many parts of it which were developing economically acquired a hunger for all sorts of things, which showed itself in rising prices and in a lively tone of business. The development of the world's economic life was not steady; fluctuations which involved not only prices but also production and real income blotted out the rising trend from time to time. In days and months of crisis they might break, as they did in 1857 and 1873, in waves of panic and despair over men in the commercial and financial cities. But the years of prosperity outweighed the years of depression. Over the whole period there was a growth in the world's effective demand for foodstuffs and raw materials, for the capital goods required by industrialists and the articles of immediate use required by the consumer, whether he was Eastern coolie or Western townsman. This was the beginning of large-scale international trade, migration and finance.

Down to about 1880, Great Britain was the only thoroughly developed industrial State in this expanding world economy. She was not without competitors and they were increasingly effective. The industrialization of the Continent, which had been so imperfect in 1848, went on apace in the next two decades, although interrupted by wars and rumours of wars from time to time in this age of nationality, of Bismarck and Cavour. In the greatest of the countries of new settlement, the United States, the development of resources depended upon communications, and the transcontinental railways were not built until after the Civil War was over. The major phase of the industrialization of the United States opened after 1880. In the meantime, much had been done to modernize economies both in Europe and America. The foundations of the industrial West were laid in the middle period of the nineteenth century, and every successive international exhibition after that of 1851 showed the Belgian, Frenchman, German and American improving their technical and organizing methods.

International competition was not officially recognized as a serious condition of all future British industrial growth until the report of the Royal Commission on the Depression of Industry and Trade in 1886. Down to the early 1880's, other countries were not looked upon by Britons as belonging in the same class as their own industrially, and this prejudice had a firm foundation in the circumstances of the age. Great Britain had possessed a temporary overwhelming advantage in new products or in new ways of making known products during the early and middle years of the century. No doubt it was a monopoly of the kind which is always dying; but it formed a real element in Great Britain's strength in world markets, perhaps never more so, as Marshall recognized, than at the time when the doctrine of competition was rising from the dignity of a working rule to that of a sacred dogma among British manufacturers and economists. The Manchester doc-

trines never quite did justice to the mingled elements of monopoly and competition which lay at the base of Britain's economic
predominance in the age of Cobden and for some time after his
death. That she was the sole supplier of many industrial goods
and the cheapest manufacturer of many others, determined at
every point her economic relations with the rest of the world,
especially in those years of rising prosperity in the mid-
Victorian age.

Between 1855 and 1859, the annual average value of the net
imports of the United Kingdom was £146 million. The total
merchandise imports were much larger, at £169 million, the
balance being re-exported. Domestic exports, not including
these re-exports, averaged in the same years £116 million. In
the late 1870's, between 1875 and 1879, at a time of comparatively depressed trade, when the boom of the years 1868–73
was over, the value of net imports was running at £320 million
a year. Total imports were valued at £375 million; re-exports,
at £55 million, were bigger than ever. Exports of United
Kingdom produce were valued at £202 million. Foreign trade
had expanded during the middle of the century much faster
than population. The value of the net imports of the 1850's,
per head of population, had been £5. 3s. 8d.; in the late 1870's,
it was £9. 10s. 4d., although prices then were coming down.
The value of exports of United Kingdom origin, divided by
population, had been in 1855–9, £4. 2s. 4d.; in 1875–9, it was
£6. 0s. 0d.

The years of rapidly extending trade saw a great growth of
shipping activity and of the merchant marine. The shipping
tonnage entering and clearing at ports in the United Kingdom
in 1855–9 averaged 21,694,000 tons a year; in 1875–9, it
reached 50,581,000 tons. Shipping tonnage on the British
register rose over the same years from 4,519,000 to 6,340,000
tons.[1]

BRITAIN AND THE PRIMARY PRODUCERS

The development of trade in the mid-Victorian age exhibited
many features of continuity with the commerce of the eighteenth
century, at least of the years after 1780. It was trade of a
particular type, dependent on the lines of growth of British

[1] See *Statistical Tables and Charts relating to British and Foreign Trade and Industry*, Cd. 4954 (1909), pp. 2–3 and accompanying tables.

production and the stage of economic development which the world had then reached.

The import trade in foodstuffs and industrial raw materials, made necessary by the industrialization of the United Kingdom and a population too large to be fed entirely from its own fields, came to form the heart of the great commerce of this period. An industrial raw material, cotton, valued at £35,756,000, headed the list of imports in 1860; next came corn, valued at £31,671,000; then sugar, wool, raw silk, timber, tea, oil, wine and butter in that order, to take the first ten most valuable imports. The second ten were also almost all of them raw materials or foodstuffs; they were tallow, flax, copper, hides, silk manufactures, coffee, spirits, tobacco, rice and iron in bar.[1] A considerable proportion of these imports were intended for resale abroad. For many commodities, such as cotton, wool, tea, hides and coffee, Great Britain was fast becoming, if she had not already become, a European, not to say world, market and middleman.

What was largely missing from the list of imports was manufactures. Great Britain's self-sufficiency in this respect is the measure of her solitariness as well as of her supremacy as a manufacturing nation, in the world of that time—the industrialization of Continental Europe and North America had not yet provided alternative and competitive suppliers. The import of manufactures increased, but the trade was small; net imports of manufactured and semi-manufactured goods in 1860 amounted to £22 million out of total net imports valued at £182 million. For many years past, much of the import of manufactures, to the extent of about a quarter, had been intended for re-export.[2] It was after 1860 that the volume of imports of manufactured goods began to rise significantly in relation to other imports. The first effect of the abolition of protection and the institution of free trade had been to encourage the import not of manufactures but of foodstuffs and raw materials.

The import of raw materials furnished employment. Imported corn and flour were indispensable and tea had long been the nation's drink. But imported foodstuffs did not, even in the case of wheat, satisfy the greater part of the demand for food. The mid-Victorian trade was only the strong beginning of the

[1] G. R. Porter, *Progress of the Nation* (1912), p. 528.
[2] *Statistical Tables relating to Trade and Industry*, Cd. 4954 (1909), p. 58.

huge annual bill for imported foodstuffs which became usual in the last quarter of the nineteenth century. Much of what came in, such as wines, was purchased only by the comfortable classes; much, especially in the way of tropical commodities, tea, sugar, coffee and so forth was resold on foreign markets.

The broadening stream of raw materials and foodstuffs coming in at the ports and retained for home consumption was partly paid for by a stream of British produce going out. Not all of these were manufactured goods, as they are ordinarily understood; Burton beer, for instance, was an important and old-standing export. But the main exports were manufactures and were the products of the industries whose productive methods had been shaped by the technical and organizational revolution of the previous seventy or eighty years. First on the list in 1860 stood cotton manufactures (i.e. piece-goods) valued at £42,141,000; then woollen manufactures, valued at £12,156,000; then iron and steel, valued at £12,154,000; then cotton yarn, linen manufactures, wool and woollen yarn, haberdashery and millinery, machinery, hardware and cutlery, and coal, in that order.[1] Below came a vast miscellany; copper, apparel, leather, beer and ale, linen yarn, earthenware and porcelain, silk twist and yarn, chemical products, paper, and many others, making a total value of exports of United Kingdom produce, excluding ships, of £136,000,000.

Great Britain's trade at the mid-century took the form mainly of an exchange of industrial products against imported foodstuffs and raw materials. It was the trade of an industrial State with countries still largely agrarian and, as such, it was worldwide. This was carrying on the traditions of the eighteenth century. The great trade of a hundred years before, in the years between the Seven Years War and the loss of the American colonies, had been with Western, Northern and Southern Europe; North America and the West Indies ran a good second, the East Indies trade third, and Africa accounted for an almost negligible quantity. Much trade had been bilateral, payments for imports being balanced directly against payments due for exports to the country from which the imports came. Europe and the mainland colonies of North America both bought from and sold to Great Britain in large amounts. The importance of the colonial trade, in British eyes, had lain in its being British controlled even where it was not

[1] G. R. Porter, *Progress of the Nation* (1912), p. 530.

bilateral. The indirect settlement of trading debts through a
third country appeared dangerous in time of war, even where
it could be arranged, and it could not always be done in an
age of limited commercial opportunities. Besides, it was repug-
nant to the strong national feeling and jealousies of the time, as
well as to the narrow thinking which found it difficult to view
the country's trade as a whole and tended to think of it in relation to this country and that, often with reference to current
politics as much as to economic gains. The Baltic trade, the
French trade and the East India trade had all been debated
from this point of view at one time or another. British commercial policy in the eighteenth century had been much influenced by the distrust of any trade in which a direct, satisfactory and obvious balance did not appear.

British trade of the middle nineteenth century ran along the
same main channels. The political development involved in the
breakaway of the American colonies and the creation of the
United States had made little difference to it. Britain continued to be an exporter of manufactures, only more so. The
United States down to and after the Civil War (1861–5) was
still largely a primary producer of foodstuffs and raw material.
The two communities had immediate need of one another. In
the early 1870's, the United States provided 18 per cent of
British imports and took 14 per cent of British exports. The
West Indies, on the other hand, which had played a role in the
commerce of the previous century out of all proportion to their
physical size, had dwindled into insignificance, supplying less
than 2 per cent of Britain's imports and taking not much more
than 1 per cent of her exports. This was a smaller trade than
was done at the time by Great Britain with either Holland or
Belgium. Continental Europe, including Russia (and owing
to the imperfections of the statistics Asiatic Turkey), accounted
for 34 per cent of British exports on the average of the years
1854–70, and provided a slightly smaller proportion of the
imports.

Some important additions had, however, been made to the
eighteenth-century circle of trading countries. After the
collapse of Spanish and Portuguese rule in South America and
the recognition of the independence of the new republics there
by the British government in 1824, the British trader became
a figure of influence and temporarily pre-eminent in the foreign
trade of such important countries as the Argentine and Brazil.

The British empire in the New World had fallen even earlier than the Spanish. But between the peace which acknowledged the independence of the United States in 1783, and the early years of Victoria's reign, the progress of British shipping and trade and the course of political events had created a new empire, even wider than the old. It included the colonies in Australia (founded after 1788) and in New Zealand (after 1840); conquests and acquisitions directly or indirectly due to the Napoleonic Wars, such as Ceylon, lonely Mauritius, the Cape of Good Hope, Singapore on the trade route to China, Trinidad and Tobago in the West Indies, as well as others of less economic importance; and the pre-war possessions in Africa, India, Canada and the West Indies.

The colonies were receivers of what passed for surplus population, although it included some of the ablest and most enterprising elements in the nation, and of loans out of savings which were not, for one reason or another, used in Great Britain. Settlement overseas was already considerable by the beginning of the Victorian age. A contemporary statistician, R. M. Martin, estimated the number of British living overseas in 1839 as 1,200,000, of whom the greater part were in British North America, 130,000 in Australia, 60,000 in the West Indies and 56,000 acting as garrisons of the regular army.[1] A great stream of emigration to Canada and Australia, New Zealand and South Africa, but especially the first three, flowed throughout the century. Net migration from the British Isles—the excess of outgoings over incomings—was running in 1876–80, when exact statistics first began to be compiled, at 87,000 people every year. Of these, 28,000 went to Australia and New Zealand, 8000 to British North America, 4000 to 'other places'; the great balance, 47,000, went to the United States.[2]

These numbers could never have found employment abroad but for the accompanying flow of capital. This had been going on for a long time, although investment overseas was largely a creation of the nineteenth century. The colonial investments represented by securities by 1881 included, so it was thought, £145 million in colonial government and city stocks, as well as large sums, hard to estimate, in colonial railways and banks.[3]

[1] Quoted by C. E. Carrington, *The British Overseas* (1950), p. 506.
[2] C. E. Carrington, op. cit. p. 503. The largest number of British emigrants throughout the nineteenth century went to the United States.
[3] R. L. Nash, quoted in C. K. Hobson, *Export of Capital* (1914), p. 145.

This was independent of investments in India. The sums invested in the colonies were not always spent on British goods and were seldom lent on that condition. Often, however, the loans carried with them, as an indirect consequence, not only the supply of materials but also British management and the services of British engineers, surveyors and other professional men. For technical and entrepreneurial ability, as well as capital, were in those days not easily to be found in the colonies.

Thus assisted with men and money, the colonies developed rapidly as primary producers. The export of wool from Australia to Great Britain was built up between 1820 and 1850, continued to expand despite the counter-attraction of the gold discoveries and was the staple trade of the Australian colonies in 1870. Timber formed the main Canadian export to Britain in the late 1860's, although that trade was declining in importance; the first Canadian wheat did not come in until 1874. New Zealand, like the Australian colonies, tended to concentrate on pastoral farming and the export of wool; the first export of refrigerated meat did not take place until 1882. The butter and cheese trade developed later. The Cape Colony found it more difficult to develop a staple. In the early 1870's she was becoming known for diamonds and ostrich feathers; the discovery of gold on the Rand still lay in the future. British India owed little to immigration but much to technical assistance and imported capital in constructing her Victorian economy. The indigo which had been favoured by the East India Company became of little account, as jute, coffee and tea cultivation grew after the 1830's and 1840's. Jute-growing was promoted by the Crimean war, which cut Britain off from supplies of Russian hemp; and when the American Civil War stopped the export of cotton to Liverpool from the southern states, India broke into the raw-cotton market.

The great range of countries which constituted the Victorian empire therefore performed functions in relation to the British economy which were essentially similar to those of the empire of the eighteenth century and of many countries which were not in the Victorian empire at all. They were chiefly important, from the economic point of view, as primary producers, supplying foodstuffs and raw materials, comparatively little of which competed with the produce of British agriculture, in return for manufactures—cotton and woollen textiles, iron, tin, cutlery, hardware, saddlery and many other products. But if the colonies did a great business with Great Britain in this way, so too did other countries, in Europe and North America, to an even greater extent. The United States drove a precisely similar trade with Great Britain, while it also absorbed many more British immigrants and much more British capital.

The world-wide exchange of manufactures for primary products characterized the position of Great Britain within the world economy. Together with this went the bilateral, that is, the direct settlement of many of the debts incurred in international trade, although large branches of trade were settled indirectly. The mutual offsetting of trading debts in transactions to which many countries were parties, or multilateral trading as it has come to be called, was characteristic of the trading world of the half-century before 1914, but it had deep roots in the trading practice of earlier centuries too. Where direct settlement could not be achieved, great trouble sometimes arose. The rapidly growing China trade of the early nineteenth century, like the trade with India long before, presented a difficult problem of payments, because the British demand for Chinese products was so much greater than the Chinese demand for British products.[1] By 1830 the growing sales of Manchester cotton goods at Canton suggested that this might not always be so, and forty years later China became one of the great markets for Lancashire textiles. But until this happened, opium, grown in India and exported to China by British firms, formed the main article of payment for Britain's imports of Chinese tea, silks and other products. Furthermore, in the complicated pattern of Great Britain's Far Eastern accounts, heavy annual payments due from India to Britain were remitted in the form of China tea, exported via India because the China trade was not direct between Great Britain and China but based upon Calcutta. As imports from China figured ever more heavily in British purchases overseas, the payments problem led to war when the Imperial government of China decided, on good grounds, to prohibit the opium trade. The China war of 1842 was far more than a trade war; it was the conflict of two civilizations which neither understood one another nor knew how to reach a *modus vivendi*. But it was in its immediate occasion a trade war, arising out of the peculiar difficulties of payment in Far Eastern trade and

[1] M. Greenberg, *British Trade and the Opening of China* (1951), especially chapter 1.

British lack of scruple about the means by which payments
were made. The opium trade between British India and China,
which sections of opinion in Great Britain never approved, was
tolerated by law until just before the First World War.

The great national and private interests at stake in overseas
trade and the relatively simple pattern both of its exchanges
and of its monetary settlements which made its issues easily
intelligible to the new political public, account for the fierceness
of the debate on fiscal policy which marked British politics in
the first half of the nineteenth century. This occurred just
before the vast mid-Victorian increase of overseas trade, which
was in part the consequence of the revolution in commercial
policy. The change in the law was, however, slow because the
issues were by no means easy to solve, from whatever angle
they were viewed. The solutions finally adopted were not untouched by historical accident.

The change of mind on the suitability of the old policies had
begun before the French wars, with Adam Smith and William
Pitt. It may be said to have continued during and just after
the war, in the discussion of the trading monopoly of the East
India Company. The ancient monopolistic rights of the Company in the trade to India were taken away on the renewal of
its charter by Parliament in 1813; the China trade, in which it
did not actively engage, but had conferred licences, was not
thrown open until 1834. By that time much wider matters were
in dispute. Agricultural protection, which had played a vital
part in the old system, but now seemed to impede the industrial
export trade that was growing up, while doing little to meet the
need for greater agricultural output, had been under fire since
the passage in 1815 of the unwise and impracticable Corn Law
of that year. The law had been twice revised in the 1820's,
when it became clear that no degree of protection could maintain the price for wheat which had prevailed during the war.
It was altered again by Sir Robert Peel in 1842, who substituted
a new scale of duties according to price. This helped to eliminate some of the unsteadiness of price and the speculation in
wheat stocks which had attended the Duke of Wellington's
scale of wheat duties introduced in 1828. It was a defect of the
Corn Laws that they brought no stability into prices, although

they were intended to do so, and thus injured to this extent the farmer as well as the consumer.

Peel made it clear that the country gentlemen and the farmers, who were strong in the Conservative party which he led and had never disguised their jealousy of the increasing political demands of the towns, intended to take their stand on the law of 1842. Conditions had already set in, however, which were bound to make this difficult. The trade depression of 1839 had deepened and became general. It was accompanied by much unemployment, short-time and distress among working people, heavy trading losses among merchants and manufacturers. This was fertile ground for popular agitation, and the Manchester Anti-Corn Law Association, founded in January 1839, made the most of it. The anti-Corn Law movement enlisted two of the ablest of the radical politicians of the nineteenth century, Richard Cobden (1804–65), the son of a Sussex farmer, and the slightly younger John Bright (1811–89). Both were members of the Parliament in which Peel had to defend agricultural protection. The power of these men lay in the reform of the franchise after 1832 and the skilful use they made of it to introduce into Parliament the views of the urban middle class, which had been previously largely unrepresented.

Peel had continued, in the budgets of 1842 and 1845, which he handled personally as if he had been his own Chancellor of the Exchequer, the reform and modification of the tariff. This had been resumed, when the French wars were over, long after Pitt's time, by William Huskisson, when he became President of the Board of Trade in Lord Liverpool's administration between 1823 and 1827. After Huskisson's death, the work was carried on through the budgets of the Whig Chancellors of the Exchequer in the 1830's. By Peel's time, the remissions of duty involved in replacing a high tariff by a moderate one had gone sufficiently far to create a problem of public revenue. In years such as the early 1840's, when trade was depressed and the quantity of goods coming in for tax had fallen off, there was a decline of customs revenue of some seriousness. The problem carried its own solution, in the sense that further reductions of the tariff, paring away its protective element and retaining only revenue duties, might be expected in time to increase the volume of foreign trade which came in at the lower duties. An equal amount of revenue might be gained from a lower tariff. But this was a long view of the question; there was in the meantime a gap in the national revenues. Peel filled it during the depressed years of the early 1840's by reintroducing as a temporary measure, in 1842, the income-tax. By doing so, he began a revolution in the system of public finance, for the income-tax was renewed, on one plea or another, throughout the nineteenth century and became a permanent part of the revenues. Peel's extension of direct taxation made it possible for him to carry out important reductions of duty, while balancing his budgets. This had the effect of placing the manufacturing interest, which was being slowly educated in free trade, in a position where it could ask, with some plausibility, why the landed interest continued to be protected by the state, when other men were expected to stand up to the four winds of competition?

Public affairs stood thus when, in the wet summer and autumn of 1845, the potato harvest in Ireland failed owing to disease. This was a period of agrarian distress which extended to many parts of Western Europe. Its effects on British politics were immediate. The free opening of the ports to corn importation was necessary to alleviate the famine which engulfed Ireland; but the balance of political interests in Britain was such that it was more than doubtful whether the towns, organized and represented by the Anti-Corn Law League, would ever permit them to be closed again, even by a moderate measure of agricultural protection.

There is an undetermined element in all great historical situations. The conversion to free trade in corn of Peel, round whose head the fury of party controversy raged until his death in 1850, provided this element. In a rapid series of moves, Great Britain approached the complete abolition of protection, in the budgets of 1842 and 1845 and the repeal of the Corn Laws in 1846. Peel's conversion was the turning-point in fiscal and commercial policy, and its importance was recognized at the time, for instance, by such an acute observer as the young Italian Count Cavour, then visiting London. Cavour was later to represent what came to be called liberal economic policies in his native Piedmont and in the united Italy which he helped to create.

Gladstone acted as Peel's executor in matters of economic policy, particularly when he introduced the budget as Chancellor of the Exchequer in 1853. Mid-Victorian political opinion regarded the Gladstonian budget of 1860 and the commercial treaty negotiated in that year between Great Britain and France—it was associated in this country with the name of the British plenipotentiary, Richard Cobden, but in France with the advice of the economist and member of the Conseil d'État, Michel Chevalier and the authority of Napoleon III— as marking the completion of the free trade system. The treaty led on the British side to a removal of certain duties on French products, chiefly wines, which had been retained rather for revenue than protective reasons. The French government, much against the will of French industrialists, abandoned high protection, sweeping away a number of prohibitions on trade and lowering duties, so as to allow the import of English cottons and iron manufactures.

The treaty of 1860 and the budget of 1861 left Great Britain's commercial system free from almost every vestige of protection. France, with a lower tariff than she had ever known before, proceeded in the next sixteen years to negotiate a series of commercial treaties with other European states which had the effect of lowering protective duties all round. The air of the mid-century, warmed by prosperity and growing economic activity, was favourable to liberal economic doctrines. Paris was not the only capital where they made headway. From the point of view of British free-traders of the strict school, the reciprocal bargaining which went forward on the Continent was distasteful and to be avoided. A free trade was the correct and most advantageous policy for a nation to follow in its own interest; it should be followed, whatever other nations did. On this score, even the 1860 treaty had its critics. But the decline of protection in other states was applauded. The British example, it seemed, had opened a new chapter in the history of economic policy. The prestige of 'the Manchester school', represented so ably by Richard Cobden, had never stood so high. They were the men who had grasped, twenty and thirty years before, in a less prosperous age, the supreme economic importance to Great Britain of effective demand overseas and the way to promote this by facilitating exchange. The state of British trade in the 1860's seemed to justify abundantly their doctrines and their faith.

The advantages of free trade were not, in Cobden's view, wholly economic. Politically a radical, he was against militarism even of the English variety and in favour of peace with France. The treaty of 1860, like that of 1786, had a political

purpose and was aimed to put the relations of the two countries
on a more stable basis. The growth of the commercial classes
and the decline of the aristocratic interest in Europe was also
congenial to Cobden. Like many men of his time, he identified
aristocracy with war and social oppression. Free trade for him
was a new system of international relations and a social
philosophy, as well as the only sound economics. Many
men applauded his economics, who disapproved of his other
beliefs. Their political loyalty was often given, not to any
Radical, but to Palmerston, the Whig lord, dead in the same year
(1865) as Cobden, whose robust nationalism and strong sense
of social position they found agreeable, or to Disraeli, who
became Prime Minister and leader of the Conservative party in
1868. But even Disraeli refused, in the 1870's, to return to the
agricultural protection he had defended thirty years before.
The free trade policy had made an almost complete conquest
of both parties in the State.

It was a policy congenial to the circumstances of the time. The
supremacy of Great Britain at sea and her effective detachment
from Continental and American affairs, which marked her
foreign policy between Canning's day and the Civil War in the
United States in the 1860's, freed her from the more urgent
risks of war, which might conceivably have kept alive a policy
of protection or at least of widespread and heavy revenue duties.
But the needs of war, whether in supplies or in finance, were
hardly felt until the rise of expenditure upon the fleet at the
very end of the nineteenth century. Meanwhile, the balance
of social interests in the State was, as we have seen,[1] such as to
reduce the scope of the State's functions and its outlays to a
minimum. The working men in the towns did not get the vote
until 1867, in the counties until 1884. Expenditure upon social
reforms was modest; indeed, far lower than it ought to have
been. In this posture of politics and the public finances, it was
possible for the Chancellors of the Exchequer, such as Gladstone, the main maker of the Victorian traditions of public
finance from 1853 to his retirement from politics in 1894, to
content themselves with a moderate and simplified system of
finance. Direct taxation such as income-tax was kept down to
a minimum; two-thirds of the State's income was raised from
customs and excise, charged mainly on a few articles in general
consumption, principally tea, sugar, beer, spirits and tobacco.

[1] Above, chapter x.

This enabled the Chancellors to avoid the taxation of raw materials and necessary foodstuffs and to free from taxes a great mass of other commodities which might in a different system have been protected or taxed for revenue. The structure of public finance which came to prevail in the mid-century, as a part of the free trade policy, could hardly be described as equitable or as intended to hold the scales of justice even between the classes. But it had and was intended to have an effect on employment by putting the least possible burden on the profits and the materials of industry.

To what degree free trade actively encouraged the expansion of the national economy it would be hard to say. Contemporary opinion no doubt overvalued its effects; later judgements may have underrated them. The main source of the rising economic activity of the middle years of the nineteenth century is to be found in the vast investments in agriculture, in mining (including gold-mining), in commerce and in industry, which were going forward in many parts of the world. The incitements to invest were various and the conditions surrounding investment many. The gold discoveries in Australia and California would presumably have taken place and had their consequences in the world economy, whatever Great Britain's policy had been. Similarly, the development of the United States, the greatest single fact in the economic history of the nineteenth century, although it assisted the English fiscal system, depended little on it. It can hardly be denied, however, that British commercial policy and public finance, while they did not create opportunities for investment, gave the utmost encouragement to the investor at home and abroad, sometimes at the expense of other good things.

Great Britain became something more important than a world trader, a bargainer and huckster, which she had long been. She became a pioneer in the mobilization and development of the resources of other lands. Her trade and her investments linked her with a vast circle of peoples anxious to exchange and to borrow, although they were not always content with the terms of the trade or the loan. Her policy was directed not only towards her colonies but mainly and increasingly towards that great circle. Hence the relative indifference to empire, although this was never absolute. The expansion of colonial trade became less urgent than in the more limited commercial worlds of the seventeenth and eighteenth centuries. After 1849, when the

Navigation Acts were repealed, the British shipowner was no
longer protected, whether in the trade off British coasts or in
the trade to the colonies. The budget of 1853 swept away large
parts of the old system of tariff preferences for colonial products.
Great Britain went further; in 1865 and 1867, she struck
treaties with Belgium and the German Zollverein in which she
agreed neither to give preferences to nor to receive them from
her colonies. This was in line with strict free trade doctrine. It
also appeared plain common sense. Of her rapidly advancing
trade, not more than about one-quarter was trade with her
colonies. The most effective stimulus to colonial trade lay in
Britain's need of foodstuffs and raw materials and the colonies'
lack of manufactures. But this was an exchange which she
could and did drive with the whole world.

BRITAIN AS WORLD BANKER

The surest index of the strength of the national economy in
relation to the rest of the world was to be found in the extent of
the debts which many British people were content to let lie
abroad. They were the members, as the Dutch had been before
them, only on a smaller scale, of a creditor nation. This position
they owed to the superior productivity of their economy and
the profitable terms on which they exchanged manufactured
goods for the raw materials and foodstuffs which they needed;
to the earnings of their ships, banks, insurance firms and merchant houses; to everything and everybody which brought
payments to Great Britain in most years greatly in excess of
those owed by Britons to men in other countries. Down to the
1870's there was a substantial surplus due to Great Britain in
most years, upon sales of commodities and services against
commodities and services purchased abroad. When trade was
bad and incomes fell off, the men to whom these payments were
due might bring their dividends home. They might go further
and proceed to realize some foreign assets they had bought, in
the shape of railway shares, government bonds and so forth.
But in good and merely indifferent years they left the surplus
abroad, investing it and increasing their assets in shares and
bonds in other countries. Citizens of Great Britain therefore
received, in addition to payments for commodities and services,
a third kind of income from abroad, income from their foreign
investments. The existence of this income might be used to

cushion the national balance of payments in years which were bad for exports, for, being borrowable by those who dealt on the commodity markets, it could be employed to help pay for imports. Imports tended to run high both in good years and bad.

We shall never know the extent of British foreign lendings in the nineteenth century as a proportion of the income and the capital wealth of the world. So viewed, they were certainly small, but they were a real element in the world's economic growth nevertheless. They even affected the stability of that growth. By 1875, the nominal value of British capital invested abroad was at least £1,200,000,000;[1] most of which had been invested in the previous quarter of a century, and bore interest, it is supposed, on average at about 6 per cent. This estimate relates only to government bonds and railway shares; they were of many classes, from railways in Europe, the United States and South America and United States Debt, to Indian railways and colonial government loans. But a great deal of money had also been invested, not all of it in publicly issued shares by any means, in a vast variety of commercial undertakings, from land and mortgage companies and Indian and colonial banks to steamship and cable companies. In the early years of the century, Europe had been the favourite theatre for investment; now in the century's middle years it was South America, the colonies and the United States. It was not the practice to insist on control or the purchase of materials from Great Britain; but in many enterprises, the management, the engineers or the materials, often all three, were British.

Owing to the extent and variety of their enterprises, financial as well as commercial, the British became temporarily the point of balance of the world's economic activities. The equilibrium of many countries, in Europe, North America, and other great regions, depended upon the relations and the state of payments between this, the largest of industrial States, the greatest exporter of industrial goods and of capital, and those who exchanged with her foodstuffs and raw materials.

As the Atlas of the economic world of their time, upon whose shoulders so much rested, the early and later Victorians were, it must be confessed, neither always wise nor always honest. British merchants and bankers and investors, at a time when the world depended on capital from Great Britain to a greater

[1] L. H. Jenks, *Migration of British Capital to 1875* (1927), p. 413.

extent than ever before or since, could not be said to have in-variably promoted economic stability. The commercial crisis of 1857 has been described as the first world economic crisis, coming as it did from North America, Central Europe, Liver-pool, London; but credit and enterprise from the British Isles, straying into many countries, had played a great role in the boom which then broke. So too with the vast boom and panic of 1868–73.

At all times, as financiers and merchants, doubling in them-selves the role of development banker and supplier of short-term credit, men living in Great Britain bore a certain limited responsibility for the prevailing level of employment of the world's resources. It was a responsibility of which they were only half-conscious, and it was subordinate in their minds to the aim of reaping a higher rate of interest than they could earn on their capital at home and of preserving a suitable liquidity of their assets. But given a world in which the various countries were much less directly linked than they are today and where the main links ran through London, there was something they could do to even out activity in other countries, even if in doing so they were wisely serving themselves by keeping their eggs in as many well-held baskets as possible. The existence of colonies which were in a state of active settlement, such as Australia, provided, for example, an outlet for capital and activity in years which might be bad, say in the United States. Not that London always stood by the colonies; the sudden cessation of British lendings at the end of the 1870's was largely responsible for the depression which set in in Australia and New Zealand at that time.

Unfaithful guardians of the world's economic order as they were from time to time, the power of British capitalists within that order was a real power. The trading and produc-tion of many countries was centred on Britain, and what stability the system had was to no small extent controlled and created from the City of London. After 1870, however, the system was increasingly on the change. New sources of supply for all sorts of things, with all manner of new relations between them, were coming into being. It remained to be seen how long the British could retain their pre-eminence in the world's economy and whose guidance that economy would accept, if Britain lost that position, supposing it to be prepared to accept the guidance of anyone at all.

Chapter XIII

A Leader under Challenge: Great Britain in the World Economy, 1880–1939

INDUSTRIALIZATION AND WORLD TRADE

Late in Victorian days, a new stage was reached in the economic development of the world and the trading patterns of the mid-century came to be broken up and rearranged in a new and more complicated manner. The foundation of this great change was the comparatively rapid industrialization of Western Europe, especially of Germany and France, and of the United States of America. This process brought into being a new and highly competitive international system of industrial production. Much of the new manufacturing production sprang into being in countries which, like the United States, were largely self-sufficient or were important world suppliers of foodstuffs and raw materials. But the industrialization of the West also created huge new centres of primary production, both in the tropics and in temperate countries. This could not have happened but for the currents of trade, migration and investment which linked together, both directly and indirectly, the manufacturing and the agricultural and mining halves of the world. These became deep and various, owing to the contemporary progress of steam transport by land and sea. As a consequence, economic transactions in remote countries came to form parts of a single world system as never before. On the world's markets, each country could purchase only what it could afford; but access to those markets, both physical, in the form of transport, and financial, in the form of credit and means of payment, was enormously widened as production and trade increased in so many countries. Meanwhile, the spread of banks and credit institutions and the development after 1870 of the habit of assigning a legal value to national currencies in the West and elsewhere in terms of gold, gave the world temporarily some of the advantages of a unified monetary system.

The system of world trade which appeared natural and permanent to the men who operated it just before the First World War had ancient roots, but much of its luxuriance had been a product of the growth of trade in the half-century then coming to a close. These years had created what was really a new international trading system, compared with that of the mid-nineteenth century. Both complementary and fiercely competitive in character, it brought problems as well as opportunities for a land so dependent on foreign trade as Great Britain. Some of the main controversies in public life between 1886 and 1913 turned on the significance for British interests of these vast and hurried movements in the outside world. It is of some importance to know whether and how far and by what means the late Victorians and Edwardians adapted themselves to the alteration in the conditions of their economic existence.

. The British position in world trade had been built mainly upon productive capacity in manufactures and an ability to organize and finance a trade in industrial goods with other parts of the world. Industrial power made it possible to sustain the heavy imports of food and raw materials on which the material standard of living of Britain was coming to depend.

One of the apparent paradoxes of the years after 1880 was a marked increase of this dependence, at a time when the Victorian monopoly of much of the industrial trade of the world was beginning to pass away. Prices in this country early in the 1880's were roughly comparable with prices just before the First World War. If we compare the rise in the value of imports with the rise in population between the two periods, it becomes clear that imports per head of population had very considerably increased. The value of exports per head of population rose also, but not fast enough to prevent the emergence of a gap between the value of imports and exports which was truly formidable—of the order of about £150 million annually in the years 1905–9 compared with about £60 million annually in the early 1870's. What the excess of imports over exports might be in any one year varied, for it was affected by almost every influence which played upon the trade of the world; but it had become a standing feature of the nation's economy.

We hear little or nothing during those years of difficulties arising in the balance of payments between Great Britain and other countries. They did appear, in a mild form, from time to time, as in the late 1870's and the mid-1890's, at periods of exceptional trade depression in Great Britain and the countries with which she did business. But few heard of them, except men in the City. The state of payments with the rest of the world was in most years acknowledged to be favourable, even highly favourable to Great Britain, who enjoyed the repute of being the largest creditor in world trade.

How was the gap filled and a debtor turned into a creditor, on a reckoning of annual income? The answer is by this time familiar. Sales of exported goods by no means exhausted the total revenues drawn privately by Britons from foreign transactions. Other activities and other types of transaction have to be taken into account.

SHIPPING

The exceptional position of Great Britain in the nineteenth century as a manufacturer and a trader went with an equally exceptional position as a builder, owner and operator of shipping. Technical and economic changes after 1880 reinforced this advantage.

Great Britain had been a land of shipowners and shipbuilders for centuries, with a merchant fleet since Napoleonic times which was the largest in Europe. But until iron came into use for shipbuilding, she was not a land where ships were built cheaply. As British woods became worked out and timber dear, shipbuilding wood had to be imported, from Eastern Europe through the Baltic, or from Canada under a preference first granted for the navy's sake. Hence the keenness of competition from countries where forests grew freely and where the shipbuilder's art was cultivated, such as the United States. American competition remained highly effective for many years; its decline appears to have been due not only to technical factors but also to the increasing absorption of American capital in opening up the resources of the continent after the Civil War. There were many enterprises in which the returns to be got were higher than in shipping.

The introduction first of steam, then of iron, gradually tilted the balance in favour of Great Britain. Steam slowly bore down sail in the middle decades of the century. It owed something to the opening of the Suez Canal in 1869, which gave an advantage to the powered ship on one of the main trade routes of the world, that from Europe to the East. The iron-built steamship began to come in fast in the 1870's. The economic problems of steamship operation were difficult, however; for the amount of space taken up by engines and bunkers in the ocean-going ship made it difficult to make profits on what the ship could carry in the way of passengers and cargo. Without the subsidy obtained from government mail contracts, the principal steam packet lines of the 1840's and the 1850's could hardly have established themselves. The Cunard Company on the North Atlantic, the Peninsular and Oriental Company on the route to India, the Pacific Steam Navigation Company off western South America, the Royal Mail Steam Packet Company running to the West Indies and eastern South America, were heirs and successors to the government-paid Falmouth mail packets of sailing-ship days. The high cost of steamship operation was reduced in the second half of the nineteenth century, however, by the introduction of the compound and triple-expansion engines, while the use of steel in engines and hull which became universal by 1900 permitted many economies of scale.

Under the stimulus of the cable and the railway and a multitude of other forces which played upon the world's production and trade about this time, trade between nations extended. Great Britain entered deeply into it, as the result partly of the huge expansion of her own exports and imports, partly because her oceanic position enabled her to take part in lucrative cross-trades which never touched her shores. Out of these conditions emerged commercial steamship owning and building as it was known before 1914. And of all owners and builders of merchant fleets, as of warships, the British were at that date by far the most important. Almost down to 1890 there was little effective competition; even the first ships of the new German merchant marine were built in Britain. After that date, German competition in shipowning and shipbuilding became sharp. But the position of the British shipowner and shipbuilder was still extraordinary on the eve of the First World War. In June 1914, when the gross tonnage of ships of over 100 tons gross recorded at Lloyds reached 49 million tons, the amount owned in Great Britain or the British Dominions, mostly in the United Kingdom, was 21 million tons.

Shipbuilding, being an industry concerned with the production of one of the most expensive capital instruments known, was extremely susceptible to major changes in world investment and economic activity. The years 1910–14 were years of booming trade which followed a dismal slump. Other countries were beginning to build ships upon a large scale, but on the average of those immediate pre-war years about three-fifths of the world's new tonnage was launched in British yards, including many ships built to foreign account.[1] The contribution which the shipping and shipbuilding industries made towards the national income and towards meeting, through earnings from foreigners, the country's bills abroad, was important. In the last full year of peace, 1913, when the United Kingdom spent more on imports than she earned by exports to the extent of £158 million, the net earnings of British ships stood at £94 million, which went a long way to close the gap.[2] Shipping did particularly well that year.

The rapid growth of shipowning and shipbuilding did much to give a special shape to the national economy, in peace and in war. The power of the shipping interest was an important stay of the free trade cause after 1900, at a time when protectionist thought was reviving. It would hardly be possible to understand the peculiar nature of the economy, highly vulnerable, but also infinitely flexible and resourceful, which carried the nation through the First World War, without making reference to shipping.

FOREIGN INVESTMENT BEFORE 1914

Shipping offices were not the only receivers of profits from abroad. Mercantile houses and banks and finance institutions having their headquarters in this country but often with branches and agents in distant parts of the world earned considerable sums, though it would be hard to say exactly how much. Undoubtedly, however, the largest source of income from abroad, much exceeding all profits from shipping and commercial services, was the capital owned in Great Britain but lent to borrowers, who might be governments or private persons, in other countries.

Foreign investment was nearly a century old in 1914. Much of the money invested at that date, however, with foreign governments and in mining, transport, industrial and agricultural enterprises abroad, had gone there since mid-Victorian times. Towards this great business of foreign investment, many

[1] Figures from the *Balfour Committee on Industry and Trade: Survey of the Metal Industries* (1928), pp. 369 and 405.
[2] The Board of Trade figures, quoted in A. E. Kahn, *Great Britain in the World Economy* (1946), p. 127.

elements in the national life had contributed. It had grown, in the first instance, as we have seen, out of the old-time shipping and mercantile business, as with Baring Brothers. Foreign lending was the work of commercial men in a commercial age, when the search for the maximum profit and the urge to accumulate capital seemed the natural ends of man to important sections of the community and when the intimate knowledge of conditions abroad and personal connections of many English and Scottish men of business gave them every opportunity to pursue the objects of their desire. But it was also favoured by political and military circumstances; by the small burden of taxation and the unwillingness of government to concern itself with the economic activities of its subjects; by the long peace of the nineteenth century, which some men mistook for permanent; and by the protection conferred by the fleet throughout that century upon British citizens and interests in those many parts of the world which sea power could reach.

Considering the economic side of the matter more closely, foreign investment represented the working together of some of the most characteristic activities of the nation's economic system and the high dynamic quality conferred upon that system by the developments of over a hundred years.[1] Foreign lending implied a real transfer of resources to other countries, where the advantage to be gained by their use, measured by interest rates and profits, seemed greater than at home. It could never have taken place without the high rate of capital accumulation and the fast-growing population of Victorian Britain; without the facilities which existed for the manufacture and shipping abroad of industrial articles of all kinds, but particularly of the capital goods, in the way of railways and rolling stock, mining and plantation machinery, steamships, dock and harbour equipment and the many other things which new countries wanted; or without the migratory habit of Britons and the power to transfer oneself and one's belongings and savings easily abroad, which provided some of the new countries, such as Australia and New Zealand, with most of the labour they required for their development, and made the English or Scots engineer, manager, rancher or prospector a common figure the world over. Much investment followed

---

[1] The place of foreign investment in the growth of the national economic system as a whole has been discussed by A. K. Cairncross: *Home and Foreign Investment* (1953). These remarks draw heavily upon his admirable study.

emigration and encouraged emigration, both from the United Kingdom and other countries.

The actual transfer of resources being essential to foreign investment, foreign investment tended to take place in periods when for one reason or another it appeared that home resources could be spared. Trade fluctuations, which involved sudden rises and falls in the investment of capital, took place more or less simultaneously in the various countries of the world and had their immediate effects upon foreign lending. In the long period it was significant that the building industry, which was closely linked with home investment, was most active in years such as the 1890's, when foreign investment was low and that house-building suffered severely as a result of the immense foreign lending boom of 1909–13. The pace and volume of foreign investment tended to be influenced very much by the phases of setback or progress in which lands of new settlement stood at the time and by prices obtaining on world markets for their products. The products being chiefly foodstuffs and raw materials, articles of which Great Britain was herself the largest purchaser, a national case could be made out for foreign investment,[1] irrespective of the gains of investors. As the primary producing countries began to industrialize and their industrial product to compete with that of Western Europe, the argument of national advantage might tilt the other way. But although foreign loans cannot be held to have been free from serious political and ethical objections, the economic gains down to 1914 were large and indisputable.

The practice of foreign investment, the banking side of which was concentrated in a relatively few hands in London, much of it among men who specialized in the business and did not concern themselves with home investment, had become established by 1870. Well over half of the loans at that time were in the form of European and United States government bonds, although railways and other enterprises took a large share.[2] The 1870's brought disappointment to the investor and he began to turn elsewhere. North and South America and the countries of the Empire, particularly Australia and South Africa, were heavy borrowers between 1880 and 1900, the

---

[1] The question of public policy was debated at the time by, among others, C. K. Hobson, in *Export of Capital* (1914), who also made one of the earliest statistical investigations.

[2] Cairncross, op. cit. p. 184.

share of the Empire distinctly rising. After the beginning of the present century, Canada replaced Australia as the leading Empire borrower. Europe, being well supplied from its own funds, ceased to be important. The United States and South American countries, particularly the Argentine, continued to borrow on the grand scale, the former being in 1914 the largest single borrower of British capital in the world, as well as, of course, a borrower in other European capital markets.

The total of foreign investments—so far as we can estimate them, and no exact figures exist—had risen from about £800 million in 1871 to about £3500 million in 1913. Something less than a half of this sum was lent within the Empire, and large sums were lying in the Argentine and Brazil and above all in the United States. The luxurious days of the mid-nineteenth century, when the income due to Britons for exports and shipping and commercial services compared with sums owing for imports left a comfortable surplus in most years for loans abroad, were no more. But the annual interest due on foreign investments was now sufficiently large to help pay for imports and not only filled the gap but left large sums available for investment abroad. So the large excess of imports could be afforded and a favourable balance of payments which appeared unshakeable was built up. In 1913, at the height of the boom such sums available for new lendings abroad may have reached £180 or £190 million.

COMPETITION ON WORLD MARKETS

While these conditions prevailed, it might be thought that no doubts could arise about Britain's trading future. This was not so. On the contrary, a considerable agitation arose on this very question in the early 1900's. But it was much influenced by the particular conditions of the time, and it turned less upon the actual state of the foreign balance than upon industry's contribution towards it and what the future might hold in store. The whole matter is unintelligible without reference to the contemporary industrialization of other Western States, the tariffs which they levied upon one another's goods and the complicating, sometimes the dominant, factors of political interest and military power.

The industrial growth of other nations was very marked between 1870 and 1914. At the end of the third quarter of the nineteenth century, the population, capital and trade of Great Britain had still given her a position which looked unassailable. The population of the United Kingdom, in the years 1871–4, was 32 million people. It compared with a population of 40 million in the Germany which had just won the Franco-German war; of 36 million in defeated France; of 40 million in the far-distant United States. Thirty years later, this relative uniformity in the size of the leading Western nations had been broken by fresh population growth. The last censuses taken before the First World War disclosed a significantly altered state of affairs. The Americans were then, in 1910, a people of 91 million; the Germans of 64 million; the British (in 1911, including the Irish) of 45 million; the French, of 39 million. In a world which rated nations very much in terms of their size, Great Britain was ceasing to stand out as a land of large population.

No simple relation exists between population growth and economic development. But the rising numbers of Germans and Americans corresponded, in a rough kind of way, with the progress of German and American production and trade since 1870, in the classical period of American and German industrialization. In the early 1870's, British coal output had exceeded the combined French, German and American output; so too had her output of pig-iron, and the number of her cotton spindles exceeded their combined outputs. Thirty years changed all these relations. By the early 1900's American coal output was well ahead of the British; German and American pig-iron output, separately, each larger than the British. In cotton, Lancashire still led the world; but the development of mechanical textile industries elsewhere had been remarkable and a great trade had sprung up from Britain herself in the export of textile machinery to the East, to India, China and Japan.

Industrial production strode forward with prodigious steps in the comparatively calm interval in the world's affairs between 1870 and 1914. Germany and the United States were by no means the only countries undergoing industrialization. Development was rapid in Sweden and Russia from the 1890's, in Canada and Japan in the early 1900's. The rise of the United States to the rank of the first manufacturing country in the world by value and volume of product, and of Germany to that of second, by 1914 was part of a world-wide process which created some ten or eleven industrial states.

There was much discussion, from the 1880's onwards, of the bearing of these immense developments abroad upon the industrial position of Great Britain. German and American competition was felt particularly strongly. The alarm it roused was most evident in the recurrent times of depression before 1905; less was heard about it during the great boom of 1909–13. The dominant mood of Englishmen in face of a changed world and their own altering position in it was one of composure and confidence; a Scotsman, the late Lord Tweedsmuir, making his way in ruling circles and public life in the early years of the century, marvelled at the coolness of the nerve with which the passing of so much mid-Victorian certitude was met. But the anxiety was there, flowing through and under the composure and the confidence. On the industrial side it raised some difficult questions.

The greater part of the new industrial production never entered into international trade, and when it did, Great Britain was by no means always a loser. On the contrary, considerable advantages accrued to her from industrialization abroad. She supplied much of the industrial capital equipment, as she had done in mid-Victorian times; she sold consumer goods to those in receipt of the new industrial incomes; and she found a most important market in the primary producing half of the world, which was selling foodstuffs and raw materials to the industrial West.

Down to 1914, the growth of industrialization in the world was favourable to the growth of international trade.[1] Great Britain was on balance a gainer, not a loser, by this first phase in the industrialization of the world. Her exports, not only to primary producers, but also to industrial States, increased rapidly between 1870 and 1914. When in 1914 she fought Germany, she fought her second-best customer, and was at the time one of Germany's best customers herself.

The effect of new industrialization upon an old industrial State was, however, a new experience. There were inconveniences and difficulties to be met, losses to be suffered, not always by those who made the new gains. The process of adaptation was rough and the alarm sometimes considerable.

The particular significance of German and American in-

---

[1] Cf. the evidence gathered in the League of Nations report, *Industrialization and Foreign Trade* (1945).

dustrial developments lay in those countries having been great markets of Great Britain before 1870. The loss of American markets was more important for some manufacturers than the growth of German competition. Early in the 1900's, in the depressed years after the Boer War, American competition in British markets rose' to the dignity of a newspaper scare; but little more was heard of it when good times returned and when American capital, which had been helping to build the London underground railways, was wholly absorbed by an immense internal boom in the United States after 1907.

German competition caused more popular excitement and genuine concern from the 1880's onwards. On the Continent, for very natural reasons, German trade made great strides and won something resembling a monopoly in Central and South-Eastern Europe. German competition in markets outside of Europe, such as South America, was often the more resented because Englishmen had been singularly exempt from competition there before. Shipping competition was keen, especially from the North German ports in the North Atlantic passenger trade. German competition in the home market caused more talk, as can be imagined, than anything. Low German costs in sugar, iron and steel, textiles and chemicals were severely felt by British interests from time to time, especially in periods of bad trade, as before 1905.

Much competition was experienced in the world markets served by the export industries. It drew attention to the extraordinary concentration of British exports in half a dozen industries whose future might be threatened by the growth of similar industries in other countries, and raised the question whether the existing pattern of British industrial investment and of industrial exports was wise. There was some slight tendency towards a greater diversity in British exports between 1896 and 1913. But over half of the exports in those immediate pre-war years continued to come from industries belonging to the coal, iron and steel, engineering and textile groups.[1] This appeared a dangerous weighting of the export trade to some contemporaries, who felt that Great Britain was making too much of industries which exported her wealth in the raw, such as coal, or that she held on to lines in which her comparative advantages were ceasing to be marked, and did not make enough of industries which through high manufacturing skill

[1] G. D. H. Cole, *British Trade and Industry* (1932), p. 103.

added a high value to the product.[1] The critics maintained that German and American competition were already showing the dangers of such a distribution of resources. Their point would have been weakened, if the predominant export industries had shown marked increases in efficiency. But the heavy concentration of resources lay where diminishing costs were no longer evident.

Part of the answer to this problem, it later appeared, was to be found in the creation of new export industries in fields where comparative costs lay unexploited. This happened between the wars and after 1945, when a pattern of industrial investment quite different from that of Victorian and Edwardian times came into being. But in the years between 1880 and 1914, much discussion went forward upon the assumption that the existing pattern of investment could not be substantially altered and that it must be protected.

Protection could not extend to world markets. Recognition of this simple fact and an awareness that the efficiency of industry had as much to gain as to lose from foreign competition kept the larger part of industrial opinion Cobdenite in its views of economic policy down to the 1920's. It was then that the misfortunes of the staple trades made the first great breaches in the free trade citadel.

COLONIES AND TARIFFS

At a much earlier date, during the years of falling prices and repeated slump in the 1870's, 1880's and 1890's, when foreign competition was first acutely felt, a certain longing for security had made itself evident in the attitude of the business community. This appeared clearly in a keen interest in the extensive additions to the Empire which were made about then and a disposition to defend them as necessary for the maintenance and furtherance of trade.[2] Additions to the Empire were not

[1] The argument of W. J. Ashley, *The Tariff Problem* (1903). He was comparing her industry, rather unfavourably, with that of Germany. With the main point, Marshall would probably have agreed, no doubt with characteristic reservations.

[2] Thus, the Leeds Chamber of Commerce resolved in November, 1892: 'The British Africa Company contemplates giving up Uganda. This Chamber is glad to hear that the British Commission is taking over in the name of trade, humanity and good government. Most countries are now building up a hostile tariff wall against our commodities, and it is of the utmost importance to preserve as much of the world as possible for our trade.' M. W. Beresford, *The Leeds Chambers of Commerce* (1951), p. 115.

new; they had gone on continuously throughout the mid-century. Great Britain was imperialist, even when she was free trade. But the vehemence of economic argument about the value of direct control over countries of interest to British traders and manufacturers was new and it betrayed anxiety. Much of the anxiety, it should be added, was not only economic, but also strategic and political. It had to do with the shifting balance of power in the world and with the perpetual conflict of French, German, Russian and British policies in the period, on the whole well called imperialist, which lay between the Franco-German War and the First World War. A special cause of conflict lay in the conditions of Africa, now being drawn into world trade for the first time after the death of David Livingstone in 1873. Africa was the last continent to be opened to Western penetration. Her conditions over wide areas where primitive conditions existed did not afford the security of law and settled political life for the trader and the missionary. The rivalry of the European powers for place and position was acute there. African disputes came to play after 1880 the same part in international relations as quarrels over the Americas a century or two before.

Colonial markets were never more than the smaller part of the markets served by Britain's trade. But they always had been an important market and source of supply, especially perhaps when other markets were depressed. The rate of increase of colonial trade was comparatively rapid in the last quarter of last century, when British overseas trade was meeting new difficulties in other quarters in the way of tariffs and growing domestic industries. The colonies took about one-quarter of British exports in 1870-4, and more than one-third thirty years later, although slightly less before 1913 at a time of high international boom and of rapidly expanding trade with all sorts of countries. More slowly, the Empire came to supply a larger proportion of British imports—about one-quarter in 1910. This commodity trade was independent of returns upon investment and the profits of shipping.

The growth of colonial trade was no more than a small part of that expansion of trade with the undeveloped and developing parts of the world which was the key to Britain's international economic position in the nineteenth century. It had, however, important political effects, all the more so since the self-governing colonies were beginning to control their own

commercial policies and to make their own tariffs. A self-governing colony such as Canada was prepared to offer preferences
to British trade, in return for concessions which a free trade
Britain found it hard to give. In 1897, however, the mother
country announced in answer to renewed colonial pressure and
to altering opinion at home that she intended in future to
regard Imperial preferences as a domestic matter not subject
to the provisions of her commercial treaties with other powers.
This was a significant move, for it involved the denunciation of
treaties arrived at with Belgium in 1862 and the German Zollverein in 1865, which pledged her not to return to imperial
preferences and to extend to any other country any preference
granted to her by a colony. Tempers had changed, in Great
Britain as elsewhere, since those brave days.

Foreign tariffs had become a principal grievance of British
traders and manufacturers. This was no doubt inevitable,
because some degree of exclusion of British goods was necessary
to the industrialization of Europe and North America—a need
which few in Britain were prepared to recognize. The demand
of primary producers for protection during the years of falling
prices after 1873, the consequent political bargaining with industrial groups and the need of governments for revenue also
played their part. The immediate change in European commercial policy coincided with the disastrous trading years of
the later 1870's and with Bismarck's search for a federal revenue
for the new German Empire. The German tariff of 1879 marked
the end of the liberalization of tariffs, following English and
French example, which had been so pronounced between 1846
and 1877. Continental tariffs began to go up. The 1890's saw
the strongest tariff movement for many years in Germany and
France, Sweden and Italy. The United States also under the
impulse of many forces had turned high tariff since the Civil
War, and the McKinley Act of 1890 marked the peak of the
new American protection. Particular British industries were
heavy sufferers by these and other changes. They were already
irked by the growth of new manufactures in their old markets
and there was a loud outcry.

The extent of the protection given by the new laws and the
damage inflicted on British interests was often exaggerated.
Protection on the Continent from the new German tariff of
1902–13 was moderate compared with protection in the same
quarter of the world after 1931; neither did American and

European tariffs nor the painful redistribution of trade they helped to force on prevent a large and satisfactory expansion of United Kingdom trade between 1870 and 1913. But the new laws came at an awkward moment for British enterprise, faced both with rising competition and (until 1900) with falling prices.

These events formed the ground for the revival of protectionism at home. This was not wholly industrial; the depression of farming and landownership after 1873 had the effect in the agricultural districts of turning the thoughts of some farmers and country gentlemen towards direct protection or the concealed protection of bimetallism and monetary reform. A drift of opinion in the towns was traceable, however, from the 1880's, although the literature of economic anxiety goes back to the previous decade. The Fair Trade League was founded in 1881. Heavy depressions in the middle 1880's and the 1890's reinforced the drift. A minority report of the Royal Commission on the Depression of Trade in 1886 recommended a change in commercial policy and there took place in the 1890's, about the time of the Transvaal crisis in 1896, a 'Made in Germany' scare which was childish in argument, but serious in dimensions.

No important political figure became associated with protection in the 1880's. When Joseph Chamberlain became Secretary of State for the Colonies in 1895 he was beginning to stand as the champion of a new-style Imperialism, which demanded closer bonds with the self-governing colonies and the development of Imperial resources, rather than a new commercial policy. Between 1903 and 1906 he came to lead the movements in political life both for Imperial union and protection. The events of those years, like the self-conscious Imperialism of the 1880's and 1890's, had no single root and cannot be explained wholly in economic terms. They were connected with the failure to reach an understanding with Germany; with the growing tension in Europe as the animosities of the powers became recognized and fixed; and with the growing burden of armaments and the pressure on public finances. The electorate turned down protection in 1906, so that no change occurred in commercial policy. But from that time forward protectionism was a political force to be reckoned with. The ground was prepared for the alliance of farmers and industrialists which, under different circumstances, carried the general tariff and other protective laws in the 1930's.

The fiscal controversy of the early 1900's had been much influenced by the depression which followed the Boer War and by memories of the depressions of the 1880's and 1890's. A revival of foreign trade and investment on the great scale and the return of full employment, for the first time since 1900, in 1909–13, overlaid the protectionist movement, and by the enormous lift it gave to the balance of payments suggested that the fears which had been expressed for the future of Great Britain's trade were groundless. The optimism of the boom was exaggerated, like the pessimism of the depression. If it was true that the trade of the world was about to grow away from Great Britain, as it had grown away from other countries in the past, the movement would be slow. It would show itself not in the boom but in a weakened position after each successive slump. Some such weakening occurred, in a world unbelievably complicated by the economic consequences of the First World War, in 1920–1 and 1929–31. It is not surprising therefore to discover that in these years the argument on external economic policy was resumed.

Neither the free-trader nor the protectionist of 1903–6 saw far. Their doctrines did not measure up to the tremendous character of later events. One or two men, however, looked beyond their time. It was a protectionist, W. J. Ashley, who perceived that the real issue was not commercial policy, but the economic role of the State in a world which had changed much since Cobden's day and would change more as the new century went on. It was a free-trader, and in matters of policy a traditionalist, Alfred Marshall, who wrote: 'Before another century has passed...there may then remain but a few small areas...which are not so well supplied with both population and capital as to be able to produce most of the manufactured products which they require....When that time comes, those who have surplus raw products to sell will have the upper hand in international bargains....'[1]

Such speculations belonged in essence to a later and more puzzling age. The business men and even the working men of the years before 1914, whatever their anxieties, continued for the most part to hold or passively to respect the doctrines handed down to them, on which, as they believed or as they had been told, their own success and that of their country had depended in the remarkable century that was drawing to a close, amid threats of the first general European conflict since

Napoleon's time. There were many circumstances of those years which propped up their faith. As for what war might do to industry or industry for war, these were matters about which few of them had thought deeply and on which their experience and their reflections seemed to throw only a dim light.

OVERSEAS TRADE BETWEEN THE TWO WORLD WARS

The trading history of Great Britain between the two World Wars was distinguished by two developments closely linked together. First, by a reversal of the axiom of nineteenth-century economic policy which regarded the control of the foreign balance as no proper business for the State. Secondly, by the beginning of a great deterioration in the condition of the balance of payments, the duration and true nature of which is still in doubt. The first development was a consequence of the second. Both were the result of complex influences which can only be glanced at and lightly sketched in here.

What the state of the balance of payments between Great Britain and other countries would have been with the exhaustion of the stimulus to exports given by the outburst of foreign investment in 1909–13, if there had been no war, we shall never know. But the arrival of a new chapter in the history of the British balance of payments, with all that that meant for a Britain dependent economically on the world and a world dependent up to that date on British capital and trade, was clearly proved by the official trade figures of the inter-war years. The table below includes the experience of the generation which had grown into adult life before 1914 for the sake of contrast. It does not carry the story beyond 1938 into years after the Second World War.

What chiefly stands out from these figures is the fluctuating character of the balance of payments at all times; the vigour of the foreign investment in the years 1906–10 made possible by a highly favourable balance, moving towards a peak in 1913, when foreign lending is supposed to have absorbed more than half the total of national savings; the relatively favourable position in 1927–9, when the brief post-war reconstruction was at its height; the steep decline of income from abroad early

---

[1] A. Marshall, 'The Fiscal Policy of International Trade (1903)' *Official Papers* (1926), p. 402.

in the 1930's and the repatriation of a small amount of the
capital invested. These figures clearly suggest an economic
revolution of the most important character, both for Great
Britain and for the countries with which she had trading relations. But the influences which lay behind the change are less
easily described.

United Kingdom balance of payments* (in £m.)

	Merchandise		Balance of com-modity trade	Net income from overseas invest-ment	Other net in-visible in-come	Move-ments of gold and silver	Income available for invest-ment over-seas
	Imports (−)	Exports (+)					
1871–80	371	280	−91	+53	+90	−3	+49
1891–1900	446	305	−141	+97	+96	−5	+47
1906–10	630	489	−141	+151	+137	−3	+144
1911–13	731	599	−132	+188	+160	−8	+208
1927–29	1212	838	−374	+250	+226	+1	+103
1933–35	721	448	−273	+172	+109	−68	−60
1938	920	532	−388	+175	+142	+141	+70

− = an international debit.   + = an international credit.

* This table, kindly supplied to me by Dr S. B. Saul of Liverpool
University, is drawn from the following sources:

1871–1913: A. Imlah, 'British Balance of Payments and Export of
Capital, 1816–1913', *Econ. Hist. Rev.*, 2nd series, vol. v (1952), pp. 208–39.

1927–35: *Statistical abstract for U.K.* and gold movements taken from
A. E. Kahn, *Great Britain in the World Economy* (1946), pp. 126 and 132.

1938: *Statistical Abstract for U.K.* and *International Monetary Fund Balance
of Payments Year Book*, 1938/46/47.

The table does not show the immense temporary setback to
the balance of payments produced by the First World War.
Export trade and the amount of industrial production available
for export were both seriously reduced at an early stage in the
war. At the same time a large volume of necessary imports,
including materials of war from the United States, had to be
paid for. Difficulties of payment for the dollar imports became
acute just before the United States entered the war. This led to
the sale of a certain quantity of investments abroad, in order to
make American payments. Between the urgent need for
foreign exchange and the defaults of debtors, from one-fifth to
one-fourth of the pre-war volume of investments was lost.[1]

[1] A. Kahn, op. cit. p. 137.

Income from other investments fell, the earnings of ships and other invisible incomes declined. It took some years for these old sources of wealth to recover, to knit together again the old web of world markets and restore to Great Britain something which resembled in its main features her international trading position of 1914.

Reconstruction was judged at the time to have been completed by the measure which restored the pound sterling to a gold standard in April 1925, for cash payments at the Bank of England and the traditional legal apparatus of the monetary system had been suspended at the outset of the war. The restoration of the gold standard was designed to facilitate trade and investment and within limits it did so. Large export trades, such as coal, were severely hampered by the decision to restore the pound sterling at the old parity with the dollar, which events proved to have been too high a rate. But for the next few years, production, trade and investment even in Europe, perhaps more so outside of it, resumed the growth which men had come to accept as natural in the previous century. A remarkable increase of wealth took place in many countries between 1925 and 1929. Then a catastrophic fall of prices on the New York Stock Market in the autumn of the latter year foretold an impending change of economic weather.

Sufficient of the wealth of the 1920's had come Great Britain's way to restore order to her foreign trading accounts and to cause many shrewd men to overlook the enormous transformations which had come over the world since 1914 and the position of Great Britain within it. Where change was noticed and where it hurt, the altered conditions were commonly put down either to the war and its effects, or to the policy of government which was blamed for its monetary or commercial policies, or to the misfortunes of particular trades. But it could escape no one's notice that, in terms of 1913 prices, the total volume of exports in 1929 was still below the level of the year 1913 and that idle resources and persistent unemployment had marred the record of the largest exporting trades in the country, such as coal, shipbuilding and cotton textiles, throughout the whole of the post-war decade.

The next few years produced even greater distress. The fury of the storm which blew up in 1929, in the shape of acute trade depression, bringing financial crisis, a demand for gold abroad and renewed disorganization of the foreign accounts, is a matter of oral tradition. It carried away much Victorian rigging, the gold standard and free trade included, within two years (1931–2) and left an altered world behind, where even the most experienced navigators were puzzled to find their bearings. A few years later, from 1936, with the rearming of Germany, Western governments had to take cognizance of the possibility of renewed war and to shape their policy accordingly. By 1938, armament expenditures were again beginning to shape national economies, including that of Great Britain.

During this decade of the 1930's, when trade depression made it impossible for men to exchange resources, and then the fear of war made them unwilling to do so, international trade, especially in manufactured goods, was in decay. Manufacturing capacity continued to rise, taking the world as a whole; much of this represented the effort to prepare for war or to cut loose from international arrangements which had ceased to offer either economic or political security. Great Britain was a heavy loser by such conditions. Her exports in 1937 were below the level, not only of 1929, but also that of 1924. Her foreign accounts had only just begun to recover before the Second World War.

If we are to follow any clue to British trade history through the bewildering events between the wars, avoiding the partial explanations current at the time, it is probably to be found in what had been the hinge of her international economic position throughout the nineteenth century; her relation with the primary producers of the world, who provided her with food-stuffs and raw materials and who bought in exchange her manufactured goods.

Her special relations with countries of this type had made her a trader of a different kind from Germany, the bulk of whose trade was in Europe and to a large extent with other industrial countries, including Britain herself. They linked her with the greater part of mankind who still lived by agriculture, in lands for the most part outside of Europe. The industrial revolution in Germany and the United States and in many other countries in the thirty years before 1914 had, of course, competed with but had not destroyed or narrowed this trade. The increased sales of their products in Western Europe and the United States, as industrialism proceeded there, gave primary producers additional income. Part of this was spent on increased purchases of British goods and at times when the prices of raw materials and foodstuffs were rising on world markets as they were after 1900 such countries, whether within the Empire or without, offered profitable openings to British capital.

This historical connection was resumed after the First World War. Renewed sales to the primary producing countries and the revival of investment there once more formed part of the British trade picture. They helped to bring incomes derived from abroad into balance with outgoing payments for the imports on which Great Britain depended, as the naval history of the 1914–18 war had just reminded her, for her daily existence.

The picture was, however, altered since 1914 and it was about to alter still more. The war scarcities and high prices for primary products of the years 1914–20 were over. Throughout the 1920's producers of primary products in many countries complained of a tendency of values to fall. The development of new countries—and some of the most important of the primary producers were countries of recent settlement—had always moved in phases of prosperity and depression and there was no boom among them in the 1920's, comparable with the Canadian boom before 1914, which would have taken the edge off British trade difficulties in other parts of the world.

Moreover, the primary producing countries had never regarded it as their destiny eternally to produce foodstuffs and raw materials, in competition with one another, for the relatively few nations supplying industrial goods. The declining value of their products and the memory of the scarcity and high prices of manufactures during and just after the First World War encouraged them to turn to manufacturing themselves; a policy which was encouraged by the stiffening of European agricultural protection in the same decade. The largest primary producer of the nineteenth century, the United States of America, had also become the foremost industrial State, at great gain to her power and the standard of living of her people. The resources and the opportunities of the United States were of course exceptional; but the ambitions of other countries inclined in the same general direction towards the securing of industrial incomes, which were doubly valuable in an unstable and unsafe world.

These general trends, towards depression among primary producers and towards industrialization, often heavily protected by tariff and subsidy, blurred and at last blotted out the line between industrial and primary producing states, as it had been known to the last century. They were strengthened by the tremendous fall of prices after 1929, which reduced the revenues of primary producers, upset their balance of payments and forced them back upon their own industrial resources, such as they were or might be made to be. The disastrous turn which European politics were taking and the prospect of a further war reinforced their desire for economic independence.

The new stage of industrialization, while it was natural and probably inevitable, even if economic and political conditions after 1920 had been different, was far less favourable to Great Britain than the developments of an earlier age had been. As a supplier of consumer goods, she lost by the impoverishment of old customers. Further, she had strong competition to meet, from manufacturing producers who knew the markets as well as she did, and were prepared to meet the demands of a small purse with a low-price article. The years between the wars saw the gradual but almost complete disintegration of Lancashire's immensely strong pre-1914 position in Eastern and Far Eastern markets, in face of Indian and Japanese manufacturing competition. Before 1914, the earnings of Lancashire abroad had gone far to supply the foreign exchange which rendered foreign investment possible. There can be no more dramatic example of the sudden reversal of fortunes in a modern industrial State.

These painful losses were not compensated for by larger sales of the fuel and machinery and general equipment of industrialization. Great Britain had been before the world a long time as a supplier of capital goods. But the pre-1914 concept of industrial structure, firmly built upon coal and steam engineering, fitted awkwardly with the new type of industrial structure, based upon new techniques and fuels and aimed often to satisfy new types of demand, which was fast becoming the pattern of the world in the 1920's and 1930's. The coal industry, an exporter to industrial lands since 1880, suffered acutely for this reason, as did large branches of the iron and steel and engineering industries. An important change was coming over the character of British exports during these years as industrial innovation went ahead; but the rise of new export industries was far from at once making up for the losses of the old.

Not only a new industrial and agricultural structure but also a new commercial policy was needed to face a world changed

beyond nineteenth-century experience. This gap was not filled
by the building up of the general tariff after 1931 and the
organization of a system of Imperial preferences at Ottawa in
1932. These were measures which did little more than recognize
the inappropriateness of past policies and register a highly
traditional protest against their failure. Neither did the *ad hoc*
bilateral agreements concluded with a number of countries in
the following years carry the matter much further.

The world economy of the 1930's was one in which the
periphery was no longer united with the centre. Things fell
apart, the centre did not hold, in the economic sphere as elsewhere. The economic life of the world was breaking loose from
its old metropolitan headquarters in Europe, while the headquarters itself was ceasing to exist as an organizing centre.
British policy during those years, like the policies of other States,
did little more than accept disintegration.

Yet the periphery could not exist without the centre, nor the
centre without the periphery. What was wanted was a policy,
backed by effective economic power, capable of binding the
parts together again in an organic whole. Perhaps the task was
beyond Britain or any other European State. The United States
of America had become the greatest of world traders; she
counted for much in the world economy, although international
trade played but a small part in her own; but the lead did not
come from her either.

If there was failure in Britain's economic role during those
years, there was little consciousness of it. From Munich onwards, if Britons thought about foreign affairs at all, their
attention was distracted by the unrolling of German policy
upon the Continent. From September 1939 it was wholly
absorbed, as their country flung herself into the second struggle
for national survival within the lifetime of the older generation
of men.

GENERAL INDEX

INDEX OF REFERENCES

Allen, G. C. *British Industries and their Organisation*, 179 n., 222 n.
Arch, J. *The Story of his Life*, 165 n.
Arnold, M. *Culture and Anarchy*, 266 n.
Ashley, W. J. *The Tariff Problem*, 330 n.
Ashton, T. S. 'The Standard of Life of the Workers in England', 145 n.
Ashton, T. S. and Sykes, J. *The Coal Industry of the Eighteenth Century*, 48 n.

Bagehot, W. *The English Constitution*, 266 n.
Balfour Committee on Industry and Trade, 209 n., 210 n., 222 n., 323 n.
Bentham, J. *Economic Writings*, 124 n.; *Fragment on Government*, 118
Beresford, M. W. *The Leeds Chamber of Commerce*, 330 n.
Beveridge, Lord. *Full Employment in a Free Society*, 228 n.; *Unemployment*, 228 n., 279 n.
Booth, C. *Life and Labour of the People in London*, 275
Bowden, W. *Industrial Society in England towards the end of the Eighteenth Century*, 110 n.
Bowley, A. L. *Changes in the Distribution of the National Income*, 249 n.; *Division of the Product of Industry*, 209 n.; *Wages and Income in the United Kingdom*, 196 n., 233 n., 254 n.
Bowley, M. *Nassau Senior and the Classical Economists*, 124 n.
Briggs, A. 'Background of the Parliamentary Reform Movement', 238 n.
British and Foreign Trade and Industrial Conditions, 182 n., 183 n.
Brown, G. H. P. and Jones, S. J. H. 'The Climacteric of the Nineties', 198 n.
Brunton, J. *John Brunton's Book*, 171 n.
Bulwer-Lytton, E. *England and the English*, 123 n.
Bunce, J. *Life of Josiah Mason*, 176 n.
Buxton, S. *Finance and Politics, 1783-1885*, 146 n.

Caird, J. *High Farming, the Substitute for Protection*, 163
Cairncross, A. K. *Home and Foreign Investment*, 196 n., 197 n., 324 n., 326 n.; 'Internal Migration in Victorian England', 233 n.
Campion, H. *Public and Private Property in Great Britain*, 299 n.
Cannan, E. *History of Local Rates in England*, 258 n.; *The Paper Pound of 1797-1821*, 99
Carrington, C. E. *The British Overseas*, 307 n.
Chadwick, E. *Report on the Sanitary Condition of the Labouring Population*, 260
Chambers, J. D. 'Enclosure and Labour Supply in the Industrial Revolution', 39 n.; *Nottinghamshire in the Eighteenth Century*, 58 n.
Chydenius, A. *The National Gain*, 114 n.
Clapham, Sir John. *The Bank of England*, 90 n., 101 n.; *John Brunton's Book* (ed.), 171 n.; *Concise Economic History of Britain to 1750*, 38 n.; *Economic History of Modern Britain*, 38 n., 41 n., 75 n., 76 n., 134 n., 161 n., 178 n., 206 n., 254 n., 261 n., 262 n., 280 n.
Clark, C. *National Income and Outlay*, 196 n., 209 n.
Clark, Sir George N. *The Idea of the Industrial Revolution*, 64 n.